CICERO AND THE PEOPLE'S WILL

This book tells an overlooked story in the history of ideas, a drama of cut-throat politics and philosophy of mind. For it is Cicero, statesman and philosopher, who gives shape to the notion of will in Western thought, from criminal will to moral willpower and "the will of the people". In a single word – *voluntas* – he brings Roman law into contact with Greek ideas, chief among them Plato's claim that a rational elite must rule. When the Republic falls to Caesarism, Cicero turns his political argument inward: Will is a force in the soul to win the virtue lost on the battlefield, the mark of inner freedom in an unfree age. Though this constitutional vision failed in his own time, Cicero's ideals of popular sovereignty and rational elitism have shaped and fractured the modern world – and Ciceronian creativity might save it.

LEX PAULSON is Executive Director of the Université Mohammed VI Polytechnique School of Collective Intelligence (Morocco) and lectures in advocacy at Sciences Po, Paris. Trained in classics and community organizing, he served as a mobilization strategist for the presidential campaigns of Barack Obama in 2008 and Emmanuel Macron in 2017. He has led projects in democratic innovation and leadership for UNICEF, the US State Department, the French National Assembly, and the National Democratic Institute. He served as legislative counsel in the 111th US Congress (2009–2011), organized on six US presidential campaigns, and has worked to advance democratic innovation at the European Commission and in India, Tunisia, Egypt, Uganda, Senegal, the Czech Republic, and Ukraine.

CICERO AND THE PEOPLE'S WILL

Philosophy and Power at the End of the Roman Republic

LEX PAULSON
Université Mohammed VI Polytechnique

CAMBRIDGE
UNIVERSITY PRESS

CAMBRIDGE
UNIVERSITY PRESS

Shaftesbury Road, Cambridge CB2 8EA, United Kingdom

One Liberty Plaza, 20th Floor, New York, NY 10006, USA

477 Williamstown Road, Port Melbourne, VIC 3207, Australia

314–321, 3rd Floor, Plot 3, Splendor Forum, Jasola District Centre, New Delhi – 110025, India

103 Penang Road, #05–06/07, Visioncrest Commercial, Singapore 238467

Cambridge University Press is part of Cambridge University Press & Assessment, a department of the University of Cambridge.

We share the University's mission to contribute to society through the pursuit of education, learning and research at the highest international levels of excellence.

www.cambridge.org
Information on this title: www.cambridge.org/9781316514115

DOI: 10.1017/9781009082587

© Lex Paulson 2023

This publication is in copyright. Subject to statutory exception and to the provisions of relevant collective licensing agreements, no reproduction of any part may take place without the written permission of Cambridge University Press & Assessment.

First published 2023

A catalogue record for this publication is available from the British Library

Library of Congress Cataloging-in-Publication Data
NAMES: Paulson, Lex, author.
TITLE: Cicero and the people's will : philosophy and power at the end of the Roman Republic / Lex Paulson.
DESCRIPTION: Cambridge, United Kingdom ; New York, NY: Cambridge University Press, 2023. | Includes bibliographical references and index.
IDENTIFIERS: LCCN 2022030496 (print) | LCCN 2022030497 (ebook) | ISBN 9781316514115 (hardback) | ISBN 9781009077385 (paperback) | ISBN 9781009082587 (epub)
SUBJECTS: LCSH: Cicero, Marcus Tullius–Political and social views. | Political science–Philosophy–History–To 1500. | Republicanism. | Will. | Elite (Social sciences)–Political activity. | Rome–Politics and government–265-30 B.C. | Rome–History–Republic, 265-30 B.C.
CLASSIFICATION: LCC JC81.C7 P36 2023 (print) | LCC JC81.C7 (ebook) | DDC 320.101–dc23/eng/20220825
LC record available at https://lccn.loc.gov/2022030496
LC ebook record available at https://lccn.loc.gov/2022030497

ISBN 978-1-316-51411-5 Hardback

Cambridge University Press & Assessment has no responsibility for the persistence or accuracy of URLs for external or third-party internet websites referred to in this publication and does not guarantee that any content on such websites is, or will remain, accurate or appropriate.

Pour la mère extraordinaire

Contents

Acknowledgments	*page* ix
List of Abbreviations	xii
Introduction	1

PART I THE PRACTICE OF *VOLUNTAS*

1 Forebears of Will — 17
    1.1 Greek Forebears — 18
    1.2 Latin Forebears — 24

2 Innocence and Intent — 32
    2.1 Legitimacy and Rationality — 35
    2.2 *Controversia ex Scripto et Sententia* — 38
    2.3 Capturing Goodwill — 41
    2.4 Guilty and Righteous Wills — 46

3 Cartographies of Power — 57
    3.1 Intentions, Alliances, and Schemes — 61
    3.2 *Sua* and *Summa Voluntate* — 63
    3.3 *Voluntas* as Affiliation — 67
    3.4 Boundaries of Political Will — 69
    3.5 Caesar's *Voluntas* — 75

4 An Economy of Goodwill — 79
    4.1 The Rules of *Voluntas Mutua* — 84
    4.2 The *Voluntas* Economy — 92
    4.3 Theorizing *Voluntas Mutua* — 98

5 *Voluntas Populi*: The Will of the People — 105
    5.1 Introduction: *In Verrem* — 105
    5.2 "I of All Men, Who to Serve the Will of the People ..." — 109
    5.3 *De republica* and *De legibus* — 122
    5.4 Ruin and Rebirth — 140

PART II THE PHILOSOPHY OF *VOLUNTAS*

6 Willpower   147
   6.1 Cicero on Platonic and Stoic Souls   150
   6.2 *Tusculan Disputations*: Cicero's Struggle for Reason   157
   6.3 Conclusion: Willing, Willpower, and the Will   164

7 Free Will and the Forum   169
   7.1 Lucretius' *Libera Voluntas*   171
   7.2 Cicero's *Libera Voluntas*   175
   7.3 The Politics of Free Will   181

8 The Fourfold Self   186
   8.1 The Four *Personae*: Background and Problems   189
   8.2 Will and the Four *Personae*   195
   8.3 Conclusion: Scipio and Foucault   214

Conclusion   218

Epilogue: The Afterlife of Cicero's *Voluntas*   220

Appendix Occurrences of Voluntas *in the Works of Cicero*   245
References   247
Index   265

Acknowledgments

This book began with a volcano. When Eyjafjallajökull filled Iceland's sky with billowing ash in spring 2010, two traveling friends, Adrien Muller and Rachel Welland (now Muller), were unable to return home from Washington, DC, to Europe. After a sumptuous dinner at Cactus Cantina, Adrien asked if I had considered moving to Paris – a city I had loved from afar – and starting a PhD. A few months later, to my parents' dismay, I traded the life of an overworked, underpaid congressional staffer for that of an overworked, underpaid doctoral student. It was the best decision of my life.

First thanks go, therefore, to Adrien and to his friend Jean-Pierre Reboul, who first helped me navigate the *milieu universitaire*, revising – to be fair, redrafting – the halting French of my Paris-bound emails, making me an infinitely more plausible potential *thésard*. That I was welcomed at the Sorbonne and survived my first brush with its bureaucracy intact I owe to their generosity and *savoir faire*.

My route to Cicero was equally circuitous. John Matthews' survey of Roman history, studied in my final undergraduate semester at Yale, kindled a fascination for the late Republic that blazed through my twenties as I knocked doors for candidates in Connecticut and New Hampshire. One of those campaigns, for a *novus homo* from Chicago in 2008, ended up returning me to my muggy hometown of Washington, DC, and its *collis capitolinus*. Those years on the campaign trail, in courtrooms and legislative chambers, brought me closer without knowing it to the man at the heart of this book.

My new home in Paris also put me two train rides away from the place that became this study's second home. The venerable footpaths to Christ's College, Clare College, and Michaelhouse Cafe in Cambridge were worn a bit deeper through many subsequent trips. David Sedley patiently cleared the debris from my understanding of Hellenistic logic, ethics, and physics.

Paul Cartledge not only guided me to the vistas of δημοκρατία but put his painstaking pen to work in revisions to these pages. And over many cups of tea and scones, Malcolm Schofield illuminated the corners of Cicero's corpus as no one else could. That David and Malcolm then offered to serve as jury members for the resulting thesis was a great honor. For the time, generosity, and insights of this eminent trio, I owe tremendous thanks.

At the Sorbonne, my path was made perennially smoother by the kindness of Hélène Casanova-Robin. Her friendly counsel was critical at many stages of this work, as was that of Margaret Graver, Valentina Arena, Jean-Michel David, François Prost, Paul Demont, Sabine Luciani, and Jean-Louis Ferrary. I owe a special word of thanks to Philippe Rousselot and Ermanno Malaspina, who welcomed me with hospitality into the Society of Cicero's Friends. The *secrétaire adjoint* of my initial draft was Guillaume Peynet, a young scholar of astonishing brilliance, who contributed his mastery of this work's four main languages. Whatever felicities of expression were in the French version of my thesis, I owe them to Guillaume; any faults were purely my own. Tina Bouffet kindly offered her generous translation help – and much-needed good humor – at a critical phase. I add my thanks to my editors, Michael Sharp and Katie Idle, as well as to the two anonymous readers of this manuscript, whose corrections were invaluable in its final phases. The staff of Café Le Sevigné and Le Rendezvous des Amis kept me equipped with green tea – and stronger fare – during editing sessions that were long even by the standards of Parisian table-lingering. And I owe gratitude to my students and colleagues at the UM6P School of Collective Intelligence, tested and annealed the ideas herein.

As for the director of the thesis, I would need the Arpinate's tongue to give proper words of praise. From his (to me, still baffling) decision to accept me as a doctoral student, to his proposal to make *voluntas* my subject, to the encyclopedic command of ancient thought he has shared, Carlos Lévy is a mentor beyond my hopes and desert. He has taught me the meaning of goodwill.

Finally, an offering to my own *maiores*. To Donna Sabin, my *maman deux*, who made my Paris transhumance possible. To Pat Howell, who planted philosophical seeds on Faraday Place that I will take a lifetime to harvest. To my magnificent teachers at St. Albans, and in particular Donna Denizé, Jim Ehrenhaft, Paul Barrett, Thierry Boussard, Paul Piazza, Tom Carroll, and the inimitable Ted Eagles, each of whom spurred and guided me to new vistas of the mind. To Marshall Ganz, who taught me that noble ideas and effective politics could be woven together in a common story. And to my departed hero and mentor, Harold Bloom – O *papa gnosticorum*, Odyssean overhearer – I give libations of Levon and bear our Gnosis forth to wilder strands.

This thesis is dedicated, at last, to my mother, the extraordinary Elizabeth Custis; to my father, Bill, a poet-in-residence at the end of the mind; and to my wife, Rahma, and our daughter, Illi Zahra, for whom my love would fill the Tiber and cover the seven hills. Whatever spark of humanism lights my soul, I have it from you.

Abbreviations

Aesch.	Aeschylus
Supp.	*Supplices*
Aët	Aëtius
Alex. *Fat.*	Alexander of Aphrodisias, *On Fate*
Arist.	Aristotle
Eth. Eud.	*Ethica Eudemia*
Eth. Nic.	*Ethica Nicomachea*
[*Mag. mor.*]	*Magna moralia*
Pol.	*Politica*
August.	Augustine
Conf.	Confessions
De civ. D.	De civitate Dei
Aul. Gell.	see Gell.
Cic.	Cicero (Marcus Tullius)
Acad.	*Academicae quaestiones*
Acad. post.	*Academica posteriora* (= Plasberg, Bk. 4)
Acad. Pr.	*Academica Priora* (= Plasberg, Bk. 1)
Ad Brut.	*Epistulae ad Brutum*
Amic.	*De amicitia*
Arch.	*Pro Archia*
Att.	*Epistulae ad Atticum*
Balb.	*Pro Balbo*
Brut.	*Brutus* or *De Claris Oratoribus*
Caecin.	*Pro Caecina*
Cael.	*Pro Caelio*
Cat.	*In Catilinam*
Clu.	*Pro Cluentio*
De or.	*De oratore*
Deiot.	*Pro rege Deiotaro*
Div.	*De divinatione*

Div. Caec.	Divinatio in Caecilium
Dom.	De domo sua
Fam.	Epistulae ad familiares
Fat.	De fato
Fin.	De finibus
Flac.	Pro Flacco
Font.	Pro Fonteio
Har. resp.	De haruspicum responso
Inv.	De inventione
Leg.	De legibus
Leg. agr.	De lege agraria
Leg. Man.	Pro lege Manilia or De imperio Cn. Pompeii
Lig.	Pro Ligario
Luc.	Lucullus or Academica posteriora
Marcell.	Pro Marcello
Mil.	Pro Milone
Mur.	Pro Murena
Nat. D.	De natura deorum
Off.	De officiis
Orat.	Orator ad M. Brutum
Part. or.	Partitiones oratoriae
Phil.	Orationes Philippicae
Pis.	In Pisonem
Planc.	Pro Plancio
Prov. cons.	De provinciis consularibus
QFr.	Epistulae ad Quintum fratrem
QRosc.	Pro Roscio comoedo
Quinct.	Pro Quinctio
Rab. Post.	Pro Rabirio Postumo
Red. pop.	Post reditum ad populum
Red. sen.	Post reditum in senatu
Rep.	De republica
Rosc. Am.	Pro Sexto Roscio Amerino
Scaur.	Pro Scauro
Sest.	Pro Sestio
Sull.	Pro Sulla
Top.	Topica
Tusc.	Tusculanae disputationes
Vat.	In Vatinium
Verr.	In Verrem

List of Abbreviations

Cicero, *Comment. pet.*	Cicero (Quintus), *Commentariolum petitionis*
Dig.	*Digesta*
Dio Cass.	*Dio Cassius*
Dio Chrys. *Or.*	Dio Chrysostomus *Orationes*
Diod. Sic.	Diodorus Siculus
Diog. Laert.	Diogenes Laertius
Epicurus	Epicurus
Ep. Men.	Epistula ad Menoeceum
Sent. Vat.	Vatican Sayings = Gnomologium Vaticanum
Hom.	Homer
Euseb.	Eusebius
Praep. evang.	Praeparatio evangelica
Gell.	Aulus Gellius
NA	Noctes Atticae
Hdt.	Herodotus
Hom.	Homer
Il.	*Iliad*
Od.	*Odyssey*
Hyp.	Hyperides
Liv. Andron. *Ter.*	Livius Andronicus, *Tereus*
Lucil.	Lucilius
Lucr.	Lucretius
M. Aur. Med.	Marcus Aurelius, Meditations
Men.	Menander
Dys.	Dyskolos
Phld.	Philodemus
Pl.	Plato
Grg.	Gorgias
Leg.	Laws
Phd.	Phaedo
Phdr.	Phaedrus
Resp.	Republic
Plaut.	Plautus
Curc.	Curculio
Men.	Menaechmi
Merc.	Mercator
Mil.	Miles gloriosus
Poen.	Poenulus
Pseud.	Pseudolus
Rud.	Rudens

Stich.	Stichus
Trin.	Trinummus
Plin.	Pliny (the Younger)
Ep.	*Epistulae*
Plut.	Plutarch
An seni	*An seni respublica gerenda sit*
Cic.	Cicero
Quaest. conv.	*Quaestiones convivales*
Polyb.	Polybius
Quint.	Quintilian
Inst.	Institutio oratoria
Rhet. Her.	*Rhetorica ad Herennium*
Sall.	Sallust
[*Ad Caes. sen.*]	*Epistulae ad Caesarem senem*
Cat.	*Bellum Catilinae* or *De Catilinae coniuratione*
Hist.	*Historiae*
Iug.	*Bellum Iugurthinum*
Sen.	Seneca (the Younger)
Ep.	*Epistulae*
Sext. Emp.	Sextus Empiricus
Math.	Adversus mathematicos
Stob.	Stobaeus
Suet.	Suetonius
Tac.	Tacitus
Agr.	*Agricola*
Ann.	*Annales*
Ter.	Terence
Ad.	*Adelphoe*
An.	*Andria*
Eun.	*Eunuchus*
Haut.	*H(e)autontimorumenos*
Hec.	*Hecyra*
Phorm.	*Phormio*
Varro, *Ling.*	Varro, *De lingua Latina*
Xen.	Xenophon
Hell.	*Hellenica*

Introduction

> It is clear that there is a problem about the will in ancient philosophy, but it is not so clear just what the problem is.[1]

Whose idea was the will? Many of us may share the intuition of an inner force by which we try to direct the course of our lives. So, too, may we feel caught in a contest of forces – of matter or spirit – that limits our ability not only to live the life we want, but even to choose what we know is best. How much of "us" is fixed in place by our genes, or our culture, or the force of our habits? If we have a will, is it free?

In the face of such doubts, politics may seem a distant concern. Yet the same word recurs. A profound and complex issue affecting millions is narrowed into a binary choice – "yes" or "no," that party or this one. The votes are counted. And then, says the winning more-than-half to the losing almost-half, "the will of the people has spoken." The phrase is so common that its strangeness can fail to register. How could any large and diverse body of individuals, many of whom bitterly disagree, share a single will? Who has the right to declare what that is? And why would it stay binding even as minds and circumstances change?

Most of us would shudder to think that partisan squabbles could hinder our ability to live a good life. But what if these two realms of will – the psychological and political – were linked together from the start? And what if this story, steeped in ancient history and thought, could teach us something about the dysfunctions of today's world – about why our republics are not democracies, and how to create meaning in a broken age?

Genealogies of the will have traditionally centered upon Augustine of Hippo (354–430 CE), whose treatises in Latin framed the debates of medieval Christians and secular moderns in turn. Those pushing further back find antecedents to Augustine's notion of will in the ideas of Plato,

---

[1] Kahn 1988, 234.

Table 1 *Cicero's* voluntas: *occurrences by genre*

Opera ciceronis	Voluntas	Voluntarius
Rhetorica (6)	84	5
Orationes (52)	280	15
Epistulae (931)	206	6
Philosophica (13)	74	33
Total	**644**	**59**

Aristotle, and the Stoics. And yet, these scholars largely agree: *voluntas*, Augustine's word for will, has no direct equivalent in Greek.[2] The etymological problem is compounded by a historical one: Augustine admits he did not enjoy reading Greek, nor did he ever master it.[3] But he loved Cicero.

Until now, the statesman and philosopher Marcus Tullius Cicero (106–43 BCE) has played a minor role in the history of will.[4] As some have remarked, his is the best-documented life of any man or woman before the Christian era.[5] His orations, treatises, and letters were recopied through the centuries out of reverence, not necessarily for his achievements, but for his language. Readers of all faiths agreed that the magnificence of Cicero's prose was without precedent or peer. And regarding the will, digital archives confirm a curious fact. All extant texts prior to the 1st century BCE yield around two dozen occurrences of *voluntas* and its cognates.[6] In Cicero's corpus it appears 644 times (see Table 1).[7]

---

[2] Voelke 1973, 5; Kahn 1988, 248; Frede 2011, 19–21, 158.   [3] August. *Conf.* 1.13.20, 1.14.23.

[4] See Gauthier 1970, 256: "If Cicero seems to have played a decisive role in the development of the notion of will, it is not by the originality of his thoughts ... but rather by the clumsiness of his translations." Voelke 1973, 56–58, skips directly from Panaetius to Seneca and Epictetus in his genealogy, mentioning Cicero only as a translator of *boulēsis*. Dihle 1982, 133–34, credits him with the "correct translation" of *boulēsis* but says that "there is no indication whatsoever that Cicero came to reflect" on its unique "voluntarism." Kahn 1988, 241, only cites Cicero to affirm *voluntas* as "the standard Latin rendering for *boulēsis*." Frede 2011, 25, 37, 92–93, invokes Cicero strictly as an often imprecise translator of philosophical terms.

[5] See Rawson 1975, xiii; Dyck 2008, ix; Tempest 2011, 2–3; Woolf 2015, 1.

[6] As I explore later in this Introduction, these primarily take the ablative form *voluntate*, though *voluntas, voluntatem, voluntates,* and *voluntatibus* also occur. The genitive *voluntatis*, "of or belonging to the will," and the more technical *voluntarius* are both unattested before Cicero.

[7] Some 74 of these occurrences are found in the philosophical treatises, 84 in the rhetorical treatises, 280 in the orations, and 206 in the letters. At least four of these occurrences are questioned in the manuscript tradition (e.g. *voluntatem* for *voluptatem*); following scholarly consensus, I also do not credit Cicero for authorship of the *Commentariolum petitionis*, in which *voluntas* occurs seventeen times.

Cicero's references to the will are wide-ranging and lifelong. In his early letters and speeches, *voluntas* measures criminal intent and maps hidden lines of influence. As the Republic tumbles into civil war, Cicero theorizes the will of the Roman people as the sole lawful source of power (*De republica* and *De legibus*, late 50s BCE). And with Rome in the grip of Caesarism, his treatises name the will as the seat of virtue (*De finibus*, 45 BCE), give the first account of willpower (*Tusculan Disputations*, 45 BCE), link human and divine will (*De natura deorum*, 45 BCE), and, in *De fato* (44 BCE), defend the will's freedom in a causally determined world. The earliest surviving occurrences of "will of the people" (*voluntas populi*) and "free will" (*libera voluntas*) are both found in Cicero.

This book seeks to unearth a long-ignored chapter in the intellectual history of the will. It is a Roman story, springing from and woven into the fall of its Republic. Dio Cassius observed that some essential concepts such as *auctoritas* are indigenous to Latin and not mere translations of Greek ideas.[8] I argue likewise that the will is an original Latin contribution to the Western mind. In making this case, I borrow Carlos Lévy's distinction between a concept, which "encloses reality in a unity of meaning," and a notion, which "accepts approximation, a multitude of elements, preferring suggestion to the imposition of one framework, at the risk of offering contradictory signs."[9] In its staggering variety, Cicero's *voluntas* is better seen as a notion than a concept. As we will see, in this one capacious word he joins multiple streams of debate that had not intersected in Greek, opening new fields of meaning for the will as a rational force in society and the soul.

Consider a passage from one of Cicero's late courtroom speeches, the *Pro Ligario* (46 BCE). His client, Q. Ligarius, briefly led the Pompeian forces in Africa during the civil war and is now accused by a political rival of *perduellio*, siding with a presumed enemy against the Roman people and their new dictator.[10] With Caesar himself presiding, Cicero pleads for a different view of his client's intentions, which he claims are even more blameless than his own:

> [Ligarius] went out as legate in time of peace, and in an utterly peaceable province he so bore himself that peace was its highest interest ... [While] his departure implied a will which did him no discredit [*voluntatem habuit non turpem*], his remaining was due to an honorable necessity ... You have

---

[8] Cass. Dio. 55.3.5. Despite a Roman-sounding name, Dio makes his observation in Greek.
[9] Lévy 2018, 1 (translation mine). [10] Loeb edition (Watts, ed.), 454–57.

then, Caesar, up to this point no evidence that Ligarius was alien from your goodwill [*nullum . . . signum alienae a te voluntatis*] . . .

. . . When Marcus Cicero maintains in your presence that another was not of the same will that he admits of himself [*in ea voluntate non fuisse, in qua se ipsum confitetur fuisse*], he feels no fear of what unspoken thoughts may fill your mind . . . Not until war had been engaged, Caesar, not indeed until it had run most of its course, did I, constrained by no compulsion but led only by a deliberate judgment and will [*nulla vi coactus, iudicio ac voluntate*], go forth to join those who had taken arms against you.[11]

In a single passage, the will appears as Ligarius' righteous state of mind (*voluntatem habuit non turpem*), as Caesar's goodwill (*nullum . . . signum alienae a te voluntatis*), as a partisan adherence Cicero regrets (*in ea voluntate non fuisse . . .*), and as the inner force carrying out a reasoned judgment (*iudicio ac voluntate*). *Voluntas*, in other words, is not a specific and determined concept; it is a notion that assembles a constellation of meaning. Though the agile orator uses different senses of will to refer to Ligarius, Caesar, and himself, its rapid recurrence creates an effect: Three men, seemingly at odds, are subtly conjoined. Cicero wins his friend's acquittal.

Though evidence is scarce, we can infer from the two dozen occurrences of *voluntas* before Cicero and a handful of later references where the notion may have stood as he found it. As we will see in Chapter 1, *voluntas* seems always to have held a dynamic, "onrushing" quality, denoting a deliberate, uncoerced choice. In these early Latin texts, *voluntas* is a legal or political desire-in-motion, a force by which actors with status shape their world. It is a "willing" but not yet "the will." By the 2nd century BCE, we find the playwrights Plautus and Terence adding psychological shadings that likely informed Cicero's study of politics, oratory, and the soul.

Why did Cicero need this notion? Though we find no full-blown "theory of the will" in his corpus, he deploys the word for each of his most important purposes. The first of these is survival. In an age of politician–generals, Cicero has no army. He is a "new man" (*novus homo*) in a republic led by noble families.[12] From his youthful prosecution of the wealthy Verres to his suppression of Catiline's conspiracy as consul, Cicero's career is a series of risky bets underwritten by intellectual gifts.

---

[11] *Lig.* 4–6 (after Loeb trans.).
[12] In the republican period, a *novus homo* or "new man" was the first in his family to be elected to high office. It was rare for any *novus* to ascend to the consulship and rarer still to do so at the earliest legal age, a feat Cicero accomplished in 63 BCE. See Rawson 1975, 57–59.

Introduction 5

His letters and speeches show how his skill for language gives him a subtler take on events and a richer repertoire of persuasion. In Part I of this study, these practical uses of will are foremost: mapping alliances, winning elections, and navigating what I call the "economy of goodwill." From his earliest writings, however, *voluntas* emerges in normative claims about how law and politics should work: that Rome's tangled mass of precedents could be rationalized through Greek ideas; that chief among these is Plato's precept that reason must rule; and that an alliance of philosophy and tradition must rescue the republic.

Some intellectual context is useful here. In Cicero's Rome, Greek philosophy had circulated for decades in elite circles but had yet to enter the cultural mainstream.[13] He is born around a half-century after the famous "embassy of the philosophers" in 155 BCE, in which the heads of three Greek schools – the Academy, Stoa, and Peripatos – lectured before rapt audiences at Rome and won tax relief for Athens besides. What the Hellenistic schools largely shared – including the Epicureans, popular in Rome but allergic to politics and thus absent from the embassy – was a concern with the material over the transcendental. The leading schools in the period after Plato and Aristotle considered reason an immanent presence in the world, with our mental states governed by physical laws. For the Stoics, perhaps the best-received school in Rome, the universe was itself a perfectly rational being. Uniquely among living creatures, humans participate in the *logos* via the act of rational assent (*synkatathesis*) and thus bear the strictest responsibility for our actions. This central Stoic claim would become a touchstone of great importance to the young Marcus.

On a visit to Athens in 79 BCE, Cicero studies with Antiochus of Ascalon, an integrator of Stoic ideas into the Academic tradition.[14] As he later reports in the *Academica* (45 BCE), Antiochus divided the physical world into two principles:

> [T]he active principle they deemed to constitute force [*vis*]; the one acted on, a sort of "material"; yet they held that each of the two was present in the combination of both, for matter could not have formed a concrete whole by itself with no force to hold it together, nor yet force without some matter ... (1.24)

---

[13] See Moatti 2015, 47–49, 78–79. Cicero could even play down his own philosophical interests to win advantage in a public argument; *Mur.* 61–65. Cf. *Tusc.* 4.74.
[14] See Plut. *Cic.* 4.1–4; cf. Schofield 2012, 240–49; Corbeill 2013, 13; Woolf 2015, 11–16. On Antiochus' thought, see generally Sedley 2012.

Further along, Cicero relates this idea to one given by the Peripatetic Strato, "that whatever either is or comes into being has been caused by natural forces of gravitation and motion."[15] Lévy has argued that these early influences were crucial to Cicero's view of oratory – his lifelong passion and profession – as a contest of physical forces that unfolds between speakers and their audience. This "physics" of oratory, quantifiable and scientific, may in turn reflect an early understanding of "a world that can be reduced to an ensemble of forces without the intervention of an intelligent creator."[16] As I explore in Chapter 3, these influences may have inspired Cicero to view his endangered republic in similar terms: as a matrix of forces, formerly aligned and now in need of repair.

The stakes were not simply theoretical. Following the assassination of Tiberius Gracchus in 132 BCE, the rivalries of Rome's political elite had solidified into two principal affiliations: the *populares* ("people's men") and *optimates* ("best men"). At various periods before Cicero's birth and during his life, leaders of each side proved ready to demolish precedent and murder their opponents *en masse*.[17] An orator, not a fighter, Cicero wants to refound Rome by the force of persuasion. His project is as politically conservative as it is intellectually radical. The principles of Plato and the Stoics not only accord with Rome's ancestral customs, but philosophy itself demonstrates Rome's perfection. Status and custom alone can no longer hold together a society whose institutions have been compromised by bad men. Only *ratio* – the irrevocable reason of natural law – can justify the wills of politicians and people. In practice, this means a reinforcement of collegiality and self-restraint, a balance between the forces of law (*ius*) and personal ambition – each useful for the public when properly constrained. This equilibrium of will is *concordia ordinum*, the amicable hierarchy of classes that Cicero presents as his ideal.[18]

Following the trauma of his exile (58–57 BCE), Cicero finds a new arrow for his quiver of argument. With Pompey, Caesar, and their armies now dictating public affairs, a balance of wills may no longer be possible. Though never abandoning *concordia*, Cicero proposes a new ideal in *Pro Sestio* (56 BCE): *consensus bonorum*, an unshakeable bond of all moral citizens, rich and poor, against the wicked few.[19] This ideal of consensus grounded in natural law – of intrinsic collaboration rather than balanced

---

[15] Cic. *Acad.* 2.121.   [16] Lévy 2012a, 268. See also Lévy 2008, 5–20.
[17] See generally Brunt 1971; Mouritsen 2001; Arena 2012, chs. 4 and 5.
[18] See *Cat.* 4.15; *Att.* 1.17.9–10; *Sest.* 137; *Rep.* 2.69. Cf. Morstein-Marx 2004, 101; Connolly 2010, 10–12.
[19] *Sest.* 97.

competition – is crucial to understanding what Cicero means by "the will of the people." Here, again, intellectual daring and conservative politics go hand in hand. Yes, his protagonist Scipio declares in *De republica*, *res publica* is *res populi*, the people's possession. At the same time, tradition and nature's law require the people to express their liberty not in participatory self-government but through a ruling class that relies upon their votes. In these dialogues, *voluntas populi* becomes the binding force of a nominally popular but functionally elitist constitution.

If this state of affairs looks familiar in today's "democratic" republics, we have Cicero in part to thank. Equality under the law, diffusion and rotation of power, the transaction of public affairs in public view – these are the republican ideals to which Cicero dedicated his life and that continue to inspire. But Cicero was also the first to argue that the quintessential use of a citizen's freedom is to elect better men to office. He was the first to argue (with help from Plato) that this elite must be specially educated in an art of rational rule unavailable to the masses. And he was the first to argue that the citizens – though free and sovereign – be kept as far as possible from actual governing. Rulership in sovereign republics would be strictly reserved for enlightened statesmen like himself.

In the 18th century, the republican model embodied in Cicero's writings was indeed a great leap forward; here in the 21st century, his ideal of a rational elite has cracked. Insistence on the singularity of popular will and mistrust of the common citizen lie at the heart of today's political crisis. And populists today, as *populares* did before, capitalize on the failures of elites to play the virtuous role Cicero intended. It is only logical that voters, denied education or experience of public affairs, increasingly use the one power left to them – the ballot – to detonate a system that neglects and humiliates them. And, like Caesar, the "people's champions" who grasp at their votes may prove the greatest threat to free society.

How does the story end? In Cicero's case, Rome's ensemble of forces collapses into a single man's all-powerful will. With Caesar ascendant, Cicero turns *voluntas* inward; the will of the people is reimagined as an inalienable force of the soul. In *De finibus* (45 BCE), the *Tusculan Disputations* (45 BCE), *De fato* (44 BCE), and *De officiis* (44 BCE), *voluntas* becomes the locus of individual responsibility, the power to conquer our defects, and the mark of a free conscience in an unfree age. Transmuting political failure into philosophical innovation, Cicero develops a new idea – the will and its freedom – with tremendous consequences for Western thought.

Through his astonishingly varied career, the force of *voluntas* is inflected and enriched. A mind as fertile as Cicero's defies exhaustivity.

Nevertheless, I will argue for three critical qualities that emerge in Cicero's notion of will: (1) its durability, (2) its measurability, and (3) its moral bivalence.

The *voluntas* Cicero inherits from Roman tradition denotes a single "willing," not a continuous power of mind. From the evidence available to us, it is Cicero who gives durability to the will. Early signs appear in his analysis of the *voluntas* or "spirit" of a law, which outlasts its legislator and maintains its power on posterity.[20] Cicero also links *voluntas* to *mens*, insisting as consul that it was not he alone who foiled the conspirators, but rather, "I received this mind and will [*mentem voluntatemque*] from the immortal gods . . ."[21] A similar durability is present in *voluntas mutua*, the goodwill transacted over years by distant friends and allies. *Voluntas populi*, too, retains its power beyond the moment of election – it is public will, for example, that underwrites his suppression of Catiline's plot.[22] In his treatises, the ex-consul brings the durability of *voluntas* into his architecture of the soul. Will, in the *Tusculans*, becomes "that which desires something with reason [*quae quid cum ratione desiderat*]" (4.12); in *De finibus*, it is the part of our soul where nature places the cardinal virtues (5.36); and in *De officiis*, the *persona* or role we choose in life "sets forth from our will [*a nostra voluntate proficiscitur*]" (1.115). In all of these genres, and centuries before Augustine, Cicero completes the word's transformation from a specific instance of will to a unified capacity for them all.

As Cicero gives durability to the will, he expands its measurability as well. His path to legal and political success is made by ceaselessly (if not always correctly) divining the intentions of others. In his letters and speeches *voluntas* is not binary, as *hekōn* or *eunoia* are in Greek,[23] but protean. Will varies in kind, as when a friend has "such ample goodwill for me" (*in me tali voluntate*) that he "do[es] more for my friends than perhaps I should do myself";[24] it varies in strength, as when a prosecutor shows "how much will and devotion" (*quantum voluntatis et studii*) lay in a

---

[20] See the discussion of *controversia ex scripto et sententia* and *De inventione* in Chapter 2.
[21] Cic. *Cat.* 3.22.
[22] Ibid. 4.14: All of Cicero's plans have been made "in accordance with the will of the Roman people to defend their supreme power and preserve their common fortune [*populi Romani ad summum imperium retinendum et ad communis fortunas conservandas voluntate*]."
[23] Whatever the complexity of the surrounding facts, in Greek an action is either "willing" (*hekōn*) or "unwilling" (*akōn*) – it cannot be "*hekōn* to a certain extent." Similarly, *eunoia* is a binary consideration in Greek: goodwill is either present or absent. See discussions in Chapters 1, 4, and 6.
[24] *Fam.* 3.293.2.

defendant;[25] and it varies over time, as when he complains that a friend's will is "more obstinate [*obstinatior*] than before."[26] Cicero is a master psychologist *avant la lettre*: Tracing the shifts in Pompey's intentions or lecturing his rivals on the "inmost feelings" (*intimos sensus*) of the Roman people, he both describes and practices the interpretation of will.[27] He carries this talent into the late treatises, where volition is given prime importance in quelling inner turmoil and establishing reason's rule in the soul. The measurability of *voluntas* propels his account of moral progress: To overcome our vices, the will must be trained and grow stronger. This markedly Roman account takes the Platonic notion of a divided soul and heightens it with the language of manly combat. Since the origin of our suffering lives within us, our duty is to oppose it or, in the terms of Stoic physics, to "intensify" our souls. In his magnum opus of moral philosophy, the *Tusculan Disputations*, willpower is what makes reason effective and progress possible.

The third essential quality of Cicero's *voluntas* is its hesitation between good and evil – what I call its "moral bivalence." In the *Tusculans*, Cicero identifies *voluntas* with the Stoic *boulēsis* or rational desire. Though not always directed toward proper ends, *boulēsis* is firmly and fully rational. Elsewhere, however, Cicero follows more conventional usage and makes *voluntas* akin to *hormē*, an impulse unhinged from reason.[28] He contrasts the *voluntates* of his legal clients with the rationality of law; Catiline's coconspirators look *honesti* but have "a most shameless will and cause" (*voluntas et causa impudentissima*);[29] with Caesar in power, all matters depend "on someone else's will, not to say his lust [*in alterius voluntate, ne dicam libidine*]."[30] These more negatively charged references to will are not confined to his oratory: In the *Tusculans* themselves, his definition of *voluntas* as a rational force is followed quickly by warnings against the "willing" (*voluntaria*) disturbances of our minds.[31] The moral bivalence of *voluntas* is clearest, perhaps, in the competing schemata of *De inventione*,

---

[25] *Inv.* 2.90. [26] *Att.* 1.7.1.
[27] *Sest.* 119–20. See also *Off.* 1.59, his counsel to young Romans to become "good calculators of duty" (*boni ratiocinatores officiorum*).
[28] Though the original sense of *hormē* covered various kinds of impulse or forward motion (as illustrated earlier in this Introduction), the Stoics positioned *hormē* within a monist view of the soul (i.e. fully partaking in reason). See Graver 2007, 26–28, discussed in Chapter 6.
[29] *Cat.* 2.18. [30] *Fam.* 2.190.3.
[31] See *Tusc.* 4.60, 4.65, and 4.83. Though he occasionally substitutes *voluntate* and *voluntaria* for one another, the latter term occurs far less frequently in Cicero's corpus and generally in more technical contexts: five times in his rhetorical treatises, fifteen times in his orations, six times in his letters, and thirty-three times in his philosophical treatises. Its most common use is to signal that an act that is typically coerced is in fact occurring willingly (e.g. *mors voluntaria* for suicide, *Fam.* 3.183.3, or

where it signifies criminal intent in one scheme and a righteous state of mind in another. Anticipating Christian thinkers who will explain human will as a battlefield between angelic and demonic powers, Cicero makes the *voluntas* of an audience an orator's prize that can "incline" (*inclinare*) in his favor or against him. Neither entirely rational nor irredeemably wicked, the will becomes – for the first time, it seems – the contested terrain of a moral life.

The notion of will helps Cicero confront a final problem, one that almost led him to suicide. In the theater of politics, Roman identity was forged in moments of public validation and rejection. In his rapid ascent, Cicero's sense of self is fed by popular goodwill and the (occasional) embrace of highborn peers. When fortune turns, however, the exiled Cicero despairs: "What am I really [*quid enim sum*]?"[32] Marked by bitter experience and deprived of public favor, Cicero turns to philosophy for a new foundation of self, secure from tyrants and the crowd. The pursuit of fame is a "mistaken path" (*error cursus*), he writes in the *Tusculans*:[33] Life's only true meaning is virtue, which depends on us alone. His final word for posterity, the *De officiis*, offers a view of selfhood at a crossroads of Western thought, applying Hellenistic ideas to reaffirm republican duty. Adapting the Stoic Panaetius' theory of four *personae*, Cicero makes will the fourth and freest "role" of moral lives. In so doing, I argue, he makes possible the later idea of the will as the battleground of moral choice and driver of self-consciousness. With Augustine and the church fathers, divine will submerges terrestrial politics, and many more centuries would pass before Cicero's republican values could find new life.

The problems he poses for rational self-rule still remain. Will we continue to place the hopes of free citizens in the hands of an elite or will we discover that the most effective government, *contra* Plato and Cicero, is the one that can harness collective intelligence? In politics as in the soul, the will may yet provide a vital force for good – what Arendt calls the power "to bring about something new."[34]

The principal method of this study is a close reading of Cicero's corpus. Given the state of our sources, a few points of caution should be raised. The first of these relates to Cicero's originality. Contemporary scholarship has mostly, if not entirely, discarded the caricature of Cicero as an

---

justifying his reconciliation with the hated Crassus as "voluntary forgetfulness", *oblivio voluntaria*, *Fam.* 1.20.20). For a full list of such uses, see Chapter 2, note 73.
[32] *Att.* 1.60.2; see discussion in Chapter 8.   [33] *Tusc.* 3.4.   [34] Arendt 1971, vol. 2, 7.

Introduction 11

unoriginal thinker and clever parrot of his Greek sources.³⁵ Moreover, occurrences of *voluntas* in letters from his correspondents, as well as from contemporaneous texts like Varro's *De lingua Latina* and the *Rhetorica ad Herennium*, suggest where Cicero's usages may have diverged from or gone beyond what was current in his time. Nevertheless, the superabundance of his pen in the surviving record should not lead us to rash conclusions. He was certainly not the only politician at Rome to invoke *voluntas populi*, nor – as we will see with Lucretius – was he the only Roman of his time to posit a free will. On the other hand, given Cicero's outstanding intellectual gifts, his prolific output, and his eminence in Roman society, we should not be at all surprised to find both original and influential ideas in his corpus.

A second point of caution relates to genre. I resist the tendency to detach Cicero's ideas from his *vita activa*, and I do not view his political and philosophical projects as nonoverlapping pursuits.³⁶ It is certainly the case that the genres of oratory, correspondence, and dialectic carried different codes for their practitioners, norms we may struggle to identify. A usage from one genre might not carry its meaning to another. On the other hand, Cicero lived a life of uncommon breadth, combining and alternating his pursuits in unprecedented ways – most notably in his defense of skeptical freedom as Rome's civic freedoms were extinguished. What I propose in this work, therefore, is to supplement these considerations of genre and usage with a "wide-angle view" of *voluntas* as it served Cicero throughout his life.

Finally, there is the polysemy of *voluntas* itself. As we have already seen, the notion of will Cicero inherits already contains multiple coexisting senses, from criminal intent to the goodwill of an audience. Though the evidence does suggest that *voluntas* is indigenous to Latin thought,³⁷ it does *not* suggest a teleological progress of the word from one sense to another. Rather, we will see how all throughout Cicero's career multiple coexisting senses of will are activated by context and mature in dialogue with one another. An analogy could be the development of a multicellular

---

³⁵ See, e.g., Plut. *Cic.* 40.2. A typical comment is Brunt 1988, 353: "It is true that he was not an original thinker and that where he is concerned with the more abstract philosophic themes ... he perhaps does no more than expound the doctrines of others, whether or not he indicates his own approval or dissent." See also Gauthier 1970, 260; Rawson 1975, 3; Kahn 1988, 241; Frede 2011, 25, 37, 91–93.
³⁶ Steel 2017b gives an enlightening overview of this debate in Ciceronian scholarship.
³⁷ As an illustration, in his treatises Cicero does not immediately translate *voluntas* in its first occurrence, as he does with terms such as *adsensio* for the Greek *synkatathesis*. See *Acad.* 2.37; Plut. *Cic.* 40.2. I am grateful to David Sedley for highlighting this point.

organism: New cells can add to the complexity and character of the whole without displacing older ones.

I do think Caesar's consolidation of power marks a decisive moment in this organic process. The "inward turn" of Cicero's *voluntas* is only one result – if a fascinating and consequential one – of the philosophical project he embarks upon in 46 BCE. Caesar's subsequent assassination and Cicero's sudden reentry onto the public stage only underscore the nonlinearity of history and language. If we can posit a truly Ciceronian contribution to the will, it almost certainly lies at this intersection of politics and philosophy of mind – which was, as we will see, a politics by other means.[38] Cicero's dual eminence in the practice of politics and the transmission of ideas is nearly unique and, in my view, must inform any argument regarding his notion of will. I do not think it a coincidence, in sum, that the earliest surviving mentions of "the will of the people" and "free will" are found with him. Again, his development of *voluntas* should not be seen as a "project," but rather as the natural result of an extraordinary mind pushing on inherited boundaries to meet new needs. While we will never know his intent in opening these fields of meaning, two millennia of intellectual history bear their imprint.

My study of Cicero's *voluntas* unfolds in two parts. Part I centers upon Cicero's writings and speeches as a student, as an advocate of increasing prominence, and finally as a mature politician. Chapter 1 examines the forebears of his notion of will in Greek thought and Roman usage in the period before his birth, with special attention given to the playwrights Plautus and Terence. Chapter 2 examines how the multiform legal use of *voluntas* helps the young lawyer argue and relate to his clients, witnesses, and juries. In the *De inventione* and forensic speeches, we see an ingenious and not always successful struggle to merge Roman tradition with new intellectual tools. In Chapter 3, I employ the concept of powermapping to show how the rising politician uses *voluntas* to reveal hidden intentions and reframe partisan divides. Here, again, Cicero uses will both to analyze Roman practice as he finds it and to argue for its rational improvement. Chapter 4 draws on Cicero's letters to propose an "economy of goodwill" in the late Republic. Through *voluntas mutua*, Cicero and his correspondents handle the sensitive transactions of a fast-growing empire, though his treatises show an intriguing ambivalence about a system that served him well in practice. Chapter 5 is dedicated to the *voluntas populi* and the role

---

[38] Schofield 2021, 7. See generally Barnes and Griffin 1989; Lévy 1992; Powell 1995; Baraz 2012; Nicgorski 2012; Steel 2017b.

of the people in Cicero's ideal republic. In his speeches, he endows the people's will with four principal qualities: It is fundamental, singular, fallible, and dependent on wise elites. I then explore the arguments of *De republica* and *De legibus* in favor of the people's sovereignty and against their participation in government. The trusteeship principle from *ius civilis*, buttressed by Plato and Stoic natural law, creates an entirely new constitutional dynamic: the people's will, guarantor of public liberty, guided and fulfilled by a rational elite.

Part II focuses on the notion of will in Cicero's philosophical works. In Chapter 6, we see how he links together lines of debate that in Greek had run in parallel, rendering *hekōn*, *boulēsis*, and *prohairesis* by *voluntas* and *voluntarius*. The "struggle for reason" depicted in the *Tusculan Disputations* moves originally beyond Greek accounts of *askēsis*, a regime of moral improvement that emphasized mental clarity, not concerted effort. With the *Tusculans*, I argue, willpower enters Western thought. In Chapter 7, we see how Cicero and Lucretius first turn a Greek debate on what is "up to us" into one on the freedom of the will. I propose that Cicero's idea of the will's *libertas* in *De fato* – the opportunity to conquer vice and win honor – is antithetical to the Epicurean ideas of *De rerum natura*. For Cicero, free will is the locus of civic virtue, justification of "praise and honors," and a way to reconcile with his own political failures. Chapter 8 is dedicated to the theory of self Cicero presents in *De officiis*: each person inhabiting four *personae*. The good life, Cicero explains, lies in learning to play the roles of universal reason, inborn nature, changeable fortune, and, finally, the role that "sets forth from our will" (*a nostra voluntate proficiscitur*) (1.115). In his final treatise, *voluntas* comes most clearly into view as a power of the human soul that fashions and refashions a conscious self.

In the Epilogue, I briefly explore the legacy of Cicero's *voluntas* in politics and philosophy of mind. Passages from the *De natura deorum*, in which the power of will is shared by gods and men, prefigure the struggle Augustine depicts in his *Confessions* to subdue his will with the help of divine grace. Closer to our time, echoes of Cicero in the works of Jean-Jacques Rousseau (*la volonté générale*) and Thomas Jefferson ("the will of the people") show how the problematic notion of *voluntas populi* has shaped our politics and suggest how these problems may still, with a dose of Ciceronian creativity, be resolved.

PART I

The Practice of Voluntas

CHAPTER I

Forebears of Will

The problem of the will, however snarled, is at least not etymological. The English "will," including its use in the future auxiliary, derives from Old English *willan* ("to wish, be willing, be about to"), and from there to the Proto-Germanic *willjan*. Its earliest forebear, the Proto-Indo-European root *wel-* ("to wish, will"), is also ancestor to the Latin *velle*, whose substantive form is *voluntas*.[1] The shared genealogy of *voluntas* and "will" has been reinforced by many centuries of debate in Western philosophy, law, politics, and theology, whose protagonists took direct inspiration from Latin sources or argued in Latin themselves. These debates were served not only by the clarity and richness of the Latin tongue but also by the texts and exemplars of the Roman world. Its *res publica*, in particular, was a touchstone and cautionary tale for Enlightenment defenders of "the will of the people" and *la volonté générale*. More recently, a consensus has emerged that the post-classical, pre-Christian eras – the "Hellenistic and early imperial" – were the crucible for notions of will to which thinkers like Augustine and Rousseau would later give shape.[2]

Though these compositions were in Latin, their preludes were sung in Greek. Tracing the philosophy of mind through antiquity is bewitchingly complex.[3] Histories of will tend to depart from Socrates' provocation that if we truly knew what was good for us we could not fail to act accordingly – in other words, that "weakness of will" (*akrasia*) is impossible.[4] Plato takes a different line on the problem in the Republic, where he proposes that

---

[1] "uoluntas" in Ernout and Meillet 1960; "will" in the *Oxford English Dictionary* (Simpson and Weiner 1989). A still more direct route links *velle/voluntas* to the French *vouloir/volonté*.
[2] See, e.g., Arendt 1971, vol. 2, 84; Dihle 1982, 144; Kahn 1988, 255–59; King 2010, xxxi; Brann 2014, 23–37.
[3] Key references for this study include Hatinguais 1958; Pohlenz 1964; Gauthier 1970; Arendt 1971; Voelke 1973; Kenny 1979; Dihle 1982; Foucault 1981–82; Inwood 1985; Kahn 1988; Bobzien 1998b; Gill 2006; Graver 2007; Frede 2011; and Long 2015.
[4] The traditional rendering of *akrasia* in English as "weakness of will" is problematic for reasons explored infra; cf. Frede 2011, 22–23.

reason and appetite reside in different parts of the soul; though we succumb to appetite despite "knowing better," in a harmonious soul as in a just city, reason must rule. Plato's star student is the first to propose a full theory of human action, but neither Aristotle's *boulēsis* (the desire for ends) nor his *prohairesis* (the choice of means) maps onto the faculty that Latin speakers would call *voluntas*.[5] It is the Stoics, and particularly Epictetus, who have been credited by some as inventors of the will due to their intense focus on regulating our inner responses to external events.[6] Leaving aside the problem of how these Greek texts might have found their way into Latin-speaking Christendom, there is a more serious problem: The word *voluntas* contains meanings absent from *prohairesis* or any other counterpart in Greek.[7] How, indeed, did the notion of will become central within two strikingly different debates: one about political sovereignty, the other about whether the universe determines our actions in advance?

A useful first step, therefore, is to take stock of the menagerie of Greek terms that encircle the will, as well as the evolution of the word *voluntas* in Latin before Cicero. While I cannot give this "prehistory of will" the scope it deserves, a brisk overview will help compass the range of senses upon which the young Cicero drew. These include four contexts that will be especially interesting for the budding politician and person of letters: (1) volition and legitimate command; (2) goodwill, both individual and collective; (3) political or constitutional power; and (4) free will and moral responsibility.

1.1 Greek Forebears

In his pioneering work on Stoic philosophy, Voelke observes, "The term 'to will' does not translate into Greek; *thelein* indicates that the subject is ready to, disposed to, consenting, without having taken a particular decision; *boulesthai* marks the wish or preference for a determined object, a choice tied to deliberation."[8] Indeed, *thelein* – perhaps the closest

---

[5] See Kenny 1979, 13–26, 69–80; Frede 2011, 19–30; Merker 2016, *passim*.
[6] See Gauthier 1970, 259: "[O]f the traits of the 'will' that we find in Augustine, there is not a single one that cannot already be found in the Stoics." Cf. Kahn 1988, 252–55, on Epictetus. Frede 2011, 44–48, provides the fullest and most convincing case for Epictetus' *prohairesis* as a faculty of will.
[7] See Kahn 1988, 248: "[W]hether it reflects linguistic poverty or strength of character, the fact is undeniable that *voluntas* and its cognates play a role in Latin thought and literature for which there is no parallel for any term in Classical or Hellenistic Greek."
[8] Voelke 1973, 5.

1.1 Greek Forebears

Greek equivalent to *volo* – bears a critical difference from its Latin counterpart. Where *volo* implies the active pursuit of an object (as do "*je veux*" and "I want"), *ethelō* is a statement of consent or favorable disposition. It tends to imply negotiation with another party: In Book 23 of the *Iliad*, when Achilles asks Agamemnon to award his spear to Meriones, his words are "if you consent [*ethelois*] in your spirit : so at least would I have it." Agamemnon's desire is the obverse of Achilles', and they are inseparable: one Greek's desire implying another's consent. The linguistic relationships here and elsewhere in archaic texts testify to a milieu of decentralized authority in which men constantly vie with one another for support. The forward motion of *volo* finds a correspondence in *hormē*, an impulse or appetite, used by Homer to describe the onrushing force of an invading army.[9]

If *thelein* consents, *boulesthai* commands. In its early usage, *boulesthai* is something much closer to the will ascribed to gods and rulers in English, announcing the decision of an individual with authority over another. The highest form of *boulēsis* is divine, as in Homer's Apollo: "[H]e willed victory to the Trojans [*Trōessin ... ebouleto nikēn*]."[10] Though *boulesthai* is generally available to all thinking subjects, unlike *hormē*[11] and like the English "will" it implies a choice justified by status and deliberation.[12] As Liddell and Scott note in their lexical entry, "Homer uses *boulomai* for *ethelō* in the case of the gods, for with them *wish* is *will*."[13] The same is true for *boulesthai*'s close cousin *bouleuesthai*, used in Homer to describe the councils of war and political deliberation more generally.[14] This

---

[9] See ibid. 9.355. Already in Homer, *hormē* could take on psychological connotations, see *Il*. 4.466, *Od*. 5.416; and also of an impulse received from another, *Il*. 10.123; cf. *Od*. 2.403. The term assumes an important role in the Stoic theory of action; see discussion in Chapter 5.

[10] Hom. *Il*. 7.21; cf. 23.62.

[11] Indeed, *hormē* could be used to describe the desires or impulses of a ruler that were less legitimate or respectable in the author's opinion. See, e.g., Polybius' description of Philip of Macedon: "For both owing to the splendor of his position and the brilliancy of his genius the good and evil impulses of this prince [*tas eis hekateron to meros hormas*] were very conspicuous and widely known throughout Greece"; Polyb. 7.11.3, same phrase at 7.11.4.

[12] I mean "legitimate" here in the sense of establishing or following a rule; the status and deliberation behind a *boulēsis* – even simply "I am a human and I've thought about this" – reproduce higher kinds of collective or divine lawmaking at an individual level. *Thelein*, *hekōn*, and *hormē* do not carry this conceptual weight.

[13] "βούλομαι," LSJ (Liddell–Scott–Jones Greek–English lexicon; emphasis added). The dialectic of *boulomai* and *ethelō* echoes throughout the classical period; see Pl. *Grg*. 522e.

[14] See, e.g., Hom. *Od*. 9.299, *Od*. 9.420, *Od*. 14.491, *Od*. 16.234, *Il*. 2.379. Cammack 2021 emphasizes the interior quality of *bouleuomai*/*bouleuesthai* – that is, a "deliberation" that may be unspoken or informal rather than explicit and formal – in her study of the Athenian *ekklēsia* in the classical period.

legal or political will can be subverted for comic purposes, as by Menander, who has young men and even slaves make lordly pronouncements of intent.[15]

As the language of Greek philosophy develops in the classical and Hellenistic eras, a new term assumes importance: *prohairesis*. Its root, *hairein*, originally connotes a "taking," especially of a town or city.[16] By the classical age *hairesis* could refer to the election of magistrates, a system of philosophical principles, or the affiliation of individuals to a given school or sect.[17] The prefix *pro-* adds the sense of "prior": *prohairesis* becomes the mental "taking" or choice that precedes the outward act. A distinction thus emerges in 4th-century BCE thought between *boulēsis*, the determination of an end (e.g., "what I'd like right now is a muffin"), and *prohairesis*, the selection of means to that end ("I'll go to the bakery on the corner").[18] *Hormē*, *boulēsis*, and *prohairesis* play sharply different roles in the Hellenistic schools' theories of action, but their relation is loosely that of "impulse," "willing," and "choice."[19] Both *boulēsis* and *prohairesis* will play starring roles in later genealogies of the will, but in the Hellenistic period their main association is with rational thought – a limitation that will not apply as strictly to *voluntas*.

There was no "will of the people" in classical Greece. As the *dēmos* earned political rights in Athens, it wielded power not by delegation but in active, autonomous decision. The key term of art was *dokein*, "to be resolved" (literally "to seem [best]"), most often expressed as a perfective verb: A law entered into force when "resolved by the council and people [*edoxen tē boulē kai toi dēmoi*]."[20] The relationship between the Athenian

---

[15] For example, in Act II of Dyskolos, the urbane and shiftless Sostratos hesitates at the door of the girl's house before deciding, "I'll knock on the door; that will stop any further debate [*hin' ei moi mede bouleusasth'eti*]"; Men. *Dys.* 267 (trans. Miller). When blocked by her brother, Sostratos haughtily retorts, "If I've come here with any criminal purpose, or with any intent [*boulomenos*] to plot mischief against you ... may Pan here, sir, and the Nymphs strike me dead ..."; ibid. 310–13. See also Men. *Epit.* 162; *Fab. Incert.* 5 at 21.

[16] "αἵρεσις," LSJ.

[17] Ibid. See Polyb. 6.7.3: "In the natural development of monarchy the people come to choose their kings and rulers [*tauta tēn hairesin tōn arkhontōn*], no longer for strength and courage but for judgment and reason."

[18] "προαίρεσις," LSJ. *Hairesis* also retains the sense of "choice," as in Polyb. 6.2.9: "[T]he study of causes and the consequent power of choosing [*hairesis*] what is best in each case."

[19] See discussion in Chapter 6.

[20] See Meiggs and Lewis 1989, 90; Rhodes 1972, 244–83. This phrase of formal enactment continued until at least the 3rd century CE; see ibid. at 308. Rhodes 1972, 64, also discusses the more literal *psephizesthai*, "to cast a vote by pebble"; see, e.g., Aeschin. *On the disloyal embassy* 60: "And whatever the people shall decree [*psephisētai ho dēmos*], this shall [count as] a common resolution of the allies."

1.1 Greek Forebears

Council (*boulē*) and the popular Assembly (*ekklēsia*) bears superficial resemblance to that of the Roman senate and the people's *comitia*, in that the smaller – and probably more well-off[21] – Council prepared texts for the larger Assembly to ratify. But the differences were stark. The *boulē* had nowhere near the constitutional preeminence of the Roman senate or its modern equivalents. Their core function was the preparation of draft decrees and laws that the people had full rights to amend or, if they chose, to tear up and start again.[22] Unsurprisingly, then, members of the *boulē* – chosen by lottery, not election[23] – did not describe themselves as representatives of public "will" or opinion. They took an oath to "do what was best for the people," but this exhortation to act in the common interest did not include any sense of trusteeship or elite status,[24] as they later would in Rome.[25] As Rhodes concludes, "the *boulē* was a selection of citizens taking their turn in office, not a powerful governing class with vested interests to protect."[26] There is no special discourse of representation in classical Athens, because in the democracy – we might say, in any democracy worthy of the name[27] – there is no permanent governing class.

---

[21] Rhodes 1972, 4–5, admits that "the very rich occupied almost twice as many places [in the *boulē*] as their numbers entitled them to … [such that] a certain amount of bias towards the rich must have been inevitable."

[22] Rhodes 1972, 52–53, notes that there is some uncertainty as to which body had true power of initiative as well as under what conditions the council made a recommendation and when it merely "invited the *ekklēsia* to debate." Nevertheless, all evidence suggests that the primary role of the *boulē* was procedural, not deliberative; there is no evidence of a council claiming to "represent" the *dēmos*, nor – since the *ekklēsia* was unquestionably the central locus for decision – was there a constitutional basis for such a claim.

[23] See Rhodes 1972, 6. Though elections played a larger role in earlier periods (the archons were elective under Cleisthenes, at which point they still wielded significant executive power), Rhodes observes that selection by lot "seems to have been regarded as an essential characteristic of a democratic *boulē*."

[24] According to two passages from Lysias, members of the *boulē* swore "to advise [*bouleusein*] what was best for the city"; Lys. 31.2, 30.10. Demosthenes mentions councilors swearing to advise "what was best for the People"; Dem. *Neaer.* 59.4. See generally Blackwell 2003, 5.

[25] See, e.g., Cic. *Sest.* 38: "I carried out measures for which I was not the sole author, but rather the leader of the general will [*eas res gesseram, quarum non unus auctor, sed dux omnium voluntatis fuissem*]." The special discourse Cicero develops in relation to *voluntas populi* is my main subject in Chapter 5.

[26] Rhodes 1972, 214. Unlike the Roman senate, the entire membership of the *boulē* turned over each year, and each citizen could serve a one-year term on the Council only twice in his lifetime; see Arist. *Ath. Pol.* 62.3. But see Lysias' accusations that the Council of the period before the Thirty Tyrants had developed an "appetite for oligarchy" and become corrupt; Lys. 13.19–20. I am grateful to Paul Cartledge for suggesting this argument.

[27] Cartledge 2016, 3–5, 306–11. On the centrality of representation in Roman public discourse, Garsten 2006, 160, notes that whereas Romans were represented in court by advocates like Cicero, Athenian defendants spoke on their own behalf.

Even the demagogues who populated the *agora* did not claim to represent a singular "will" of the *dēmos*.[28] In a political order where elections were not the main locus of power, politicians entreated their audience to vote with them, not instill them with representative power.[29] In foreign affairs, policies were announced as *dogmata tou dēmou*; again the key emphasis is on concrete decisions, not collective will.[30] Conversely, in debates over large-scale political relationships, the key term is *eunoia*, literally "good disposition of mind," most often rendered as "goodwill."[31] *Eunoia* is not a decision but rather the favorable sentiment underlying a decision, as when the people of Ceos grant citizenship rights to "Naupactus and the council of the Aetolians ... [who] have shown all goodwill and respect to the cities of Ceos."[32] As with *boulesthai/bouleuesthai*, a state of *eunoia* can exist between individuals, communities, or a combination of the two.[33]

Only Polybius, describing Rome's republic to the Greek-speaking world, comes close to naming what Cicero would call *voluntas populi*. He inventively combines *eunoia* with both *dokein* and *prohairesis* to render an argument on the legitimacy of political power: Hippocrates claims that his grandfather, Pyrrhus, was "the only man whom all the Sicilians had accepted as their leader and king deliberately and from goodwill [*kata*

---

[28] The standard trope was to call upon an audience to "vote my way"; see, e.g., the speech of the ephor Sthenelaidas at Thuc. 1.86 ("Therefore, Spartans, cast your votes [*psēphizesthe*] for the honor of Sparta and for war!").

[29] "The overt purpose of most orations was to persuade the mass audience to act – specifically, to vote – in a particular way"; Ober 1989, 43. Compare Demosthenes' praise for the superior judgment of the assembly: "I, being one, would be more likely to be mistaken than all of you"; Dem. *Ex.* 45; see also Hyp. 1.14 (no one in the polis can deceive "the mass of you").

[30] See, e.g., Aeschin. *Ctes.* 69–70: In their debate over peace with Philip, "the allies submitted a *dogma* recommending peace only, which any of the Greeks might join within three months"; Xen. *Hell.* 6.3–5. On the "resolution" (*dogma*) of the *synedrion* of the Second Athenian League, see Rhodes 1986, 263.

[31] See, e.g., Hdt. 6.108: "The Lacedaemonians gave this advice not so much out of goodwill [*kata tēn eunoiēn*] toward the Plataeans as wishing to cause trouble for the Athenians with the Boeotians." Conversely, when Aeschylus' suppliant women throw themselves at the feet of King Pelasgus, he reassures them that "all men show goodwill [*eunoias pherei*] to the weaker cause"; Aesch. *Supp.* 489.

[32] *Sylloge Inscriptionum Graecarum*, 522.iii. See also *Orientis Graeci Inscriptiones Selectae*, 265: "Resolved by the council and people; proposal of the generals: Since the people of Temnus are well disposed towards the people of Pergamum, for good fortune, the council and people shall resolve to send two envoys to go [to Temnus] and declare the goodwill [*eunoian*] which the people of Pergamum continue to have towards them."

[33] See, e.g., Polyb. 7.9.8 (on the enactment of a treaty between Hannibal and Philip of Macedon: "[W]ith all zeal and goodwill [*prothumias kai eunoias*], without deceit or secret design, we will be enemies of such as war against the Carthaginians ..."); ibid. 6.1147 (Tarquinius Priscus, through his liberality, "won the gratitude of many and gained the goodwill [*eunoian*] of all"); ibid. 7.11.4 (due to Philip's genius, "all his hereditary dominions were more submissive and had more goodwill [*eunoiais*] toward him than to any king before him").

prohairesin kai kat'eunoian]" (7.4.5). Intriguingly, he describes the Roman senate as in quasi-mystical thrall to their *dēmos*: "[T]herefore for all these reasons the senate is afraid of the masses and must fasten itself to the people's mind [*toi dēmoi ton noun*]" (6.16.5).³⁴ Yet the key qualities of Cicero's "will of the people" – its sovereignty, unity, fallibility, and dependence on elites – remained unexplored.³⁵

The final shades of *voluntas* anticipated in Greek thought are terms of responsibility and autonomy. In both popular and technical use, *hekousiōs* designated an act that could justly be ascribed to the actor performing it, with *akousiōs* being its opposite. "Actor" is a better term than "person" because in philosophical settings, and notably in Aristotle, nonrational actors such as animals and children are capable of acting *hekontes* and thus can bear moral responsibility.³⁶ As Michael Frede observes, both the Latin *voluntarius* and the English "willing" are common but inaccurate translations of *hekousion*; determining an act to be *hekousion* involves questions of objective fact – was there coercion or ignorance? – not of personal intent, as the English "willing" implies.³⁷ The *hekōn* or *akōn* quality of an actor is significant in determining whether or not the actor is praiseworthy;³⁸ it is equally useful in pointing out a lack of force in situations where it might be expected, as in "voluntary exile" [*hekousion ... phugadeian*] or in the acceptance of a claim to kingship.³⁹ We will see Cicero using both *voluntas* and, less often, *voluntarius* in similar contexts of praise and blame.

---

³⁴ See also ibid. 6.16.1 (the senate is obliged "to pay attention to the commons in public affairs and respect the wishes of the people [*stokhazesthai tou dēmou*]"); 6.16.5 (tribunes "are always obliged to act as the people decree [*to dokoun toi dēmoi*] and to pay every attention to their wishes [*stokhazesthai tēs toutou bouleseōs*]"). In the latter passage, Polybius confuses the *plebs* (what he calls the *dēmos*) with the *populus*. See discussion in Chapter 5.

³⁵ In his admirable survey of Roman political theory, Atkins 2018b, 112–13, cites Plato's *Gorgias* for the notion that "even the most independent-minded and strong-willed political leader in democratic Athens is bound to the will and desire of the people." *Pace* Atkins, the passage he cites (*Grg.* 513a–c) gives no Greek word corresponding with "will"; rather, Socrates advises Callias that he would need to "make [him]self *as like as possible* [*se hōs homoiotaton gignesthai*] to the Athenian people if you intend to be pleasing to them [*ei melleis toutō prosphilēs einai*] and have great influence in the city" (emphasis added). Straumann 2016, 220, falls prey to a similar anachronism translating Arist. *Pol.* 3.1281a11–24.

³⁶ I give special attention in Chapter 6 to Aristotle's terminology of choice and responsibility in relation to the *Tusculan Disputations*.

³⁷ Frede 2011, 24–29.

³⁸ See Polyb. 6.39.4: Honors go to those soldiers who "have of their own accord and by choice [*hekousiōs kai kata prohairesin*] thrown themselves into the danger"; 6.39.6: Soldiers rescued in battle crown their saviors of their own accord (*hekontes*) or under compulsion by tribunes; 6.54.4: Single combat performed of one's own accord (*hekousiōs*) to save the Republic.

³⁹ Polyb. 6.14.7–8, 6.4.2, "It is by no means every monarchy which we can call straight off a kingship, but only that which is voluntarily accepted [*hekontōn sunkhōroumenen*] by the subjects and where they are governed rather by an appeal to their reason than by fear and force."

Finally, scientific breakthroughs of the Hellenistic period brought about a renewed focus on human autonomy and fate, this time in terms that reflected a materialist view of nature and psychology.[40] As I examine in Chapter 7, the key term of debate for the Greek schools was not *eleutheria* (freedom) but *eph'emin*, "what depends on us" or is in our power. It is Lucretius and Cicero who introduce freedom and will into the free will debate, with their two versions differing sharply – not to say vehemently – from one another.

1.2 Latin Forebears

Voluntas first comes into view in Rome as the force of lawful judgment. From its earliest years, Roman law honored two main poles of *auctoritas*: the *paterfamilias* and the magistrate. The range of their powers was not fixed in a single code, operating instead through a web of statutes, case law, and custom.[41] It is in this multiform setting that a father's will (*voluntas patris*) becomes a principle of civil law. Though earlier references are thin, evidence from Cicero's time and thereafter indicate its antiquity and scope.[42] Like the Greek *boulēsis*, it announces the decision of an actor with authority; like *hekōn*, a legitimate *voluntas* implies a lack of duress; like *hormē*, it marks an "onrushing" that is not necessarily or even typically rational – for it is status, not reason, that underpins Roman law. This "onrushing" character of *voluntas* is the defining feature of volition in Latin. Varro will write in his 1st-century BCE treatise *De lingua Latina*, "*Volo* is said to come from *voluntas* and from *volatus* ['flight'], because the spirit is such that in an instant it *pervolet* ['flies through'] to any place it wills [*volo a voluntate dictum et a volatu, quod animus ita est, ut puncto temporis pervolet quo volt*]" (6.6.47). From its origins, then, *voluntas* is a "desire-in-motion," a lawful if not always rational force.

To this richness of sense, the Romans added a talent for punctilio. In a largely illiterate society, precise oral formulations – such as "*spondeo*,"

---

[40] See generally Annas 1992, 2–33.
[41] The Twelve Tables, though a venerable source of legal precedent, was not a "constitution" and existed within this web rather than atop it. Cf. Tac. *Ann.* 3.27–28; Crook 1967, 24, 28; Lintott 1999, 3–8.
[42] See Quint. *Inst.* 12.2.9; *Dig.* 50.17.5 Ulpian. Its earliest surviving occurrence seems to be literary; in Terence's *Andria*, a father laments his son's defiance in dallying with a low woman: "How can he be so headstrong as to defy social custom and the law and the wishes of his own father [*praeter civium morem atque legem et sui voluntatem patris*]? He's determined to have this woman whatever the disgrace"; Ter. *An.* 879–81. On *voluntas patris* and *patria potestas*, see generally Villey 1945, 16–18; Crook 1967, 103–13; Dihle 1982, 135–42; Arena 2012, 23–25; Vuolanto 2016, 491–93.

1.2 Latin Forebears

spoken to seal a marriage contract – were the main proofs of *voluntas* in the event of later dispute.[43] No matter the intent of the actors, if the appropriate formula had not been verbalized – or had been verbalized incorrectly – the agreement was empty of force.[44] Importantly, at this stage of Roman legal practice the function of *voluntas* was to characterize, not constitute, an agreement. The analysis it serves is both retrospective and binary: A prior act was either "willing" (*voluntate*), and thereby lawful, or not.

Conversely, in its political setting *velle* seems to have constitutive or self-enacting power. A late 2nd-century BCE inscription in Roman Spain announces,

> *extarent eis red(d)idit dum populus [senatusque]/Roomanus vellet deque ea re eos [qui aderunt —]/eire iussit legatos Cren[— f(ilius)]/Arco Cantoni f(ilius) legates [—]*[45]

Public law, in other words, is law insofar as it is what the senate and people of Rome have willed.[46] Though extant texts from the period are rare, it appears that in a political context *velle* and the ablative *voluntate*, a "willing" decision, were more common in the republican period than the substantive *voluntas*.[47] For quite some time, in other words, the Romans may have willed or been willing without needing "a will."

As Roman legal culture evolved from its oral roots, an urbanizing society needed new tools to prove the intent behind written documents, and new subtleties of will emerged.[48] Texts from Cicero's youth show how the

---

[43] On *sponsio* as an indicator of fatherly *voluntas*, cf. Varro, *Ling*. 6.69–72. On the role of consent in Roman marriage, see Lewis 2015, 165–67.

[44] See Varro, *Ling*. 6.61: "From this, *iudicare* ['to judge'] because then *ius* ['right'] *dicitur* ['is spoken']." Cf. Villey 1945, 12: "In the absence of rich legislation, an entire juridical regime resides in these formulas." On the importance of oaths and ritual formulae in Roman law, see generally Crook 1967, 76–77; Ibbetson 2015, 25–28.

[45] Inscription from Castillejo de la Orden, Lusitania (Spain), 104 BCE; cf. inscription at Callatis, Moesia inferior (modern Romania), c. 106–101 BCE, "*quid ad hance [socie]/[tatem poplus Romanus ac poplus Call]at[inu]s adere exime[rev]e [ve]/[lint communi poplico consilio utriusque] voluntate liceto/ [quodque adiderint id inesto quodque e]xe[mer]int id societat[i]/,*" available at http://edh-www.adw.uni-heidelberg.de/edh/inschrift/HD021778; Delos (-aus), Achaia, 58 BCE: "*pro]/[tribu] A(ulus) Gabinius A(uli) f(ilius) Capito prei[mus scivit rogamus vos Quirites ve]/[litis iu]beatis quom res publica pop[ulei Romanei deorum immortalium].*"

[46] Though the phrase *velitis iubeatisne* ("Do you will and order it?") appears to have been the standard enacting phrase in the assembly, there is no occurrence in the nominative, *voluntas senati* or *voluntas populi*, in the extant record prior to Cicero. See Williamson 2005, 119–22.

[47] This appears to be the case both for legal/political and literary uses of the word. Of the twenty-five or so occurrences of *voluntas* and its cognates before Cicero's lifetime, only three were in a nominative or accusative form, and each of these in the works of Plautus and Terence. By far the majority of these early occurrences are the form *voluntate*, qualifying or "coloring" a given act.

[48] See Dihle 1982, 135–42.

precise, "did-he-or-didn't-he" rules of law were giving way to more complex hermeneutics. The *Rhetorica ad Herennium*, commonly dated to the 80s BCE,[49] suggests rules for analyzing the *indicia* of an actor's *voluntas* in cases of ambiguous expression or when literal readings produced seemingly incongruous results. This "letter and spirit controversy" (*controversia ex scripto et sententia*) seems to have been well established by the time of Cicero's student years, yet his study of the question in *De inventione* is more intricate and interesting than that of its contemporary, as we will see in Chapter 2. As concerns the "will" of a Roman official, though legal handbooks long predated Cicero, the record suggests that these were practitioner's guides, not critical studies, and certainly had no lawful force in themselves.[50] For all its complexity and centrality in Roman society, the encounter of law and *logos* had barely begun.[51]

Turning to the literary record, we find in Rome's early annalists instances of *voluntas* that anticipate Cicero's political views. The 2nd-century BCE historian Calpurnius Piso uses the term to trace the latent conflicts typical of Roman politics: "He feared his colleague L. Tarquinius because he was of the Tarquin name, and begged him to leave Rome willingly [*metuere eum/que orat, uti sua voluntate Roma concedat*]."[52] The "willingness" of Tarquinius' exit from Rome is not strictly a question of law, but rather of the legal system's greatest aim: settling conflict without violence. By Cicero's age, though, the sanctity of the courts and stability of the laws were under severe threat. A concern for public order seems to animate a fragment from the historian L. Cornelius Sisenna,[53] showing a slightly different usage: "[A]lthough the city was fearful and uncertain, due to a diversity of wills, Pomponius and his soldiers occupied a high piece of ground ... [*denique cum variis voluntatibus incerta civitas trepidaret, Pomponius cum velite superiorem locum insedit*]."[54] Here in embryonic form is another idea Cicero will develop as a core principle: A *varietas* of wills endangers the community and, conversely, only unity of will can save it.

---

[49] Enos 2005, 331.
[50] See Dyck 2004, 4; Moatti 2015, 111. Dyck and Moatti each cite the *magistratuum libri* of C. Sempronius Tuditanus (cos. 129) and the *de Potestatibus* of M. Junius Gracchanus, also mentioned by Cicero at *Leg.* 3.49.
[51] See generally Moatti 2015.
[52] L. Calpurnius Piso Frugi, *Annalium fragmenta in aliis scriptis seruata*, LLA 164, fr. 19, p. 129, line 1.
[53] Since Sisenna (c. 120–67 BCE) was only fourteen years older than Cicero, his annals may or may not precede the publication of Cicero's first speeches, notably the Verres trial of 70 BCE, in which Cicero uses *voluntas* and its cognates ninety-one times.
[54] LLA 253, fr. 78, p. 288, line 1.

1.2 Latin Forebears

It is onstage where psychological shadings of will first appear. Indeed, the earliest extant occurrence of *voluntas* in any form is not from a legal text, but rather from a play by Rome's first dramatist, Livius Andronicus. A curious line from his play *Tereus*, a tragedy first performed in the mid-to-late 3rd century BCE, reads: "Believe me that he never, with my consent, rubbed his head against [his? hers?] [*Cum illoc olli mea voluntate numquam limauit caput*]."[55] Though we miss the dramatic context, the implied relationship resembles that of *voluntas* and *sponsio* in a marriage contract: an individual giving consent, presumably verbal, for an action performed under his authority. "Reading" the will of the speaker is not yet at issue; the focus is on the relative status of the two parties, and the relation is that of *boulesthai* to *thelein*, command to consent.

By contrast, misreadings of will are critical to the intrigues of Rome's two great dramatists, Plautus and Terence. The word *voluntas* and its cognates occur eight times in Plautus' twenty-one extant comedies and six times in Terence's six. Plautus' play *Pseudolus* shows his familiarity with the "transactional" will of legal tradition. In Act I, the eponymous clever slave[56] faces a mock trial by his master and a family friend for swiping a large sum of money. Having taken the money to help his master's son buy a slave girl, Pseudolus converts the mock-criminal-trial into a mock-contract-negotiation: "Will you not at once give me the money of your own free will [*tua voluntate*] for me to pay to the procurer?" (v.536). "He makes a fair claim [*ius bonum orat*]," the friend chimes in, "say, 'I grant it.'" As in the fragment from Andronicus, the character's will is confirmed orally rather than investigated. From blessing marriages to selling goods, *voluntas* still implies a commitment whose legality stems from verbal agreement and the status – often comically inverted – of the speaker.[57]

But Plautus adds two more important shades of sense that Cicero later develops. In *Miles Gloriosus*, a trick is hatched by this play's clever slave to free the entrapped maiden Philocomasium. Persuaded that another woman seeks his affections, the swaggering soldier agrees to eject the maiden, warning, "if she will not go out of her own accord, I'll turn her out by

---

[55] Liv. Andron. *Tragoediarum fragmenta*, LLA 115, v.28.
[56] Segal 2001, 188, names the *servus callidus* as Plautus' "consummate creation."
[57] See also Plaut. *Men.* 640–45; *Stich.* 170. Karakasis 2008, 206, in reference to a Plautine scene in which a brother seeks his sister's approval before giving her away in marriage, cites Ulpian ("unless this has all been done with the girl's consent [*nisi forte omnia ista ex voluntate puellae facta sint*]"), suggesting another link between *voluntas* and *sponsio* in Roman law; *Dig.* 23.1.6. For a similar verbal contract in Greek comedy, this one using *hekōn*, see Men. *Dys.* 815–18.

force [*quin si voluntate nolet, vi extrudam foras*]."⁵⁸ Unlike the uses from Andronicus and *Phormio*, where the consent of one party allows the action of another, here lies a more complex interpretation: Is the maiden's act "willing" or not? The humor value arises from the ironic gap opened between the choice the bully claims to be offering – being removed willingly or by force – and what the audience knows, which is that the maiden not only consents to leave, but has tricked him to make this possible.⁵⁹ We also see, for the first time, *voluntas* as a force in competition with others – here, the maiden's (misread) will and the soldier's aggression.

In Plautus, therefore, will becomes an object of investigation. Though his purposes are dramatic rather than philosophical, he gives the term a broader psychological range.⁶⁰ From the well-worn premise that only a willing act can be credited or blamed, his characters spar over each other's motivations and the invisible forces that propel them. When a slave girl in the final scene of *Curculio* insists to the enraged Therapontigonus that her former master had treated her kindly, he retorts: "That was through no inclination of his own [*haud voluntate id sua*]; give thanks to Æsculapius that you've preserved your chastity; for if he had been well, he'd long ago have packed you off wherever he could." By *haud voluntate*, Plautus signifies a hidden compulsion that annuls the apparently decent behavior; "willingness" is no longer a plain fact.⁶¹ As these investigations intensify, we note a passage from *voluntate*, "willingly," to *voluntas*, "the will." In Act 2 of *Mercator*, the elderly Demipho confides to his friend Lysimachus that he is enjoying a "second youth," having contracted a case of love at first sight. He continues:

> There's no reason for you to be angry with me now: other respected men have done such a thing before. It is human to go astray and it is human to forgive. Do stop castigating me, it's not my own will that drove me to it [*ne sis me obiurga, hoc non voluntas me impulit*]. (v.321–22)

Unlike most of Plautus' pseudo-legal conflicts, here no one accuses Demipho of impropriety – except for Demipho. "Me" and "my will" are now on opposite sides of *impulit* ("urged, impelled"); perceiving his ridiculousness in the eyes of his friend, the character steps outside himself

---

⁵⁸ Plaut. *Mil.* 1120.
⁵⁹ The humor of the scene is heightened by its juxtaposition with an earlier one in which the soldier's henchman threatens to drag the girl toward the very house from which she is later "ejected": "No; by force and against your will, in spite of you, I'll drag you home, unless you'll go of your own accord [*vi atque invitam ingratiis, nisi voluntate ibis, rapiam te domum*]"; ibid. 449.
⁶⁰ See generally Garbarino 2014, 41–63.
⁶¹ See also Plaut. *Trin.* 1165: "Why, sir, if that came about with my approval [*si id mea voluntate factumst*], you'd have reason to be incensed at me."

to interrogate his volition, "overhearing" his own guilty conscience.[62] Demipho thus becomes both spectator and participant in this contest of force. In this earliest attested use of "the will" (*voluntas* in the nominative case),[63] Plautus' character achieves a new kind of self-awareness, an avenue Cicero would fruitfully explore.

Patronized by Scipio Aemilianus and possibly an associate of Panaetius and Polybius,[64] Terence further expands the psychological frontiers of comedy. And whereas Plautus plays upon inversions of status, Terence deconstructs and reassembles the phrases themselves.[65] In *Adelphoe*, the country father Demea is entreated to recall his son to the side of a woman he has apparently spurned, now in labor: "Ah! she is now imploring your protection [*vestram fidem*], Demea; let her gain of your own free will what the force of law demands [*quod vos vis legis cogit, id voluntate impetret*]."[66] As in Plautus, *voluntate* lends the coloring of willingness to an act, whose humor lies in the privileged knowledge of the audience (the accusation of abandonment is untrue). In the urgency of the moment, his *voluntas* and the law's *vis* are forces that can be aligned; the law will compel Demea's assistance, but even better if he gives it right away.[67] A similar twist lies in the admonition of the father in *Phormio*, buying his way out of a son's embarrassing marriage: "It's not enough to do your duty if popular opinion doesn't approve what you've done [*non id fama approbat*]. I want this to be done with her own consent, so that she won't claim she was forced out [*volo ipsius quoque voluntate haec fieri, ne se eiectam praedicet*]."[68] Once again, *voluntate* signifies the legally relevant consent,

---

[62] See Bloom 1998, xix (emphasis in original): "In Shakespeare, characters develop rather than unfold, and they develop because they reconceive themselves. Sometimes this comes about because they *overhear* themselves talking, whether to themselves or to others. Self-overhearing is the royal road to individuation ..."

[63] A contested occurrence is found in the comic poet Caecilius Statius: "By heaven it is rarely that [will/goodwill/pleasure] comes to a man [*Edepol* [*voluntas/voluptas*] *homini rarenter venit*]"; Warmington 1935, fr. 126. Since in no other text before Cicero, or indeed in his corpus, does *voluntas* "come to" (*venire*) a man, I find *voluptas* to be the more likely reading; cf. ibid. 514, n.524 (noting an alternative reading of *voluptas*).

[64] Each of these three men plays an outsized role in Cicero's thought: Scipio is his political exemplar and the protagonist of *De republica*; Polybius gives the first theoretical account of Rome's constitution (in Greek), which Cicero seeks to refute; and Panaetius is the inspiration for his valedictory treatise *De officiis*. See generally Grimal 1953.

[65] Segal 2001, 226, posits that by dispensing with the summary prologues of Menander and Plautus, Terence's legacy "[is] quite simply the invention of dramatic suspense." Suetonius records that in Cicero's opinion Terence had "conveyed and replayed Menander in a Latin voice [*conversum expressumque Latina voce Menandrum*]"; Suet. *Vit. Ter.* 7. On Terence's innovations in Latin literary style, see Goldberg 1986, 171–81.

[66] Ter. *Ad.* 489–91.   [67] For similar uses of *voluntate*, cf. Ter. *Phorm.* 5.3; *Haut.* 5.4.

[68] *Phorm.* 724–25.

but the duality between appearance and intent is spun around: The girl's willingness matters much less to him than public perception and the legal action he can thwart.

Like Plautus, Terence's most subtle treatment of willingness lies in the experience of love. In Act 4 of *Andria*, the smitten lover Charinus confronts his friend Pamphilus, affianced to Charinus' love but only as a ruse to solve his own troubles. Charinus is incensed; against the assurances of his friend, he retorts: "Yes I know, you were compelled [to marry] – of your own free will [*tu coactus tua voluntate es*]."[69] Here, the trope of the "coerced" lover has been turned on its head; it is the accuser that is carried away by his feelings (v.638–42) and the purported lover behaving rationally. Terence's phrase merrily explodes the binary choice of *voluntas* or coercion; Pamphilus is "willingly forced" to marry. In the very incoherence of the phrase, and the gap between the accusation and what his audience knows, lies Terence's humor. As in Plautus, the word has evolved from the coloring of an action to an inner force in competition with others.

A final Terentian innovation is his subversion of the comedic prologue. He abandons its traditional purpose as plot summary, leaving his audience in suspense as to the characters' fates. What good, then, is a prologue? Terence opts to do what no dramatist we know of had done before: address the audience in his own voice.[70] He answers charges of plagiarism (*Andria*), recounts the toils of production (*Hecyra*), and denies receiving help from his aristocratic friends (*Adelphoe*).[71] Where customarily the audience is entreated to applaud by one or more of the play's characters, in *Phormio* the playwright makes a personal appeal:

> Now listen carefully to what I want to say. I bring you a new comedy which is called in Greek "The Claimant"; its Latin name is "Phormio," since the man who plays the leading part will be Phormio the parasite, through whom most of the action will be carried out, if your goodwill comes near the poet [*voluntas vostra si ad poetam accesserit*]. (v.24–29)

We are thus introduced to a final, critical sense of *voluntas*: a favorable disposition, counterpart to the Greek *eunoia*.[72] The notion of collective

---

[69] *An.* 658.
[70] To this point, both tragic and comic prologues had been delivered either by a chorus or by an "omniscient" individual, often divine; see Segal 2001, 228.
[71] In a meta-theatrical flourish, Terence even explains his own decision to keep the audience in suspense; *Ad.* 22–25.
[72] Compare the appeal of Menander's Demeas at the close of *Samia*: "Gentlemen, now all together loudly give applause that's prized by our god of theater, as evidence of your goodwill [*eunoias*]"; Men. *Sam.* 735. For *eunoia* in a political context, see the discussion of Polybius supra.

goodwill captured in speech will play heavily in Cicero's rhetorical training and ultimately in his elaboration of the *voluntas populi Romani*.[73] The survival of Terence's entire corpus – a unique event in antiquity – suggests that his bid for *voluntas* was a roaring success.

Plautus and Terence mark a key transition in the story of *voluntas*. The passages in *Mercator* ("stop castigating me, it's not my own will that drove me to it [*ne sís me obiurga, hoc non voluntas me impulit*]") and *Andria* ("you were compelled of your own free will [*tu coactus tua voluntate es*]")[74] show a new, psychologically richer sense of will emerging alongside the legal and civic formulae. For both poets, *voluntas* is the inner force of a character's desire, "onrushing" from him[75] into a contest with other forces. Perhaps unexpectedly, in both cases a character's will is used to complicate rather than clarify his responsibility; the relation of "me" to "my will" is left intriguingly open. It is in these multiple senses and fertile ambiguities that Cicero's exploration begins.

---

[73] A related sense in Cicero, the interpersonal goodwill of friends and allies, is anticipated by the satirist Lucilius (c. 180–102 BCE), who in his definition of *virtus* includes prizing his fellow man, "wishing them well [*bene velle*] and being a life-long friend to them." Lucilius, in Warmington 1938, fr. 1206. For Lucilius' influence on Roman intellectual life, see generally Lévy 2016.

[74] Plaut. *Merc.* 321–22; Ter. *An.* 658.

[75] Though these two passages relate to male characters, the term *voluntate* is applied to both men and women. See, e.g., Plaut. *Mil.* 1120; Ter. *Phorm.* 724–25.

CHAPTER 2

Innocence and Intent

Of the *personae* Cicero would inhabit in his long career – consul, philosopher, litterateur, even *imperator* – he was firstly and remained an orator. A career in law was not merely his means of political ascent, though alternatives were scarce for a young man with no famous name nor taste for war. With his friend and rival Hortensius, Cicero was foremost a member of the Roman bar for the better part of his life.[1] In speeches and treatises, he decrypts the puzzles of his profession – how to marshal precedent, prove intent, and persuade a jury – with a richness unexampled in antiquity. In each of these tasks, his notion of will points in two directions: backward to a hallowed if untidy heritage; and forward to the rationalized legal system he thought possible.

Cicero joins the vanguard of reason in Roman law. Bright child of a modestly connected provincial family, he seems to have learned Greek at a very young age.[2] The young Cicero showed a keen interest in his own language as well, devouring Plautus and Terence and studying with the prominent grammarian and antiquarian Aelius Stilo, a specialist in obsolete words and advisor to conservatives seeking a historical sheen for their speeches.[3] The dean of his legal studies was the eighty-four-year-old Q. Mucius Scaevola, an eminent and kindly jurisconsult who had known the great Scipio Aemilianus in his youth. The model of Scipio – glorious in battle, defender of *mos maiorum* (the "way of the ancestors"), patron of philosophers and poets – is one to which Cicero would always return, notably for his seminal dialogue on the Republic in which Scipio takes lead role. In the cursus Scaevola would have taught, legal status afforded a vast

---

[1] Quintilian calls Cicero "king of the law-courts" (*regnare in iudiciis dictus est*); Quint. *Inst.* 10.1.112.
[2] Rawson 1975, 7–8. Rawson notes that Cicero's generation had a fuller mastery of Greek than any previous or subsequent one in Roman history.
[3] Ibid. 14. Stilo was also the teacher of Varro, author of *De lingua Latina* and, with Cicero, one of the leading minds of his generation; Moatti 2015, 96.

scope of action.⁴ This was true for public status, such as the praetor whose edict set the law for the year;⁵ for "semi-public" status, as with the *iuris prudentes* whose views held sway in court; and for private status, as in the near-absolute power of a Roman *paterfamilias* over his household.⁶ No one code unified these practices and no arbiter had final say over the boundaries of *ius Romanus*.⁷

The compilation and criticism of Roman precedent was given new energy by Greek ideas. Carneades, head of Plato's Academy and lead ambassador to Rome in 155 BCE, dazzled and appalled his hosts by arguing brilliantly for the norms of justice in a first lecture and then with equal force against them the day after.⁸ Though shocking to some traditionalists, the skeptical methods of the New Academy aligned very well with the needs of a young orator who, through his career, was likely to find himself on either side of a given argument. Just as Cicero revered his teachers Scaevola and M. Antonius – later to become protagonists of *De oratore* – so, too, was he deeply influenced by Philo of Larissa, then head of the Academy and a refugee in Rome, from whom he learned dialectic and rhetoric together.⁹ Along with the Stoic Diodotus, whose stringent ethics would also leave a lifelong impression,¹⁰ Cicero was acquiring the tools of rigorous, critical argument that would make him so formidable in court. Outside his library, though, the Republic's crisis deepened: Cicero's studies were interrupted by junior service in the War of the Allies and the bloody purges of Marius and Sulla, in which Antonius and Scaevola each lost their lives.¹¹

In her magisterial work on the period, Claudia Moatti argues that exploring Greek reason and excavating Roman tradition were two sides of a common pursuit. For elite Romans of Cicero's generation, "the movement outward, to others, and the movement inward, to themselves, that opening-up combined with a putting-down of roots, were part of a single process that was at once intellectual and imperialist, a combination of comprehension and appropriation."¹² A product of this vibrant

---

⁴ On the Roman law of status, see generally Villey 1945, 51–78 ("*Classification des personnes*"); Crook 1967, ch. 2; Dihle 1982, 139–42; Lewis 2015, 151–74.
⁵ See Crook 1967, 24–25; Mousourakis 2003, 86–88, 185–88; Lintott 1999, 108–09.
⁶ See Polak 1946, 251; Crook 1967, 99–113; Dihle 1982, 139–40; Ruelle 2012, 62–63; Lewis 2015, 157.
⁷ On the variety of sources of Roman civil law available to Cicero, see *Top*. 28. Cf. Villey 1945, 39–40; Mousourakis 2003, 115–26; Harries 2009, 51–52, 68.
⁸ Lactant. *Div. inst*. 5.14.3–5.   ⁹ See Rawson 1975, 12–14, 18; Harries 2016, 151–53.
¹⁰ Rawson 1975, 19.   ¹¹ Ibid. 16–17.
¹² Moatti 2015, 94. Schofield 2021, 13, agrees with Moatti and proposes that amid this decline of ancestral practice scholars of Cicero's age were "turning living tradition (so far as it still lived) into

intellectual climate, Cicero took on the unkempt heuristics of civil law with fresh methods and new shades of expression. Reason and persuasion: His ideals for a troubled age were also his means to win cases and move up in the world.

As his career in court begins, Cicero quickly discovers that the standards of reason and the wills of his clients can diverge. This uneasy rapport between *voluntas* and *ratio* – and the role of each in making law – is a keystone theme for Cicero throughout his long reign at the bar. A second problem concerns the interpretation of legal texts. Comparing his early treatise *De inventione* and its contemporary *Rhetorica ad Herennium*, we gain insight into how Cicero may have sought to reshape the practice of law. Both works treat the *controversia ex scripto et sententia*, a disagreement over whether applying a text literally would frustrate its intent. Whereas *Ad Herennium* puts "text" and "will" on either side of the dispute, Cicero reframes the question to ask where *voluntas* really lies.[13] Even where a legislator's or testator's will is *non simplex* (2.123), the "spirit" of his text is to be kept safe (*conservanda*, 2.128). In winning over a jury, Cicero's more complex notion of will is also in evidence: The *voluntas* or goodwill of one's audience is not a mere function of party affiliation but an elusive prize to be won by acuity and adaptation.

Finally, the will is Cicero's locus of evaluation in "hard cases" of criminal intent. Much of *De inventione* is dedicated to fact patterns where strong emotions or unusual circumstances complicate the question of guilt. Here, the young scholar presents not one but three different schemata for evaluating such cases, and *voluntas* figures centrally – but differently – in each. Through these explorations, Cicero adds force to the psychologizing shift in Roman law: from treating morality as a fixed property of certain acts to divining and judging the mental states behind them.[14]

Already in the "unfinished and crude"[15] *De inventione* appear the qualities that would come to characterize the will for Cicero: the passage from *ad hoc* decision to durable faculty; its variety and measurability; and the will's bivalence, its tendency toward virtue or vice. This is not to

---

text – indeed into a database. Once internalized ancestral knowledge becomes objectified ancient history." See generally Harries 2009, 52–54; Ibbetson 2015, 26–29; Giltaij 2016, 188–99.

[13] *Inv.* 1.70.

[14] See Kunkel 1966, 24–32, 64–74; Mousourakis 2003, 181–94; Powell and Paterson 2004, 1–9, 35–36, 43–52; Lintott 2015, 301–07, 313–14, 326. For a detailed comparison of arguments in *Inv.* and *Rhet. Her.*, see Hilder 2016.

[15] Cicero's later description of the work; see *De or.* 1.2.5: "[T]he unfinished and crude essays which slipped out of the notebooks of my boyhood [*quae pueris aut adolescentulis nobis ex commentariolis nostris inchoate ac rudia exciderunt*]."

overestimate his theoretical concerns: The value of these legal concepts may simply have lain in the verdicts he won or lost. Yet even as a young man the force of Cicero's analysis overflows the local and transactional. His grasp is systematic, and his ambition is for rational and stable order – a law-bound society in which a man of his own gifts could thrive.

2.1 Legitimacy and Rationality[16]

What place does the will hold in Roman law before Cicero? Though sources in the republican period are scarce, the earliest sense of *voluntas* seems to be a lawful choice. The word's specificity is easier to see in comparison with its relatives *sententia*, *consilium*, and *iudicium*. Speaking very broadly, a *sententia* is understood as an opinion or preference, a *consilium* as the product of deliberation, and a *iudicium* as the statement of a rule applied or dispute resolved.[17] Cicero often uses *consilium* or *iudicium* to refer to a position or judgment in a certain case.[18]

By contrast, as shown in the pseudo-legal disputes of Plautus and Terence, *voluntas* is a desire-in-motion, an intention with legal consequence. To state one's will is to assert a status and the rights attaching thereto. Depending on the role occupied in Roman society,[19] one can express a *voluntas* to create and dissolve partnerships, alter citizenship status, distribute property, and create edicts that others must obey. In the *Pro Quinctio*, his first recorded case, Cicero argues that his opponent mistreated a man that, by *voluntas* or *fortuna*, had become his legal partner.[20] In the matter of a daughter's inheritance, he accuses Verres of robbing the deceased father of his *voluntas*[21] and of preventing certain freedmen from carrying out the will of their dying master (*mortui voluntatem*).[22] An expression of will is

---

[16] Translation note: For the sake of consistency, in the citations that follow I will almost always translate *voluntas* as "will" even where this yields a less felicitous sentence in English. Such consistency is meant to underscore the word's polysemy and the vast range of contexts in which Cicero employs it. The main exception will be the sense of *voluntas* as a durable positive disposition, for which "goodwill" is its natural English counterpart. I note finally that while *bona voluntas*, a term of import in later Latin philosophy, seems already current in the mid-1st century BCE (see, e.g., Gn. Plancus's letter, *Fam.* 3.371.2–3; Sall. *Ad Caes. sen.* 2.3), the phrase never appears in Cicero's corpus.

[17] Hellegouarc'h 1963, 254–56.

[18] For *consilium* see, e.g., *Rosc. Am.* 151; *Caecin.* 29, 51; *Mur.* 60, 81; *Planc.* 9, 15, 44. For *iudicium* see, e.g., *Verr.* 1.11, 2.2.154, 2.5.37; *Att.* 1.17.7; *Sest.* 106; *Rab Post.* 45.

[19] Though Roman women had the power to devise property and thus theoretically could have *voluntas testatoris*, there is scant evidence for such a usage during the republican era; Jakab 2016, 502. See also Halbwachs 2016, 443–53. By and large, legal *voluntas* was a male affair.

[20] *Quinct.* 52.   [21] *Verr.* 1.114; cf. ibid. 1.104, 1.113.

[22] Ibid. 1.124. Cf. *De or.* 1.242; *Brut.* 198.

required to effect any change in citizenship status, as with Archias the poet, "who is ours by his will and by the laws [*qui et voluntate et legibus noster est*]."²³ In each of these questions, the *voluntas* of an individual with recognized status – a citizen, a father, a testator – substantiates the validity of the decision. Interestingly, there is nothing to suggest that the word *voluntas* was itself part of a legal formula, as was, for example, the spoken "*spondeo*" to seal a marriage contract.²⁴ Rather, the term becomes part of a retrospective inquiry in which an advocate seeks out all possible *indicia*, *testimonia*, or *significationes*.²⁵ As such, *voluntas* occupies a liminal space in the legal lexicon, connoting both an inner decision and the outer manifestation of that decision – much as in English, "will" denotes both the intent of a testator and the piece of paper enacting it.

Though firmly tied to status, will could be unmoored from reason. We see the potential for unreasonable or thoughtless *voluntas* most clearly in Cicero's legal clients.²⁶ In the *Pro Cluentio*, the accusation is murder but the client is more intent on repairing his reputation from a prior misdeed. Though Cicero declares that he would rather focus on the present case, he digresses at length to address the earlier controversy. Why? As the young advocate explains:

> [W]hen engaged in the trial of a man of honour and good sense it has not been my habit merely to be guided but my own ideas: I defer also to the plan and will of my client [*et consilio et voluntati obtempero*].²⁷

Here, *voluntas* indicates both the status and the impaired thinking of his client. He depicts Cluentius as "tearful" (*lacrimans*) and "begging" (*obsecrare*) for his help. Following this display by Cluentius, Cicero says, "I gave way to him … which we ought not to do always."²⁸

Why this hedge? Because two fundamental but potentially incompatible norms are at play. An advocate must follow the dictates of reason, but so,

---

²³ *Arch.* 19. On the inviolability of individual *voluntas* on matters of citizenship, cf. *Caecin.* 96–98; *Balb.* 27; *Dom.* 77–78.
²⁴ See Varro, *Ling.* 6.69–72; *Dig.* 23.1.6 (Ulpian). Cf. Villey 1945, 11–12; Lewis 2015, 165–67.
²⁵ See, e.g., *Clu.* 31, where Cicero laments the case of a poisoned man who tried to alter his will as he died, who "died in the very act of expressing his will [*in ipsa significatione huius voluntatis est mortuus*]."
²⁶ For clarity, I use the English "client" when referring to a party receiving legal representation and *cliens* for a personal or political dependent.
²⁷ *Clu.* 144.
²⁸ He makes three further invocations of his client's *voluntas* as divergent from his own intentions: *Clu.* 158, 160, and 164. At *Clu.* 158, he goes so far as to say that as a matter of personal policy henceforth he will only apply the strict legal argument that his client's *voluntas* did not permit him to adopt in this case.

2.1 Legitimacy and Rationality 37

too, must he honor his client's wishes. Cicero's apparently trivial aside hints at a canny rhetorical strategy: Depicting himself as sober advocate, he affirms the logic of his case; depicting his client's anxiety, he aims to win jury sympathy. Despite appearances, he is not giving "emotional" *voluntas* the upper hand over "rational" *consilium* but harnessing the persuasive power of each.[29] The notion of will enables the precocious lawyer to show both deference to and distance from his client with a single word.

Such measured deference serves Cicero in a number of ways. He uses it to show humility before power, as when he and Pompey are co-counsel for Balbus, Caesar's majordomo. Though Cicero's *eloquentissimi* colleagues – newly allied in the Triumvirate – had no need of him,[30] he speaks at the request both of Balbus, "whose will in the hour of danger I can on no account fail to serve [*cuius ego voluntati in eius periculis nullo modo deesse possum*]," and of Pompey, "who willed me to proclaim and defend his own action, judgment, and good deed [*qui sui facti, sui iudicii, sui beneficii voluit me esse ... et praedicatorem et actorem*]."[31] Such humble posturing likely fooled no one but may have been appreciated. Conversely, a client's will could elevate Cicero above a distasteful opponent, as when he claims that an invective against Vatinius was not his own idea but rather that of Sestius, whose will overcame his own (feigned) reluctance for the task.[32]

Cicero's deference to his client's *voluntas* held true even when his client was, so to speak, an entire province. In his momentous case against Verres, ex-governor of Sicily, Cicero is nearly tripped up by a straw-man prosecutor who contends with him for the right to bring the case. Cicero proposes that the power to decide lies in "the will of those to whom injustice has been done, those, in fact, for whose benefit this Extortion Court has been appointed [*de voluntate eorum quibus iniuriae factae sunt, quorum causa iudicium de pecuniis repetundis est constitutum*]."[33] Here, *voluntas* serves both an immediate purpose and a more subtle one. To get around Caecilius' roadblock, Cicero argues that the will of the injured party is paramount in the choice of prosecutor – and Cicero has the Sicilians on his side. More urgently still, the young man needs the

---

[29] Cf. *De or.* 2.102, 2.189–92. Garsten 2006, 161, observes that for Cicero, while "the orator cultivated a degree of detachment from his client's claims, ... the ultimate purpose of even that detachment was to judge which arguments would be most likely to persuade jurors of his own client's view of the case."
[30] *Balb.* 1.   [31] Ibid. 4.
[32] *Vat.* 1.3; cf. *Sest.* 14. Cicero could ascribe an "unstable" *voluntas* to witnesses as well; see *Flac.* 6–9; *Cael.* 22; *Scaur.* 15–16. Cf. Guérin 2015, 324–38.
[33] *Div. Caec.* 11.

voluntas – both the specific choice and durable goodwill – of this wealthy province to advance a claim he lacked the *dignitas* to make alone.³⁴

Invoking the *voluntas* of a client had further political purposes. In a passage from *Pro Rabirio Postumo* (54 BCE), Cicero describes certain compromising services his client performed for the king of Egypt. Since these were services given under coercion, he exhorts the jury,

> do not, then, hold him responsible for his hard lot; do not account the outrage done to him by the king as his crime; do not judge his intentions by this compulsion nor his will by the force to which he bowed [*nec consilium ex necessitate nec voluntatem ex vi interpretari*].³⁵

In this felicitous phrase, the claim of Rabirius' *voluntas* and *consilium* is made superior to those of necessity (*necessitas*) and violence (*vis*). Whereas in *Pro Cluentio* Cicero opposes *voluntas* to *consilium* to separate his client's emotions from his own logic, here they are jointly the locus of evaluation: two inner forces outweighing those beyond his client's control. Importantly, physical force is not antithetical to reason in all cases; from the murder of the Gracchi to the suppression of Catiline's conspiracy, Cicero indeed defends violence that, in his view, has the force of law behind it.³⁶ His recurring theme, rather, is that the lawful force of reason – *voluntas* – must defeat the lawless force of his enemies. The argument is one that Cicero employs with greater frequency as violence engulfs the Republic.³⁷

2.2 *Controversia ex Scripto et Sententia*

In Book 1 of *Rhetorica ad Herennium*, its author introduces the *controversia ex scripto et sententia*, in which "the framer's intention appears to be at variance with the letter of the text [*videtur scriptoris voluntas cum scripto ipso dissentire*]" (1.19). His example is of a sailor, unable to flee a sinking ship with his comrades, who claims ownership of the ship when it miraculously comes to land. This windfall, correct according to the letter of the law, is opposed on equitable grounds by the ship's owner. The question for the court: Should the *scriptum* of the law be followed or the lawmaker's

---

³⁴ I develop this distinction between will as specific choice and durable relationship in Chapters 4 and 5. For Cicero's repeated invocations of Sicily's *voluntas*, see *Div. Caec.* 54; *Verr.* 1.10, 2.2.117, 2.5.130.
³⁵ *Rab. Post.* 29.
³⁶ See *Cat.* 4.10; *Mil.* 10; *De or.* 2.132–34; *Off.* 1.76. Cf. Straumann 2016, 165–67.
³⁷ See *Inv.* 1.2.3; *Verr.* 2.2.145, 2.2.151–52, 2.4.14; *Red. sen.* 22; *Rab. Post.* 29; *Sest.* 38; *Rep.* 3.4; *Leg.* 3.42; *Lig.* 7.

2.2 Controversia ex Scripto et Sententia

voluntas? Commonplaces are proposed for either view. For those defending the *scriptum*, the author suggests, one should argue that "the text is written clearly, concisely, accurately, impeccably, and with a sure mind [*scriptum illud esse dilucide, breviter, commode, perfecte, cum ratione certa*]" (2.13). Those taking the other side will say, conversely, that "to follow the words literally and to neglect [the legislator's] will is a pettifogger's method [*calumniatoris esse officium verba et litteras sequi, neglegere voluntatem*]" (2.14).[38] While valid arguments are offered for the *voluntas et sententia* of the legislator or the *verba et litterae* of the text, these positions are opposite and distinct.

Though scholars have disagreed on the amount of original material in *De inventione*, and Cicero himself looks back dismissively on the work,[39] his presentation of the *controversia* diverges interestingly from *Ad Herennium*. Cicero gives the paradigmatic case of the general Epaminondas, who defeats the Spartans despite having kept his troops several days past the lawful period. Here, the prosecutor must refute the argument that an *exceptionem* for Epaminondas' circumstances is implied by the law or can alternatively be added *ex post facto* by the jury. Cicero imagines a closing argument to Epaminondas' jury in which the letter of the law is defended:

> What more certain proof of his will could the author of the law have left [*testimonium voluntatis suae relinquere*] than the statement which he wrote himself with great care and pains? Therefore, if there were no written documents we should be in sad need of them to learn from them the law-giver's will; nevertheless we should not permit Epaminondas ... to interpret the will of the law-maker not by what is quite plainly written, but by what suits his case [*non ex eo quod apertissime scriptum est, sed ex eo quod suae causae convenit, scriptoris voluntatem interpretari*].[40]

In comparison with the *Ad Herennium*, legal will is transformed. First, the binary choice between *voluntas* and *scriptum* is erased; the question is no longer whether the legislator's *voluntas* will be obeyed but rather where its most faithful *testimonium* may be found.[41] A prosecutor not only claims the *scriptum* as the superior sign of his will; he asserts that in the event that no written law existed, it would have to be invented to protect that will from oblivion. As such, the interpretation of *voluntas* is not the tactic of one party against the other but the shared challenge of both.[42]

---

[38] Cf. *Caecin.* 65–66.   [39] *De or.* 1.5.   [40] *Inv.* 1.70.
[41] Cf. Scaevola's and Crassus' positions at *Brut.* 197–98; Dugan 2012, 124.
[42] Cf. *Rhet. Her.* 2.14.

In the extensive discussion in *De inventione* Book 2,[43] three new shades of will come to light.[44] It can vary in quality and complexity; interpretation *contra scriptum* will be argued for where "the writer's will is shown not to be simple" (*non simplex voluntas scriptoris ostenditur*, 2.123; i.e. where it could not reasonably be applied identically in all cases). Second, those arguing *contra scriptum* should extol the importance of juries, especially those created by the law at issue:[45]

> ... that the reason why the author of the law provided for judges from a certain class and of a certain age was that there might be a judicial body able not only to read his law, which any child could do, but to comprehend it with the mind and interpret his intentions ... For he did not think of you as clerks to read his law aloud in court, but as interpreters of his will [*neque enim vos scripti sui recitatores sed voluntatis interpretes fore putavit*]. (2.139)

In this broadened view, it is thus part of the legislator's will that his own will be interpreted.[46]

A third quality of will is suggested in an argument for those on the side of *scriptum*: "If the will of the writer is to be preserved, he will affirm that it is he, and not his adversaries, who sides with that will [*quod si voluntas scriptoris conservanda sit, se, non adversarios, a voluntate eius stare*]" (2.128). *Voluntas* is something to be preserved (*conservanda*), something upon which the advocate can stand (*stare*): Each word suggests a durability to *voluntas* absent from any prior surviving text. The durability of will is echoed in a final commonplace *contra scriptum*: "[H]ow unfair it is that words should hinder the justice and equity which *are protected* by the will of him who wrote them [*quam indignum sit aequitatem litteris urgueri, quae voluntate eius qui scripserit defendatur*]" (2.143, emphasis added). We note that the protection offered by the legislator's will is in the present tense (*defendatur*): This will is an ongoing commitment that should outlast any attempt to twist his words.[47] The continuity is affirmed in a poignant

---

[43] *Inv.* 2.121–47.
[44] Cicero's treatment of *controversia ex scripto et sententia* in Book 2 is not only five times longer than the corresponding section in *Rhet. Her.*, but it is also the longest of any surviving antique text. Cf. Plin. *Ep.* 2.16, 4.10, 5.7; *Dig.* 32.25.1 (Paulus); *Dig.* 35.1.101 and 50.16.219 (Papinian). On the possible influence of Greek philosophy on this debate, see Giltaij 2016, 190–91.
[45] Unlike most modern statutes, Roman laws of the late Republic often provided for the establishment of courts of special jurisdiction; cf. Lintott 1999, 108–09; Mousourakis 2003, 148–49. Thus, Cicero suggests, the specific membership criteria of a jury (*certo ex ordine iudices certa aetate*) must be considered when interpreting the *voluntas* of a given law.
[46] Harries 2009, 65, argues that Cicero's forensic speeches tend to emphasize "the superiority of intention over exact wording." Cf. *Caecin.* 80 and see generally Dugan 2012.
[47] And see ibid. 2.141: "We value the laws not because of the words, which are but faint and feeble indications of intention [*quae tenues et obscurae notae sint voluntatis*], but because of the advantage of

simile: That, to the legislator, the text is "as an image he leaves of his will" (*suae voluntatis quasi imaginem reliquerit*, 2.128). The *imagines* of a Roman *domus* bore an importance that is difficult to overstate; these images of illustrious ancestors were among a family's most prized possessions, displayed over many generations.[48] Cicero's analogy suggests that these qualities of preciousness and permanence are understood to reside in a lawmaker's *voluntas*: Here, perhaps for the first time in the West, it is proper to refer to the "spirit" of a law.[49]

A final word should be added concerning the political implications of this early text. In the section treating the *controversia ex scripto et sententia*, the interpretation of will connects to deeper arguments about who should have power in deciding the law. Against the argument that an *exceptio* be "read into" the law to accommodate his client, Cicero suggests the following reply: "If the jury should desire to add a provision to the law on their own authority, would the people permit it [*si ipsi vellent iudices ascribere, passurusne sit populus*]?" (2.133). In other words, if jury members will (*vellent*) to amend the law, this would mean superseding the lawmaker's will – and this is not allowed. The *populus*, in turn, is invoked as the ultimate decider in this competition of force: It is their *potestas cognoscendi et probandi aut improbandi* (power of discernment to approve or disapprove) that decides what the *lex* really means.[50] Though the line of argument may not be original to Cicero, this ability to cast specific disputes within broader struggles was among his defining talents as an orator.

2.3 Capturing Goodwill

Cicero's talent for legal theory was equaled only by his talent for winning a crowd. With the *Ad Herennium* again as a convenient baseline, we see how

---

the principles which they embody, and the wisdom and care of the law-makers. Next he may set forth the true nature of law, that it may be shown to consist of meanings, not of words [*in sententiis, non in verbis consistere*]."

[48] See Polyb. 6.54.3; Sall. *Jug.* 4.5; Lintott 1999, 167–69.

[49] The most famous instance of this debate may have been *causa Curiana*, a landmark inheritance case in which Crassus had argued that "words are snares if *voluntates* are ignored." *Brut.* 198; cf. *Part. or.* 25. See generally Pohlenz 1948, 262; Dihle 1982, 135–42; Harries 2009, 100–02; Giltaij 2016, 191.

[50] Cicero further suggests that if the people are indeed proposing to alter the law, the advocate "should like to know who is proposing the amendment, and what body is going to accept it; that he sees party strife arising and wishes to resist it [*velle se scire qui lator sit, qui sint accepturi; se factiones videre et dissuadere velle*]"; *Inv.* 2.134. Cicero would later adopt a very different position regarding the people's role in lawmaking; see discussion in Chapter 5.

the notion of will helps Cicero define his approach to rhetorical persuasion. *Ad Herennium*'s author defines a "faulty" (*vitiosum*) speech as one

> ... spoken against the goodwill of the judge or audience [*contra iudicis voluntatem aut eorum qui audiunt*] – if the party to which they are devoted, or men whom they hold dear, should be attacked, or the hearer's goodwill injured [*laeditur auditoris voluntas*] by some fault of this kind. (3.21)

In a more positive vein, the author adds, "what benefits our own voice finds favor in the hearer's will [*quod nostrae voci prosit idem voluntati auditoris probetur*]" (ibid.). Two observations can be made. First, the will or goodwill of the listener (*voluntas auditoris*)[51] is depicted as a machine with two settings, *probetur* and *laeditur*. One either pleases or offends them. Second, the author does not suggest that the *voluntas* of an audience is attacked when their beliefs or principles have been maligned but more simply when the speaker insults groups he sees represented in the crowd.

De inventione shows Cicero both echoing and dissenting from *Ad Herennium* on this question. At 1.92, he defines an "offensive argument" (*offensum*) as "one that injures the goodwill of our audience [*quod eorum qui audiunt voluntatem laedit*]." This definition is almost identical to the one at *Ad Herennium* 2.43, though stripped of its political tone. In his own treatise at 1.23–24, Cicero treats the method of "insinuation" (*insinuatio*) in the event of a hostile audience. The speaker must first shift the audience's attention from the offensive act or person toward a more favorable one, maintaining that he is also displeased by these offenses while concealing (*dissimulare*) the argument he is expected to defend (1.24). The speaker will strive in this way "by working imperceptibly as far as possible to win the goodwill of his audience away from your opponents [*et tamen id obscure faciens, quoad possis, alienes ab eis auditorum voluntatem*]" (ibid.).

As he did in the *controversia*, Cicero shows a psychological subtlety entirely missing from *Ad Herennium*. First, winning an audience's *voluntas* in Cicero's treatise is not as simple as saying what pleases and avoiding what offends: It is a painstaking process requiring sensitivity and patience. Good orators keep a constant lookout for "hints of will" (*indicia voluntatis*) and apply principle and experience to their interpretation.[52] Further, *voluntas* does not merely indicate an audience's approval: It is a durable

---

[51] Both "will" and "goodwill" are compassed by this use of *voluntas*, since both the specific judgment and the durable good feeling of the audience is at issue. See n.16, supra, and Chapter 5.

[52] For *indicium suae voluntatis*, see ibid. at 2.128, 2.141; *Rep.* 3.3. On the combination of *doctrina* and *disciplina* in Cicero's notion of *ars*, see Gavoille 2000, 167–78, 190–97.

2.3 Capturing Goodwill

presence, a prize to be won or lost, a force to be deflected "as far as possible" (*quoad possis*) from one's opponent. A final evolution from *Ad Herennium* is that whereas the former work treated *voluntas auditoris* in genitive singular, here Cicero's prize is the *voluntatem auditorum*, a genitive plural modifying a singular accusative.[53] In other words, for Cicero the wills of many listeners merge into a single shared will – a step of great consequence for his (and our) idea of "the will of the people," as we shall see in Chapter 5.[54]

In *De oratore*, Cicero develops the idea of audience goodwill as an object of expert manipulation. His protagonist, Antonius, ironically disclaims that oratory is the "highest art," but nevertheless "some very clever rules may be laid down for playing upon men's feelings and extracting their goodwill [*praecepta posse quaedam dari peracuta ad pertractandos animos hominum et ad excipiendas eorum voluntates*]."[55] He continues that, in order to win a case, "the arbitrator who is to decide in our favor must either lean to our side by natural inclination of will, or be won over by arguments for the defense, or be constrained by a stirring of soul [*aut inclinatione voluntatis propendeat in nos, aut defensionis argumentis adducatur, aut animi permotione cogatur*]."[56] As in *De inventione*, an audience's *voluntas* is the orator's prize, but here it is placed in a matrix of forces resembling Aristotle's three modes of persuasion: *Voluntas* is the attractive force of *ethos*, *argumentum* that of *logos*, and *permotio animi* that of *pathos*.[57]

---

[53] *Ad Herennium* is not clear on whether several individuals can share a single will; *voluntas auditoris* is clearly singular, but the preceding *contra iudicis voluntatem aut eorum qui audiunt* is ambiguous, and the elided accusative could be either singular or plural (such that the reader would understand either *contra iudicis voluntatem aut voluntates eorum qui audiunt* or *aut voluntatem eorum qui audiunt*). In the rhetorical context, Cicero's "collective will" may or may not be an innovation. In its political context his originality is more clear, as I will argue in Chapter 5.

[54] See Chapter 5. Compare Cicero's use of *animus* in the phrase *cum animus auditoris infestus est* – the listeners are treated as sharing one soul, just as they share one will; *Inv.* 1.23. Interestingly, the later *De oratore* is inconsistent on whether an audience shares one *voluntas* or many *voluntates*: See, e.g. *De or.* 1.30, where Crassus opines on how excellent a thing it is "to get a hold on assemblies of men, entice their minds and direct their wills [*voluntates impellere*] where he chooses"; cf. *De or.* 2.32, discussed later in this chapter. Perhaps these are mere stylistic variants or perhaps Cicero wants his readers to understand that audience goodwill should be viewed either collectively or severally according to circumstances.

[55] *De or.* 2.32. Cf. Gavoille 2000, 167–78.

[56] *De or.* 2.129. The sense of *voluntas* as a force in motion is highlighted by the verbs *pertractare* ("to draw or drag through") and *excipere* ("to catch or take out").

[57] *Inv.* 1.24. Cicero openly avows this debt via Antonius' concession at *De or.* 2.160: "Aristotle, from whose doctrines you think my own differ but little ... I read also that book of his ... [*isto Aristotele, a cuius inventis tibi ego videor non longe aberrare ... cuius et illum legi librum ...*]." Cf. Atkins 2018b, 122.

Interestingly, while verbs of motion are also used in the second passage (*adducor,* "to lead toward," and *cogor,* "to drive together"), here will has a position and orientation: The listener "leans to our side by natural inclination of will" (*inclinatione voluntatis propendeat in nos*). Even more strongly than the terms of motion, the idea of "inclination" (*inclinatio*) suggests a durability before and after the speech: An orator may lure the audience's *voluntas* his way, and if it had been leaning his way already, *tant mieux*.[58] By contrast, a *consilium* or *iudicium* may be reversed or abandoned but not "drawn out" or "inclined."[59] Though psychology is not his main subject, Cicero's use of "soul" (*animus*) in parallel with *voluntas* implies that a person's will is some kind of durable inner possession – a critical step toward the notion of will to be made Christian doctrine by Augustine.[60]

This "rhetorical" will takes a political guise in a following passage. Scholarly learning, Antonius announces, is less important to an orator than familiarity with his fellow citizens:

> For bring me a man as accomplished, as clear and acute in thinking, and as ready in delivery as you please; if, for all that, he is a stranger to social intercourse, precedent, tradition, and the ways and wills of his fellow-countrymen [*in moribus ac voluntatibus civium suorum*], those commonplaces from which proofs are derived will avail him but little. (2.131)

What would Cicero's audience understand by *voluntates civium*?[61] The association with *mores* suggests a definitional importance akin to the *mos maiorum*. In this light, the *voluntates civium* are something like the shared inclinations of a community, as much a part of its identify as its customs (*mores*), but equally something not "worn on the surface." We understand, then, why Antonius might distinguish oratory from other branches of knowledge: It consists both in elaborating ideas and in understanding people. In one sense, the art of speaking "lies open to the view" (*in medio posita*); it relies upon "the language of everyday life, and the usages approved by common sense [*a vulgari genere orationis ... atque a consuetudine communis sensus*]" (1.12).[62] An orator's language is *varia* because it

---

[58] Cf. *Mur.* 53, consular elections often feature a "sudden inclination of will" (*repentina voluntatum inclinatio*) of the voters toward one candidate or another. See also Guérin 2015, 348–59; Remer 2017, 38.

[59] See Hellegouarc'h 1963, 254–55.   [60] See Epilogue.

[61] Though its function in the sentence is clear, this usage of *voluntas* is unique: In over 640 occurrences of *voluntas* and its related forms in the Ciceronian corpus, he uses *voluntatibus* only nine times and the phrase *in moribus ac voluntatibus civium* just this once. See Table 1, Introduction.

[62] Cf. Remer 2017, 148–52.

2.3 Capturing Goodwill

must be "adapted to the feelings of common people [*ad vulgarem popularemque sensum accommodata*]."[63] His success depends foremost on his ability to feel out and accommodate himself to the tastes and beliefs of his fellow man.[64]

Common though it may be, the *sensus communis* demands painstaking effort. "When setting about a hazardous and important case," Antonius explains, "in order to play upon the feelings of the tribunal [*ad animos iudicum pertractandos*] ... I scent out with all possible keenness what they feel, judge, expect, and will [*quid sentiant, quid existiment, quid exspectent, quid velint*]" (2.186). We note again the image of persuasion as a play of forces, here with the speaker drawing forth his listeners' souls (*pertractare animos*).[65] We note as well that what the audience "wills" (*velint*) is the ultimate term of the series, as if this word – the active subjunctive of *velle* – caps and completes the argument. What Cicero is describing, in effect, is the "personality" of an audience to which the orator must adapt. Like their *mores*, the *voluntas* of an audience is something that awaits an orator's discovery and can aid or thwart his success.[66]

Yet we find hints in this treatise that the "common listener," all-powerful as he may be, is not given unqualified respect. At 1.31, Crassus extols the singular power of oratory:

> For what is so marvelous as that, out of the innumerable company of mankind, a single being should arise, who either alone or with a few others [*vel solus, vel cum paucis*] can make effective a faculty nature gives to all? ... Or what achievement so mighty and glorious as that the impulses of the people, the consciences of the judges, the austerity of the Senate, should suffer transformation through the eloquence of one man [*quam populi motus, iudicum religiones, Senatus gravitatem, unius oratione converti*]? (1.31–32)

---

[63] *De or.* 1.108. Cf. *Part. or.* 15: "[T]he prudent and cautious speaker is controlled by the reception given by his audience – what it rejects has to be modified [*nam auditorum aures moderantur oratori prudenti et provido, et quod respuunt immutandum est*]." See also *Para. stoic.* 4, where Cicero tests whether philosophical doctrines could be "brought out into the light of common daily life and expounded in a form to win acceptance, or whether learning has one style of discourse and ordinary life another [*tentare volui possentne proferri in lucem, id est in forum, et ita dici ut probarentur, an alia quaedam esset erudita alia popularis oratio*]." These passages may inform the reciprocal relationship between senate and people that Cicero defines in his political treatises; see discussion in Chapter 5.

[64] Cf. Harries 2009, 52: "[T]he forensic advocate had to adapt to popular understanding ... so that the *iudices*' idea of what was 'fair' might work in favour of his client and prevail over whatever alternative legal authority the opposition had available to them."

[65] That the audience's *animus* is an object to be moved or manipulated is captured nicely at *De or.* 2.187: Citing the poet Pacuvius, Antonius insists that even when confronting a hostile audience, eloquence is "the soulbending sovereign of all things [*flexanima atque omnium regina rerum*]."

[66] See Garsten 2006, 2–5, 147–51.

Here in two sentences lies the blueprint for Cicero's ascendance as a *novus homo* and, perhaps, for his ultimate limitations. The great orator defines his success as the product of a special excellence given not by birth or wealth but by a faculty "nature gives to all" (*omnibus natura datum*).[67] This openness of access is matched by a difficulty of mastery: Only a very few in each community achieve its summit. In his mastery, moreover, the orator heeds and reinforces the hierarchies of this community, with the *senatus*, *iudices*, and *populus* each given their proper place. We note the words accompanying each: The senate's *gravitas* denotes those of highest merit; the *iudices* are not so complimented but are granted *religio*, the piety of good men. The *populus* has no such decoration: Its *motus* ("impulse") is the orator's prize, a word befitting an unreasoning crowd.[68]

Is the people's will the sovereign power of the state or an orator's plaything? The main paradox of Cicero's politics comes into view.[69]

2.4 Guilty and Righteous Wills

Winning a conviction in a Roman court, as in most courts today, required proving not only that an alleged act took place, but also that the defendant had the requisite intent. To prove intent, an advocate of Cicero's generation would face three common questions: Are there facts to indicate the actor's state of mind? Is there evidence of compulsion (and do outbursts of emotion count?) And what version of events will best persuade a jury?[70] Texts both early and late in Cicero's corpus reveal the depth of his interest in these questions of jurisprudence. They also suggest that he never quite succeeded in establishing the standard terminology that Roman law, in his opinion, sorely needed.[71] As we shall see in this section, however, each attempt adds something new to his variegated notion of will.

The theory of criminal responsibility presented in *De inventione* is, to put it mildly, confused. Cicero proposes at least three distinct schemata to evaluate a defendant's intent, either connecting him with an act he denies

---

[67] On oratorical power as a "force of nature," see generally Lévy 2012a; cf. Guérin 2015, 348–59.
[68] At *Part. or.* 9, Cicero's defines *motus* as "an excitement of the mind to either pleasure or annoyance or fear or desire [*motus autem animi incitatio aut ad voluptatem aut ad molestiam aut ad metum aut ad cupiditatem*]"; cf. *Brut.* 279, 322; *Part. or.* 53; *Top.* 458.
[69] Atkins 2018b, 123, points out that, for Cicero, the reciprocal bonds between orator and audience do not exclude a hierarchy of *dignitas* between the two. Cf. Remer 2005, 155; Atkins 2018a, 769–70.
[70] See Powell and Paterson 2004, 43–52. On hierarchies of proof in criminal cases, Guérin 2015, 259–72.
[71] See *Leg.* 1.13–20.

2.4 *Guilty and Righteous Wills*

or excusing him from an act he admits. These three frameworks address similar questions of law but deploy notions of will and willingness in highly contradictory ways. Why would Cicero, even as a student, allow such a muddle?

For one thing, *De inventione* does not pretend to be an exhaustive treatise on civil law but rather an advocate's handbook. Cicero does not pronounce upon how an issue should be resolved but rather presumes that an advocate may find himself on either side and should be equipped appropriately. The work thus presents a range of valid arguments available to prosecutor or defendant on a given point but does not typically opine on which argument should prevail.[72] Nevertheless, Cicero occasionally comments on the probability that a given point will be accepted or rejected by the jury. For example, his warning that a prosecutor should not deny the validity of accident (*casus*) or necessity (*necessitudo*) as defenses shows that these were well-established claims and likely to be upheld (2.99). In all, his three frameworks of criminal intent tell us a great deal about how the notion of will stood in Roman law at the time of Cicero's education and thus how he develops its *réseau d'intelligibilité* over his career.

In Book 1, Cicero treats the question of *modus*, the manner in which an action is performed (*quemadmodum et quo animo factum sit*, 1.41). Cicero divides all alleged criminal acts into two categories: *prudens* and *imprudens*. *Prudentia* is not explicitly defined; rather, Cicero says that a prosecutor should seek to prove the crime was *prudens* "from the acts performed secretly or openly, by force or persuasion [*ex eis, quae clam, palam, vi, persuasione fecerit*]" (1.41). *Imprudentia* is also not defined, but examples are given: *inscientia* (ignorance), *casus* (accident), *necessitas* (necessity), and *affectio animi* (strong emotion, lit. "disposition of soul"), a subcategory that includes *molestia* (annoyance), *iracundia* (anger), and *amor* (love), among others (ibid.). Where is will in all this? First, we notice that *voluntas* and *voluntaria* are not yet a factor in evaluating guilt. Second, in this schema, an action *prudens* can be the result of several factors, *including* force (*vis*). Finally, acts from strong emotion (*affectio animi*) are here classified as *imprudens*, along with *inscientia*, *casus*, and *necessitas*.

Which of these acts are punishable? Regarding the *topica* available to an advocate, Cicero continues,

---

[72] Cicero remarks later that his enthusiasm for study was heightened by the intense disorder of the legal system wrought by the civil unrest of his youth. *Brut.* 305–07; cf. Harries 2009, 64; Lévy 2012b, 60.

in the sixth topic it is shown that the deed was done purposely and intentionally and the remark is added that voluntary misdeeds should not be pardoned, but that sometimes inadvertent acts may be forgiven [*sextus locus est per quem consulto et de industria factum demonstratur et illud adiungitur, voluntario maleficio veniam dari non oportere, imprudentiae concedi nonnunquam convenire*]. (1.102)

The word *voluntarius* is thus brought in, though at some distance from the initial definitions, as a synonym or substitute for *prudentia*. Thus, a prescription is implied: A criminal act that is *voluntarius* or *prudens* is to be punished, but *imprudentiae* may in some cases be pardoned. Reading these two passages together, we see how the schema of Book 1 may have seemed both too strict and too lenient for Cicero: Too strict in that a defendant who had been literally forced to commit murder (*vi fecerit*) would be considered to have acted *prudentia* or *voluntaria* and thus be condemned; and too lenient in that crimes committed *affectio animi*, such as murdering an adulterous spouse, would be considered *imprudentia* and thus be excused. In other words, a crime the defendant was literally forced to commit could be judged more harshly than if the same act had been spurred by his emotions – an unsatisfying result. Further, it is difficult to imagine that the adult Cicero would endorse any definition of "voluntary" that included actions performed under the threat of violence: Lack of coercion, in fact, becomes the critical sense of *voluntarius* for Cicero, a word he typically employs to emphasize willingness when it is unexpected.[73]

Tellingly, Cicero leaves this schema to one side and develops a new one in Book 2. Here, his theme is establishing the motive for a crime. Cicero divides the possible causes of an act into two parts: *impulsio* and *ratiocinatio*. *Impulsio* describes an act performed *sine cogitatione*; that is, without reflection. *Ratiocinatio*, on the other hand, is "when the mind seems to have avoided or sought something to do or not to do for a definite cause [*certa de causa vitasse aut secutus esse animus videbitur*]" (2.17–18). The prosecutor must then show that no one *else* had a similar motive and that every alternative suspect lacked either *potestas*, *facultas*, or *voluntas*. The sentence introducing will into this second scheme is rather enigmatic. Suspects can be argued to lack

---

[73] See, e.g., *mors voluntaria* for suicide (*Prov. cons.* 6, *Scaur.* 5, *Fam.* 3.183.3, *Brut.* 103, *Fin.* 3.61, *Sen.* 75); *oblivio voluntaria*, "willing forgetfulness" (*Fam.* 1.20.20); *volnus voluntarium*, a "willing wound" (*Planc.* 89); *servi voluntarii*, "willing slaves" (*Rep.* 1.64, *Phil.* 1.15); *interitus voluntarius*, "willing doom" (*Marcell.* 14); *misera voluntaria*, "willing misery" (*Tusc.* 3.32); *casus voluntarius*, "willing calamity" (*Phil.* 10.19); *cruciatus voluntarius*, "willing torture" (*Off.* 3.105).

2.4 Guilty and Righteous Wills

the power [*potestas*], if it can be said that they did not know about the possibility of the crime, or were not present or were not physically able to perform some act; the opportunity [*facultas*], if it can be shown that any one lacked a plan, helpers, tools and all other things pertinent to the deed; the will, if his mind can be said to be free of such acts and upright [*voluntas, si animus a talibus factis vacuus et integer esse dicetur*]. (2.24)

On the surface, the schema is simple enough: To disprove that an individual performed a crime, one can show that he lacked either the necessary power (*potestas*), opportunity (*facultas*), or will (*voluntas*). Yet Cicero's definition of will associates a plan's conception (having the *facta* in mind) with the *voluntas* to carry it out. This is clear enough in the negative: I cannot form the legal intent for a crime I have no idea how to commit. Its converse, though, is intriguingly ambiguous: Would "conceiving" an act (showing I had the *facta* in mind) imply *prima facie* that I willed to do it? Could I conceive the crime and yet remain blameless and "upright" (*integer*)?

Read against his first schema, Cicero takes a harder line on whether acts spurred by emotion should be punished. *Impulsio* is not described as *imprudentia*, nor is it linked to *inscientia*, *casus*, or *necessitas*.[74] Though *impulsio* acts are said to take place "without cognition" (*sine cogitatione*), such a state of mind is no longer exculpatory. In other words, proving the presence of strong emotion – for example, facts showing the defendant's jealousy of a murdered rival – would not be grounds for a defense. The opposite is true: It would substantiate his motive to commit the crime. Impulsive acts are no longer "unwilling" ones. By the connection of *voluntas* to *ratiocinatio*, we can infer that a claim of "unwillingness" might win out if an absence of preparatory steps could be shown.

Under this sense of *voluntas* as a criminal state of mind, proving an *animus integer* requires some ingenuity. Cicero describes how a defense attorney can cite, for example, a lack of previous bad acts on the part of the defendant:

> This argument will be strengthened if it can be shown that when he had an opportunity of doing a dishonest deed with impunity he had no desire to do so [*voluntas a faciendo demonstrabitur afuisse*]. (2.35)

---

[74] That a valid defense exists from *necessitas* and from chance is not stated directly but strongly implied at 2.43–44. Otherwise, the Book 2 schema is clearly derived from a different source than that of Book 1. There is no hint in Book 2 that a defendant who acted from an *impulsio*, a word described similarly to *affectio animi*, could be excused as having acted *imprudentia*. On the contrary, if a prosecutor has established facts sufficient to show *impulsio* under the scheme of Book 2, he is a large step closer to his goal of conviction; ibid. 2.19.

An absence of criminal *voluntas* is substantiated, in other words, if someone – say, a business partner accused of embezzlement – previously had the *potestas* to do the crime but did not act on it. As with the *lacrimans* client described in Section 2.1, here will is a force proper to an individual that is intentional (i.e. uncoerced and specifically directed) but not necessarily rational.

Cicero's second schema for criminal responsibility is less immediately problematic than the first, but it, too, is laid aside and a third schema offered at 2.86–110. Our first hint that a new framework is at play comes during a discussion of Horatius, an early statesman who murdered a sister for sympathizing with Rome's enemies (2.78). In a list of valid topics suggested for Horatius' attorney, Cicero says the defendant will

> speak against the audacity of the criminal on whom he took revenge ... [and say] that a deed should be judged not by the name attached to it, but in the light of the intent of the person who performed it [*non ex nomine ipsius negotii, sed ex consilio eius qui fecerit*], and of the cause and of the circumstances. (2.86)

The defendant's intent is no longer explained via a discussion of motive (*impulsio* or *ratiocinatio*) that would associate him with the alleged act. The fact of the murder is presumed: In the illustration, Horatius' defense is not that someone else committed the murder, but rather that he should be judged by the *consilium* underlying his act and not its *nomen* alone. By *consilium* we understand some state of mind that motivated the crime, but what *consilium* could excuse a murder?

Cicero continues by discussing the two defenses available where, as in Horatius' case, the alleged act is admitted. The first, *remotio criminis*, entails either "shifting the responsibility" for a defendant's act (*tum causa removetur*) or "shifting the act itself" (*tum res ipsa removetur*) (2.86–87). He illustrates the first kind of *remotio* with the example of ambassadors from Rhodes who fail to perform certain duties, claiming that this is because their city's treasurer never paid them (2.87). To "shift the responsibility" (*tum causa removetur*), it is argued, the ambassadors will identify a *causa*, in this case the negligent treasurer, that "impeded his will" (*voluntati suae fuerit impedimento*) (2.92). The prosecutor, on the other hand, will defend the treasurer by showing "how much goodwill and devotion was in him" (*quantum voluntatis et studii fuerit in ipso*) – pointing to his diligence in other duties (2.90). In this third schema, the meaning of *voluntas* has flipped! Rather than a "criminal state of mind," it now denotes a *righteous* state of mind, a provable desire to act correctly, which can either be impeded by an external actor (2.92) or indicated by prior good acts (2.90).

2.4 *Guilty and Righteous Wills*

The defense of "shifting the act itself" is illustrated in the case of a young soldier commanded by his general to sacrifice a pig as part of a treaty with the Samnites. When the treaty is disavowed by the senate and the general given over to the enemy, the question arises as to whether the young soldier should be surrendered as well (2.91–92). The plea advised for his defense is that "the alleged crime does not attach to himself or his powers or his duties [*eam rem nihil ad se nec ad potestatem neque ad officium suum pertinuisse*]" (2.93). Why is the question of legal intent "shifted away" from the soldier? We remember from the forensic speeches that will, in its legal sense, is only recognized in actors of the proper status. In this case, the soldier's state of mind is irrelevant because his status *requires* him to obey the general. Thus, the soldier's absence of *voluntas* is consonant with its presence in the ambassadors' case: Will is no longer the intent to perform a criminal act but rather the intent to act correctly where one has the status required.

The second category of exculpatory defense, *concessio*, is given by Cicero as "when the deed itself is not approved but is asked to be pardoned [*non factum ipsum probatur ab reo, sed ut ignoscatur, id petitur*]" (2.94). As with the prior defense, *concessio* comes in two flavors: *purgatio* and *deprecatio*. An interesting correspondence now emerges with Cicero's first schema. At 1.15, he includes both *concessio* and *remotio criminis* among four types of pleas *assumptivi*, in which a common set of facts are assumed by both sides.[75] The earlier definition of *concessio* is nearly identical to this one, but its *purgatio* is different indeed: "[W]hen the deed is acknowledged, [but] the guilt removed [*cum factum conceditur, culpa removetur*]" (1.15). In contrast, in this third schema *purgatio* is a plea "by which the *goodwill* of the accused is defended but not his act [*per quam eius qui accusatur non factum ipsum, sed voluntas defenditur*" (emphasis added).

What sense does *voluntas defenditur* bring to the definition that *culpa removetur* did not? For one, the earlier definition is more conclusion than explanation: The defendant should be pardoned because he is not guilty – hardly illuminating. The third schema, rather than claiming flatly that the defendant lacks *culpa*, allows the stronger proposition that behind the apparently culpable act lies an exculpatory force: the defendant's righteous will. Moreover, in his discussion of *remotio*, Cicero gave two possible ways

---

[75] These latter two are translated by Hubbell as "retort of the accusation" and "comparison," respectively.

to demonstrate this kind of will: by showing either an external impediment (2.92) or prior good acts (2.90).[76]

In the following passage, *voluntas* as righteous will comes most clearly into view. In quick succession, three distinct senses are woven together. First is the oldest attested sense, *voluntas* as lack of compulsion; the prosecutor must prove via *suspicio* that what is claimed "not to have been willingly done" (*voluntate factum negabitur*) was uncoerced (2.99). He continues that a righteous will may be thwarted by chance (*casus*). Such a claim arises "when it is shown that the defendant's *voluntas* was thwarted by Fortune's power [*cum demonstratur aliqua fortunae vis voluntati obstitisse*]" (2.96). Cicero gives the example of a Spartan herder under contract to provide animals for sacrifice but who is prevented from delivering them by a suddenly flooded river (2.96–97). Though trapped on the wrong side, "the contractor to show his *voluntas* placed all the animals on the bank so as to be seen by those across the river" (2.97). Here, *voluntas* appears to unite two distinct senses that defy an accurate English rendering. By displaying his sheep, the herder is showing his specific intent at that moment – he was ready to bring them across the river and physically could not. But parading his flock is evidence of a second sense of will: As with the Rhodian treasurer (*quantum voluntatis et studi fuerit in ipso*, 2.90), his extra efforts show "how much goodwill" lies behind the allegedly negligent act.[77] Both his specific intent and his ongoing goodwill are thus "thwarted" (*obstare*) by Fortune.

Three distinct shades of meaning – "lack of compulsion," "specific intent," and "ongoing goodwill" – are thus united in a single term of art. The defendant claiming a righteous *voluntas* will turn all of the prosecutor's arguments in his favor:

> [I]n particular, however, he will spend some time in defending his will and in magnifying the circumstances which thwarted it; saying that it was impossible to do more than he did, that in all things one should look to *voluntas* [*et in omnibus rebus voluntatem spectari oportere*] . . . finally, that nothing is more shocking than that he who is free of guilt should not be free of punishment. (2.101, after Hubbell trans.)

---

[76] In another departure from the first schema, Cicero divides the defense of *purgatio* into three parts: *imprudentia*, *casus*, and *necessitudo* (2.94). *Imprudentia* is here defined as "when the accused claims that he was not aware of something [*cum scisse aliquid is qui arguitur negatur*]" (2.95) – in other words, a plea of ignorance rather than a category of involuntary action (1.41).

[77] This sense of *voluntas* as goodwill is also evident at 2.106–07; a defendant admitting the crime but requesting pardon (*deprecatio*) should cite his family's many services to the state as evidence of "the breadth of his goodwill" (*amplitudo suae voluntatis*).

2.4 *Guilty and Righteous Wills*

Over the course of the third schema, therefore, a new kind of legal will has emerged: It is a righteous state of mind that exculpates an otherwise criminal act. It signifies a state of mind free from compulsion (2.99), an ongoing disposition of goodwill toward the opposing parties and to lawfulness itself (2.90, 2.106–107), and the specific intent of an actor with status (2.93). If one's state of mind contains each of these elements, then it is justly argued, as above, that "in all things one should look to will."

Intriguingly, this third schema brings *voluntas* into contact with *consilium* and *ratio*, two terms of consequence for Cicero's philosophy of mind. An act performed *voluntate* is linked to something done *consulto* (2.99) and *ex consilio* (2.86); conversely, a prosecutor opposing a *concessio* plea may argue that the *impedimentum* to the defendant's *voluntas* should have been rationally foreseen (*ratione provideri potuisse*, 2.99). In other words, a prosecutor can argue that a failure by a defendant to use *ratio* – his powers of reason – negates his righteous will. The implications – that conation and cognition are distinct powers of mind and can pull in opposite directions – suggest both the kinship and tension between these notions for Cicero.[78]

Taken together, the second and third schemata – criminal intent and righteous will – suggest an essential ambiguity. In some of his forensic speeches, *voluntas* clearly denotes the criminal intent of the second schema, as in the "will to harm" (*voluntas ad laedendum*) shown by witnesses against Flaccus.[79] The measurability of will is also on display: Fonteius' prosecutors are accused of lacking the courage or ingenuity to match "how much will they have for his downfall" (*quantam voluntatem habent ad hunc opprimendum*),[80] a more malevolent will meriting greater censure. Conversely, Cicero also uses *voluntas* to indicate a righteous state of mind that makes an accusation less probable. When Caelius is accused of disturbing the peace under the *lex de vi*, Cicero asserts that his client's prosecutions of similar crimes should be considered "either as hostages against dangerous behavior or pledges of his goodwill [*pignora voluntatis*]."[81] Similarly, Rabirius' jury is exhorted not to judge his *voluntas* by the acts that necessity forced upon him.[82]

---

[78] Cf. Lévy 2012b, 60.
[79] *Flac.* 11. For "evil wills" in Cicero's forensic speeches, see *Verr.* 2.1.95, 2.1.104, 2.3.57, 2.3.220, 2.3.198; *Sull.* 28; *Planc.* 33; *Lig.* 4.
[80] *Font.* 40.   [81] *Cael.* 78.
[82] *Rab. Post.* 29. Cf. *Lig.* 5. See also *Planc.* 13, Plancius' withdrawal from a previous election is no reason to doubt his *voluntas* (i.e. his righteous state of mind against the accusation of election tampering).

Voluntas, in other words, becomes a locus of moral evaluation that is both bivalent – potentially oriented toward good or evil – and measurable in its intensity. In the *Pro Scauro*, Cicero wins the acquittal of a dubious client by leaning heavily on xenophobic insinuation. He declares that his opponent's key witness, being Sardinian, must not be trusted, and that

> any witness whatever, even though refined and scrupulous, may be swayed, deterred, moulded, diverted; he is the sole master of his own will [*dominus est ipse voluntatis suae*], and has free leave to tell lies as he pleases. But an argument, such as is suited to the case at hand ... must needs remain immutable; for it is not invented, but employed, by the pleader.[83]

While Cicero warns often of fickle witnesses,[84] his phrase here is striking: Each witness is the *dominus* of his *voluntas*, the "lord of his will," and the choice between righteous and evil intent is his alone.

Cicero's attitude toward criminal responsibility seems to grow stricter over time. In the late treatise *De partitione oratoria*, constructed as a dialogue between Cicero and his son, he returns to the "hard cases" where strong emotion is at play. As he had in the first schema of *De inventione*, *imprudentia* is once again defined as a category of involuntary actions, and once again *animi permotiones* are included.[85] Interestingly, on the question of how to evaluate acts of strong emotion, he comes to the opposite conclusion to that which he had arrived at as a young student. In his earlier work, all acts *imprudentes* were grounds for pardon: *imprudentiae concedi nonnunquam convenire*.[86] Here, however, Cicero takes a harder line, claiming that "actions done from emotion and mental disturbance, and therefore irrational, afford no line of defense against the charge in a court of law, but they can provide a defense in a free debate [*nam quae motu animi et perturbatione facta sine ratione sunt, ea defensionem contra crimen in legitimis iudiciis non habent, in liberis disceptationibius habere possunt*]."[87] While *De partitione oratoria* treats fact patterns that recall the defenses of *remotio criminis* and *concessio*, their treatments are brief and *voluntas* is absent.[88] When it does reappear, it is squarely in line with the second schema of *De inventione*: *voluntas* as the will necessary to prove a crime, not excuse it.[89]

---

[83] *Scaur.* 15–16. [84] See, e.g., *Clu.* 159; *Font.* 22–23; *Cael.* 22; *Part. or.* 49.
[85] *Part or.* 38. There is some evidence of hasty drafting: Cicero initially defines *imprudentia* as *quae est aut in casu aut in quadam animi permotione*, but adds a few lines later: *Est etiam in imprudentia necessitas ponenda*.
[86] *Inv.* 1.102. [87] *Part. or.* 43. [88] Ibid. 102. [89] Ibid. 113.

2.4 *Guilty and Righteous Wills* 55

An epilogue to this story of legal *voluntas* is found in the *Topica*, written near the end of Cicero's life. In this treatise, based loosely on Aristotle's work of the same name, we see that the ex-consul's analysis of the validity of legal claims has evolved into a broader inquiry on emotion, freedom, and fate. Cicero's baseline is the law of universal cause and effect; while all actions have causes, the nature of Fortune is to reveal certain causes while obscuring others (63). Our actions, therefore, are partly "unintentional products of necessity" (*ignorata, quae necessitate effecta sunt*) and partly "willing, that is, by design" (*voluntaria, quae consilio*, ibid.). If hitting someone unintentionally (*quem nolueris*) with a weapon is "of Fortune" (*fortunae*), throwing it is "of the will" (*voluntatis*) (64). We note here a grammatical form absent from *De inventione* and occurring only once in *De oratore*. Throwing a weapon is not "voluntary" (he twice uses *voluntarius* in the preceding sentence) but "of the will." Admitting Cicero's penchant for stylistic variation, it may be that by the 40s BCE, and alongside its many other meanings, his notions of will now include "the will" as a faculty in its own right.[90]

Here, he adds a final word to the debate on moral responsibility that has marked, in one fashion or another, his entire legal career:

> Mental agitation belongs with acts performed in ignorance or lack of foresight. For though such a state of mind is voluntary [*voluntariae*] – for these conditions yield to reproof and admonition – still they produce such violence of emotion that acts which are voluntary seem sometimes to be necessary and certainly unintentional [*ut ea quae voluntaria sunt ut necessaria interdum aut certe ignorata videantur*]. (64)

Here, we see not only an appreciation of the power of emotions in driving action, but also what it is like to experience this process "from the inside": *tantos motus, ut ea quae voluntaria sunt ut necessaria interdum aut certe ignorata videantur.* Three distinct shades of psychological experience are put in close relation: volitions we feel to be such; volitions that nevertheless feel forced upon us; and volitions that "catch us unawares" (*ignorata*). These new psychological subtleties do not overshadow Cicero's moral judgment, however, which applies a Stoic strictness in

---

[90] In *De inventione*, *voluntatis* occurs solely as a genitive of possession, typically with the pronoun *suae*; see *Inv.* 1.70, 2.107, 2.128, 2.139–41. The subjective genitive "inclination of will" (or "of the will") from *De or.* 2.129, discussed in n.56 of this chapter, anticipates this occurrence in the *Topica*. *Voluntas* in the subjective genitive does not occur in any surviving text prior to Cicero; cf. discussion of Plautus and Terence in Chapter 1.

each case.⁹¹ The power of emotion may make certain decisions of ours *seem* (*videantur*) forced or accidental, but they *are* (*sunt*) voluntary nonetheless. Though extraordinarily attuned and sympathetic to the inner conflicts of his fellow man, Cicero is at the last unwilling to excuse him from responsibility.

---

⁹¹ The Stoic notion of absolute inner responsibility, to which Cicero dedicates large portions of *De finibus* and the *Tusculans*, is the main subject of Chapter 6.

CHAPTER 3

Cartographies of Power

Power in history's earliest states was typically central and singular. In the first cities and empires of the Mediterranean world, public decisions were commonly made by a sole ruler and executed by administrators, soldiers, and scribes.[1] Democratic Athens was a noteworthy exception, but its control of territory *extra muros* was brief and its capacities of judgment earned grave skepticism.[2]

Rome was different. From 509 BCE to Cicero's lifetime, its expanding empire was governed by a plural cast of magistrates, chosen by assemblies and serving a single year in each post. Elections were hotly contested and made winners and losers on each step of the ladder of power. And for all the richness of Roman public law, no constitution established these offices or defined their limits. An agglomeration of written statutes (*leges*), judicial precedent (*ius*), and ancestral custom (*mos maiorum*) were the main constraints on the ambitions of Rome's politicians.[3] If one magistrate's interpretation of law or custom conflicted with another's, no higher court save that of public opinion could resolve the dispute.

At its most successful, this distribution of power produced a dynamic equilibrium capable of great resilience – as in the Republic's recovery from staggering defeat at Cannae (216 BCE) to triumph over Carthage.[4] But by Cicero's lifetime, this model – apparently as successful as it was

---

[1] See generally van de Mieroop 1997, 118–41; Will 1998, 811–35; Chavalas 2005, 34–47, 48–62.
[2] See most notably Pl. *Resp.* 303a4–6; Arist. *Pol.* 1279a17–21, 1289a38–b11 (democracy as one of the "deviant" constitutions); Cic. *Rep.* 1.43–44. Cf. Schofield 2005, 225, 245–51; Cartledge 2016, 33 ("the tradition of thought about politics that started with the age of Herodotus was resolutely and overwhelmingly anti-democratic"). See generally Roberts 1994.
[3] Wieacker describes the Roman Republic as a conglomerate of "institutions and formalized rules of political action that, as a whole, were perceived and practically applied as a legally binding" and only occasionally "endorsed, reformed or developed by laws," that is, by statutory law; Wieacker, 1988, 345, 353. Cf. Lintott 1999, 94–104; Hölkeskamp 2010, 17; Straumann 2016, 47–62. On sources of judicial precedent in the republican period, see Chapter 2, n.84.
[4] This is of course the principal subject of Polybius's *Histories*. For Cannae, see Polyb. Bk. 3.

unprecedented – had reached a breaking point. Rome had won a vast empire, but politics at home were in disarray. A chasm had opened between rich and poor, and the popular institutions designed as counterweights – the tribunes, courts, and *contiones* – could no longer budge an intransigent senate.[5] Frustration and ambition led to increasingly radical strategies; rivalries once contained by *auctoritas* and *suffragium* now spilled onto the battlefield. The dam of civil peace broke in 132 BCE with the murder of reformer T. Gracchus, setting in motion a wave of violence that only broke with Octavian's victories a century later. Strife and emergency were the constants of Cicero's career.

The next three chapters examine how he used the notion of will to rationalize Roman politics as they came undone. Will is firstly for Cicero the animating force of this venerable equilibrium. The wills of Rome's magistrates should be a public asset, vectors to inscribe reason on the world. These forces are naturally counterbalanced by respect for colleagues and for the *maiores*. This is the system Polybius had described in other terms at its pre-Gracchan zenith and that inspired later notions of "checks and balances."[6] In his early career, Cicero describes and defends this equilibrium in which senators, magistrates, and assemblies all participate. Reciprocity is central in the constitution Cicero later frames: "For the man who governs well must have obeyed in the past, and he who obeys dutifully will be seen fit later to govern."[7]

This ideal equipoise of will, already damaged at the time of Cicero's birth, was increasingly tipped toward bloodshed. The mature Cicero watches Pompey and Caesar overwhelm all collegiality and constraint; worse still, Cicero finds himself arguing to suspend those same constraints, such as in the Catilinarian conspiracy and with Pompey's extraordinary commands. To this crisis of norms, as Straumann shows in a masterful recent study, Cicero applies constitutional thinking.[8] In the face of enactments he considers unjust, Cicero appeals to *ius* as a body of norms with superior force. Legislation by his *popularis* opponents can thus be annulled for procedural reasons – disrespect of auspices or votes carried by violence – but also for substantive or material ones. Clodius' bill to strip Cicero of his

---

[5] See Brunt 1988, 6–19; Lintott 1999, 199–213; Hölkeskamp 2010, 20–22; Arena 2012, 68–72, 137–60.
[6] Polyb. 6.11–59; see Lintott 1999, 16–26, 247–55; Straumann 2016, 151–61; Atkins 2018b, 13–24; Schofield 2021, 45–46.
[7] *Leg.* 3.5: *nam et qui bene imperat, paruerit aliquando necesse est, et qui modeste paret, videtur, qui aliquando imperet, dignus esse* (after Loeb trans.).
[8] See Straumann 2016, esp. chs. 1, 3, and 4; Steel 2017b.

house cannot properly be *lex* because it defies a central norm of Roman *ius*: Legislation targeting one citizen (*privilegium*) is forbidden.[9]

When will cannot be tempered by the diffusion of power into many hands, some new constraint must be found. This constraint, argues Cicero, is natural law (*ius naturae*), discovered by Greek Stoics but given life in Rome's legal and political heritage. *De republica* and *De legibus*, written after the crises of his consulship and exile, show Cicero at the summit of political creativity. Here, we find his strongest normative statements about how will should balance the Republic. Cicero throughout his life had presented will as subject to rational limits – and, further, as the force necessary to make reason effective. In these works, however, the constraints on will are no longer primarily horizontal and organic: They are inherent, substantive, and governed by higher-order principles of natural law as interpreted by a rational elite. As Straumann and others have capably shown, though these principles failed to save Cicero's republic, they unwittingly laid the foundation for much of modern constitutionalism and thus for much of the political fortunes and misfortunes of today.[10]

The present chapter will show how Cicero employs the idea of will to map his political environment, the intentions of its leading players, and the lawful boundaries of their power. In letters and speeches, we find both artful political commentary and heartfelt appeals to place will under reason's control. In Chapter 4, we will see how a particularly Roman coinage – *voluntas mutua* or "mutual goodwill" – serves Cicero and his colleagues in stabilizing a fast-growing empire. Here, the crisis of Caesarism impels him to engage with theories of reciprocity and friendship. Chapter 5 will bring Cicero's political beliefs most fully into view. We will explore how *voluntas* creates the relationship between sovereign citizen and governing elite, producing an idea unknown to Plato and Aristotle: the will of the people.

In its contemporary form, powermapping is the discipline that traces and interprets the dynamics of a social system.[11] Its purpose is to derive

---

[9] *Dom.* 43; Straumann 2016, 136–39.
[10] Straumann 2016, 16–21, 303–41. For a range of viewpoints on this influence, see, e.g., Lintott 1999, 247–55; Millar 2002, 100–34; Connolly 2015, 1–22; Remer 2017, 152–66; Atkins 2018b, 192–99. Atkins in particular stresses how modern theorists have tended to misread their Roman predecessors.
[11] Though network analysis is described in various ways in the many disciplines that employ it, "powermapping" begins in the academic literature in the context of social psychology. See Hagan and Smail 1997, 257–67; Noy 2008, 3–18. Interestingly, Hagan and Smail 1997, 258, present their approach as a challenge to the "regnant paradigm in clinical and therapeutic psychology," the

from the raw data of personalities, laws, and events a blueprint of influence to help an advocate advance their goals. Powermapping encompasses a range of techniques and frameworks; it has no definitive textbook. It is manifest, rather, in certain practices and habits of mind that, from the evidence of their texts, may have been as useful to ancient analysts as to their modern counterparts. Among these are: realism, an attention to informal influence as well as formal status; interdependence, an interest in the second- and third-order effects of a given event; and dynamism, a recognition that as roles shift and relationships evolve the transaction of power can undergo radical change. Each of these principles is evident in Cicero's attention to the equilibrium – and, more often, the discord – of Rome's willful politicians.

For Cicero, powermapping was literally a means of survival. Lacking an army, street gang, or family compound, he depended on intellectual gifts to stay out of harm's way. Uncovering the designs of a Pompey or Catiline required sophisticated intelligence-gathering and a new toolkit of expressions. Mapping networks of influence first helps Cicero clear a path to high office. He begins gauging the preferences of senatorial colleagues more than a year before his campaign for consul, signaling to Atticus, "when I have made out the wills of the nobles, I shall write to you" (*cum perspexero voluntates nobilium, scribam ad te*).[12] Descriptively, the notion of will helps Cicero trace finer gradations of support and opposition, notably in the phrases *sua* or *summa voluntate*. In a more normative tone, it helps him reframe party conflict and distinguish his opponents from the "good citizens" who included senate and people alike.

But powermapping was not only an instrument of self-protection. To map is to order a disorderly world. From his first speech against Verres to his final Philippic, Cicero is propelled by the duty – dimmed but never extinguished – to restore *mos maiorum* and return the republic to her better self.[13] Here, Cicero's normative claims for reason and will come to the fore. At home and abroad, *voluntas* should transact within a plural order of *auctoritas*, with rational will prevailing over violence. His acknowledgment in *De republica* that politics "may defeat reason" does not refute but rather

---

premise that the psychological problems can be solved through individual "will-power" alone. Similar techniques are common in information systems and management theory; see, e.g., DeSanctis and Gallupe 1987; Mendelow 1991. Powermapping is a technique of growing importance to community-level advocacy campaigns; see, e.g., "A Guide to Power-Mapping" by the advocacy network Move to Amend, available at www.movetoamend.org/guide-power-mapping.
[12] *Att.* 1.10.3.   [13] See Annas 2013, 222.

emphasizes the standard that reason must set.[14] With help from Stoic and Platonic ideas, Cicero takes the *voluntas* of common usage and builds a case for the priority of self-mastery over brute force. Where *vis* overwhelms *voluntas* in Roman politics, as Laelius predicts in *De republica*, "those who up to the present have obeyed us by will are held faithful by fear alone [*qui adhuc voluntate nobis oboediunt, terrore teneantur*]."[15] On the other hand, will bereft of reason is *temeritas*, a selfish ambition that "runs beyond the mark." In letters and speeches, Cicero constantly strives to raise the practice of politics to a rational plane where the rough edges of ambition are refined by wise law and prudent action. But whereas for Cicero the politics of *voluntas* stand diametrically opposed to those of *vis*, Caesar enforces his own will at the point of a sword.

3.1 Intentions, Alliances, and Schemes

Cicero's map of Roman power begins with the wills of its leading men. In the early days of his public career, this task centers upon an uncommonly changeable politician: Gnaeus Pompeius Magnus. Writing to his ally Lentulus Spinther in 56 BCE, Cicero relates that while Pompey has nominally supported his friend's appointment to restore the exiled king of Egypt, support of an alternative measure among Pompey's friends "intensifies suspicion as to Pompey's will [*auget suspicionem Pompei voluntatis*]."[16] This discrepancy between words and intentions has immediate consequences for Lentulus: To oppose the alternative bill is to risk angering Pompey, while allowing it would undermine his own standing. The interdependent stances of these actors carry serious consequences and thus must be carefully recorded.[17]

In his cartography of power, Cicero enlists the help of young Caelius Rufus. In their correspondence, they explore the hidden wills of Rome's major players. If Cicero meets Pompey, writes Caelius,

> be sure to write and tell me what you thought of him, how he talked to you, and what will he showed [*quam orationem habuerit tecum quamque ostenderit voluntatem*]. He is apt to say one thing and think another, but is usually not clever enough to keep his real aims out of view.[18]

As elsewhere with the spirit of a law and the goodwill of an audience, in this exchange will is a durable inner force that can alter over time. Unlike

---

[14] *Rep.* 2.57: "[T]he essential nature of the commonwealth often defeats reason [*sed tamen vincit ipsa rerum publicarum natura saepe rationem*]." See generally Atkins 2013.
[15] *Rep.* 3.41.   [16] *Fam.* 1.12.3.   [17] See, e.g., *QFr.* 6.3; *Fam.* 1.19.2.   [18] Ibid. 1.77.3.

with *sententia*, a stated opinion on a single issue, reading *voluntas* is an ongoing concern in which surface positions can mask true intent. Principles of political realism must apply: In the most favorable cases, a politician's *voluntas* can be "plainly noted" (*plane perspecta*), such as in the timing Pompey seeks for Caesar's withdrawal from Gaul.[19] But most often, as Cicero writes Brutus, "people's wills [are] concealed and their dispositions complex [*occultas hominum voluntates multiplicisque naturas*]."[20] Indeed, Cicero recognizes the utility of obscuring his own *voluntas* at delicate moments. When Dolabella emerges as a potential son-in-law during his prosecution of one of Cicero's allies, Caelius advises him to "show nothing whatsoever of your will [*nihil de tua voluntate ostendas*]."[21] Political will can also be weaker than it appears: Caelius recounts the soft opposition of the Catonians to public honors for Cicero following his victories in Cilicia "because they merely showed the measure of their will without fighting for their position, whereas they could have been a nuisance [*tantum voluntatem ostenderunt, pro sententia cum impedire possent non pugnarunt*]."[22]

Caelius' gifts were rare, though, and Cicero could betray frustration with those who lacked his *protégé's* subtlety. As Caesar marches from Gaul in 49 BCE, Cicero remonstrates with Atticus for making special efforts to go welcome him, adding that Pompey had blundered, too, by extolling Caesar's "most brilliant achievements" (*rebus gestis amplissimis*) in public. The smarter move was, of course, to pacify Caesar without elevating him: "[A]ll this blurs the signs that might distinguish sincerity from pretense [*quibus voluntas a simulatione distingui posset*]."[23] In Cicero's politics, prudence demanded not sincerity but a scrupulous insincerity that served both his reputation and his survival.

The flexibility required of a budding politician made *voluntas* an ideal term to denote all manner of schemes. In his speeches, the notion of will adds fire to his invective. He vilifies Catiline and his friends for their "unscrupulous will and purpose" (*voluntas et causa impudentissima*),[24] or when, though depriving his *popularis* enemies of their swords, he cannot remove their "criminal and evil wills" (*voluntates ... consceleratas ac nefarias*).[25] Conversely, he could use it to signify a righteous state of mind, as when praising the censor Gaius Cassius for erecting a statue of Concord: "His will was a lofty one, and worthy of all praise [*Praeclara*

---

[19] Ibid. 1.84.4; cf. 2.137.1.   [20] *Ad Brut.* 13.1.   [21] *Fam.* 1.88.2.
[22] *Fam.* 1.91.2. Note as well the "conjoined" *voluntas* shared by this group of political actors, to be explored further in Chapter 4.
[23] *Att.* 3.188.2.   [24] *Cat.* 2.18.   [25] *Sull.* 28. See also *Cat.* 2.16, 4.13; *Dom.* 116.

voluntas atque omni laude digna]."[26] Similarly, by presenting the will as measurable he can track it as it shifts, as when he expresses regret to Atticus that Lucceius' *voluntas* is "more obstinate" (*obstinatior*) than before, requiring a new strategy to reconcile the two.[27]

Though these expressions were useful when analyzing an individual, the functional unit of Roman politics was the network. Here, too, *voluntas* helps Cicero trace hidden lines of influence. In the courtroom, he uses *voluntas* to link two individuals in a criminal conspiracy, tying Verres to a previous judgment against an ally for illegal taxation.[28] Conversely, Cicero uses will to decouple an aggrieved Sicilian from the corrupt governor who claimed to have seized his estate *voluntate*.[29] A new level of complexity arises with the formation of the First Triumvirate. To justify his volte-face toward the three men, Cicero recalls Pompey's stern reminder that support for his return from exile was given *voluntate Caesaris*.[30] That Caesar's will lay behind Pompey's support adds leverage to the demand that Cicero reverse his opposition to Caesar in the senate, leverage to which Cicero ultimately yields.[31] Similarly, Caelius writes regarding Curio's candidacy for tribune that his newfound goodwill toward the *boni* is not as it appears: "[I]ts origin and cause is that Caesar ... has shown his indifference to Curio in no uncertain manner [*huius autem voluntatis initium et causa est quod eum non mediocriter Caesar ... valde contempsit*]."[32] The second-order reasoning of a powermapper is well in evidence here: If Caesar's rebuff was the true cause of Curio's defection to the *optimates*, despite Caesar giving funds "to get the friendship of any guttersnipe,"[33] Cicero could conclude both that Curio was not to be trusted and that Caesar must have special cause for his ill will.

3.2 *Sua* and *Summa Voluntate*

In a dynamic and realistic powermap, purely "yes or no" positions are rare. More often, a multitude of shadings lies between opposition and support. With the phrase *sua voluntate* Cicero develops a semantic middle ground, previously unattested in Latin, between political neutrality and active adherence. When Athens' municipal council, seeking to protect the ruins of Epicurus' house, comes into conflict with the Roman senator owning

---

[26] *Dom.* 131. Cf. *Planc.* 33: "It was Granius too who often employed the license granted to his brusque wit in sarcastic comments upon the wills of L. Crassus or M. Antonius [*Ille L. Crassi, ille M. Antonii voluntatem asperioribus facetiis saepe perstrinxit impune*]."
[27] *Att.* 1.7.1.   [28] *Verr.* 1.95; cf. *Div. Caec.* 34; *Sull.* 36.   [29] *Verr.* 2.18.44.   [30] *Fam.* 1.20.9.
[31] *Prov. cons.* 43.   [32] *Fam.* 1.81.2.   [33] Ibid.

the property, Cicero entreats his colleague to let it be known that the Areopagus had acted "according to your will" (*tua voluntate*).³⁴ If the senator could not explicitly reverse his stance without loss of face, *tua voluntate* will signify his implicit endorsement of the city's plans, defusing the conflict.³⁵ Similarly, when the senate debates restoring Cicero's house after his recall from exile, the tribune Serranus, dissuaded from interposing a veto, attempts to delay the proceedings. Seeing that the tide of opinion was in his favor, Cicero opts against confrontation: "[W]ith much ado, and with my willingness, the point was conceded him [*vix tamen ei de mea voluntate concessum est*]."³⁶ By taking the middle path designated by *mea voluntate*, Cicero again defuses a politically tense moment without harm to his own position: A decree in his favor passes the next day.

The sense of *mea voluntate* as implicit endorsement had a range of uses for Cicero. The phrase could save him time or annoyance, as when he importunes Atticus to handle a conversation with Clodius he would rather avoid.³⁷ Near the end of his career he uses the phrase counterfactually to ease political suspicions: In the fourteenth Philippic, Cicero accuses the Antonians of attempting to entrap him by offering fasces "as if done by my will" (*quasi mea voluntate factum*), a putative coup d'état they wanted as a pretext for murder.³⁸ A surviving letter from Antony shows that Cicero was not the only statesman to exploit the phrase. A month after Caesar's murder, Antony expresses his wish to recall from exile a henchman of Clodius convicted for burning down the senate house seven years before. Antony claims to be recalling him with Caesar's permission, but that he will only do so *tua voluntate*; that is, with Cicero's consent.³⁹ Antony's ploy is transparent: Though Cicero is a well-known enemy of Clodius, Antony wants to equate the absence of Cicero's active opposition as a tacit endorsement of the man's recall. (Whether he overestimated his own power to muzzle Cicero is another matter.)

The particular sense of *sua voluntate* comes into clearer relief in contrast with the related *sua sponte*, "of one's own accord." While *voluntas* is for

---

³⁴ *Fam.* 1.64.5.   ³⁵ See also *Att.* 2.104.6, debriefing Atticus on the affair.
³⁶ *Att.* 1.74.4. Here, I think that "my willingness," though a bit awkward in English, splits the difference between "willingly" and "by my will," neither of which quite capture the subtlety of Cicero's phrase. Though *voluntate* identifies a position relative to a specific act (as it had for Plautus and Terence), here it also signals Cicero's *dignitas* as a political actor, making the *mea* or "my" important as well.
³⁷ *Att.* 3.270.1: "[Y]ou can do so with my willingness, in fact that is more convenient than what he asks of me, i.e. that I should write to Clodius myself [*potes id mea voluntate facere commodiusque est quam quod ille a me petit, me ipsum scribere ad Clodium*]."
³⁸ *Phil.* 14.15.   ³⁹ *Att.* 4.367A.

3.2 Sua *and* Summa Voluntate

Cicero a specifically human faculty, all creatures can act *sua sponte*; the phrase also implies, as *voluntate* does not, that its subject initiated the given action.[40] For example, Cicero writes to Atticus regarding a letter he has apparently sent at Atticus' behest, "recommending me to do something I had already done of my own accord [*mea sponte*] the day before."[41] To perform an act *sua sponte* was to do so deliberately and thus take ownership of the consequences – in this case, credit from one's friends. By contrast, *sua voluntate* allowed Cicero and his colleagues another shade of remove from acts they did not want too explicitly to endorse.

Similarly, the phrase *summa voluntate* allowed Cicero to keep himself at a comfortable distance from a given political act. In his defense of Murena, Cicero accuses the prosecutor, Servius, of having spoiled his campaign for consul by wasting time and capital on antibribery legislation. Though some of his bills had passed,[42] there were others "which a crowded Senate rejected with my strong approval [*quae mea summa voluntate senatus frequens repudiavit*]."[43] Cicero frames a battle of wills between himself and Servius; but whereas Servius has actively exerted himself, *summa voluntate* denotes Cicero's support – perhaps even his engineering – of the bills' rejection without deigning to oppose them openly. *Voluntas* thus maps Cicero in clear opposition to Servius while creating enough semantic distance to frame the conflict as one concerning principles, not personalities, and that in any event costs Cicero no effort to win.[44]

In some cases, *voluntas* could express strong favorability toward an event that Cicero had neither initiated nor actively supported. In his first political speech, he exhorts the senate to approve the granting of Pompey's special commission against Mithridates. He gently defuses his senior colleague Catulus, who opposes the motion on the grounds of its novelty (*novum*), by praising him and noting that such powers had recently been granted *summa Q. Catuli voluntate*.[45] The word *summa* serves the rhetorical purpose of emphasizing, without accusing his elder colleague of hypocrisy, that his past and present positions do not match. Moreover, Cicero submits that

---

[40] See, e.g., *Verr.* 2.5.18; *Clu.* 79, 138; *Att.* 1.1, 6.2; *Cat.* 1.13; *Dom.* 12; *Fin.* 1.25.
[41] *Att.* 4.25.27.
[42] *Mur.* 46: "[Y]our wishes and your standing were deferred to [*gestus est mos et voluntati et dignitati tuae*] ..."
[43] Ibid. 47.
[44] Ibid. See also *Att.* 1.19.9, a decree passed *summa voluntate* of senate rank and file, but not with our *auctoritas*; cf. *Pis.* 46, where Cicero gloats that Piso's loss of his army and his popularity were "beyond my prayers, but absolutely in accordance with my will [*praeter optatum meum, sed valde ex voluntate*]."
[45] *Leg. Man.* 61.

Catulus had actively participated in granting these powers, that these prior innovations "were brought about on the initiative of Quintus Catulus and the other honorable men of the same rank [*sunt in eundem hominem a Q. Catuli atque a ceterorum eiusdem dignitatis amplissimorum hominum auctoritate*]."[46] The notion of his colleague's "honorable" if inconsistent will lets Cicero keep a pointed riposte within respectful bounds.

The phrase *summa voluntate* could also create protective distance from political liability. In the early stages of his campaign for consul, Cicero is contemplating defending Catiline against charges of extortion, and he reports to Atticus, "we have the jury we want, with full willingness of the prosecution [*iudices habemus quod volumus, summa accusatoris voluntate*]."[47] At least for the moment, Cicero was contemplating the defense of Catiline via collusion with Clodius – skirting the law with his soon-to-be bitterest foes! The phrase *summa voluntate* serves Cicero by adding semantic distance from this collusion, implying that Cicero and Clodius were working together while not explicitly assigning responsibility. Cicero creates a similar distance in writing to Quintus that the elections for 53 BCE have been continually postponed due to contrary omens "by the great willingness of all good men [*magna voluntate bonorum omnium*]."[48] Cicero knows that political opposition, not divine disfavor, is behind these "omens"; his phrase preserves a pious fiction by distancing the *boni* from their own tactics.[49]

Cicero seeks the same kind of protective distance in his famous "palinode" for Caesar, *De provinciis consularibus*. The speech to his fellow senators aims at a delicate and awkward goal. Though having vocally opposed Caesar's land redistribution bill, and with his personal distaste well known, Cicero must now both support Caesar's tenure in Gaul and suggest their relationship is sounder than it looks:

> If you also thought it important to the good cause that Caesar's will should not run counter to my well-being [*voluntatem Caesaris a salute mea non abhorrere*]; and if I have his son-in-law [Pompey], who is at once my witness for Caesar's goodwill to me [*mihi testis de voluntate Caesaris*], and guarantor of my own to him ... should I not eradicate from existence those most unhappy matters, at least wholly banish them from my heart? (43)

---

[46] Ibid. 63.   [47] *Att.* 1.11.1.   [48] *Qfr.* 23.2.
[49] Divination is a Roman institution that presents a special challenge for Cicero. It is part of the *mos maiorum*, it is a useful tool for suppressing *popularis* agitation, and yet its claims to reading divine will in entrails cannot be taken literally. As he explains in a letter to Aulus Caecina, he believes the practice of divination – like the rest of Roman politics – can be reimagined as augury by reflection on history and nature's laws; *Fam.* 2.234.2–12. Cf. *Sest.* 33–34; *Leg.* 2.21, 3.27; Polyb. 6.56.11; Lintott 1999, 187–90; Lévy 2020b.

The awkwardness of the moment impels Cicero to try not one but three rhetorical tricks: (1) the association of Caesar with his "son-in-law" Pompey, still a senate favorite; (2) the association of the senate with Caesar's support; and (3) a qualified reference to his own rapprochement. The "reconciliation" of Caesar and Cicero is not between the two men personally, but rather between Caesar's *voluntas* and Cicero's *salus*. These semantic niceties help Cicero navigate a most uncomfortable turn of events.

3.3 *Voluntas* as Affiliation

A well-attested sense of the Greek *prohairesis* was an individual's choice of life path.[50] Though this sense of *voluntas* was probably not original to Cicero,[51] he makes inventive use of it in his account of Rome's civil strife. For decades, rival coalitions of *populares* and *optimates* had vied with one another with increasing violence.[52] Unwilling and unfit to join a battle of arms, Cicero attempts a maneuver in the combat of ideas. In his speech for Sestius (56 BCE), he explains:

> There have always been two classes of men [*duo genera*] in this State who have sought to engage in public affairs and to distinguish themselves in them. Of these two classes, one willed to be, by repute and in reality, "the people's men," the other, "best citizens" [*alteri se populares, alteri optimates et haberi et esse voluerunt*]. (96)

He continues:

> "Who then are these best citizens of yours?" In number, if you ask me, they are infinite; for otherwise we could not exist ... All are "best citizens" who are neither criminal nor vicious in disposition, nor frantic, nor harassed by troubles in their households [*Omnes optimates sunt, qui neque nocentes sunt nec natura improbi nec furiosi nec malis domesticis impediti*]. (97)

In a move much imitated by modern politicians, Cicero thus reframes party labels to his and his allies' advantage. Against the idea that Rome's two political *genera* represent a recent emergency, Cicero claims that it was *always* the case that Roman leaders willed to be *optimate* or *popularis*. *Voluerunt* thus carries a double kind of permanence: lifelong commitment

---

[50] See Merker 2016, 364–71.
[51] In the opening lines of the Verres prosecution (70 BCE), his first major case, Cicero anticipates the criticism of abandoning the defense bar, of "a sudden change of will toward prosecution [*subito nunc mutata voluntate ad accusandum descendere*];" *Div. Caec.* 1. It is likely that this usage was already current if Cicero uses it without explanation in a forensic speech.
[52] See Brunt 1971, 74–111.

to one of two political tribes, themselves a permanent feature of the Roman landscape.⁵³ Interestingly, Cicero first gives equal treatment to the two camps, saying that these partisans sought to *habere* and *esse* their affiliation. He then shifts course, expanding the definition of *optimate* from the moneyed elite to all Romans rich and poor who seek "calm with dignity" (*cum dignitate otium*, 98).⁵⁴ Cicero's new framework excludes only those who are "by their natures unsound" (*natura improbi*) – an unsubtle reference to his *popularis* opponents. In other words, the "party spirit" first presented as a venerable choice of sides is refashioned such that only criminals could fail to be considered "best citizens."⁵⁵

In the seventh Philippic, Cicero attempts a similar argument to reframe the political affiliations of his enemies – here, the allies of Mark Antony who remain in Rome:

> Hence we see that all along they disliked the best condition of the community, and that they were not willingly the "people's men" [*non voluntate fuisse popularis*]. How else does it happen that the same folk who were "people's men" in evil causes prefer to be criminal rather than "popular" in the most popular cause that ever was, being also for the good of the Republic?⁵⁶

We see the great distance that "willingness" has traveled from its Plautine origins as a lack of compulsion.⁵⁷ Cicero is certainly not claiming that these allies of Antony were forced to be *popularis*; rather, their current criminal behavior proves the insincerity of their previous *voluntas* (here, "adherence") for the *popularis* cause. In a deft rhetorical turn, Cicero argues that whereas these men were false *populares*, he is now – due to the present emergency – a truer *popularis* than they are!⁵⁸ Here, the bivalence of will – its ability to serve good or evil – collides with Cicero's normative ends. Instead of condemning his opponents' "evil wills," he wants instead to argue that they do not really have a "will" at all: Their *voluntas* is faulty, derived from a shaky grasp of public affairs.⁵⁹ Will as party affiliation can also be weighed and measured, as when Cicero laments that the gifted

---

⁵³ This type of *voluntas* as political affiliation should not be confused with *voluntas in* (or *erga*) *rem publicam*, a form of "public goodwill" more closely related to the *voluntas mutua* between statesmen, as explored in the following chapter. See, e.g., *Verr.* 1.34; *Cat.* 4.9; *Phil.* 1.10, 2.13, 2.30.

⁵⁴ There is a rich body of scholarship on this phrase that can only be acknowledged in passing here. See, e.g., Boyancé 1941, 172–91; Wirszubski 1954, 1–13; Wood 1988, 193–99; Frede 1989, 83–84; Kaster 2006, 32; McConnell 2014, 33–34; Zarecki 2014, 57–58.

⁵⁵ In an inverse and particularly daring act of reframing, in his first speech before the Roman people as their consul Cicero "reveals" himself as a *popularis* and proceeds to redefine *popularis* toward his own political views. See *Leg. agr.* 2.6–7. Cf. Morstein-Marx 1998, 262–63.

⁵⁶ *Phil.* 7.4. ⁵⁷ See Chapter 1. ⁵⁸ *Phil.* 7.4–5. ⁵⁹ Cf. Yavetz 1969, 41–57.

popularis C. Gracchus was not "turned toward a better mind and will [*ad meliorem mentem voluntatemque esse conversa*]."[60]

As conflict deepens between triumvirs and senate, Cicero faces a dilemma over where his own *voluntas* should lie. In a letter to Lentulus Spinther in 54 BCE, he describes feeling caught between the ideals of a *bonum civem*, loyalty to the Republic over faction, and a *bonum virem*, honoring his friendship with Caesar and Pompey.[61] In this tour de force of rationalization, Cicero floats three separate arguments, each of which hinges on *voluntas* as a deep but alterable affiliation. He first pleads the superior claim of Pompey's service to the Republic and their bonds of friendship. How could Cicero be criticized if "in certain speeches I changed my tack a little and aligned my will with the dignity of this great man [*me immutassem meamque voluntatem ad summi viri de meque optime meriti dignitatem adgregassem*]?"[62] Second, he complains that even if he had kept his former stance, there are no longer *optimates* worthy of the name: "[A]ccordingly, men of sense, of whom I hope I am and am considered to be, have now completely to reshape their will and position [*et sententia et voluntas mutata esse debet*]" (20.18).[63] In a final appeal to Lentulus, Cicero maintains that, after all, it was the *boni* who shifted their wills first (*ac bonorum voluntatibus mutatis*, 20.21), and therefore, "we must move with the times [*temporibus adsentiendum*]."[64] Besides suggesting what we would call a guilty conscience, this variegated plea shows the importance of *voluntas* as affiliation and the lengths to which Cicero went to justify his own.

3.4 Boundaries of Political Will

3.4.1 The Status Quo and Its Problems

As Straumann demonstrates, Roman constitutionalism was, somewhat paradoxically, the result of political failure. Derived in great part from unwritten norms,[65] the principal constraints of the early republican

---

[60] *Har. resp.* 41.   [61] *Fam.* 1.20.10.   [62] Ibid. 1.20.11.
[63] An echo of this rationalization can be heard in the famous remark of the conservative US President Ronald Reagan, a former trade unionist: "I didn't leave the Democratic Party, the Democratic Party left me." Remarks delivered at Rosemont, Illinois, August 12, 1986 (video available at https://commons.wikimedia.org/wiki/File:President_Reagan%27s_Remarks_at_Illinois_State_Fair_on_August_12,_1986.webm).
[64] *Fam.* 1.20.11; cf. *Prov. cons.* 25, referring to Caesar's persuasion of the senate, *posteaquam rebus gestis mentes vestras voluntatesque mutastis*.
[65] Straumann 2016, 47–62. On the Republic's diverse sources of constitutional law, see also Lintott 1999, 3–8.

constitution were procedural and temporal, not substantive. Despite endemic tensions between patricians and plebeians, laws passed by proper order in the assemblies were typically perceived as legitimate, especially following the *Lex Hortensia* of 287 BCE.[66] As we have seen in this chapter, a magistrate's scope of action was limited by the complementary powers of his colleagues and the expiration of his term of office – following which, in extreme cases, he could be prosecuted for abuses of power.[67] While "entrenched" norms such as the individual right to a trial before the people (*provocatio*) are in evidence prior to the Gracchan crisis,[68] explicit arguments for those norms – properly "constitutional" claims – only emerge, in Straumann's view, in the partisan battles of the late 2nd and early 1st centuries BCE.[69] Only as the constitution was collapsing, in other words, did constitutional thought come into its own.

Could a people's assembly give Sulla the power to declare Roman citizens enemies of the state?[70] Could a law to redistribute land be held invalid in the face of a higher-order right to property?[71] Though sources for disputes like these are often from Cicero's lifetime or later, Straumann shows how *ius* and *mos maiorum* may have been increasingly evoked after 132 BCE to annul otherwise lawful acts. His main area of focus involves the limits to popular legislation, a topic I examine more fully in Chapter 5.[72] For the purpose of individual magistrates, the point is that by Cicero's lifetime the collapse of traditional "checks and balances" required new forms of argument to counter the willful and ambitious.[73]

The problem of legitimacy was mirrored in the essential instability of *voluntas* in common usage: The same word marked both a lawful decision and the personal desires one might place above the law. This linguistic ambiguity was reflected in the problem of self-help: Since Rome had no state police force, when a magistrate invoked emergency powers, he was not only able but expected to enforce those powers with violence.[74] As

---

[66] Livy, *Per.* 11; Pliny, *HN* 16.37; Gell. *NA* 15.27.4.
[67] See Lintott 1999, 14–15, 26, 94–104. The standard legal language was "as they judge to be in accordance with the public interest and their own good faith." Ibid. at 94.
[68] I use Straumann's term. For *provocatio*, see also Brunt 1971, 64–67; Lintott 1999, 33–34.
[69] Straumann 2016, 30–62; cf. Lintott 1999, 89–93.
[70] Brunt 1971, 104–11; Lintott 1999, 210–13; Straumann 2016, 77–100.
[71] Brunt 1971, 77–79; Lintott 1999, 96; Straumann 2016, 139–45.
[72] Straumann 2016, 119–29.
[73] Lintott argues that the principle of collegiality should not be seen "as a form of constitutional check" *de jure* but notes many examples of magistrates having power to assist or obstruct their colleagues in practice. Lintott 1999, 99–120.
[74] Finley 1983, 130, relates the institution of the *senatus consultum ultimum* to habits of military obedience "deeply embedded in the psyche of the ordinary Roman citizen." In a society without

a young orator, Cicero exploits this ambiguity when it suits his needs. He could argue that the seemingly dubious *voluntas* of a magistrate was legitimate, as in the case of Sulla, for whom "the people of Rome passed a law that gave his own will legal force [*legem populus Romanus iusserat ut ipsius voluntas ei posset esse pro lege*]."[75] Conversely, in another case he cautions a jury not to accept the censors' judgment against his client as binding, being "their will or opinion, whichever it was [*sive voluntas sive opinio*]."[76] Similarly, he describes the augurs' assignment of Verres to the city praetorship as "more gratifying to his own will and Chelidon's than to the will of the Roman people [*magis ex sua Chelidonisque, quam ex populi Romani voluntate*]."[77] Even where Cicero admits that a magistrate's *voluntas* was used legally, he can signal that political will and public interest may not be the same.[78]

3.4.2 *Cicero's Bounded* Voluntas

As he confronts the rise of violence and the shattering of old norms, Cicero pleads more strenuously for rational limits to the exercise of political will. Reading together references from his letters and speeches, we find the primary tenets of the pluralist system he envisions.

Firstly, each of Rome's public officials has a scope of action within which he can exercise independent judgment. In his letter to Quintus on how best to govern a province, Cicero advises his brother that his signet ring, symbol of his magistracy, be "not the tool of other men's wills but the witness of your own [*minister alienae voluntatis sed testis tuae*]."[79] Like *imperium*, will carries the double sense of the governor's decision at a given moment and a durable faculty or power.[80] Depending on his place in the hierarchy, a magistrate should be expected to carry out the wills of others;[81] so, too, was he free to alter his own will as circumstances

---

prisons, moreover, "force" meant either exile or, more often, death. See Nippel 1995, 16, 25; Lintott 1999, 149–62.

[75] *Verr.* 2.3.82 (after Loeb trans.).   [76] *Clu.* 125.

[77] *Verr.* 1.104. See also ibid. 2.3.69, certain Sicilians submitted to a rigged judicial proceeding "rather than to submit to any terms dictated by [Verres'] own will [*quicquam cum isto voluntate denique*]"; cf. *Leg. Agr.* 2.64, if unprecedented powers are given to agrarian decemvirs, they will "buy whatever and from whomever suited his will [*ex sua voluntate fecisset, tum denique emeret, a quibus vellet*]."

[78] See, e.g., *Att.* 1.19.4, Pompey "set his will upon the bill going through [*ad voluntatem perferendae legis incubuerat*]"; *Mur.* 46, the prosecutor Sulpicius passed superfluous antibribery legislation by "your will and standing [*et voluntati et dignitati tuae*]."

[79] *QFr.* 1.1. See also *Prov. cons.* 18.43; *Att.* 1.17.7; *Fam.* 1.91.2.

[80] See *Verr.* 1.153; *Caecin.* 56; *Att.* 1.17.7; *Phil.* 2.13. On *imperium*, see Lintott 1999, 96.

[81] *Fam.* 1.68.5.

changed.[82] Critically, his will operates within a framework of written law, as when Cicero accuses Verres of subverting *voluntate ac sententia legis*.[83] In sum, a magistrate's will, though unforced, should align both with the statutes and customs of the past and with the *consilia* of Rome's best men.[84] As such, a wise statesman both honors and augments the *voluntas* of Rome's ancestors.[85]

Secondly, in Cicero's republic, will is not singular and self-regarding but one voice in a polyphony. Though independent in judgment, a leader must take account of where his colleagues stand, as does the consul-elect Plancius in "elicit[ing] the wills of my fellow governors and commanders in adjoining provinces [*eliciendae etiam voluntates reliquorum*]."[86] Those of more senior rank will expect and deserve deference on certain matters,[87] requiring prudent compromise; Cicero affirms to Atticus that even in the second speaking slot reserved for ex-consuls, "one's will is not too much fettered by one's sense of the consular favor [*voluntatem non nimis devinctam beneficio consulis*]."[88] In all things, one must respect the wills of one's colleagues and not harm or diminish (*laedere*) them.[89] Hard cases arise when private and public status collide. When the tribune Flaminius carries a land bill "against the wishes of the senate and in contrary to the wills of the best men [*invito senatu et omnino contra voluntatem omnium optimatium*]," his father exerts *patria potestas* and drags him off the rostrum.[90] But

---

[82] See, e.g., *Fam.* 1.20.18–21; *Rosc. Am.* 95. [83] *Verr.* 2.3.193.

[84] See *Caecin.* 56, in which the rejected line of argument flouts "the principles of law, the force of the injunction, the will of the praetor, the policy and authority of wise legislators [*ratio iuris interdictique vis et praetorum voluntas et hominum prudentium consilium et auctoritas*]"; cf. *Leg. Man.* 69; *Mur.* 70.

[85] When referring to rules established by the *maiores*, Cicero characterizes them of having "willed" (*velle*) these laws. See, e.g., *Rosc. Am.* 151 (that both juries and senate hold *consilium publicum*); *Clu.* 120 (that judges be accepted by both disputants; *Leg. agr.* 2.15 (that tribunes be guardians of liberty); 2.18 (that the *pontifex maximus* be elective); 2.26 (that certain offices be elected by two *comitia*); *Flac.* 15 (that *contiones* be subject to *comitia* process); *Dom.* 74 (that urban *plebs* have *conventicula*, "little councils").

[86] *Fam.* 3.371.3.

[87] Cf. *QFr.* 6.3, Cicero's duty was to "[meet] Pompey's wishes in fine style [*voluntati Pompei praeclare satis fecimus*]"; see also *Fam.* 1.19.2, 1.61.1.

[88] *Att.* 1.13.2. See also *QFr.* 1.32, Cicero's warning to Quintus, regarding the thorny matter of the Roman tax farmers in Asia, of the "great obstacle to this your will and endeavor [*difficultatem magnam ... huic tuae voluntati ac diligentiae*]."

[89] See *Flac.* 6, the accusation that Flaccus' administration of justice "flouted the wills of many men of influence [*tot hominum gratiosorum laesae sint voluntates*]"; cf. *Rosc. Am.* 145. Cicero's use of *laedere* recalls the definition of an "offensive argument" (*offensum*) in *De inventione* as "one which wounds the sensibilities of our audience [*quod eorum qui audiunt voluntatem laedit*]"; *Inv.* 1.92.

[90] *Inv.* 2.52. Cicero gives the example of Flaminius as a classic "hard case" of *lèse-majesté*. Later sources are clearer that *patria potestas* does not carry into the exercise of a son's public functions; see *Dig.* 1.6.9: "A *filius familias* counts as a *paterfamilias* in public affairs, e.g. for holding magistracies or

3.4 Boundaries of Political Will

these hard cases underscore the general principle that the *voluntas* of each man be proportional to his place in a common order.

Thirdly, a statesman should use the notion of will to temper conflict. In its legal sense, to act *contra voluntatem* meant to defy a person with *auctoritas* over oneself; Cicero uses this sense in reassuring his ill servant Tiro that he has not acted *contra meam voluntatem* in remaining absent.[91] In his politics, however, he often seeks to portray opposition not as defiance but rather as a temporary dissonance of will. When assigned the second slot in the speaking list of ex-consuls, Cicero counters the slight by observing that it will allow him to speak *contra voluntatem* of the first-place Piso, a former legal client he doesn't much like.[92] Positioning himself between *optimates* and triumvirs after the conference at Luca, Cicero notes bitterly that since speaking *contra Pompei voluntatem* had not won over the *boni*, he might as well tack toward Pompey again.[93] In both of these cases, the phrase *contra voluntatem* makes clear that speaking against Piso or Pompey in the senate does not mean that the men are eternally *inimici*. Cicero's opposition is not aimed at their persons but their *personae*.[94] Some of his peers apparently accepted this usage; Lepidus, on the march against Antony, pardons Silanus and Culleo out of considerations of past friendship, despite their having assisted Antony *contra meam voluntatem*.[95] The phrase thus gives a stable frame to an otherwise provocative act, depersonalizing the conflict and favoring a reconciliation.[96]

3.4.3 Outer Limits: Violence and Temeritas

As we have seen, the earliest surviving use of *voluntas* is the ablative *voluntate* to signify willing action.[97] In Cicero's corpus, the word underpins one of his closest-held convictions: that brute force should yield to free choice in public affairs. In *De inventione*, he proposes that justice first arose in human society when, by the power of oratory, men abandoned

---

guardianships"; *Dig.* 36.1.14: "[T]he right of parental control does not apply to the duties of public office [*quod ad ius publicum attinet non sequitur ius potestatis*]." Cf. Crook 1967, 109; Lintott 1999, 35–36; Arena 2012, 23–25.

[91] *Fam.* 2.185.1. In a less formal sense, it can signify any act of speech contravening someone of greater power. See, e.g., *Rosc. Am.* 18, 48, 60; *Verr.* 2.3.39, 2.3.135; *Fam.* 1.65.1; *Mur.* 42.

[92] *Att.* 1.13.2. [93] Ibid. 1.80.2.

[94] The idea of *persona civitatis* ("role of state") is one Cicero later develops in *De officiis*; see *Off.* 1.124, discussed in Chapter 8.

[95] *Fam.* 3.396.2.

[96] For other occurrences of *contra voluntatem* to reduce political conflict, see, e.g., *Att.* 1.42.2, 4.310.2; *Sull.* 32. The usage had resonance in Cicero's personal life as well; see *Att.* 1.17.7.

[97] See discussion in Chapter 1.

rule by the strongest and learned "to obey others willingly [*aliis parere sua voluntate*]."⁹⁸ Similarly, in Book 3 of *De republica*, Laelius argues that the Republic will decline "if the habit of lawlessness begins to spread and changes our rule from one of justice to one of force [*ad vim a iure traduxerit*], so that those who up to the present have obeyed us willingly are held faithful by fear alone [*qui adhuc voluntate nobis oboediunt, terrore teneantur*]."⁹⁹ Both at the Republic's beginning and at its end, the primacy of lawful will over brute force is Cicero's criterion of civilization.

Free choice is, Cicero insists, the very soul of Roman law. In his defense of Caecina, Cicero asserts that no citizen can be compelled to renounce his citizenship: Those Romans who downgrade their status by joining colonies do so "either of their own will or to avoid a penalty imposed by law [*aut sua voluntate aut legis multa profecti sunt*]: had they been willing to undergo the penalty, they could have remained within the citizen body."¹⁰⁰ He employs a similar argument to ensnare Verres' lawyers, who had accused his Sicilian witnesses of bias. Cicero argues that certain statues erected in Verres' honor were either *sua voluntate statuisse* ("set up of their own will"), refuting the alleged bias, or were extorted illegally by Verres himself.¹⁰¹ "Will anyone doubt," Cicero concludes, "that a man who is bound to be your deadly enemy, who has sustained the heaviest wrongs at your hands, paid the money supposed to be for your statue because he was ordered and forced [*vi atque imperio adductus*], and not because he was obligated or willed it [*non officio ac voluntate*]?"¹⁰² The contrast of *vis* and *voluntas* and the link between the farmers' will and their duty frame the justice of Cicero's claim.¹⁰³ At the other end of the moral spectrum, Cicero decries the evil *voluntas* of Catiline's cronies and links Clodius' *voluntas* to his *impudentia, audacia*, and *cupiditas*.¹⁰⁴ Rather than resolve the bivalence in

---

⁹⁸ *Inv.* 1.3.
⁹⁹ *Rep.* 3.41. Cf. ibid. 1.11, a wise man does not generally descend *sua voluntate* into statecraft but does not decline the duty when circumstances require.
¹⁰⁰ *Caecin.* 98. The more natural English expression is "of their own free will." I take up the relation of *libertas* and *voluntas* in Chapters 4 and 6. On lack of coercion as a principle of Roman law, cf. *Balb.* 27: The legal principle governing citizenship "depends not merely upon the laws of the State but also upon the will of individuals [*non solum in legibus publicis positum, sed etiam in privatorum voluntate*]."
¹⁰¹ *Verr.* 2.2.151.   ¹⁰² Ibid. 2.2.153.
¹⁰³ In a telling contrast, years later Cicero relates to Quintus that the communes of Asia had proposed to dedicate temples to him "by their highest will [*summa sua voluntate*] in recognition of their great indebtedness to me and the signal benefits of your government"; *QFr.* 1.26 (60 or 59 BCE). The phrase is infelicitous in English but captures that the dedication was not only "willing" (i.e. uncoerced), but that the communes themselves initiated it. Cicero claims to have graciously declined the offer.
¹⁰⁴ *Dom.* 166.

his notion of will, Cicero heightens it for rhetorical effect. This nebulous space between lawful and self-serving will is the gap through which Caesar will march his legions.

The utmost expression of will was *temeritas*. The word's etymology is complex. It shares the same root as *tenebra*, a shadow, yet Cicero also links it to the Greek *propeteia*, "running beyond the mark" in a moral sense.[105] In nonphilosophical use, the word covers a wide spectrum from simple thoughtlessness to criminal ambition.[106] Its political purpose, however, is to mark the responsibility of actors whose volition carries them beyond ancestral norms. Cicero locates *temeritas* in the arrogance of his *popularis* enemies;[107] in his speech for Plancius, he accuses them of carrying the Roman people along with them in their recklessness, "by impulse and temerity [*impetu . . . et quadam etiam temeritate*]."[108] *Temeritas*, Cicero wants to say, is will unbridled by reason.[109] But whereas Cicero's typical adversaries can be painted as reckless monsters, the case of Caesar is not so simple. His cognitive gifts are beyond question; his excesses cannot be compared to the *temeritas* of a grasping child, as Cicero does with Piso.[110] Cicero insists that Caesar's unbounded will is *temeritas*, but rather than emphasizing its lack of self-control, he focuses instead on the "error of opinion" (*opinionis error*) that led such a brilliant man to a misguided use of his will.[111] Unsurprisingly, Caesar rejects this label – *nihil temere agendum*, he writes in *Bellum Gallicum*[112] – and he may also have applied Greek ideas to suit his needs. Lévy observes: "Caesar, perhaps because he had learned from Epicureanism that action is determined by calculation, asks his soldiers for an unwavering will, which is something else entirely from *temeritas*."[113] Cicero calls for a rationally bounded will; Caesar, only an unfailing one.

3.5 Caesar's *Voluntas*

Caesar had several assets in his drive to refashion the rule of law around himself. There was the immediate pretext of Pompey's overreach and

---

[105] *Temere, temeritas*. Ernout and Meillet 1960, 683; Hellegouarc'h 1963, 247, 258. Cicero uses *temeritas* over 200 times in his corpus. See generally Lévy 2018.
[106] See, e.g., *Inv.* 1.25, 2.10; *Prov. cons.* 11; *Att.* 9.10.2, 11.8.1. Cf. Lévy 2018, 6. [107] *Rep.* 1.52.
[108] *Planc.* 9. On *temeritas multitudinis*, see *Sest.* 103; *Mil.* 11; *Flac.* 19.
[109] Cf. *Marcell.* 7; *Tusc.* 2.47. [110] *Pis.* 39.
[111] *Off.* 1.26: "We saw this proved but now in the effrontery of Gaius Caesar, who, to gain that princely power which by a depraved imagination he had conceived in his fancy, trod underfoot all laws of gods and men [*Declaravit id modo temeritatis C. Caesaris, qui omnia iura divina et humana pervertit propter eum, quem sibi ipse opinionis errore finxerat, principatum*]."
[112] Caes. *BGall.* 5.28.3. [113] Lévy 2018, 4.

the senate's dubious treatment of his allies.[114] More importantly, he could call on the venerable principle of self-help: Victims of a crime, whether private or public, bore the primary responsibility to redress it. Where the danger was particularly grave and urgent, Roman tradition allowed for the emergency use of force, as Cicero himself had sanctioned against Catiline and his allies. Curiously, in that very case Caesar may have argued to constrain the will of Rome's consul by citing a law that extended *provocatio* to the military sphere – a speech in which, if Sallust is correct, Caesar warned about the precedent of removing limits to individual power![115] Caesar famously exploits the institution of the dictatorship – to which he had been elected by a vote of the assembly[116] – and the precedent of Sulla, whose *voluntas* Cicero admits had been given the force of *lex*.[117] Consequently, Caesar did not need to invent a new vocabulary to justify his regime – only stretch the one that already existed.[118]

If Cicero's *voluntas* is a force governed by ethical restraint, the dictator's will obeys only itself. Merely describing this new order could be a struggle. Cicero writes to a friend that Caesar's consolidation of power has made all things uncertain, "when the path of legality has been forsaken, and that there is no guaranteeing the future of what depends on someone else's will, not to say his whims [*quod positum est in alterius voluntate ne dicam libidine*]."[119] Each of the principles Cicero had defended – that individual will be constrained, balanced, and uncoerced – Caesar rejects. Freedom of speech is gone; Cicero must "say nothing offensive to his will or those of people he likes."[120] Caesar's intentions are now the only ones worth mapping: Cicero finds himself reassuring the senate that no one could doubt "what is Caesar's will with regard to war [*quae Caesaris de bello voluntas fuerit*],"[121] and he is at pains to excuse any wartime actions "less according to Caesar's will" (*minus ex Caesaris voluntate*) as "extremely unwilling" (*invitissimum*) and "someone else's idea" (*aliorum consilio*).[122] A man's orientation to Caesar's will is now the sole indicator of his standing, as when Cicero pleads to Caesar that Ligarius had never been

---

[114] See Rawson 1975, 184–90.   [115] Sall. *Cat.* 51.21–36; cf. Straumann 2016, 130–32.
[116] Caes. *BCiv.* 2.21.5; Dio Cass. 41.36.1. On the evolution of the dictatorship, see Straumann 2016, 74–88.
[117] *Verr.* 2.3.82.   [118] See Yavetz 1969, 41–57.   [119] *Fam.* 2.190.3.
[120] Ibid. Atkins 2018a, 768–70, argues that the blow to Cicero's freedom is not primarily due to his submission to Caesar's arbitrary will, but rather that Caesar has foreclosed the political space needed by Cicero and his elite colleagues to enhance their own *dignitas* through political action.
[121] *Marcell.* 15.   [122] *Fam.* 3.282.7. Cf. *Att.* 3.176.1, 3.200.1.

"distant from your will [*alienae a te voluntatis*],"[123] or when Caecina worries that Caesar has judged some of his writing to be *contra suam voluntatem*.[124] To act *contra voluntatem Caesaris* was no longer to create a temporary opposition in a stable order, but rather to defy the *voluntas patris* of Rome itself.

After Caesar's death, Cicero was briefly optimistic that Rome's traditional equilibrium could be restored. He thanks Oppius for his advice that Cicero join Pompey's camp, in which "you thought more of my duty than of [Caesar's] will [*antiquius tibi officium meum quam illius voluntas fuit*]."[125] The restoration of Rome's liberty is, in Cicero's retelling, a triumph of many wills over one: "And so, all decent men killed Caesar so far as it was in them to do so: some lacked design, some courage, some opportunity; none lacked the will [*aliis consilium, aliis animus, aliis occasio defuit; voluntas nemini*]."[126]

Yet history shows that Caesar accelerates a semantic process in which an *imperator*'s will would not only be unbound by constitutional restraint, but would become the very source of law. As the dictator's heirs take control of the "restored" republic, they cannily adjust the language of authority. The jurist Modestinus writes, regarding the crime of electoral bribery (*ambitus*) against which Cicero had so often inveighed: "[T]his law is obsolete in Rome today, because the creation of magistrates belongs to the care of the emperor, not the favor of the people [*quia ad curam principis magistratuum creatio pertinet, non ad populi favorem*]."[127] The overturning of republican tradition is accomplished not by direct attack but by the introduction of new phrases – "the care (*cura*) of the emperor" – suggesting a benevolent *paterfamilias*, not a domineering *tyrannus*. In civil disputes, a citizen's *voluntas* remains a key criterion of justice,[128] but in high public matters, as Ulpian writes, "that which has been decided by the emperor has the force of law [*quod principi placuit, legis habet vigorem*]."[129] And yet, an idea of constraint lingers in the Roman legal psyche. To the above dictum, the jurist adds this explanation: "because the emperor himself is given his *imperium* and power by a law of the people [*utpote*

---

[123] *Lig.* 6; see discussion in the Introduction.
[124] *Fam.* 2.237.2. See also ibid. 3.319.1, Cicero praises a legate for carrying out his orders "according to the will of Caesar [*ex voluntate Caesaris*]."
[125] *Fam.* 3.335.1.   [126] *Phil.* 2.29.   [127] *Dig.* 48.14.1.
[128] See, e.g., *Dig.* 1.6.8pr., 1.7.5, 1.7.18. Cf. *Dig.* 1.1.10pr (Ulpian): "Justice is the constant and perpetual will to render to each what is his [*Iustitia est constans et perpetua voluntas ius suum cuique tribuendi*]."
[129] *Dig.* 1.4.1.

cum lege regia, quae de imperio eius lata est, populus ei et in eum omne suum imperium et potestatem conferat]."¹³⁰ Centuries after Cicero, the unboundedness of imperial will continued to complicate Rome's greatest idea: its rule of law.

---

¹³⁰ Ibid. See also *Dig.* 1.3.32: "For given that statutes themselves are binding upon us for no other reason than that they have been accepted by the judgment of the populace, certainly it is fitting that what the populace has approved without any writing shall be binding upon everyone. What does it matter whether the people declares its will by voting or by the very substance of its actions [*nam quid interest suffragio populus voluntatem suam declaret an rebus ipsis et factis*]?" (trans. Watson).

CHAPTER 4

An Economy of Goodwill

The Caecilii Metelli had become a problem. At the denouement of Catiline's conspiracy in late 63 BCE, the loyal and lordly Q. Metellus Celer takes an army in pursuit of the rebels. Just after this, Celer's brother Nepos unleashes a tirade against Cicero, condemning him at *contiones* and preventing the consul from giving his valedictory address.[1] In the senate, Cicero awkwardly laments the Metelli's opposition – if only because he had so nearly made Celer his friend. The other senators laugh.[2]

In the wake of this embarrassment, Celer sends a letter complaining of the insult to his family and accusing the ex-consul of violating their "mutual sentiments" (*pro mutuo inter nos animo*). Cicero's reply is five times the length of Celer's rebuke. He praises the nobleman's fraternal feeling, justifies his own actions as self-defense, and points out that he had helped Celer secure his province for the coming year. Why had Cicero passed up a governorship and delivered it to Celer? "As for your reference to 'our mutual sentiments,' I do not know how you define reciprocity in friendship [*amicitia mutuum*]. I conceive it to lie in goodwill equally received and returned [*voluntas accipitur et redditur*]."[3] At this delicate moment, Cicero wants to leverage an asset that could counterbalance Celer's family pride. That asset is their *voluntas mutua*.[4]

What does Cicero mean by the phrase? Is "mutual goodwill" the same as friendship? In *De inventione*, the young scholar had defined *amicitia* as "a will toward someone to do good things simply for the benefit of this person whom one loves, with a requital of goodwill on their part [*voluntas erga aliquem rerum bonarum illius ipsius causa quem diligit cum eius pari voluntate*]."[5] In his letter to Celer, Cicero is evidently trying to

---

[1] Kept only to a recitation of the traditional oath, Cicero famously responded with an improvised oath that by his efforts, and his efforts alone, Rome and the Republic had been saved; see Rawson 1975, 86.
[2] *Fam.* 1.2.1–2.   [3] Ibid. 1.2.3.   [4] Ibid. 1.2.1.   [5] Ibid. 2.166.

repair a breach between them. Nevertheless, this "exchange" of *voluntas* does not concern, even superficially, a mutual affection or desire for the other's company.[6] Is Cicero merely being insincere, or is another set of rules at play?

To bring *voluntas mutua* into relief, we might contrast it with Aristotle's *eunoia*, a sentiment also rendered as "goodwill" in English.[7] Books 8 and 9 of the *Nicomachean Ethics* give *eunoia* a starring role in the story of friendship. Aristotle defines goodwill as *boulēsis t'agathou* – rational desire for the good of another and makes it the first step in the cultivation of friendly love (*philia*) (8.2.4, 1156a2).[8] *Eunoia* can "spring up suddenly" (9.5.2, 1166b35–36), without the knowledge of the other party (8.2.3–4, 1155b35–1156a1), but it is insufficient in itself to produce friendly acts (9.5.3, 1167a13–14). To flower into *philia*, both parties must be aware of the other's *eunoia* (8.2.4, 1156a3–4), then give form to their goodwill through acts of service, returning each favor according to the moral intent (*prohairesis*) of the giver (8.13.11, 1163a21–24). Finally, both time and intimacy are each indispensable to true friendship: One cannot have *philia* with a large number (8.3.8, 1156b25–30), just as "a hundred thousand is a city no longer" (9.10.3, 1170b32–33). Aristotle's political analogy is by design, for the *philiai* of citizens produce acts of moral goodness that, summed together, bring the city to its fulfillment (9.8.7, 1169a8–12).

But should we choose our friends for the good they bring us? For Aristotle, utility poses a difficult problem for friendship. While true friends may indeed be useful to one another (8.4.1, 1157a2–3) – indeed, they only actualize their *philia* in mutual service – these acts of *prohairesis* must always be made of one's own accord (*hekōn*) and for the sake of the friend himself, not in expectation of repayment (8.13.9, 1163a21–24; 9.5.3, 1167a13–22). A friendship based on self-interest (*chrēsimon*) is both inferior from a moral standpoint and unstable in practice (9.5.3, 1167a13–18); since it depends on our interests in the present moment, these friendships vanish when those interests change (8.3.1–3, 1156a19–29). Nevertheless, Aristotle adds

---

[6] Cf. Konstan 1997, 126.

[7] Griffin 2007, 85, 95–97, has argued, from the evidence of *De amicitia* and his late letters, that Cicero "subscribes to the Peripatetic view of friendship, first developed by Aristotle in *Eudemian Ethics* 7 and in Books 8 and 9 of the *Nicomachean Ethics*." On the influence of Aristotle's theory of friendship on Cicero, cf. Brunt 1988, 354; Konstan 1997, 130–31. On the question of his familiarity with the Aristotelian corpus, see *Fin.* 5.12–14, and see generally Fortenbaugh and Steinmetz 1989.

[8] *Philia* is broader than the English "friendship" and includes kindly feelings toward parents, family, and lovers, as well as toward friends. Cf. Arist. *Eth. Nic.*, Loeb edition (ed. Rackham), p. 450 ff.

knowingly, we are natural hypocrites: "[W]hile it is noble to freely give, we wish what is noble but choose what is profitable" (8.13.8, 1162b34–36).[9]

This chapter explores Cicero's notion of mutual goodwill and his attempt to reconcile ideals of friendship with the realities of an expanding empire. Accounts of friendship in surviving Hellenistic texts center upon intimacy, selflessness, and constant company.[10] By contrast, a Roman statesman of the late Republic relied upon a diffuse network of political allies – but were these his friends? If so, what level of intimacy or sincerity did these friendships require?[11] And what if, politics being politics, one needed the *amicitia* of an odious but highly useful person?[12] Complicating the matter further, the philosophical tradition that most clearly embraced the role of utility is friendship – the Epicureans – was the one Cicero most fiercely opposed.

Historians have long debated the role of power politics in *amicitia*. L. R. Taylor calls it simply "the good old word for party relationships"; Syme concurs, declaring *amicitia* "a weapon of politics, not a sentiment based on congeniality."[13] "[I]t is implausible to suppose," counters Brunt, "that the Romans, whose word for friendship (as Cicero points out) derives from *amo*, had no native acquaintance with genuine affection of a non-sexual kind." In an extensive review of texts from the late Republic, Brunt concludes that "the range of *amicitia* is vast":

> From the constant intimacy and goodwill of virtuous or at least of likeminded men to the courtesy that etiquette normally enjoined on gentlemen, it covers every degree of genuinely or overtly amicable relation. Within this spectrum purely political connections have their place, but one whose all-importance must not be assumed.[14]

With respect to Cicero in particular, Brunt adds that what is stressed "is often not so much the services actually rendered as the constant and

---

[9] On the contrast between the accounts of utility in friendship offered in the *Nicomachean Ethics* and *Eudemian Ethics* and the dubious authorship of the latter work, see Schofield 1999, 82–99.
[10] Here, the major exception was the school of Epicurus, who placed the origin of friendship in pleasure gained to oneself and argued not only that it should be restricted to a small, intimate number, but also that friendship and politics should never mix. On the compatibility of Stoic and Aristotelian accounts of friendship in Cicero and his rejection of the Epicurean view, see Griffin 2007, 95–96, 106–107.
[11] On the account of "political friendships" in the *Eudemian Ethics*, see Schofield 1999, 86–94. While more sympathetic (or realistic) about the transactional nature of friendship in the political context, the emphasis that the text places on the strictly egalitarian and temporary nature of these friendships may have limited its applicability to Cicero's circumstances, even in the event that he read it.
[12] In perhaps the most flagrant example, Cicero privately complains of Antony's incompetence and mischief while assuring him of his constant love; *Att.* 4.367.6., 4.367B.1 (April 44 BCE).
[13] Taylor 1949, 7; Syme 1939, 157.   [14] Brunt 1988, 381.

known will or readiness to render them."[15] This insight – that the *verified disposition* to perform a service has value independent of or even superior to the service itself – is the starting point for understanding what Cicero means by *voluntas mutua*.

In a footnote to the passage above, Brunt defines *voluntas* as "the will to realize one's opinions," political or otherwise.[16] *Pace* Brunt, the evidence of Cicero's correspondence indicates a much broader notion at play. The *voluntas mutua* he invokes to Celer does not connote a need to realize an opinion. As we will see, goodwill in Cicero is a finely graded social currency to be measured, verified, and maintained. *Voluntas* is only one term in a rich social lexicon that included *fides, gratia, officium, beneficium*, and many other notions that Cicero mastered and deployed.[17] The singularity of *voluntas mutua* is its interiority – its power to stabilize relationships through the exchange of assurances rather than gifts. Just as he finds new ways to map political alliances, Cicero finds new shades of language to encompass both decorous appearance and hidden intent. Real money, power, and lives were at stake in these exchanges of gentlemanly favor. As with the *voluntas* of magistrates, one's success often depended on anticipating the second- and third-order effects of rivalries and reconciliations. The republican economy of goodwill that Cicero reveals to us is ubiquitous, highly valuable, and often invisible.

An indigenous Roman antecedent may be found in the *mutuom argentum* or "friendly loans" that animate the comedies of Plautus.[18] In the frank negotiations of his star-crossed lovers, we find both kinships and tensions with Cicero's economy of goodwill. Like *mutuom argentum*, the practice of *voluntas* could often resemble the haggling of a marketplace. Its exchanges bound together a broad array of participants under a common set of rules, requiring neither intimate feeling nor constant presence. And where Aristotle's *eunoia* is spontaneous and unidirectional, *voluntas mutua* operates as a "joint account" of goodwill that statesmen create in one another – accounts whose balance is monitored, augmented, and drawn

---

[15] Ibid. Konstan 1997, 128, makes the related point that "services may be interpreted as a sign of good will or amicableness," such that "[m]utual support is the point at which the vocabularies of friendship and exchange of benefits intersect." He concludes that Cicero "moves naturally between the two issues."

[16] In the same note, he criticizes Hellegouarc'h's definition of *voluntas*, "*la notion d'opinion publique*," as "at once too narrow and too weak." Brunt 1988, 356 n.25.

[17] *Fam.* 1.109.2. See Hellegouarc'h 1963, 149–50, 152–69, 181–85; Brunt 1988, 355–59; Konstan 1997, 122–24, 127.

[18] See, e.g., Plaut. *Trin.* 3.3, 4.3; *Curc.* 1.1; *Pseud.* 1.1, 1.3; *Stich.* 1.3; *Asin.* 1.3, 2.1; *Heaut. Tim.* 3.3; and the prologues to *Poen.* (vols. 79–82) and *Men.* (vols. 54–55).

down in *officia* as needed. This is a discourse tailor-made for Rome's unusual constitution, a distributed constellation of power in which high office was temporary and networks were built to last.[19] *Pace* Taylor, these networks did not offer the clarity and stability that membership in a political party does today. Given the highly fluid alliances of the late Republic, argues Brunt, "the usual character of friendship in the political class did not favour the formation of [durable and cohesive] factions."[20] Whatever the causes, the challenges of managing a vast political network are beyond dispute. Under Cicero's pen, goodwill becomes a currency to measure these relationships and to harness them to a common rulebook.[21]

Whatever its similarities to the marketplace,[22] *voluntas mutua* is not merely the tallying of credit and debt. First, unlike hard currency, "spending" *voluntas* can increase its supply. As Cicero explains in *Pro Plancio*, "in a moral debt, when I pay I keep, and when I keep, I pay by the very act of keeping" (68).[23] Friendly favors reinforce an account of *voluntas* instead of spending it down. Second, this currency creates an alternative channel of political support when material support is temporarily unfeasible. Requesting a favor to the consul Paullus from his post in Cilicia, Cicero affirms that "I think it must be fated somehow that you are always given opportunity to do me honor, whereas I find nothing but the goodwill with which to requite you [*mihi ad remunerandum nihil suppetat praeter voluntatem*]."[24] In the rapid turnabouts of politics and the distances of empire, these virtual exchanges of support play an increasingly visible role. Finally, unlike commercial transactions, but similar to Aristotle's *philia*, exchanges of *voluntas* are linked, at least rhetorically, to the public interest. Whatever one's true motivations, respecting the codes of friendship testifies to

---

[19] Vogel 2020 reviews several interesting studies applying social network analysis to the Roman Republic, with a focus on Quintus Cicero's governorship in Asia. See also Rosillo-López 2020.
[20] Brunt 1988, 378.
[21] Unsurprisingly, statesmen of Cicero's era used an array of terms to describe this common system. What Cicero gave as *voluntas mutua*, Metellus Celer might call *mutuo inter nos animo*, Marcellus *benevolentia* (*Fam.* 2.233.1), Plancius *bona voluntas* (*Fam.* 3.371.2), and Lepidus *studia offici mutuo inter nos* (*Fam.* 3.400.1). For analysis of this goodwill and its relation to *fides*, *gratia*, and *beneficia*, see Hellegouarc'h 1963, 23–51, 80–90, 149–50, 181–85. Though this chapter focuses on *voluntas mutua*, each of these terms figures in the rich Roman lexicon of friendship.
[22] Roman jurisprudence characterized a loan as "more an affair of goodwill and duty than necessity or convenience [*voluntatis et officii magis quam necessitatis est commodare*]"; *Dig.* 13.6.17.3. See Crook 1967, 209.
[23] Cf. the inverse statement in the prologues to Plaut. *Men.* (vols. 54–55): "For unless a person gives the money, he will be mistaken; except that he who does give it will be very much more mistaken [*argentum nisi qui dederit, nugas egerit / verum qui dederit, magis maiores nugas egerit*]" (trans. Riley).
[24] Cf. *Att.* 2.145.1, in the absence of volunteers, it is not goodwill they lack but hope (*deficit enim non voluntas sed spes*).

voluntas erga rem publicam, goodwill toward the Republic as a whole. Personal favor transacts in an argot of civic duty.[25]

While we lack the evidence for a more comprehensive study, the originality of Cicero's *voluntas mutua* may lie in its interiority. The defining element of goodwill was not the active favor but the durable *possibility* of favor; as Brunt observes, a particularity of Roman goodwill was its value as a latent disposition, convertible to active support.

Though the rules of the goodwill economy are revealed principally in his letters, throughout his career we find Cicero testing them by the rigors of Greek philosophy – an endeavor that, while perhaps not unique, surely distinguished him from the majority of his peers. Cicero's philosophy of friendship describes an arc of three phases. Early texts show a civic-minded pragmatism: In political settings, Cicero writes in *De inventione*, friendship is and should be beneficial. As he climbs the *cursus honorum*, he draws on Stoicism to justify *voluntas mutua* in universalist terms: These reciprocities are natural, just, and universal. Mutual obligation binds Roman society together, and the thorny matter of *utilitas* goes unaddressed. When he finally confronts the question in *De amicitia*, he rejects the Epicurean position as un-Roman: True friendship derives not from self-interest but virtue, any accounting of favors is sordid, and the "entire profit" of the relationship is "in the love itself."[26] But Cicero returns to civic pragmatism in his final work, the *De officiis*. His theory of *decorum*, adapted from the Stoic Panaetius, joins utility to sincerity and propriety in a proper accounting of mutual duty. These carefully ordered rules do justice to hard experience while agreeing finally with Aristotle that without integrity even the most apparently useful friendships will fail.

4.1 The Rules of *Voluntas Mutua*

In what follows, I draw on Cicero's correspondence and speeches to propose a working model of the goodwill economy. I trace the life cycle of an "account" in *voluntas mutua*: how it was monitored, drawn upon, and liquidated. I then examine how these rules brought together different strata of Roman society into a single system of reciprocal exchange. As with many economies, Cicero's system looked healthiest just before its crash, and his late letters show how Caesar's ascent upends the venerable system of goodwill. *De amicitia* and *De officiis* become Cicero's elegy to the

---

[25] Cf. Brunt 1988, 351; Konstan 1997, 126–27.   [26] *Amic.* 31.

4.1.1 (Re)opening an Account

Where does mutual goodwill begin? As with certain songbirds, *voluntas mutua* is rarely sighted at birth. An important reference comes in a letter to Matius, whom Cicero had admired as a young man: "[Y]our subsequent departure for a long period, together with my pursuit of a political career and the difference between our modes of life, debarred us from mingling our wills by constant intercourse [*voluntates nostras consuetudine conglutinari*]."[27] As Miriam Griffin observes, this account bears close resemblance to Aristotle's *philia*: Mutual admiration is necessary but insufficient for friendship; only regular companionship gives the intimacy necessary for real goodwill to emerge.[28]

In the political context, however, such requirements rarely obtain. Cicero often speaks of regaining or reinforcing *voluntas* among politicians but almost never about "mingling our wills by constant intercourse" or other conditions necessary to become friends in the first place.[29] In a typical example, Cicero reassures Lentulus of his success in convincing the senate of Lentulus' *voluntas* toward their *ordo* such that "we regained the senate's goodwill [*reconciliata nobis voluntas esse senatus*]."[30] On the surface, this choice of words suggests a polite fiction: Each man has always been worthy of the other's regard, and any appearance to the contrary was misunderstood. But Cicero's emphasis on the "restoration" rather than creation of *voluntas* gives an important first indication of its departure from Aristotle's scheme of *eunoia* and *philia*. Whereas *eunoia* can "suddenly spring up" and then be transformed into *philia*, Cicero's *voluntas mutua*, at least rhetorically, has always been there.

Cicero's word *conglutinare* ("to mingle" or "to glue together") marks a second key difference from Aristotle's scheme. For Aristotle, one-sided *eunoia* is actualized into reciprocal *philia*; not so for Cicero. For the

---

[27] *Fam.* 3.348.2.   [28] Griffin 2007, 95.
[29] Griffin 2007, 109, notes that the ideals of friendship expressed to Matius and similarly witty correspondents coincide with periods "when there was less chance of political and forensic activity than usual."
[30] *Fam.* 1.13.1. Cato credits Cicero's record as an honest governor for winning back Rome's Asian allies (*sociorum revocatam ad studium imperi nostri voluntatem*); *Fam.* 1.111.1. L. Plancus (not to be confused with the defendant in *Pro Plancio*) follows this usage in urging Lepidus "to be reconciled with me and collaborate in aiding the commonwealth [*reconciliata voluntatem nostra communi consilio rei publicae succurreret*]"; *Fam.* 3.390.1.

Roman, "goodwill" is dual from the start. He claims that King Deiotarus is "bound to me by goodwill of hospitality" (*hospitium voluntas utriuque coniunxit*);[31] he laments having to argue in opposition to Laterensis, with whom he shares "a sympathetic union of thought and goodwill [*consensus et societas consiliorum et voluntatum*]";[32] and he entreats L. Plancus on Atticus' behalf, "linked as I have always been to you by goodwill and hereditary friendship [*quem voluntate et quem paterna necessitudine coniunctum*]."[33] Roman goodwill is not an individual sentiment but a joint account, the durable disposition both parties can rely upon.

This notion of a joint account, in turn, suggests an entirely new conceptual relationship from the one Aristotle had given between goodwill, mutual service, and friendship. For Aristotle, *eunoia* is both one-sided and temporary; regular companionship and acts of mutual service (*prohairesis*) actualize this goodwill and transform it into *philia* (8.13.11, 1163a21–24). He emphasizes, moreover, that this level of intimacy cannot be achieved with a large number of people (8.3.8, 1156b25–30). In Rome's diffuse and dynamic politics, Cicero faces a problem that Aristotle's theory cannot solve: How is one to ensure the support of a great number of allies without (1) sharing direct contact with them and (2) constantly performing expensive favors? His answer is an imaginary currency holding value in the form of latent support and confirmable at a distance: *voluntas mutua*.

Rather than favors turning goodwill into friendship, then, favors for Cicero are *indiciae* that a joint account of *voluntas* is intact. These signs could be in the form of electoral support, as when Verres "gave so clear a token of goodwill" (*dedit enim praerogativam suae voluntatis*) by bribing voters on Metellus' behalf.[34] Goodwill could be manifested in the acclamation of a crowd,[35] a kind word in a letter,[36] or even a facial expression – Lepidus gives a *signum* of his goodwill by "a groan and a sad countenance" when Antony offers Caesar a crown.[37] In each case, we see how Cicero reapplies key senses from his early studies: As in *controversia ex scripto et sententia*, *voluntas* is a force to be interpreted and conserved; like the goodwill of an audience, it is a durable disposition to be inclined in one's

---

[31] *Deiot.* 39.   [32] *Planc.* 5.
[33] *Att.* 4.407B. See also ibid. 4.407A.1, to Plancus, "powerfully reinforced by our personal feelings for each other, mutual and equal on both sides [*magnam attulit accessionem tua voluntas erga me meaque erga te par atque mutua*]"; *Pis.* 41, "men closely identified with ourselves in purpose and position [*cum publicanos nobiscum et voluntate et dignitate coniunctos*]"; ibid. 80, Lentulus joined his will with Caesar's (*adiunxit huius voluntatis*) to help Cicero.
[34] *Verr.* 1.26.   [35] *Leg. agr.* 2.24.   [36] *Fam.* 1.3.2.   [37] *Phil.* 5.38.

4.1 *The Rules of* Voluntas Mutua

favor.³⁸ As such, mutual service does not replace goodwill as in Aristotle but, rather, evinces and proves it.

This latent and durable quality of goodwill has important political benefits for Cicero and his fellow statesmen. First, an account in *voluntas* creates the possibility of joint action beyond what a statesman could accomplish alone. Cicero extols the patriotism of 2nd-century BCE consul M. Lepidus, who on the day of his election as censor approached a new colleague on the Campus Martius, formerly his enemy, and reconciled with him "so that they might uphold their common responsibilities as censors with a common purpose and goodwill [*ut commune officium censurae communi animo ac voluntate defenderent*]."³⁹ This joint *voluntas* allows each party, in turn, to share credit for the other's accomplishments. Writing to Furnius, who is in the field against Antony's army, Cicero advises him to return for the praetorian elections only "provided that such haste in the furtherance of your career does not in any degree detract from the reputation we have won."⁴⁰ Additionally, sharing *voluntas* signifies that an alliance can withstand changing circumstances and differences of judgment, even serious ones. When Cicero criticizes Brutus for his fecklessness following the Ides, his reproach of the Liberator's *consilium* is situated within the solidarity of their mutual goodwill.⁴¹

Finally, affirming one's *voluntas* in writing opens an alternative channel of support at moments when more concrete favors are impossible or unwise. Thanking Atticus for the gift of a book that had restored him to health, Cicero adds, "I am prepared to make payment of goodwill in full measure [*voluntatem tibi profecto emetiar*], but the debt itself [*rem ipsam*] I do not now seem able to pay ..."⁴² Conversely, when Caesar as Triumvir apparently proposes to include Cicero in his projects, Cicero tells Quintus, "I am not thirsty for honors nor do I hanker after glory. I look forward to

---

[38] See also *Inv.* 1.24; *De or.* 2.32, 2.129, 2.200.

[39] *Prov. cons.* 21. Cf. *Fam.* 3.390.1, where Plancus describes urging Lepidus "to be reconciled with me and collaborate in aiding the commonwealth [*reconciliata voluntatem nostra communi consilio rei publicae succurreret*]."

[40] *Fam.* 3.403.2. Shackleton Bailey adds in an editor's note: "As often, Cicero politely affects to consider his correspondent's affairs as his own." Cicero's distaste for military affairs makes it equally likely that the sentiment is one of borrowed glory in the fight against Antony rather than mere politesse.

[41] *Ad Brut.* 5.1: "My goodwill has always been identical with yours, my dear Brutus; my policy in certain matters ... has perhaps been a little more forceful [*Voluntas mea, Brute, de summa re publica semper eadem fuit quae tua, ratio quibusdam in rebus ... paulo fortasse vehementior*]." Brutus apparently shared Cicero's view that these discrepant *consilia* did not damage the two men's underlying *voluntas*; see ibid. 26.6.

[42] *Brut.* 16. Cf. *Fam.* 1.109.1; *Att.* 2.145.1.

his lasting goodwill more than to the outcome of his promises [*magisque eius voluntatis perpetuitatem quam promissorum exitum exspecto*]."[43] It appears that Caesar's latent goodwill is a more valuable asset for Cicero than any specific honors, and at a delicate political moment gives him a means to create distance between Caesar's radical agenda and his own dignity. Aristotle's *eunoia* is not an asset to be held in reserve; Cicero's *voluntas* clearly and crucially is.

Nevertheless, Cicero emphasizes that the rules of goodwill are not simply those of commerce. He inserts a short lecture on the economics of *voluntas* into his defense oration for Gn. Plancius:

> He who discharges a debt in money, ceases forthwith to possess that which he has paid; while he who remains a debtor keeps what does not belong to him. But in a moral debt, when I pay I keep, and when I keep, I pay by the very act of keeping. If I discharge this debt to Plancius, I shall not thereby cease to be his debtor, and *I should be repaying my debt to him none the less by my goodwill*, if the present unfortunate situation had not occurred [*Neque ego nunc Plancio desinam debere, si hoc solvero: nec minus ei redderem voluntate ipsa, si hoc molestiae non accidisset*].[44]

The repayment of *voluntas* is thus not a transaction to discharge a responsibility but rather a reciprocal bond growing stronger with each "payment." Cicero adds that these rules of goodwill are the province of gentlemen, requiring a subtlety of understanding the masses may lack.[45]

4.1.2 Checking a Balance

As he had in his legal studies, Cicero depicts *voluntas mutua* in various gradations and types. While in exile, Cicero entreats the consul Metellus, a near relative of his enemy Clodius, to find a solution acceptable to them both "with however much goodwill you can bring to bear" (*quantum tua fert voluntas*);[46] he marvels that Servius has shown "such ample goodwill" (*voluntatem tantam*) to Atticus and himself when they least expected it;[47] and he jokes, in a separate letter, that Servius has "the kind of goodwill in me" (*in me tali voluntate*) that he does more for Cicero's friends "than perhaps I should do myself..."[48] In these references, we see how *voluntas* can vary in kind (*tali*), quantity (*quantum*), and extent (*tantum*).

Why were these expressions useful? First, these shadings of goodwill reflected the fact that political relations among "equals" could in fact

---

[43] *QFr.* 25.3. [44] *Planc.* 68 (emphasis added). [45] Ibid. 73. [46] *Fam.* 1.10.2.
[47] Ibid. 3.284.1. [48] Ibid. 3.293.2. Cf. *Phil.* 1.2; *Dom.* 9.

4.1 *The Rules of* Voluntas Mutua

involve wide disparities of power. When Pompey alone cannot achieve Cicero's recall from exile, he "adjoins Caesar's aid to this will [sc. project]" (*huius voluntatis ... sibi et adiutorem C. Caesarem adiunxit*), despite Cicero's opposition to Caesar in the past.[49] When Plancius is accused of insufficient aid to Cicero during his exile, Cicero responds that his lack of service was due "not to any deficiency of goodwill on his part [*non huic voluntatem defuisse*], but to the fact that, being already under such great obligations to Plancius [*quum tantum iam Plancio deberem*]," Cicero was satisfied with the aid of others.[50] A second reason was that an account of *voluntas*, though not dischargeable like a monetary debt, was not guaranteed to hold its value. Brutus reassures Atticus that despite his (perhaps spurious) diatribe against Cicero's handling of the Antonian war, "you may be sure that there has been no falling off in my goodwill [*de voluntate propria mea nihil esse remissum*], though my judgment has changed considerably."[51] Metellus Nepos, caught in a dispute with Clodius, expresses his hope that Cicero will "conserve the goodwill you had for me in the past [*pristinam tuam erga me voluntatem conserves*]."[52] The measurable gradations of *voluntas* thus provided Cicero with a sharper analysis of his political landscape, comparing the strength of his alliances and tracking the changes in each.[53]

Not surprisingly, verifying one's stock of *voluntas* was as common a habit for politicians of the late Republic as checking opinion polls is today. Writing to Ligarius, the anti-Caesarian exile whose cause Cicero would champion, Cicero reassures the distraught man that his letter would "make clear to you both my opinion and my goodwill [*tibi et sententiam et voluntatem declararem meam*]."[54] To this end, third parties could be sent as "*voluntas* auditors" to assess whether and why someone's goodwill had changed.[55] In several early letters to Atticus, Cicero tries and fails to complete this audit with regard to a certain Lucceius, whose *causa ... immutatae voluntatis* he fails to ascertain.[56] In especially delicate cases,

---

[49] *Pis.* 80.   [50] *Planc.* 77.
[51] *Ad Brut.* 26.6. Cf. *Red. Sen.* 21. In his litany of gratitude, Cicero includes Marcus Cispius, whose family's interests in a private action ran counter to Cicero's (*cum a me voluntas eorum in privato iudicio esset offensa*).
[52] *Fam.* 1.11.2. Cf. ibid. 1.1.2, Metellus Celer's earlier complaint to Cicero that he didn't expect Cicero's "disposition so changeable towards me and mine [*animo tam mobili in me meosque*]." Cicero counterclaims that he had heard from some travelers of Metellus' "change of spirit [*animum immutatum*]" toward him; ibid. 1.10.1.
[53] Cf. Brunt 1988, 360: "[A]micitia had imperceptible gradations in quality and degree."
[54] *Fam.* 2.227.1.   [55] The phrase is my own.
[56] *Att.* 1.7.1. This confirmation could take place without the knowledge of the third party, as when Cicero writes that "Lentulus' friendly attitude, evinced in actions, promises, and letters, makes me

confirmation could even come via a fourth party, as when the exiled exconsul acknowledges receipt of a letter from Atticus concerning "the confirmation of Pompey's goodwill which you say Varro has given you [*quod a Varrone scribis tibi esse confirmatum de voluntate Pompei*]."[57]

In a number of *epistolae*, confirmation of *voluntas* is sought to answer a more tangible need. Writing from the field in a vulnerable position against Antony, D. Brutus pleads to Cicero: "If I had any doubts of your goodwill towards me [*si de tua in me voluntate dubitarem*], I should use many words in requesting you to defend my public standing; but the fact surely is, as I am convinced, that you have my interests at heart."[58] The fact of the letter belies its content – as consul-elect, Decimus was apparently quite keen to reconfirm the support of the senate's *de facto* leader. Conversely, at a moment of fragile détente, M. Brutus and Cassius request urgently that Antony, now consul, confirm "your goodwill in us [*tuae voluntatis in nos*]" before they return to Rome.[59] Similarly, Cassius, in sore need of money for his Eastern troops, tells Cicero of his soldiers' devotion to the venerable statesman: "[B]y dint of constantly hearing of your goodwill they have developed an extraordinary regard and affection for you [*de cuius voluntate adsidue audiendo mirifice te diligit carumque habet*]."[60] Between the lines of Cassius' flattery we sense an urgent appeal for cash.

As useful as these reconfirmations could be, Cicero knew that they came with their own transaction costs. Nervous for the unsoldierly Trebatius in Caesar's Gaul, Cicero warns his protégé that there are limits to how often he could check the young man's account:

> How pressingly I have written to Caesar on your behalf, you know; how often, I know. But to tell the truth, I had temporarily given it up, because in dealing with so generous a man and so warm a friend of mine I did not want to risk appearing to lack confidence in his goodwill [*ne viderer liberalissimi hominis meique amantissimi voluntati erga me diffidere*].[61]

Though he admits having finally written the requested letter, the reminder illustrates that in checking a balance of goodwill with Caesar, hidden fees could apply.

---

somewhat hopeful of Pompey's goodwill [*spem nobis non nullam adfert Pompei voluntatis*], as you have often told me that he is completely under Pompey's thumb"; *Att.* 1.67.2.

[57] *Att.* 1.60.1. Cf. ibid. 2.125.5, where Cicero, nervous about confirmation of his triumph after his service in Cilicia, rejoices at the news of Pompey's support and praises Atticus especially as "you had visited him in order to ascertain his sentiments toward me [*ad eum venisse ut animum erga me perspiceres*]."

[58] *Fam.* 3.342.1.   [59] Ibid. 3.329.1–2.   [60] Ibid. 3.387.4.   [61] Ibid. 1.33.3.

4.1.3 Making Withdrawals

Depending on circumstances, latent goodwill could be converted into a variety of concrete favors. Given Cicero's talents, the courtroom is often his preferred venue. In the preface to his speech for Balbus, he pledges to his client "a talent by no means equal to my goodwill [*ingenii minime voluntati paris*]."[62] Letters of recommendation are another staple. In a letter to Caesar that opens with the eyebrow-raising line, "you are my other self [*te me esse alterum*]," Cicero requests the safety of the aforementioned Trebatius, whom Cicero has given assurances "amply of your friendly disposition [*prolixe de tua voluntate*]."[63] Similarly, Cicero entreats Culleolus to resolve a matter of provincial business for Lucceius, positing that since "no man's word and influence counts for more with you than mine, ... we urgently need your goodwill, influence, and power [*opus est nobis et voluntatem et auctoritatem et imperium tuum*]."[64] We note that while Cicero draws on his account for another's benefit, he elides this fact for politeness' sake (*opus est nobis*, "we urgently need").[65] A naked transfer of favor to a third party could look like ungentlemanly horse-trading; the discourse of shared *voluntas* gave a moral sheen to his realpolitik.[66]

Such three-way transactions could be thwarted if a key link was missing. When Sallustius[67] asks Cicero for a letter on his behalf to his superior, Bibulus, Cicero bridles at the request:

> The goodwill on my side is not lacking [*mihi voluntas non deest*], but I think I have a bone to pick with you in this connection. Of all Bibulus' entourage you are the only one who had never told me how causelessly unfriendly his disposition towards me is [*quam valde Bibuli voluntas a me sine causa abhorreret*].[68]

For Cicero's *voluntas* to redound to this man's benefit, in other words, Cicero requires his own goodwill in Bibulus and Sallustius' in himself. But

---

[62] *Balb.* 1.1.   [63] *Fam.* 1.26.1.   [64] Ibid. 1.54.2.
[65] Also noteworthy is the complementarity of bringing both *auctoritas* and *gratia/voluntas* to bear: Whereas *auctoritas* is a measure of personal prestige (i.e. an account one builds in oneself), *gratia* and *voluntas* measure reciprocal obligation (i.e. an account one builds in others). Cicero combines them because they appeal to parallel and distinct sources of motivation.
[66] In one of his most amusing letters, Cicero grits his teeth and recommends Atticus to his former co-consul Antonius, with whom his relations were glacial. Noting the jokes Antonius has made at his expense, Cicero sniffs that "what I have already done for you was first out of goodwill and later for consistency's sake [*quae tua causa antea feci, voluntate sum adductus posteaque constantia*]"; *Fam.* 1.5.3. For evocations of *voluntas* in letters of recommendation, see, e.g., *Ad Brut.* 19.1; *Fam.* 2.129, 3.283; *Att.* 4.407B.
[67] A proquaestor in Syria of no apparent relation to the historian.   [68] *Fam.* 2.117.6.

Cicero's account in Bibulus had apparently been closed, and Sallustius has failed to alert him: ample reason to abort the transaction. Nevertheless, the ex-consul's commitment to the system – or, less charitably, his fear of alienating either man – impels him to write the letter anyway.

Demonstrations of goodwill could matter critically on questions of political timing. Cicero favors a quick return to Rome from Cilicia before the departure of that year's magistrates, "having had a sample of their goodwill in the matter of the Supplication [*quorum voluntatem in supplicatione sum expertus*]."[69] Nevertheless, Cicero could also overestimate the *voluntas* he had accrued; as Clodius prepared his bill for Cicero's exile, Cicero maintains to Atticus that he is protected by a bastion of goodwill (*benevolentia hominum muniti sumus*); his very next letter is from the road to Macedonia.[70] Thus, the interiority of *voluntas* was both its unique power and great risk; the goodwill Cicero presumes in others could disappear unannounced.

4.2 The *Voluntas* Economy

4.2.1 Hierarchies of Exchange

Cicero's letters testify to the complexities of exchanging goodwill with fellow statesmen. His orations, in turn, illustrate how the *voluntas* economy operated at all levels of Roman society. *Voluntas* could be exchanged between client and patron, as when the citizens of Syracuse establish a festival *maxima voluntate* in the name of the Marcelli.[71] At the other end of the social spectrum, Cicero relates how the Syrian prince Antiochus, robbed of a sacred statue, cries out to Jupiter "to witness his piety and goodwill [*testem ipsum Iovem suae voluntatis ac religionis adhibere*]."[72] Between provincials and gods stretched a long social ladder for which *voluntas* was a shared currency of exchange. Or nearly so: When the tribune Sestius decides to arm himself and his allies against Clodius' gang, Cicero declares that the entire state stood behind him: "The goodwill of

---

[69] *Att.* 2.120.2. Cf. *QFr.* 1.26: The *communes* of Cilicia vote Cicero a memorial in thanks for having lightened their tax burdens as governor, a welcome demonstration of *voluntas* at a delicate political moment.

[70] *Att.* 1.45.2. Similarly, in the long letter to his ally Lentulus after his return to Rome, he partially justifies his volte-face toward Caesar with the complaint that, regarding restitution for Cicero's losses at Clodius' hands, the *optimates* had "showed a less forthcoming goodwill than I had expected [*neque ... eam voluntatem quam expectaram praestiterunt*]"; *Fam.* 1.20.5.

[71] *Verr.* 2.2.51.   [72] Ibid. 2.4.67.

4.2 *The* Voluntas *Economy*

the Senate was extraordinary, the spirit of the Roman Knights was aroused in his cause, Italy was on the tiptoe of expectation [*senatus incredibilis voluntas, equitum Romanorum animi ad causam excitati, erecta Italia*]."[73] On the sliding scale – *voluntas, animus, erecta* – we infer a reluctance to equate the crowd's favor with gentlemanly goodwill.[74]

Where he does use *voluntas* for the goodwill of common citizens, as in his speech for Milo, Cicero warns that it is of a fragile and fickle sort: "[F]or there is nothing so pliable, so delicate, so easy to break or to bend, as the goodwill and feelings of our fellow citizens [*nihil est enim tam mobile, tam tenerum, tam aut fragile aut flexiblile quam voluntas erga nos sensusque civium*]."[75] Nevertheless, when turned in his favor, the *voluntas multitudinis* is an asset:

> [N]othing can be more glorious and more illustrious than the fact that at the *comitia* at which I was elected you did not hand in your voting-tablet, whose secrecy guarantees the freedom of your vote, but showed by universal acclamation your goodwill and attachment to me [*sed vocem unam prae vobis indicem vestrarum erga me voluntatum ac studiorum tulistis*].[76]

In this usage, we see a blending of the senses of "specific intent" and "durable disposition" explored in *De inventione*.[77] As we will see in Chapter 5, *voluntas populi* comes to signify both the people's specific choice at election time and the ratification of an ongoing bond that both sides maintain.[78]

Was the *voluntas* offered by the Roman people to Caesar and Cicero truly reciprocal? Though statesmen could bestow *beneficia* on their tribes and clients,[79] the goodwill they returned to the people as a whole was described not as *voluntas in populo*, a phrase absent from Cicero's corpus, but rather as *voluntas in* (or *erga*) *rem publicam*.[80] When the young advocate, prosecuting Verres, cites the injustice of Romans "oppressed by the hand of recklessness and crime," he declares that in his crusade

---

[73] *Sest.* 87.
[74] See also *Cat.* 4.1; *Sull.* 10; *Mur.* 70–74. On the semantics of reciprocal service among Roman patrons and clients, see generally Konstan 1997, 136–37.
[75] *Mil.* 42. [76] *Leg. agr.* 2.4. [77] See discussion in Chapter 2.
[78] Cf. *Leg. agr.* 3.1.2, Cicero's entreaty to the assembly, "[w]herefore I beg those of you, who have not believed anything about me [that the tribunes have said], to retain the goodwill which you have always shown towards me [*ut eam voluntatem, quam semper habuistis erga me, retineatis*]"; cf. *Planc.* 103; *Lig.* 37.
[79] On *beneficia*, see Hellegouarc'h 1963, 163–69.
[80] Cf. *Verr.* 1.34; *Cael.* 78; *Cat.* 4.9; *Att.* 3.240.2; *Ad Brut.* 5.1; *Phil.* 1.10, 7.6, 8.30, 13.8, 13.13, 13.50. For alternatives to the phrase used by Cicero's peers, see, e.g., *Fam.* 3.408 (Lepidus, *qua mente et quo animo semper in rem publicam*); *Ad Brut.* 26 (Brutus, *optimo animo*); *Fam.* 3.371.2–3 (Plancus, *bona voluntas*).

against corruption, "the Roman people [should] perceive my goodwill to my country [*meam in rempublicam voluntatem populus Romanus perspicere posset*]."⁸¹ In Cicero's view, the *populus* offer their *voluntas* to statesmen, and in return statesmen show their *voluntas* to the Republic: something less, we might say, than true reciprocity. Actions for the common good, and not specific *officia* or *beneficia*, were what the *populus* should expect from Cicero and his fellow *optimates*, who should expect constancy from one another and caprice from the mob. Even when Cicero casts doubt on Laterensis' *voluntas* for the people, it is for his unwillingness to stand for tribune rather than for his noncompliance with popular demands – and this after likening the *populi voluntates* to the waves of a stormy sea.⁸²

Where statesmen may have found the phrase most useful, finally, was in praising one another.⁸³ In the thirteenth Philippic, Cicero praises the senate's envoys "whose steadfast goodwill toward the Republic you know well [*quorum habetis cognitam voluntatem in rem publicam eamque perpetuam atque constantem*]."⁸⁴ And as seen in the previous chapter, complimenting Brutus' patriotism created room to criticize his tactics:

> My patriotism has always been identical with yours, my dear Brutus; my policy in certain matters ... has perhaps been a little more forceful [*Voluntas mea, Brute, de summa re publica semper eadem fuit quae tua, ratio quibusdam in rebus ... paulo fortasse vehementior*].⁸⁵

This flourish was especially fit for the patriotic consolations attending political failure: Cicero declares in the first Philippic that he will follow Piso in criticizing Antony, such that even if their cause falters, his words will be "the testament of my goodwill to the Republic [*testem rei publicae ... voluntatis*]."⁸⁶

4.2.2 *Expansion and Crisis*

The exchanges of goodwill that animated Rome's domestic politics also sped the consolidation of its empire. Though largely indomitable in battle,

---

⁸¹ *Verr.* 1.35.
⁸² *Planc.* 11–13. The scion of a well-known plebeian family, Laterensis had lost an election for aedile to Gn. Plancius, Cicero's young benefactor during his exile in Greece. Laterensis' subsequent prosecution of his rival for electoral bribery is the occasion for Cicero's speech. The outcome of the case is uncertain. See Loeb ed., 402–05.
⁸³ See *Cael.* 78 (Caelius); *Cat.* 4.9 (Caesar); *Phil.* 1.10 (Piso), 13.50 (M. Pompeius).
⁸⁴ *Phil.* 13.13.
⁸⁵ *Ad Brut.* 5.1. The phrase could lend a patriotic gloss to pleas for personal amity; cf. *Fam.* 1.3.2 (Cicero and Pompey), 3.390.1 (Plancus and Lepidus).
⁸⁶ *Phil.* 1.10. Cf. *Sest.* 113; *Phil.* 7.6.

4.2 *The* Voluntas *Economy*

Rome lacked the resources to subdue unwilling peoples *ad infinitum*; the same ends could be achieved more cheaply by integrating its new subjects into the reciprocities that made Roman life attractive. And whereas the *beneficia* of baths and aqueducts could not be forthcoming every day, assurances of *voluntas mutua* could.[87] Such assurances from the distant capital were a key factor in imperial policy. On his arrival as governor of Cilicia, Cicero quickly sends his colleagues an evaluation of the deteriorating military situation: Though King Deiotarus can be depended on "for both goodwill and troops" (*et voluntatem et copias*), due to the recent harshness of Roman rule, no remaining regional ruler can be relied on "either for money or goodwill" (*neque opibus ... nec voluntate*).[88] For the provinces, these exchanges could bolster their relative standing: Sicily should receive special consideration, argues Cicero, as "the first jewel in our imperial crown," in that no other province has surpassed it "in loyal goodwill toward the Roman people [*fide benivolentiaque erga populum Romanum*]."[89] Similarly, Cicero implores a magistrate to let Caesar settle a dispute involving a city in Cisalpine Gaul, given "the high standing of the community, the equity of their cause, and also their goodwill toward himself [*voluntatis erga se habiturum*]."[90] These exchanges abroad could enhance *dignitas* at home: Cicero crows that he and King Deiotarus are "bound together in mutual hospitality and goodwill [*hospitium voluntas utriuque coniunxit*]."[91]

Cicero's arrival in Cilicia in 51 BCE illustrates the critical importance of *voluntas mutua* to Rome's empire. In his tortuous correspondence with the outgoing governor, we can infer both the standard operating procedures and the pitfalls lining their path. Before assuming office, Cicero writes to its current occupant, Appius Claudius Pulcher, regretting "the long period of suspension of our intercourse," adding a pleasantry about acquiring a statue from the man's collection and renaming it "the Appian Minerva."[92] Later, on the eve of his departure from Italy, Cicero reconfirms his

---

[87] See, e.g., *QFr.* 1.26.
[88] *Fam.* 1.104.5–6. Cf. *Lig.* 24, where Cicero accuses Tubero of opposing Caesar by setting off for Africa, a province alienated from Caesar's *voluntas*.
[89] *Verr.* 2.1.2.
[90] *Fam.* 3.320.3. These ties of *voluntas* were relevant to economic transactions in the provinces as well; see *Fam.* 2.139.1.
[91] *Deiot.* 39. Cicero similarly uses provincial goodwill to boost his client Rabirius; see *Rab. Post.* 3.8.
[92] *Fam.* 1.64.1–2. Cicero must push rather hard to pretend a social parity with the lordly Appius, citing connection to his daughter's father-in-law (Pompey) and their collegial relations as augurs (*collegique coniunctio*); ibid. 1.67.2. These "college ties," useful then as now, apparently did not suffice to win Appius' favor; cf. ibid. 1.71.5.

goodwill to Appius, now making more explicit his hope, given their "reconfirmed" friendship, that the province will be "consign[ed] to me in as orderly and unembarrassed a state as possible."[93]

On his arrival to the province, however, Cicero learns that, despite a mounting Parthian threat, Appius has discharged large numbers of soldiers. Gritting his teeth, Cicero "repeats the request" of his previous letter, bearing in mind "the perfect harmony of goodwill which exists between us [*pro nostra consociatissima voluntate*]," and urging a "minimum of reductions" in the troops he will command (1.66.1–2). Then, a sharp turn for the worse: Appius not only fails to honor this request, but, with his successor now ashore, continues to hold official assizes. Cicero pretends to put the blame on meddling junior officers attempting to "separate my goodwill from yours" (*alienare a te voluntatem meam*), but he notes with fraying patience, "those who do not know our mutual sentiments might well regard your conduct as that of a person indifferent (to use no harsher word), avoiding his successor, whereas mine would appear that of the closest of friends" (1.69.3–4).

In a coda to this duel, Appius returns to Rome after the botched handover and, hoping for support of his sought-after triumph, promptly changes his tone (1.72.1). Cicero rapidly acquiesces in this "reconciliation" and reaffirms his *constantis erga te voluntatis* ("my unswerving goodwill towards you") (ibid.). Appius has apparently offered to support a triumph for his successor in return for Cicero's influence in the senate. Seeking a veil for so naked a transaction, Cicero denies that his support for Appius will in any way be related to his own future self-interest, which he says would be the "Epicurean" way of doing business (1.72.2). The mess in Cilicia has been cleaned up and gentlemanly goodwill secured: Only at this point Cicero can conclude, with a perceptible roll of the eyes, "the gain I promise myself from our friendship is – friendship itself, [which] nothing rewards more richly [*ipsam amicitiam, quo nihil est uberius*]" (1.76.2). At each act in this drama, the code of *voluntas mutua* stabilizes the rapport of two men who clearly cannot stand each other.[94] With no permanent bureaucracy or single ruler in charge, pretended goodwill is Rome's safeguard against paralysis or bloodshed.

The *voluntas* economy received a shock in the form of the First Triumvirate. Opposing Verres, Catiline, and Clodius, Cicero has no difficulty associating his personal opposition to those men with the good

---

[93] Ibid. 1.65.1.   [94] On this episode, see also Brunt 1988, 356.

of Rome. By the time of Luca (56 BCE), however, we see how the goodwill he shares with both Pompey and Caesar casts him into doubt. He cannot seemingly be a *bonus vir*, honoring his *voluntas* in the two great men, while remaining a *bonus civis*, loyal to senate and people.[95] Ultimately, the war between Caesar and Pompey breaks the system that the Triumvirate had bent. Cicero gives an early warning to Atticus after an assembly in 59 BCE at which Caesar as consul had tried unsuccessfully to turn the crowd against his co-consul Bibulus: "[I]n short, they realize that they hold no goodwill in any section of society, which gives us all the more reason to fear violence [*sentiunt se nullam ullius partis voluntatem tenere, eo magis vis nobis est timenda*]."[96] Here, again, is the theme of *voluntas* versus *vis*, the force of collective reason against lawless brutality.[97] Cicero may have sensed it was a losing fight.

Despite his unprecedented aims, Caesar cleverly invokes the codes of goodwill to which his peers were accustomed. On the brink of war, he takes pains to confirm his *voluntas* in Cicero through an intermediary, as Cicero had so often done: Caesar's fairness is evident, says Balbus, in the decision to excuse Balbus from fighting against Pompey, his old patron. Balbus then makes a similar request of Cicero: Stay neutral in the conflict and instead "lend your goodwill to both parties [*utrique . . . tuam benevolentiam praestare*]."[98] The *coup de grâce* is an appended letter from Caesar to two lieutenants, in which his mastery of the old forms is clear. Caesar proposes that they "make mercy and generosity our shield," rejecting the retributive model of Sulla and affirming that with clemency "let us win back the goodwill of all [*possemus omnium voluntates recuperare*]."[99] To Cicero's credit, he rejects these advances and – in the face of a final, direct appeal *pro nostra benevolentia* – joins Pompey and the rump senate in their unpromising but righteous cause.[100]

With Pompey dead and Caesar in charge, Cicero despairs of the networks of goodwill that had sustained the Republic. To Mescenius Rufus he laments, "some are dead, others away, others have altered their goodwill [*alii interierint, alii absint, alii mutati voluntate sint*]," and he will

---

[95] *Fam.* 1.20.10; cf. discussion in Chapter 3.   [96] *Att.* 1.41.5.
[97] See Chapter 2, note 36 and discussion.
[98] *Att.* 3.174B.1–3. In this passage, Balbus uses a phrase "he signified to me entirely of his own goodwill" (*mihi ipse sua concessit voluntate*), which never appears from Cicero's pen, demonstrating the varieties of expression possible in this common discourse.
[99] Ibid. 3.174C.1–2.
[100] Ibid. 3.199B.1; cf. ibid. 3.185.3, using Cicero's son-in-law Dolabella's *benevolentia* toward Caesar to help lure Cicero back to Rome.

seek refuge instead "in my literary dabbling ... and also in my political conscience [*litterulis nostris, praeterea conscientia etiam consiliorum meorum*]."[101] An epilogue of sorts emerges in an exchange with Matius, the old friend who had followed Caesar's line in politics and served as an intermediary during the dictator's reign. Matius seems to have kept his old attachments beyond the Ides of March, and Cicero frames his friend's ethical position thus:

> But a scholar like yourself will not be unaware that Caesar was a despot ... On the one side it can be maintained ... that in caring for your friend even after he is dead you show commendable loyalty and good feeling. According to the other view ... the freedom of one's country should come before a friend's life [*libertatem patriae vitae amici anteponendam*].[102]

Matius insists, in a gracious reply, that while he demurs from Cicero's view of his patriotism, his goodwill in him is secure nevertheless (*perpetua fuisset atque esset benevolentia*).[103] Despite divergent views on the duties of friendship and patriotism, their continued goodwill shows the resilience of this economy through the horror of civil war.

4.3 Theorizing *Voluntas Mutua*

In his jurisprudence and constitutional theory, Cicero turns to Greek philosophy for normative arguments that might order his disordered republic. His explorations of friendship, too, show a creative, inconsistent, and desperately patriotic mind at work. The first phase of this journey is a muddled pragmatism. In his earliest treatise, the *De inventione*, *voluntas* sits at the center of his definition of friendship: *Amicitia* is "a will to do good for someone simply for the benefit of that person whom one loves, with a similar will on his part [*voluntas erga aliquem rerum bonarum illius ipsius causa quem diligit cum eius pari voluntate*]."[104] The reciprocity of friendship is strictly selfless. He adds, however, that "there are some who think that friendship is to be sought solely for advantage [*utilitas*], others, for itself alone, and others for itself and for advantage."[105] As to which view is the right one, he hedges: This is "a matter to be considered at another time," but "since we are here discussing speeches about public issues, we associate friendship with benefits to be derived from it, so that it

---

[101] *Fam.* 2.182.1.   [102] Ibid. 3.348.8.   [103] Ibid. 3.349.10.   [104] *Inv.* 2.166.
[105] Ibid. 2.167.

4.3 *Theorizing* Voluntas Mutua

may seem desirable because of these as well as for its own sake."[106] Thus, friendship is by definition strictly selfless, except there are those who disagree, and its political benefits should be noted: a less than coherent view. Nonetheless, we can surmise that these claims reflected the range of positions a Roman orator might espouse.[107]

This pragmatic approach is in evidence in Cicero's early speeches as well. In one of his first cases, the young lawyer links an opponent's breach of trust to the interests of society as a whole, observing, "that is why friendships are formed – that the common interest may be furthered by mutual services."[108] Similarly, arguing to Metellus Celer that proper friendship is *voluntas accipitur et redditur*, Cicero's purpose is not to expound a theory but to resolve an impasse.[109] Nevertheless, there are hints that Cicero is approaching these issues in an increasingly systematic vein. He chides the young jurist Trebatius for neglecting his duty to send dispatches from Caesar's camp, which would not have occurred "if you had cared to study the rules of friendship as thoroughly as those of court procedure [*si tu maluisses benevolentiae quam litium iura perdiscere*]."[110]

As the cases of Metellus and Appius illustrate, the conduct of Roman politics depended on alliances not of intimacy and admiration but of reliable support. The *Commentariolum petitionis*, ostensibly a letter from Quintus Cicero to his brother, advises a panoply of tactics to win over influential supporters;[111] nowhere do its authors advise limiting one's electoral strategy to those whom one admires. Nevertheless, as he confronts the ethical tensions of a public career, Cicero gives new arguments that justify the practice of *voluntas* on its own terms. We have seen in *Pro Plancio* earlier in this chapter the special rules that distinguish goodwill from low commerce – that in repaying it, "when I pay I keep, and when I keep, I pay by the very act of keeping" (68). Later in the same speech, Cicero re-emphasizes the need for reciprocal service in politics and families alike, calling *gratia* "the mother of all virtues" (*mater virtutum omnium*):

---

[106] Ibid.: *Hic, quia de civilibus causis loquimur, fructus ad amicitiam adiungimus ut eorum quoque causa petenda videatur ... Quorum quid verissime constituatur, alius locus erit considerandi.* (I reverse the order the phrases in the main text.)

[107] Cf. Brunt 1988, 355; Griffin 2007, 104. Remer 2017, 50, 69, suggests that this flexibility had philosophical as well as pragmatic value: "[Cicero] also selects this type of argumentation because he considers truth to be *multiplex*, and arguing different sides points up different aspects of the truth."

[108] *Rosc. Am.* 111.   [109] *Fam.* 1.2.3.   [110] Ibid. 1.38.2.

[111] On the contested authorship and political ideas of the *Commentariolum*, see generally Balsdon 1963; Gelzer 1969, 62, 139; Nardo 1970; Brunt 1988, 428–29; Morstein-Marx 1998; Lintott 2008, 130–33; Alexander 2009; Sillett 2016; Mouritsen 2017, 134–35.

> What is filial affection, if not grateful goodwill to one's parents [*voluntas grata in parentes*]? What is patriotism, what is service to one's country in war and peace, if it is not a recollection of benefits received from that country? What is piety and religion, save a due reverence and remembrance in paying to the immortal gods the thanks that we owe?[112]

In this second, universalizing phase, Cicero places *voluntas* in league with the duties of family, citizenship, and religion – the three pillars of Roman identity.[113] Each of these relationships is animated by reciprocal *gratia*, of which Cicero concludes "nothing is more essentially human [*nihil tam proprium hominis*]."[114] Importantly, the conceptual justification Cicero gives for these reciprocal services is duty, not utility or political gain.[115]

In *De legibus*, Cicero adds another arrow to his philosophical quiver: *ius naturae*, the Stoic doctrine of natural law. On the question of friendship, he deploys their concept of "right reason applied to command and prohibition" (*recta ratio imperandi atque prohibendi*) to distinguish the inherently just from the merely customary or advantageous.[116] If Nature is not to be the foundation of justice, he asks,

> where then will there be a place for generosity, of love of country, or loyalty, or the inclination to be of service to others or to show gratitude for goodwill received [*referendae gratiae voluntas*]? For these virtues originate in our natural inclination to love our fellow men, and this is the foundation of Justice. (1.43)

Mutual goodwill is thus grounded still more rigorously in the principle of Nature's law. What *ius natura* firmly rules out, though, is *utilitas* as a barometer of friendship. If a friend is not loved sincerely, he will be "deserted and cast aside as soon as there is no longer hope of benefit and profit from his friendship" (1.49). He concludes, "if, on the other hand, friendship is to be sought for its own sake, then the society of our fellow men, fairness, and justice, are also to be sought for their own sake. If this is not the case then there is no such thing as justice at all, for the very height

---

[112] *Planc.* 80. [113] See *Off.* 1.161.
[114] *Planc.* at 81: "I consider no faculty to be so essentially human as the power of recognizing the obligation not merely of a kindly act, but even of anything which betrays a kindly thought [*Equidem nihil tam proprium hominis existimo quam non modo beneficio, sed etiam benevolentiae significatione alligari*]."
[115] In his speech for the poet Archias, Cicero gives a stirring image on the theme of reciprocity and community: "Indeed, the subtle bond of mutual relationship links together all arts which have any bearing upon the common life of mankind [*Etenim omnes artes, quae ad humanitatem pertinent, habent quoddam commune vinculum et quasi cognatione quadam inter se continentur*]"; *Arch.* 2.
[116] *Leg.* 1.42.

4.3 *Theorizing* Voluntas Mutua

of injustice is to seek pay for justice" (1.50). Anchoring reciprocal service in the law of Nature, the ex-consul sets his earlier pragmatism aside.

In the treatise Cicero dedicates to friendship, *De amicitia*, his stance is sharpened by a perceived Epicurean threat. The school of *hēdonē*, he insists, is incompatible with Roman tradition and the public good.[117] Just as detestable as their rejection of civic duty, in his view, is their suggestion that friendship derives from the pursuit of pleasure.[118] In *De amicitia*, Laelius refutes this position with regard to his friendship with Scipio:

> Although many and great advantages did ensue from our friendship, still the beginnings of our love did not spring from the hope of gain. For as men [of our class] are generous and liberal, not for the purpose of demanding repayment – for we do not put our favors out at interest, but are by nature given to acts of kindness – so we believe that friendship is desirable, not because we are influenced by hope of gain [*non spe mercedis adducti*], but because its entire profit is in the love itself. (31)

Cicero's rejection of Epicurean selfishness hints at the gentleman's traditional disdain for commerce.[119] The anti-mercantile *topos* is made even more explicit in Laelius' scoff at the idea of friendship as *paribus officiis ac voluntatibus*, rejecting this "close and petty accounting ... [requiring] an exact balance of credits and debits" (58). What knits true Romans together in friendship is not profit but virtue, which alone animates "the return of goodwill and the interchange of zealous service" (49).[120] Interestingly, the anti-Epicurean stance also takes him further from another critical element of *voluntas mutua*: its extensibility over great space. Laelius emphasizes that a friendship as uncommon as his own with Scipio can unite only two or at most a few persons (20).[121]

Nevertheless, Cicero's rejection of Epicurean utility is not his final word on the subject. We see hints of a final, reconciling turn in *De partitione oratoria*. In giving practical advice to the orator, Cicero allows that he may appeal to considerations of both expediency and moral goodness (*honestas*) (83–88). Rome's civic customs, including its exchanges of *gratia*, are thus honorable and align with Nature's law. These rules are not any less powerful

---

[117] Cf. Griffin 2007, 106, on anti-Epicureanism as a central theme of the late treatises. Cicero's jeremiad carried over into his letters as well; see, e.g., *Fam.* 1.72.2, to Appius, condemning the practicing of *quid pro quo* triumphs as reflecting an "Epicurean point of view."
[118] See *Fin.* 1.69.   [119] Cf. Rawson 1975, 34–36; Tempest 2011, 105–06.
[120] At *Fin.* 3.70, the Stoic Cato makes a similar case: "[T]he school I am discussing emphatically rejects the view that we adopt or approve either justice or friendship for the sake of their utility. For if it were so, the same claims of utility would be able to undermine and overthrow them." Cf. *Nat. D.* 1.122.
[121] Cf. Brunt 1988, 358.

for being unwritten; rather, they are maintained either by custom or "by the conventions and virtual consensus of mankind" (*conventis hominum et quasi consensu*), which Nature obliges us to preserve for posterity.[122] The longevity of *voluntas mutua* in Roman tradition becomes an argument in its defense.

Cicero produces a triumphant and fully Roman solution to the problem of useful friendship in *De officiis*. At the heart of its ethical system is *decorum*, the principle of just proportion in the relations of men.[123] Society flourishes not when each individual is treated identically, but rather when each gives what is owed and receives what is deserved. By treating friends according to their merits, each citizen serves the needs of all: "[T]he interests of society and its common bonds will be best conserved, if kindness be shown to each individual in proportion to the closeness of his relationship" (1.50).[124]

This principle of proportionality provides an ethical foundation for the exchanges of goodwill Cicero so diligently pursued in public life.[125] Not only is friendship strengthened by the "mutual interchange of kind services," but these services regulate our duties in turn.[126] In deciding what we owe another, we must account for "his moral character, his attitude toward us, the intimacy of his relations to us, and our common social ties, *as well as the services he has hitherto rendered in our interest [et animus erga nos et communitas ac societas vitae et ad nostras utilitates officia ante]*" (emphasis added) (1.45). Political utility is thus reconciled with moral goodness, but under the strictest conditions. First, we must take a long view, judging friendships by their *stabilitas* and *constantia*, not their short-term advantage (1.47).[127] Second, under no circumstances may our

---

[122] *Part or.* 130. Cf. *Nat. D.* 2.62: "Human experience moreover and general custom have made it a practice to confer the deification of renown and gratitude upon distinguished benefactors [*Suscepit autem vita hominum consuetudoque communis ut beneficiis excellentis viros in caelum fama ac voluntate tollerent*]."

[123] See discussion in Chapter 8.

[124] See ibid. 1.12: *Beneficentia* and *liberalitas* must be "proportioned to the worthiness of the recipient" (*pro dignitate cuique tribuatur*); ibid. 1.59, in performance of all these duties, "consider what is most needful in each individual case and what each individual person can or cannot procure without our help." Cf. Griffin and Atkins 1991, xxii–xxv; Burchell 1998, 108–09.

[125] Panaetius' Stoicism may play a decisive role in this return to a more plural and flexible ethical system. I discuss his influence on *De officiis* at length in Chapter 8.

[126] Cf. ibid. 1.56: "Another strong bond of fellowship is effected by mutual interchange of kind services; and as long as these kindnesses are mutual and acceptable, those between whom they are interchanged are united by the ties of an enduring intimacy [*Magna etiam illa communitas est, quae conficitur ex beneficiis ultro et citro datis acceptis, quae et mutua et grata dum sunt, inter quos ea sunt, firma devinciuntur societate*]."

[127] This resonates with *Amic.* 82, in which Laelius asserts that stable friendships are the result of virtue compounded over time.

4.3 *Theorizing* Voluntas Mutua

calculations of interest run counter to the public good, as with those men who butchered the Republic (1.57).[128] Finally, in tallying the *beneficia* of friends and allies, sincerity is paramount: We must only repay those in whom we can see "the spirit, the devotion, the affection, that prompted the favour [*in quo ... quisque animo, studio, benivolentia fecerit*]" (1.49). The decoupling of *voluntas* from *facultas* – so useful to Cicero in practice – is here given an Aristotelian flavor: The spirit of a favor preponderates over the favor itself.[129]

Crucially, in *De officiis*, Cicero maintains the distinction he had always insisted upon between the laws of commerce and those of goodwill. He posits, following Hesiod, that one should repay well beyond the favors given, just as the "fruitful fields ... return more than they receive" (1.48).[130] Furthermore, Cicero's temple of *voluntas* has space enough for charity. Just as Ennius praised those who lit the lamp of "a wand'rer on his way," helping another at no expense to himself, the statesman exhorts his readers to bestow favors on those with nothing to give back (1.51–52). Though he acknowledges that our will inclines more toward those who can repay us (*in eum fere est voluntas nostra propensior*), we do better in helping the honest poor who "cannot return a favor in kind, but if he is a good man ... can do it at least in thankfulness of heart" (2.69).[131] Though we do not reckon as merchants, Cicero encourages his readers to become "good calculators of duty" (*boni ratiocinatores officium*), prudent actors in a moral marketplace of goodwill (1.59).[132]

A few months before his death, Cicero urges Plancus to recommit himself to public service and join the resistance to Antony. "To be sure," he admits,

---

[128] Cf. ibid. 2.26: "[A]s long as the empire of the Roman people maintained itself by acts of service, not of oppression, wars were waged in the interest of our allies or to safeguard our supremacy [*quam diu imperium populi Romani beneficiis tenebatur, non iniuriis, bella aut pro sociis aut de imperio gerebantur*]."

[129] Cf. *Off.* 1.44, 2.32; Arist. *Nic. Eth.* 8.13.11, 1163a21–24.

[130] See also *Brut.* 16: Citing Hesiod's admonition "to repay with what measure you have received, or if possible with larger [*quod eadem mensura reddere iubet quae accerperis aut etiam cumulatiore, si possis*]," he continues, "I am prepared to make payment of goodwill in full measure, but the debt itself I do not now seem able to pay and for this I ask your forbearance [*ego autem voluntatem tibi profecto emetiar, sed rem ipsam nondum posse videor, idque ut ignoscas, a te peto*]."

[131] Here, Cicero returns to the distinction he made in *Pro Plancio*: "As someone has happily said, 'A man has not repaid money, if he still has it; if he has repaid it, he has ceased to have it. But a man still has the sense of favor, if he has returned the favor; and if he has the sense of the favor, he has repaid it' [*Commode autem, quicumque dixit, 'pecuniam qui habeat, non reddidisse, qui reddiderit, non habere, gratiam autem et, qui rettulerit, habere et, qui habeat, rettulisse*']"; *Off.* 2.69.

[132] Cf. Griffin and Atkins 1991, xxii–xxiii; Burchell 1998, 109–10; Remer 2017, 54–60.

in my judgment love of country transcends all other sentiments; but love and goodwill undeniably exercise the greater charm [*est omnino patriae caritas meo quidem iudicio maxima, sed amor voluntatisque coniunctio plus certe habet suavitatis*]. And so your reminder of my relations with your father, of the goodwill you have bestowed upon me since your childhood ... made me a happier man than you can well believe.[133]

Though the *voluntas* economy lay ruined by Caesarism, patriotism and goodwill would, for Cicero, always be bound.

[133] *Fam.* 3.359.1.

CHAPTER 5

Voluntas Populi
The Will of the People

5.1 Introduction: *In Verrem*

Prosecuting the governor of Rome's oldest province would have been an uphill challenge for any politician. For a thirty-six-year-old lawyer of undistinguished birth, no military record, and modest connections, it was close to folly. Though undoubtedly crooked, Gaius Verres was massively wealthy and well ensconced in Rome's elite. By accusing Verres, Cicero was also assailing the system through which most of the jurymen – senators all – had made their money or aspired to do so.[1] Add in a traditional suspicion of provincials and self-serving prosecutors and the task would have seemed hopeless even with a strong family network and personal fortune, both unavailable to Cicero.

What he brings to bear instead is a keen legal mind and a daring rhetorical strategy. He diverts attention from his modest status: It is not Marcus Tullius Cicero, with no history of prosecuting anyone,[2] but the province of Sicily that brings this momentous case.[3] "For the province it is that prosecutes," he asserts, "when her claim is made by the man whom she has clearly chosen to maintain her rights, to avenge her wrongs, and to conduct her case throughout."[4] Deflecting attention from his own vulnerability, he places it on the trial's political stakes, warning the jury of "the unpopularity of your Order and the discredit attaching to these Courts of Law."[5] Cicero's aim is not merely to convict Verres but "to restore the lost good name of these Courts." Will he accomplish this grand mission by his own *dignitas* or *auctoritas*? No. He does so *cum*

---

[1] See, e.g., Rawson 1975, 40–43; Wood 1988, 28–29; Ryan 2012, vol. 1, 114.   [2] *Div. Caec.* 1.
[3] As quaestor, Cicero was responsible for ensuring an uninterrupted supply of corn from Sicily to Rome, in which capacity he seems to have built a substantial network of supporters, both Greek-speaking local gentry and the expatriate *equites* who comprised the business elite. See Rawson 1975, 32–36.
[4] *Div. Caec.* 54.   [5] *Verr.* 1.1.

summa voluntate et exspectatione populi Romani, "by the highest will and hope of the Roman people."[6]

This phrase marks the earliest surviving reference to "the will of the people" in the Western tradition: not in a constitution or treatise, but from a young orator in a trial he was set to lose.[7] Cicero locates the prime insecurity of the senators on his jury – that popular legislation would strip them of their monopoly – and makes it the point of his spear. He cautions the senators that they will earn the same condemnation as Verres if, in the face of all evidence, they "refuse what the Roman people had so strongly willed [*tantae populi Romani voluntati restitisse*]."[8] The crooked governor had perverted the political order, winning the praetorship "more by his and his mistress's will than by the will of the Roman people [*magis ex sua Chelidonisque, quam ex populi Romani voluntate*]."[9] His crimes are not the private matter of certain Sicilians but rather a betrayal of the *populus Romanus*, in whose cause Cicero is champion. Against long odds, he wins the case.

Claiming a special right to speak for the people was not unprecedented in Roman oratory.[10] But both Cicero's political stance and his choice of words were starkly different from the *popularis* tradition his audience would have known.[11] Cicero calls for reconciliation with, not vengeance against, the senatorial elite. He explicitly seeks to revitalize – and ascend within – this establishment, not defeat and replace it. His ideal is *concordia ordinum*, the harmony of the orders, a goal that requires each to know his place and occupy it with integrity.[12] Though "strongly backed" by the *voluntas populi*, he prosecutes Verres not to assail the senate but "to help in allaying the discredit which is mine as well as yours."[13] Finally, the political newcomer claims that he is uniquely qualified to bring the people's voice to the senate's attention:

---

[6] Ibid. 1.2.
[7] The fact that a young Cicero employs the phrase without further explanation suggests that it was already current in Roman usage; see discussion of *velle* as part of official legal pronouncements in Chapter 1. Nevertheless, the phrase *voluntas populi* does not appear in any extant text before this speech.
[8] *Verr.* 2.1.10–11.   [9] *Verr.* 1.104.
[10] See Morstein-Marx 2004, 212, 229–34; Atkins 2018b, 116–17.
[11] Though sharing a hometown and family ties with the *popularis* Gaius Marius, Cicero also enjoyed *optimate* connections through his family and early education; see Rawson 1975, 2–6. On the *popularis* tradition, see generally Brunt 1971, 92–96; Lintott 1999, 174–76; Mouritsen 2001, 128–48; Morstein-Marx 2004, 217–40; Hölkeskamp 2010, 42–43.
[12] See *Cat.* 4.15; *Att.* 1.17.9–10; *Sest.* 137; *Rep.* 2.69. Cf. Morstein-Marx 2004, 101; Connolly 2010, 10–12.
[13] *Verr.* 1.2.

5.1 Introduction: In Verrem

I of all men, who to serve the will of the people must bear a heavier burden than those which it is every man's duty to perform [*qui praesertim plus etiam quam pars virilis postulat pro voluntate populi Romani oneris ac muneris suscipere debeam*].[14]

Why indeed "of all men" must Cicero serve the people's will?[15] He claims that his zeal for the task derives from his close ties to Sicily and his faith in equal justice – standard fare.[16] More interestingly, he adds that Verres' crimes cannot go unpunished "while we honest men ... make our merit, and not our money, the means whereby we maintain our dignity and justify the favors conferred upon us by the Roman nation [*populique Romani beneficia non copiis sed virtute tueamur*]."[17] As he argues later, he "had not, to plead for me ... a crowd of kinsfolk,"[18] "no influential connections, no menace of armed men rising to back my cause."[19] A famous name, money, and military clout: Of the politician's three surest assets, Cicero has none.

Converting necessity to principle, he invents a new *persona* in Roman politics: the conservative *popularis*. Speaking for the people's will allows Cicero to downplay his vulnerabilities; yet schooled as he was at the feet of leading conservatives, he is no Gracchan or Marian.[20] So while he claims to "have given many hostages to the Roman people,"[21] in policy and temperament his conservatism is steadfast. His daring and counterintuitive strategy is to claim the *populus* as a political base without embracing the reforms – from land distribution to debt relief – that he both opposed and was in no position to deliver.[22]

Why do the people need a will? Cicero's Greek forebears had apparently done without such a notion. In Athens and other democracies, the *ekklēsia*

---

[14] *Verr.* 2.3.7.
[15] The word *pro* in the phrase *pro voluntate populi Romani* suggests both that Cicero acts "in favor of" the people but also that he understands his duty "in proportion to" what the people have willed (cf. *pro* in *pro rata*). The implication is that the people's *voluntas*, as in so many previous contexts, has a measurability that assigns a certain duty to each politician in accordance with his station and opportunity to act – a duty that Cicero claims he has both met and surpassed (*plus etiam*).
[16] Ibid. 2.3.6. [17] Ibid. 2.3.9. [18] *Red. sen.* 37. [19] *Red. pop.* 7, 16.
[20] Though Cicero occasionally refers to fellow Arpinate Gaius Marius in positive tones, he makes clear that his family did not share Marius' politics (e.g. his grandfather opposed the introduction of the secret ballot in town elections); see Rawson 1975, 4. With very few exceptions, Cicero abhors the Gracchi and extols Scipio Nasica's political murder as a patriotic act. See generally Murray 1966, 291–98.
[21] *Div. Caec.* 72.
[22] Cicero announces he will be a *popularis* consul in his maiden speech, saying that what the people really desire is liberty (*libertas*) and peace (*otium*), not free land; *Leg. agr.* 2.6–7. Similarly, his argument for *consensus omnium bonorum* in *Pro Sestio* artfully reframes the term *popularis*; see discussion in Chapter 3. See generally Seager 1972; Morstein-Marx 1998.

or Assembly was the unquestioned center of power. As we saw in Chapter 1, the *dogmata tou dēmou* were specific statements of policy, not a permanent force to glorify and interpret. While elite actors figured prominently in democratic politics, there is no evidence that they claimed to represent the "will" – the *boulēsis* or *prohairesis* – of the masses.[23] Such special terms were superfluous because the *boulē* or Council did not comprise a governing class; though probably wealthier than the mean, its members were selected by lot and served a single-year term repeatable only once in their public careers. There was little need to speculate as to the will of the *dēmos*; one simply called a vote. Conversely, in cities where a *tyrannos* or *oligoi* had power, they were understood to exert this power for their own interests or (at best) for the general good, not by "the will of the people."[24] Where power was shared between few and many, the relationship was characterized in terms of cooperation and competition, not delegation and representation.[25]

It is in Cicero that the people's will first finds a voice. The phrase appears fifty-three times in his extant corpus.[26] Like *voluntas mutua*, *voluntas populi* is a concept viewed primarily in action; prior to his treatises *De republica* and *De legibus*, the notion of will serves his arguments without itself becoming an object of theory. Nevertheless, his ideal of elite representation marks a qualitative leap beyond the mixed constitutionalism of Polybius and Aristotle. What is more, in his oratory emerge the key claims that would ignite revolutions and that bedevil us today: The *populus* is both semidivine sovereign and fallible mob; the community has a single will even when a large minority shouts "no"; and, most consequentially, the people's will needs a ruling class to fulfill it.

---

[23] See discussion in the Introduction.

[24] The term *eunoia* (goodwill) was used to express the favorable feeling of a population toward a ruler or ruling family; see discussion in the Introduction. Though suggesting consent of the governed and thus the legitimacy of a regime, the context is monarchic, with *eunoia* designating a favorable relationship but not an election or choice of policy. The discourses of *dogmata tou dēmou* and *eunoia* apparently did not intersect, as they do in the Latin *voluntas*.

[25] See, e.g., Pl. *Resp.* 462a–d (the best cities' parts must collaborate); Pl. *Leg.* 628a–b (civil strife should lead to reconciliation, not destruction of one part by another); Arist. *Pol.* 1279a25–39 (government must be in the hands of one, or a few, or the many); ibid. at 1298b–300b (advantages to blending aristocracy and democracy in deliberative functions of the *polis*); Polyb. 6.15.1–2, 6.18.2–3. On the evolution of mixed constitution theory, see generally Lintott 1999, 214–32; Hahm 2009, 178–98; Straumann 2016, ch. 5. On political representation in ancient thought, see Pitkin 1967; Remer 2017, ch. 5 (responding to Pitkin).

[26] Of these fifty-three occurrences, thirty-four are found in the orations, eight in the letters, seven in the philosophical treatises and dialogues, and four in the rhetorical treatises.

As I will explore in this chapter, Cicero's political treatises give equally vigorous cases for popular sovereignty[27] and against popular power. He goes well beyond Greek tradition in asserting that a *liber populus* both defines and owns the Republic – encapsulated in his famous phrase *res publica res populi*.[28] The relationship he proposes between senate and people is one of trusteeship: By the *voluntas populi*, magistrates wield power and manage public affairs.[29] Critically, though the *populus* must be *liber*, it must not have *potestas* to decide policy or enact reform. In practice, he must concede that the people in assembly express their will in *leges*, but as a theorist Cicero cannot abide popular initiative. Consequently, in *De legibus* he frames a Roman constitution with a sole locus of the *voluntas populi*: the election of wise leaders. Having risen by the people's will, this elite is then duty-bound to defy it: With reason, prudence, and moral authority, they will shape laws to reflect the people's *utilitas*, regardless of their *voluntas*. They must serve the people's will while ignoring their shouts in the street.

I will examine finally how the new dictator of Rome subverts Cicero's language, justifying his coup d'état in the people's name. It was a sad irony that Cicero had himself elaborated the *voluntas populi* as both the people's constitutional power and their personal goodwill, offering Caesar a rhetorical trick that dictators have played ever since.

5.2 "I of All Men, Who to Serve the Will of the People ..."

Following the eye-catching success of the Verres trial, Cicero evokes the *voluntas populi* at each stage of his political ascent. In his first political oration, Cicero declares that his efforts will only earn him honors "if borne by your will [*si vestra voluntas feret*]."[30] In this he esteems the people's *voluntas*, and the *dignitas rei publicae*, more than his own "convenience and purposes" (*commodi et rationes*).[31] With each new office he wins, the people's will prevails over Cicero's opponents: Verres tries to bribe voters

---

[27] The translation of "sovereignty" into a Roman context requires careful handling. Schofield 2021, 49, observes: "The Romans may have had no word meaning 'sovereign' or 'sovereignty.' But they did have the genitive case. And in the collocation *res populi*, the genitive *populi* is a genitive of belonging or ownership. To state that the public interest and the conduct of public affairs are something owned by the people is effectively to assert that they have ultimate rights in them superior to those of any possible contender. Such an assertion may reasonably be construed as tantamount to a doctrine of popular sovereignty, or even as the first clear articulation of the idea of it in Greek or Roman thought."
[28] *Rep.* 1.39. [29] Cf. Remer 2017, ch. 5, discussed infra. [30] *Leg. Man.* 70 (66 BCE).
[31] Ibid. 71.

against Cicero in his race for aedile, but the Roman people "with prompt enthusiasm" (*animo libentissimo*) rise up to save him.[32] In his speech for Fonteius, he asserts that the *voluntas civium* should outweigh the prosecutors' designs,[33] and he insists that his election to the consulship was as pleasing to the *boni* as it was *cum universi populi Romani summa voluntate*.[34] Nor was this merely a public posture: As praetor, he crows to Atticus that his handling of Macer's case won "the people's will to a quite extraordinary degree [*incredibili ac singulari populi voluntate*]."[35]

Why did this notion – unattested before Cicero and absent from contemporary texts[36] – have such resonance for him? His rhetorical training offers one answer. As a young man, he had been taught how to win the *voluntas* of an audience away from his opponents.[37] The notion of goodwill as an orator's prize helps him explain the ups and downs of election campaigns, where "a sudden shift of will is critical [*magna est ... repentina voluntatum inclinatio*], particularly when swung toward a good man whose candidature has many other sources of support."[38] In his speech for Sestius, Cicero posits that the *voluntas populi* can be most clearly seen in three places – the *contio*, the assembly, and theatrical or gladiatorial shows[39] – and that he himself can divine "the inmost feelings of the country [*intimos sensus civitatis*]."[40] Thus, Cicero's gifts of interpretation distinguished him (or so he thought) in both the intellectual and public spheres.

The Republic's crisis gave new urgency to this task. In the previous chapters, we saw how *voluntas* signified a rationally guided command and how *voluntas mutua* marked a currency of reciprocal goodwill. Against the bloody demagogues, Cicero wants to affirm the people's uncoerced – though properly guided – power to choose. In his deeply divided society, Cicero insists upon reciprocal trust and service. Thus, in Cicero's "will of the people" these two distinct forces – specific, lawful choice and collective, personal goodwill – are united. Deciding the case *pro voluntate* – a turn of phrase unattested before Cicero – means not only that the people consent to the trial's outcome (the "Plautine" *voluntate*), but that the trial is also "for" them or on their behalf. *Voluntas populi* thus compasses both a

---

[32] *Verr.* 1.25.
[33] *Font.* 32 (69 BCE). See also his rhetorical question at 15: "As for the citizens of Rome, what is their will [*Civium Romanorum quae voluntas est*]?"
[34] *Vat.* 2.6 (56 BCE). Cf. *Brut.* 93.321; *Pis.* 3.7.   [35] *Att.* 1.9.2.
[36] The phrase does not appear in any extant text of Caesar, Varro, or Sallust. *Voluntate plebes* appears once in Sallust, see *Frag. hist.* 2.44.
[37] See, e.g., *Rhet. Her.* 2.43, 3.21; *Inv.* 1.24, 1.92; *De or.* 2.32, 2.129.   [38] *Mur.* 53 (63 BCE).
[39] *Sest.* 106–27 (56 BCE).   [40] Ibid. 119–20.

5.2 "I of all men ..."

specific choice and a special relationship – in this case, their bond of goodwill with Cicero, the people's representative and champion. Their will is expressed in the reward of elective office, a decision that reinforces the *voluntas mutua* he enjoys with them. Though manifest when ballots are cast, the *voluntas populi* remains a durable asset to be interpreted and kept on one's side.

In his early speeches and letters, this notion of popular will takes on four distinctive qualities. First, the force of the *voluntas populi* is not limited to elections but radiates through the Roman system at all times, giving legitimacy to actors and acts favored by the people. Second, though the *populus* is fractious and divided – or possibly because of this fact – its will is single and unanimous. Third, the people's will is capricious and, especially when beguiled by demagogues, can run contrary to their own *utilitas* and the *ratio* of state. Finally, because the *voluntas populi* is at once sovereign and fallible, enlightened leaders must intervene to form it by persuasion, interpret it when obscure, and enact it as their trustee. Unsurprisingly, Cicero believes himself uniquely capable in these roles of state.

5.2.1 The People's Will Is Fundamental

In Cicero's speeches, the Roman *populus* is the first and final authority in public affairs.[41] "Nothing can be sacrosanct save what has been enacted by the people or the plebs,"[42] he declares in his speech for Balbus. Clodius' attempt to expropriate his house runs counter both to the ancestral ban on *privilegia* and to a decree of the *populus*, "who has the greatest power in all things [*cuius est summa potestas omnium rerum*]."[43] For having ratified his recall from exile, Cicero announces his gratitude to the Roman people, "who are endowed in my thoughts with the power and sanctity of the immortal gods [*qui apud me deorum immortalium vim et numen tenetis*]."[44]

---

[41] The only rival in legitimizing power in Cicero's oratory is, of course, the *mos maiorum*. Not coincidentally, Cicero draws correspondences between the "way of the ancestors" and "will of the people"; see discussion infra.

[42] *Balb.* 33: *Primum enim sacrosanctum esse nihil potest, nisi quod populus plebesve sanxit.* Livy held this to be a norm given by the Twelve Tables: "[W]hatever was the last order that the People made that should have the force of law [*ut quodcumque postremum populus iussisset id ius ratumque esset*]"; Livy, *Ab urbe cond.* 7.17.12. On the controversial historicity of this claim, see Straumann 2016, 36–37.

[43] *Har. resp.* 11 (57 BCE); *Dom.* 43 (57 BCE).

[44] *Red. pop.* 25 (57 BCE). For the equation of popular and divine power in Roman affairs, cf. *Rosc Am.* 136: "[A]ll these results are due to the will of the gods, the zeal of the Roman people, and the felicitous plan and power of L. Sulla [*deorum voluntate, studio populi Romani, consilio et imperio et felicitate L. Sullae*]."

And in a world of autocrats, it is a point of pride that by the command of the Roman people (*imperante populo Romano*), defeated kings are restored and live under Rome's protection.[45]

Though Cicero recognized that the people could enact their will directly into law, in his speeches its most typical setting is election day. The magistracies bestowed by the *populus* on its favorites are "the reward of merit proffered by the judgment and goodwill of his fellow citizens [*praemium virtutis iudicio studioque civium delatum ad aliquem*]."[46] By contrast, those who obtain power *invitis suis civibus* have "the title of honor, but not the honor itself."[47] At the moment of election the will of the people is manifest,[48] and the winners are illegitimate unless the whole *populus* has been called to vote.[49] As a constitutional force, the people's *suffragium* can oppose and offset the wills of other actors: The sanctions of a censor can be vacated "by the elections of the Roman people," and a consul-elect's jury is exhorted to acquit "[so] that your opinion ... may tally with the will of the Roman people expressed in their votes [*cum populi Romani voluntatibus suffragiisque consentiant*]."[50] The electoral process is itself an expression of that will: Cicero warns that Bibulus' plan to delay elections would *populi voluntatem offendere*.[51]

Critically, the force of *voluntas populi* is not merely felt at the moment of a magistrate's election but extends through his mandate. In his counter-insurgency against Catiline, Cicero announces that his plans were made "in accordance with the will of the Roman people to defend their supreme power and preserve their common fortune [*populi Romani ad summum imperium retinendum et ad communis fortunas conservandas voluntate*]."[52] Just as the people's will can be harnessed while in office, so too can it be lost; even prior to his trial, Verres "[was] condemned long ago by the will and judgment of all [*omnium voluntate iudicioque damnatam*]."[53] This durability of *voluntas* is brought out in contrast with *iubere*, another term marking the people's *potestas*. When the *populus iussit*, the phrase connotes

---

[45] *Sest.* 57.   [46] *Brut.* 281 (46 BCE).   [47] Ibid.   [48] *Planc.* 54 (54 BCE).
[49] *Leg agr.* 2.18, 28–29. By this Cicero means that special election procedures in which only a portion of citizens may participate do not carry the same legitimacy as those in which all are eligible (even if only a small portion of those eligible participate). Cicero also implies that "unanimous" election results give more force to a magistrate's actions than closely divided ones do – the modern idea of a "political mandate" in embryo. Cf. *Vat.* 11–12: Whereas Sestius wins "unanimous" election to the quaestorship, Vatinius is elected "not by the favor of the Roman people, but of a consul, just stuck on to the end [*non populi beneficio, sed consulis extremum adhaesisse*]." On election procedures in the republican period, see generally Lintott 1999, 43–49.
[50] *Clu.* 121–22; *Mur.* 1.   [51] *Att.* 1.41.5 (59 BCE).   [52] *Cat.* 4.14.
[53] *Verr.* 1.10. Cf. *Rep.* 1.64: The *populus* would have kept the same *voluntas* toward Rome's kings had it not been for the injustices of Tarquin.

a specific command taking place at a given moment and having a specific legal duration.[54] In contrast, just as the goodwill of an audience is a perennial prize, the *populus Romanus* always had and will always have a *voluntas*, of which their *suffragium* is merely one instance.[55]

Proof of the durability of the people's will lies in the continuous scrutiny given it between elections. Cicero claims that in the people's spontaneous ovation for certain lines of a play, and for his ally Sestius at the games, his enemies "could see the will of the entire people [*voluntatem universi populi viderent*]."[56] Similarly, when Pompey proposes to restore powers to the tribunes, the attendees at the *contio* only murmur – but when he proposes to eliminate corruption from Roman courts, "with the mightiest roar, the people of Rome showed their will [sc. gave their accord]."[57] Again, these *indicia* do not comprise the people's will: They indicate it. Even when silent, the *populus* retains its force to approve or disapprove.[58] A telling ambiguity emerges: May the people express its will for policies it favors or only for individual politicians? In his speeches, Cicero remained flexible. An orator could not plausibly deny that certain provisions like land distribution or the grain dole were popular regardless of who proposed them.[59] Only in his treatises does Cicero take a firm normative position: Incapable of understanding *ius*, the people's will is confined to their choice at the ballot box.

Nevertheless, the *populus* can lose its lawful power if certain conditions go unmet. In Chapter 3, we observed how increasing polarization in the late Republic led to new kinds of arguments for "higher-order" or substantive constraints on popular enactments. Even a measure proposed by the proper magistrate and carried in assembly could be held invalid if "the people," properly understood, had been absent.[60] When Clodius has an assembly ratify his proposal to annex Cyprus, Cicero accuses him of

---

[54] See, e.g., *Verr.* 2.2.161, 2.3.17, 2.3.82; *Planc.* 42; *Rab. Post.* 12; *Rep.* 2.25; *Off.* 3.109.

[55] Cf. Remer 2017, 148: "Cicero's view of the orator-statesman as beholden to the people rests on the orator's ongoing need for the audience's approval – less of a concern for the modern representative, who is elected only at intervals."

[56] *Sest.* 124.   [57] *Verr.* 1.45: *maximo clamore, suam populus Romanus significavit voluntatem.*

[58] For the passive force of *voluntas* in other contexts, see, e.g., *Inv.* 2.67: "Customary law is thought to be that which lapse of time has approved by the common consent of all without the sanction of statute [*consuetudine ... ius esse putatur id quod voluntate omnium sine lege vestustas comprobarit*]." Cf. ibid. 2.162; *Cat.* 1.20: "Why are you waiting for them to voice their decision, when you see clearly their wish expressed by their silence [*Quid exspectas auctoritatem loquentium, quorum voluntatem tacitorum perspicis*]?"

[59] See Morstein-Marx 2004, 230–40.

[60] The *Lex Hortensia* of 287 BCE made *plebiscita* – decrees of the *consilium plebis* – legally binding. See Lintott 1999, 37–38.

"involving the Roman people in your criminal act."[61] Similarly, a certain tribune failed to win election to the praetorship because he confused the desires of a *contio* with "what the true people approved" (*vero populo probaretur*); in this, Cicero concludes, "the *populus* is itself not *popularis*."[62] Alternatively, flawed procedure could annul a putative expression of popular will. In his defense of Flaccus, Cicero contrasts the inadequacies of a Greek *contio* – which "are not based upon considered votes or affidavits nor safeguarded by an oath" – with the orderliness of Rome's *comitia centuriata*. Here, we see an idea of the protocol that gives legal power to popular will:

> As for what the commons might approve or the people might order, when the meeting had been dismissed and the people distributed in their divisions ..., when the proposers of the measure had been heard, when its text had been published well in advance and understood, then they wished the people to give their orders or their prohibitions. (*Flac.* 15–16)

Since this procedure has been flouted by the Greeks, he entreats his audience, "allow me to distinguish the crimes of the mob from the position of the city."[63]

Here, Cicero was likely developing a strand of argument begun by *optimates* of the previous generation on limits to popular will. Straumann illustrates how debates over popular legislation, from the time of the Gracchi down to Sulla, came to feature both procedural and substantive arguments against bills that had been carried in assembly.[64] At times, these arguments anticipate modern notions of individual due process, as when a promising young aedile is banned from public life "not by a deliberate vote of censure but by the shouts of the crowd [*clamore hominum*]."[65] In Cicero's political framework, as we have seen in Chapters 3 and 4, the force of a lawful choice is antithetical to – and gravely threatened by – the

---

[61] *Dom.* 20.
[62] *Sest.* 114. See also ibid. at 127: "Do you see, then, how great is the difference between the Roman People and a meeting [*inter populum Romanum et contionem*]?" The same charge is made against the Antonians at *Phil.* 1.6, who pass "many important measures ... through the popular assembly – in the absence of the people and against their will [*absente populo et invito*]."
[63] Ibid. 57–59. Cf. ibid. at 96: "[T]hey see that the mind and will of the Roman people have not changed [*etenim populi Romani perspicunt eandem mentem et voluntatem*]."
[64] Straumann 2016, 123–29, discusses key examples of controversial legislation including bills for land redistribution and the bestowal of extraordinary commands.
[65] *Clu.* 79 (66 BCE). Cf. ibid at 90, 93–94; *Dom.* 33: The "peculiar mark of a free community" is that citizens cannot be deprived of property or privilege "without a verdict of senate, of people, or of the courts constituted to deal with each type of offence."

vis of armed demagogues.⁶⁶ *Cedant arma togae.*⁶⁷ Yet it is admittedly Cicero himself, not a neutral tribunal, who opines as to when the people wields its lawful force – and, in the case of the murdered Gracchi, when violence is acceptable in the interests of the state.⁶⁸ As such, we observe both the defensible limitations Cicero gives to the people's will and the inherent difficulty, even arbitrariness, in deciding what exactly they have willed.

5.2.2 The People's Will Is Singular

In its very familiarity to us, it is easy to miss the striking metaphysical claim in the phrase "the will of the people." How, we may wonder, does a fractious and mutable body of citizens express a single will? The beginnings of an answer lie long before Cicero's time. The phrase *velitis iubeatisne* ("Do you will and order it?") appears to have been the standard enacting phrase in the assemblies through the republican period.⁶⁹ This discourse of unified power arising from a body of individuals apparently ran deep with the Romans, who derived their institutions not from a Lycurgus or Solon but from the *mos maiorum*, the "genius of many" expressed as the one "way" of the ancestors.⁷⁰ Another relevant correspondent, given Cicero's (occasional) exaltation of the *populus*, is the *voluntas deorum*, the singular will of Rome's many gods.⁷¹ Still another factor may be the scale of empire; as its influence swelled, Rome may have found a need to embellish its official pronouncements. As such, the Roman senate and people

---

⁶⁶ See, e.g., *Sest.* 37, Metellus' refusal to observe a law that had been passed by violence; *Red. sen.* 22, Fabricius' efforts at Cicero's restoration were prompted by *voluntas*, checked by *vis*, and revived by the senate's *auctoritas*; *Att.* 1.41.5, regarding Caesar, "they realize that they have no support in any section of society, which gives us all the more reason to fear violence [*sentiunt se nullam ullius partis voluntatem tenere. eo magis vis nobis est timenda*]"; *Caecin.* 5, "the use of force, which is the absolute antithesis of law [*vis ea quae iuri maxime est adversaria*]"; *Sest.* 92, there is no clearer opposition among civilized peoples than *ius* and *vis*.
⁶⁷ *Off.* 1.77.   ⁶⁸ Ibid. 1.76.   ⁶⁹ See Williamson 2005, 119–22.
⁷⁰ *Rep.* 2.2. Cicero often uses *velle* to describe how this collective body of ancestors set the rules of the Republic; see Chapter 2, note 47. Cf. Ferrary 1995, 55: "Even if the proper mixture [sc. in Scipio's ideal constitution] ... had been achieved by 449 BCE, there was no dislocation between an original period of creation and the day-to-day running of affairs, and hence no opposition between lawgiving and politics. On the contrary, it is the same political virtue of prudence that creates the proper mixture, maintains it against the forces that threaten it, and tries if necessary to reestablish it."
⁷¹ Cf. *Dom.* 107. The correspondence of divine will with individual human will in Cicero is a perhaps underappreciated legacy in Western thought. I examine this correspondence and its possible influence on Augustine in the Epilogue.

developed a lexicon as elevated as those of its neighbor empires whose policies were those of a single emperor or king.⁷²

Whatever its origin, we see that the singularity of *voluntas populi* has the effect of occluding dissent. For the champion of *concordia*, it is axiomatic that "the divergent wills of citizens" (*diversae voluntates civium*) represent a warning sign for the Republic.⁷³ Alongside his traditionally Roman emphasis on unity we surmise the influence of Plato, for whom public discord evinced an uneven grasp on necessarily universal truth. When under threat, Cicero inevitably employs the conceit of the people's unanimous will in his favor, even when circumstances clearly refute him.⁷⁴ Time and again, he insists, the only reason for disagreement is that some bloc of citizens has been bought and paid for.⁷⁵ This position becomes increasingly untenable when faced with the persistence of pro-Catilinarian sympathies following his consulship. In the wake of judicial reprisals against him, he maintains that he has the entire *populus* on his side:

> They see that the spirit and will of the Roman people have not changed. The Roman people shows what it feels in every way it can; men are unanimous in what they think, in what they will and in what they say [*nulla varietas est inter homines opinionis, nulla voluntatis nulla sermonis*]. (*Flac.* 96)⁷⁶

Nor was this merely a rhetorical *topos*: Cicero crows to Atticus in the same year that "all with one accord [*una voce*] groan of the present state of affairs, yet no one does or says a thing to better it ... [T]he will of the community is free while its courage is in chains [*civitatis voluntatem solutam, virtutem adligatam*]."⁷⁷

Did Cicero's insistence on a unified *voluntas populi* blind him to changing currents of opinion? He must surely have known that large portions of the *populus* were not with him, and yet the vote for his exile

---

⁷² I am grateful to Paul Cartledge for suggesting this point.   ⁷³ *Marcell.* 30.
⁷⁴ Cf. Ryan 2012, vol. 1, 65, on Plato's "unpolitical politics," where "the idea of legitimate but conflicting interests has no place."
⁷⁵ See *Sest.* 106: "What meeting has not been held within these years – I mean one that has not been packed with hirelings, but a real one worthy of the name – in which the unanimous agreement of the Roman people [*populi Romani consensus*] could not be clearly seen?" Cf. Lévy 2012a, 261–62.
⁷⁶ Cf. ibid.: "Are we, who tore the sword and the brand from the hands of Publius Lentulus and trusted the judgment of the ignorant crowd, afraid of the votes of the cream of our citizens and our most distinguished men?"
⁷⁷ *Att.* 1.38.1. Cf. ibid. 1.43.2: Though Clodius "flings out formidable threats of wrath to come," "a greater unanimity of will and words has never been seen [*consensionem universorum nec voluntatis nec sermonis umquam fuisse*]."

seems to catch Cicero very much off guard.⁷⁸ Suggestively, in speeches following his return, his discourse of unanimous will undergoes a subtle change. In a struggle between tax farmers and subject cities, Cicero lucidly observes that "it is no easy matter to unite the wills of those differing in material interest and in their very natures."⁷⁹ He no longer presumes the unity of public opinion but takes pains to point out, as in Plancius' election, "when not merely a small fraction, but the whole of the electorate, has shown its will."⁸⁰ This is not to say that Cicero suddenly appreciates the value of dissent. As before, where the public is concerned, disagreement is a prelude to violence; when a controversial question is put to an assembly, "first comes an uproar, and then a sort of taking of sides within a meeting."⁸¹ Cicero will not accept that *voluntas populi* can be divided, even when public opinion inevitably is.

5.2.3 The People's Will Is Fallible

Cicero's respect for the people's sovereignty does not imply his respect for their judgment. In an early case, he observes: "This is the way of the crowd; its judgments are seldom founded on truth, mostly on opinion."⁸² He admonishes Verres for diverting funds owed to Sicilian farmers, "if the people have willed that it should be paid to the farmers, *and if it is just* that it should be so paid [*sin autem et populus Romanus voluit et aequm est*]."⁸³ In his speech for Caecina (69 BCE), he posits that all laws passed in the assembly contained a clause that any proposal "contrary to law" therein would be null and void.⁸⁴ Despite the dubious historicity of this claim,⁸⁵ Cicero's contention is that *ius*, understood as a body of higher-order norms, puts substantive limits on popular will: "[I]f the people commanded [*populus iusserit*] that I was to be your slave, I would still not be."⁸⁶ The same advocate who once distinguished his *ratio* from the *voluntas* of an overwrought client⁸⁷ now raises this distinction to the constitutional plane.

---

⁷⁸ See *Att.* 1.47–49.
⁷⁹ *QFr.* 1.36 (60 or 59 BCE): Regarding the Roman tax farmers and their Greek targets, "it is indeed difficult to join together that which is opposed by material interest and almost by nature and will [*difficile est autem ea quae commodis <et> utilitate et prope natura diversa sunt voluntate coniungere*]."
⁸⁰ *Planc.* 49; cf. *Sest.* 122; *Vat.* 6.   ⁸¹ *Sest.* 77.   ⁸² *QRosc.* 29.
⁸³ *Verr.* 2.3.182 (emphasis added). On Cicero's emphasis on *aequitas* in Roman law, see Pagnotta 2007, 67–84; Schofield 2014, 120–21.
⁸⁴ *Caecin.* 95: *si quid ius non esset rogarier, eius ea lege nihilum rogatum.*
⁸⁵ Straumann 2016, 60–61.   ⁸⁶ *Caecin.* 96–98. Cf. Straumann 2016, 60–62.
⁸⁷ See discussion in Chapter 2.

At this middle stage in his career, the people's constitutional powers remain ambiguous. In the examples above, *ius* is presented as a counterweight to *voluntas populi*, or, alternatively, an enactment *contra iuris* proves that "the people" had not truly acted. Cicero's speech for Sestius (56 BCE) presents the intriguing case of the ex-consul Opimius, tried for the murder of tribune Gaius Gracchus in 120 BCE. The prosecutor argued that the Senate's "last decree" (*senatus consultum ultimum*), the putative basis for Opimius' violence, itself violated written statute.[88] In his defense, the consul Carbo asserted that Gracchus' killing was lawful (*iure*) since it was "for the public safety" (*pro salute patriae*) as required by the emergency decree.[89] Cicero concludes that the acquitted Opimius had "brilliantly earned the republic's gratitude" and that "*the Roman people itself* [*ipse populus Romanus*] rescued him from danger."[90] As Straumann points out, this suggests that in a conflict between higher-order *ius* (the norm of public safety) and written *lex* (a statute contrary to the senate's decree), it is "the people itself" who decide the issue!derived[91] The qualifier *ipse* leaves room for doubt: Cicero may simply mean that "even" the people endorsed what *ius* required, not that their verdict was decisive.[92] Adding to the complexity, in the same speech he enumerates several policies – including the secret ballot, Gracchan land reforms, and the corn dole – to illustrate how "in many ways the desire of the masses and the advantage of the people did not match the public interest [*cum multis in rebus multitudinis studium ac populi commodum ab utilitate rei publicae discrepabat*]."[93]

The people's judgment at election time is equally unreliable. Defending Plancius against a vote-buying charge, he ironically reassures the runner-up Laterensis:

> For the multitude is a stranger to deliberation, to reason, to discernment, and to patient scrutiny; and all great thinkers have held that acquiescence, but not always approval, should be accorded to acts of the people [*Non est enim*

---

[88] See *De or.* 2.132. On the much-discussed "last decree," see, e.g., Mommsen 1871, vol. 1, 690–97; vol. 3.2, 1240–51; Burckhardt 1988, 88–110; Lintott 1999, 89–93; Arena 2012, 200–20; Straumann 2016, 57–62, 88–100.
[89] See *De or.* 2.106.   [90] *Sest.* 140 (emphasis added).
[91] In the fourth Catilinarian, given several years before, Cicero observes that "the man who carried the Sempronian law himself paid the penalty to the state by the command of the people [*iussu populi*]," apparently a reference to Opimius' acquittal; *Cat.* 4.10. See Straumann 2016, 59.
[92] Straumann 2016, 59–60, notes that the "last decree" seems to have become a more "entrenched" part of constitutional *ius* after the Opimius trial, yielding the possible interpretation that "the introduction of a new constitutional device was subject to the People's imprimatur." Garsten 2006, 158, points out the similarities between Opimius' case and Cicero's with regard to the Catilinarian conspiracy.
[93] *Sest.* 103.

consilium in vulgo, non ratio, non discrimen, non diligentia: semperque sapientes ea, quae populus fecisset, ferenda, non semper laudanda dixerunt (?)].[94]

Nevertheless, Cicero concludes, "we must bear contentedly with the people's will, win it to ourselves when it is estranged, grapple it to us when we have won it, and pacify it when it is in turmoil."[95] In these passages we see Cicero at his least flattering, his snobbery and self-regard all too evident. He cannot stifle his schadenfreude for candidates who strike a *popularis* pose and still fail to win votes ("you see that the people themselves are no longer 'for the people' [*videtis igitur populum ipsum ... iam non esse popularem*]").[96] Nevertheless, the fickleness of the people's will presents an opportunity as well. To a losing candidate for praetor, Cicero affirms, "[n]othing is more fickle than the crowd, nothing harder to discover than the will of men, nothing trickier than the conduct of any campaign."[97] If the people's will were reasonable and self-evident, elite statesmen like Cicero would be out of a job.

5.2.4 The People's Will Needs an Elite to Guide It

In republican practice, the *voluntas populi* could "announce itself" in lawmaking assemblies, a venerable form of popular initiative won by struggle and negotiation.[98] Even in this context, however, the people's will is not *sui generis*. As a practical matter, assemblies needed magistrates to convene them, and it was the magistrates who decided the agenda and speakers' list.[99] For Cicero, however, the people are dependent on the ruling elite not just procedurally but metaphysically: The force of an orator's persuasion forms their will, and elected magistrates interpret and fulfill it. We saw in Chapter 2 how Cicero frames the act of persuasion as a competition of forces: Opposing orators contend with one another; the listener weighs their respective power; and the listener's *iudicium* is given motion by his will, which joins with others' to produce the *voluntas* – both the "choice" and the "goodwill" – of the community.

Once formed, the people's will must still be enacted. It is here, in the rules of political representation, where Cicero's originality shines. In his

---

[94] *Planc.* 10. [95] Ibid. 11.
[96] *Sest.* 190. See also Cicero's assertion that the theater crowd's acclamation of the abovementioned actor showed "how the whole Roman people declared their will in favor of a man who was not *popularis* [*declaratio voluntatis ab universo populo Romano in causa hominis non popularis*]"; ibid. 122.
[97] *Mur.* 36. [98] See Lintott 1999, 32–39; Connolly 2015, 26–64.
[99] Lintott 1999, 43–49; Arena 2012, 52–56; Connolly 2015, 53–54; Straumann 2016, 123.

first purely political speech, *Pro Lege Manilia*, he commends the proposal of new powers to Pompey:

> Gaius Manilius, in the first place I applaud and most heartily support this your law, your will, and your proposal [*et legem et voluntatem et sententiam*]; and in the second I exhort you, with the authority of the Roman people behind you [*auctore populo Romano*], to stand by that proposal undeterred by the violence or the threats of any man. (69)

Here, Manilius' personal *voluntas* is the object of Cicero's praise, and the people's *auctoritas* underwrites it. As his career matures, this phrasing is given a half-turn. The consul Lentulus, Cicero's great ally against Clodius, is described as "the bulwark of the Senate, the champion of your will, the promoter of the general unanimity, the restorer of my civic rights [*propugnator senatus, defensor vestrae voluntatis, patronus publici consensus, restitutor salutis meae*]."[100] Though he does not specify from whom the people's will needs "defending," we see how Cicero now portrays the people's will as safeguarded by the statesman's *auctoritas* and spliced away from the *populares* he detests.

How should a statesman weigh the claims of the *populus* against the standards of *ius*? In *De domo sua*, Cicero gives some indications of the expertise required. Against the "fickleness" (*varietas*) and "inconstancy" (*inconstantia*) of the "ignorant mob" (*imperita multitudo*) that voted to deprive him of his property, Cicero praises the college of Pontiffs, "whose high seriousness bids them shrink from inconstancy, and who are deterred from capricious changes of view by the strict and precise ordinances of religion, by the precept of history, and the by the study of approved literary record."[101] Behind the flattery of his jurors, Straumann comments, "there is probably something to his claim that the Pontiffs had expertise in a well-defined body of religious law, constitutional precedent, and antiquarian writing as well as knowledge of institutions."[102] Here in germ is the argument for the true statesman's mastery of natural law, soon to become the centerpiece of *De republica* and *De legibus*.

In *Pro Sestio*, Cicero's principles of elite representation begin to take form. The ex-consul, threatened equally by the Triumvirate and *popularis* street gangs, finds himself again as vulnerable as he was in the Verres trial fifteen

---

[100] *Mil.* 39. As consul for 57 BCE, Lentulus Spinther had proposed several measures for Cicero's recall, ultimately succeeding in August of that year; see Rawson 1975, 119–21.
[101] *Dom.* 4: ... *quos ab inconstantia gravitas, a libidinosa sententia certum et definitum ius religionum, vetustas exemplorum, auctoritas litterarum monumentorumque deterret.*
[102] Straumann 2016, 137.

years before. Fascinatingly, he employs the same three tactics of that earlier speech, each of which centers upon the people's will. He first shifts the audience's attention from his own weakness to the invisible mass of supporters behind him. He justifies his flight into exile by comparison to the *optimate* ex-consul Metellus, who had fled Rome a generation earlier. Of all senators, Metellus alone refused to swear an oath to uphold a *popularis* agrarian law, a futile act of resistance showing "greater regard for some sort of glory of his own than for the manifest welfare of the State."[103] In contrast, Cicero as consul "carried out measures for which I was not the sole author, but rather leader of the general will [*eas res gesseram, quarum non unus auctor, sed dux omnium voluntatis fuissem*]."[104] Despite setbacks and failures, Cicero draws strength from his service as champion (*dux*) of the people.[105]

Second, just as he made the Verres trial a referendum on judicial integrity, he situates *Pro Sestio* in a centuries-old partisan struggle. Rejecting the idea that this conflict is between deprived masses and entitled elite, Cicero insists that "all who are neither criminal nor vicious" – that is, all good Romans, rich and poor – are really *optimates*. With this radical idea, the play of political forces is transformed. Cicero's older notion of *concordia ordinum* – the cornerstone of his early speeches – was grounded in the equipoise of classes. Cicero's new aim is *consensus bonorum*, the harmonious alignment of all moral citizens, rich and poor.[106] The unit of this *consensus*, critically, is not the group but the individual. A new dynamic of forces is thus made possible – the *voluntas ac iudicium* of each citizen merging into a collective will that can quell violence and rout the demagogues. Under this new banner, the forces of the senate and of the people – so long in bitter conflict – finally align: "[T]hose who serve the will, interest, and opinions" of good Romans will be called "defenders of the best" (*defensores optimatium*) and "leaders of the community" (*principes civitatis*).[107] The master orator transmutes the story of Rome's partisan divide into one of hidden moral alliance.

---

[103] *Sest.* 37. Interestingly, this is the converse of his argument at *Rep.* 5.8 that a true statesman should uphold the people's *utilitas* over their *voluntas*.
[104] Ibid. 38.
[105] Cf. *Sest.* 113: Tribunes Domitius and Ancharius were given credit by the *populus* and made praetors despite not having been able to accomplish anything, on account of "the mere goodwill they showed [*tamen voluntate ipsa gratum fuisse*]"; *Mur.* 38: "How important do you think this is for winning the fame and goodwill of men [*ad famam hominum ac voluntatem*]?"
[106] An important background factor to this rhetorical strategy was the recent expansion of Roman citizenship across Italy, which had brought many thousands of "unaffiliated" voters into the Roman political scene; see generally Lepore 1954.
[107] *Sest.* 97.

Having mitigated his own weakness and redefined the stakes, Cicero puts himself center stage. Just as augurs use special skills to read the will of the gods (*voluntas deorum*),[108] Cicero claims to be master diviner of the Roman people. "The will and judgment [*iudicium ac voluntatem*] of the Roman people in public affairs," he instructs, "is most clearly expressed on three occasions: at a meeting [*contio*], at an Assembly, and at the theatrical and gladiatorial shows."[109] He takes each of these settings in turn to illustrate how silences, lamentations, and ovations at certain moments reveal the people's *voluntas*.[110] To correct the errors of his enemies and enlighten the youth, Cicero will reveal "the true and uncorrupted judgment of the whole people, and the inmost feelings of the country [*universi populi iudicium verum et incorruptum et ... intimos sensus civitatis*]."[111] Those who serve the people's will must first know how to take its measure, and "there is nothing so pliable, so delicate, so easy to break or to bend, as the will and feeling of our fellow-citizens towards us [*nihil est enim tam molle, tam tenerum, tam aut fragile aut flexibile, quam voluntas erga nos sensusque civium*]."[112] The ex-consul thus constructs a game of political divination he purports to master.

5.3 *De republica* and *De legibus*

The *Pro Sestio* is a prologue to Cicero's two seminal treatises on politics and the state. In *De republica*, he proposes a theory of popular sovereignty as trusteeship, in which the people "own" the Republic but entrust an elite to govern on their behalf. In *De legibus*, Cicero fills in the content of this arrangement with a legal code that both vaunts and circumscribes the people's power. Together, these two works propel the people's will into Western political thought. As in his orations, he insists that the *voluntas populi* derives its lawful force from reason, not the whims of the crowd or the designs of demagogues. Only the guidance of an educated and virtuous senate – whose absence Cicero laments – can, by correcting a fallible *populus*, preserve the freedom of all.

---

[108] *Dom.* 107; *Fam.* 2.234.2–12; *Leg.* 2.21. Cf. Polyb. 6.56.11; Lintott 1999, 187–90; Lévy 2020b.
[109] *Sest.* 106.
[110] Cf. *Att.* 4.356.1: Theater demonstrations are "good signs of popular accord [*bona signa consentientis multitudinis*]."
[111] *Sest.* 119–20. Cf. *Vat.* 10; *Pis.* 7, 57.   [112] *Mil.* 42.

5.3.1 De republica: *Will and Freedom*

In *De republica*, Cicero seeks to prove by philosophical argument that Rome's ancestral constitution is *optima* (1.34). Heir to Socratic tradition, Cicero embarks from first principles: What is a republic? Scipio Aemilianus, paragon and protagonist of the dialogue, offers a definition:

> Well, then, a commonwealth is the property of a people [*res publica res populi*]. But a people is not any collection of human beings brought together in any sort of way, but an assemblage of people in large numbers associated in an agreement with respect to justice and a partnership for the common good. (1.39)

Here emerge two critical claims. First, the Republic is first and finally the *res* of a *populus*. The people not only constitute the *res publica*; properly considered, they are its owners. Second, the formation of a *populus* is a very specific kind of act, not brought about by chance or force but by voluntary agreement.[113] Crucially, this is not just a pact about who will rule, but an agreement about justice itself (*iuris consensu*) and a "collaboration for the common good" (*utilitatis communione sociatus*).[114] From its first moments, the people's voluntary action is both essential and constrained: Their "free act of will" creates the polity,[115] but only to the extent that it aligns with *ius*, a body of higher norms, and *utilitas*, the wisdom of experience.

A third definitional claim follows from these first two: As the Republic's true sovereigns, the *populus* must be *liber*. The argument is made first in weaker, then in stronger form. In Book 1, Scipio asserts the prudence of freedom: Even when the wisest men rule – such as the Persian king Cyrus or the aristocrats of Massilia – these governments are not the most desirable since the former is directed "at the nod and caprice of one man [*unius nutu ac modo*]," and the latter is "like slavery for a people [*populi*

---

[113] Here, *consensus* and *concordia* are the critical terms marking agreement; 1.39–40. Scipio emphasizes that this voluntary union is one to which human beings are drawn not by weakness but by natural affinity. Schofield argues that this marks a departure from the "origin stories" of *Inv.* and *Sest.*; see Schofield 1995, 70–71. What ties all of these accounts together in my estimation is Cicero's emphasis on a voluntary choice at the community's founding.

[114] But see Schofield 2021, 67–68, who notes that the genitive *iuris* suggests that the phrase means something closer to an "agreement or consensus or a common mind *created* by justice, or characteristic of a just order in society." For my purposes, what is striking is the conceptual link Cicero makes between *voluntas* and *res*, each a venerable term from Roman legal tradition, in his theory of the commonwealth.

[115] Cf. *Inv.* 1.1–3 on the role of voluntary choice in establishing human society. In the earlier work, Cicero emphasizes the centrality of the orator in persuading his fellow proto-citizens to live by the rule of reason and not of brute force. See discussion in Chapter 3.

similitudo quaedam servitutis]" (1.43). In other words, while a state led by one or several good men might be superior *a priori*, a republic's owners will not bear to be treated as property.[116]

Scipio presents the stronger claim in Book 3: Though glorious in wealth, Syracuse was ruled by a tyrant, such that "nothing belonged to the people, and the people itself was the property of one man [*nihil enim populi et unius erat populus ipse*]" (3.43).[117] "Therefore," he concludes to Laelius, "wherever a tyrant rules, we ought not to say that we have a bad form of commonwealth, as I said yesterday, but, as logic now demonstrates, that we really have no commonwealth at all" (ibid.). Though the word *libertas* does not figure directly, the clear implication is that a republic without a *liber populus* (i.e. where the people, like slaves, are another's property) is no republic.[118]

To appreciate the originality of this claim, we must contrast Cicero's definition of a political community with those of his Greek forebears. Though arguing that the "best" or "truest" governments would be those in which reason ruled, neither Plato nor Aristotle had asserted that a badly governed *polis* ceased to be one.[119] The Stoics, on the other hand, seem to have adopted precisely this view. Schofield argues that Dio Chrysostom, writing in the 1st century CE, gives orthodox Stoic doctrine in affirming that the term *polis* "is not appropriate for any of the so-called cities which are foolish and lawless ... For just as he who does not have rationality as an attribute is not a human being, so what does not have law-abiding as a property is not a city."[120] Schofield finds no evidence that Zeno or Chrysippus had emphasized freedom (*eleutheria*) as a defining criterion of a city and in fact concludes that classical Stoics "never attempt to elaborate a concept of political freedom" at all.[121] Cicero's definition of

---

[116] He adds the pragmatic argument that monarchies have a tendency to produce tyrants; ibid. 1.65.

[117] The genitive *populi* carries the sense of "belonging to" the *populus*.

[118] Cf. Schofield 1995, 76: "[A]lthough the definition of *res publica* makes no mention of liberty, consideration of the conditions under which there can be a *res publica* leads Cicero to identify these with the conditions of political liberty, provided that *res populi* is construed in terms of the property metaphor." See also Arena 2012, 95–97, 119–20, 250; Straumann 2016, 170–71. Atkins 2013, 132, shows how Scipio's definition in *Rep.* is prefigured by Cicero's arguments for the superior force of *ius* and *utilitas* in *Sest.*

[119] See Pl. *Resp.* 4.445c–d, 8.544c–e (both superior and inferior forms are classified as cities); Arist. *Pol.* 1252a1–7, 1252b29–30, 1279a 25–39. Aristotle's description is especially neutral: The *polis* is a hylomorphic (matter-form) compound consisting of a particular body of citizens in a given territory (material cause) and a constitution (formal cause). The constitution itself is fashioned by the lawgiver and is governed by politicians, who are like craftsmen (efficient cause), and the constitution gives the aim of the *polis* (final cause, 1289a17–18). Schofield 1995, 65, notes a lack of the "general problem of legitimacy for the commonwealth" in Aristotle.

[120] Dio Chrys. *Or.* 20; Schofield 1991, 60–62. [121] Ibid. 54.

res publica thus takes up Plato's doctrine of rational rule, adds the Stoic exclusion of "so-called cities," and puts both in service of Rome's highest ideal: *libertas*.[122]

Notwithstanding his definitional claim for popular liberty, Cicero holds equally tenaciously to another tradition: distinctions of rank. The democracy of Athens "could not maintain its fair renown" because "it had no definite distinctions in rank [*distinctos dignitatis gradus non habebant*]" (1.43). It is axiomatic for Cicero that Rome's hierarchies are a positive good and that attempts to equalize these differences are unnatural and unwise.[123] When all political affairs are managed *per populum*, "the resulting equality itself is inequitable" (ibid.). In terms that recall Plato's preference for geometric over arithmetic equality, Cicero affirms that in times of difficulty, "citizens should be weighed, not counted" (6.1).[124]

Cicero's challenge, to which most of the extant *De republica* is dedicated, is thus to defend popular liberty and sovereignty while simultaneously rejecting democracy. *Voluntas populi* is the key that unlocks this puzzle.

His first move is to demonstrate that *libertas*, while definitional of a republic, is not an unqualified good. History has proven that too much liberty leads to *licentia*, the despotism of the mob. He cites Plato's warning that when the throats of a *populus* "become dry with the thirst for liberty" and swallow a draught that "instead of being moderately tempered, is too strong for them," then even wise magistrates will be tarred as tyrants (1.65–66). The denial of every natural distinction transforms liberty into its opposite: "Just as an excess of power in the hands of the aristocrats [*principes*] results in the overthrow of an aristocracy, so liberty itself reduces a people who possess it in too great degree to servitude" (1.68).[125] As such,

---

[122] Cf. Schofield 1995, 64 (Cicero's definition of *res publica* operates as the "criterion of legitimacy"); ibid. 74 (the requirement that the *res populi* be "conducted well and justly" is "no doubt an authentically Ciceronian formulation").

[123] See Arena 2012, 96–98; Straumann 2016, 174–78; Atkins 2018b, 53–54; Schofield 2021, 45–46, 74.

[124] See Pl. *Leg.* 757c: Of the two types of equality, the "better and higher kind" is the one "which gives to the greater more, and to the inferior less and in proportion to the nature of each; and above all, greater honor always to the greater virtue, and to the less less; and to either in proportion to their respective measure of virtue and education." Cf. Rawson 1975, 151: "To [Cicero], as to Plato, justice is involved in the preservation of proper ranks and hierarchies, though there is a sympathetic insistence on the equality of all citizens before the law." Arena posits a Pythagorean influence; Arena 2016, [4–5]; cf. Pagnotta 2007, 108–19.

[125] Cicero's comparison of regime change to an unpredictable "ball game" marks another deliberate departure from Polybius, whose account of *anacyclosis* is schematic and invariant; see *Rep.* 1.65–70; Polyb. 6.5.4–6.9.14.

even a state nominally administered by the whole *populus* can forfeit its claim to be a republic; once it becomes a despotic multitude "inflict[ing] punishment on whomever it will," it is no partnership in justice and thus no *populus* but a mob.[126] "There can be nothing more horrible," Scipio poignantly concludes, "than that monster which falsely assumes the name and appearance of a people."[127]

His second move is to show that the people can be *liber* without participating equally in government.[128] Here, Cicero exploits a crucial ambiguity in the term *populus*. In Scipio's definition at 1.39, the *populus* that forms the state by common agreement is clearly *omnes*, the entire civic body.[129] Constitution by a voluntary act and the criteria of *ius* and *utilitas* are universal, relating to all citizens. Nevertheless, when he takes up the Greek framework of the three forms – how to apportion power among one, few, and many – the *populus* is no longer the entire citizen body but rather the *multitudo*, the masses.[130]

These two senses of "the people" as *omnes* and *multitudo* help Cicero reconcile the norm of universal *libertas* with elite *potestas* (1.69).[131] When considered as the whole community, the *populus* shares in the universal guarantee of *libertas* for all. But only constrained powers are given to the *populus* as *multitudo*, being but one actor in a tripartite scheme alongside magistrates and senate.[132] In the mixed constitution Scipio recommends, "the magistrates have enough power [*potestas*], the counsels of the eminent

---

[126] Cf. Schofield 1995, 72; Schofield 2021, 37.

[127] *Rep.* 3.45: *hoc etiam taetrior, quia nihil ista, quae populi speciem et nomen imitatur, immanius belua est.*

[128] In *Rep.* the term *consilium* denotes the choice of policy as distinct from the election of leaders; cf. 1.41: Once formed, a republic must be ruled by some deliberative body (*consilio quodam regenda est*), which can either be a single man, certain selected citizens, or the people as a whole (*multitudini atque omnibus*).

[129] Cf. *Verr.* 1.10: Verres has been condemned by "the will and judgment of all" (*omnium voluntate iudicioque*); *Sest.* 38: "I carried out measures for which I was not the sole author, but rather the leader of the general will [*eas res gesseram, quarum non unus auctor, sed dux omnium voluntatis fuissem*]."

[130] See *Rep.* 1.42. Cf. 1.69: Certain matters should be left "to the judgment and will of the masses [*esse quasdam res servatas iudicio voluntatique multitudinis*]." On Cicero's reworking of the Greek mixed constitution tradition, see Powell 2012, 23–26; Schofield 2021, 41–42. Ryan 2012, vol. 1, 141–42, observes that whereas Polybius had asserted the "negative virtue" of each element's power to check the others, Cicero makes the first positive case for combining the singular virtues of each.

[131] I am grateful to Malcolm Schofield for guiding me to this point.

[132] Cf. *De or.* 1.31–32: "What achievement so mighty and glorious as that the impulses of the people, the consciences of the judges, the austerity of the Senate, should suffer transformation through the eloquence of one man [*Quid est enim ... tam potens, tamque magnificum, quam populi motus, iudicium religiones, Senatus gravitatem, unius oratione converti*]?"

citizens have enough influence [*auctoritas*], and the people enough liberty [*libertas*]" (2.57). His *optimus status rei publicae* is thus both universal and aristocratic, offering "in a high degree a sort of equality, which is a thing free men can hardly do without," but also the stability in which "every citizen is firmly established in his own station."[133] With this fertile ambiguity, Cicero thus integrates two sacred traditions – the *liber populus* and *gradus dignitatis* – whose uneasy coexistence was a through line of Roman history.[134] As we will see later in this chapter, the quintessential expression of the people's will is the free choice of leaders wiser than themselves.

Is Scipio's *libertas populi* merely a façade? On the one hand, Scipio asserts that the people's *libertas* must connote actual *potestas*, not merely the "flavor" thereof (2.50).[135] On the other hand, his is clearly a balance in which the senate rules. In the Republic's golden age, "the government was so administered by the senate that, though the people were free, few political acts were performed by them, practically everything being done by the authority of the senate."[136] By creating a centuriate assembly with greater power for wealthy citizens, Servius Tullius ensured that the majority "would neither be deprived of the suffrage, for that would be tyrannical, nor be given too much power, for that would be dangerous" (2.39–40).[137] And though skeptical of the innovations introduced by Publicola, Scipio concludes that "it was a man of no ordinary talents who, by granting the people a moderate amount of liberty, the more easily maintained the power of the leaders of the State" (2.55).[138] Though he might have protested the point, popular liberty is clearly "moderated" by Cicero in

---

[133] *Rep.* 1.69: *[H]aec constitutio primum habet aequabilitatem quandam magnam, qua carere diutius vix possunt liberi, deinde firmitudinem ... [N]on est enim causa conversionis, ubi in suo quisque est gradu firmiter collocatus ...*

[134] See Wirszubski 1950, 17: "The crucial problem of *libertas* at Rome was how to make the fitting adjustment between the equality of the fundamental rights of all and the supremacy of some." See also Arena 2012, 5–10, 251–52; Connolly 2015, 26–64; Atkins 2018a, 769–70; Atkins 2018b, 49–54; Schofield 2021, 33–34.

[135] Scipio's argument for "real *potestas*" is framed as a prudential concession rather than a respect for the judgment of common citizens. Cf. *Rep.* 4.8: "[I]t is not easy to resist the people in their might if you give them no legal rights or only a few."

[136] Ibid. 2.56: *Tenuit igitur hoc in statu senatus rem publicam temporibus illis, ut in populo libero pauca per populum, pleraque senatus auctoritate ... gererentur.*

[137] This plan also follows Cicero's Platonic preference for geometrical over arithmetic equality. See *Rep.* 2.39: It "put into effect the principle which ought always to be adhered to in the commonwealth, that the greatest number should not have the greatest power." Cf. Pl. *Leg.* 757c.

[138] Among the popular innovations Cicero notes are the lowering of the rods before the people, which he criticizes, and the right of *provocatio* or appeal for capital crimes, which he says had already been "previously recognized"; *Rep.* 2.53–54.

that it is shorn of real *potestas*.[139] Conversely, the senate's *potestas* does not abridge the *libertas populi* because, as citizens, senators are part of the "*populus* as *omnes*." There can be no *dominatio* if, in the broadest sense, the *populus Romanus* rules itself.

Thus, we come to understand why *res publica res populi* is the crux of Cicero's argument. Polybius had argued that Rome's success depended on competitive tension among the powers of one, few, and many.[140] Conversely, though Cicero recognizes that the Republic's divisions are severe – the analogy of "two suns" and "two peoples" is the treatise's starting point (1.31) – he does not accept that the best state is a kind of ceasefire. Rather than treat the few and the many as competing claimants for power, he reimagines their relationship. Drawing upon doctrines of Roman civil law, Cicero thus offers his two strikingly original claims: The people are owners of the Republic; and "leading citizens," far from usurping the people's *potestas*, wield it by their consent and on their behalf.[141]

In the extant record, this notion of trusteeship, though well established in *ius civile*, had never before been applied to constitutional theory.[142] In a recent work, Remer argues that the standard view of representation as a strictly modern concept – often traced to Pitkin's seminal work of 1967 – overlooks the contribution made by Cicero.[143] Remer finds four terms that

---

[139] Intriguingly, Cicero puts a blistering attack on this position in the mouth of his own protagonist. Pure aristocracies (*dominatio optimatium*) are rejected on the grounds that the *multitudo* has no real *potestas* nor role in *consilium communi*, and thus no *libertas*; *Rep*. 1.43. He singles out for criticism states where the people are ostensibly free (*in quibus verbo sunt liberi*) and have electoral and ratifying powers but no practical share in *imperium, consilium*, or in the courts – as we will see later in this chapter, almost exactly the system recommended in *De legibus*! The crucial difference is that in the state Scipio criticizes at *Rep*. 1.47, "real" power is given according to birth or wealth (*familiarum vetustatibus aut pecuniis*), where the code in *Leg*. establishes an aristocracy of virtue and merit. But see Arena 2016, [1], who argues that *Leg*. represents a "significant strengthening" of Cicero's aristocratic bias.

[140] See Polyb. 6.18.6–8, 6.15.1–2, 6.18.2–3. On Cicero's advances upon Polybian theory, see Harries 2009, 58; Ryan 2012, vol. 1, 139. Schofield 1995, 81, notes Polybius' use of the "entrustment" of power to nobles by the people, but concludes that "the legal connotations of guardianship are exploited only by Cicero."

[141] Concluding that these claims go well beyond Platonic or Aristotelian theories about ruling in the common interest, Schofield 1995, 82, observes: "What makes the difference is the conceptual framework of Roman law, for it is Roman law which enables questions to be formulated about the rights a free people has to own, lend, transfer, or place in trust powers conceived on the model of property."

[142] Ibid. 79–81. Polybius observes that the senate is obliged "to pay attention to the commons in public affairs and respect the wishes of the people [*prosekhin tois pollois kai stokhazesthai tou dēmou*]," but his terms suggest a relationship of collaboration and deference, not trusteeship; Polyb. 6.16.1.

[143] See Pitkin 1967; Remer 2017, ch. 5.

recur in Cicero's descriptions of the ideal orator-statesman: *rector*, *princeps*, *procurator*, and *tutor*. The former two of these terms emphasize the idea of outstanding leadership (*rector* and *princeps*) and the latter two emphasize the idea of guardianship or action on another's behalf (*procurator* and *tutor*).[144] The term *procurator* is particularly suggestive: In Roman law it means "representative of interests," especially to manage property, and in contrast with the related term *cognitor*, the represented party does not forfeit his legal power.[145] Thus, Remer concludes, "by using the *procurator* as the metaphor for the orator-statesman, Cicero suggests that like the *dominus*, who has power to act, the people – the true master of the Roman orator – play a significant role independent of their representative."[146] As we will see later in this chapter, though, Cicero is careful to distinguish the crowd's ability to judge oratorical excellence from its ability to decide matters of state.

Trusteeship is Cicero's remedy for a divided society. Just as Laelius playfully posits joint ownership of the sky to solve the problem of "two suns" (1.20), Scipio uses a legal analogy to show the interdependence of Rome's commoners and its elite:

> But if a free people [*liber populus*] chooses the men to whom it is to entrust its fortunes, and, since it desires its own safety, chooses the best men, then certainly the safety of the State depends on the wisdom of its best men. (1.51)[147]

Though ostensibly part of Scipio's defense of "pure" aristocracy, later set aside in favor of the mixed constitution, the sole critique that emerges to this arrangement is that the common people, confusing fame and wealth for virtue, choose the wrong men for the job.[148] The risk lies not in the soundness of trusteeship, therefore, but in the quality of the trustees.

To whom should the people entrust their property? Like Thrasymachus in Plato's *Republic*, Philus asserts that political justice is at best a *pactio*

---

[144] Ibid. 142–44.
[145] Ibid. 144–46 (citing Zetzel 1995, 205). For Cicero's use of *procurator*, see *De or.* 1.215, 1.249, 3.131; *Rep.* 1.35, 2.51; *Leg.* 2.34, 2.66, 3.18; *Off.* 1.85, 2.75.
[146] Remer 2017, 146. Whereas Pitkin 1967, 131, had argued that the Roman view of representation "does not suggest an independent role for the 'someone else' who is taken care of or whose interests are acted for," Remer contends that Cicero's *procurator* model satisfies this requirement.
[147] Cf. *Sest.* 137.
[148] Ibid. He makes the point more explicitly much later in *De officiis*: "For the administration of the government, like the office of a trustee, must be conducted for the benefit of those entrusted to one's care, not of those to whom it is entrusted [*Ut enim tutela, sic procuratio rei publicae ad eorum utilitatem, qui commissi sunt, non ad eorum, quibus commissa est, gerenda est*]"; *Off.* 1.85. Cf. ibid. 1.124.

between *populus et potentes*, the stronger ruling the weaker (3.23).[149] In his refutation, Scipio reminds his friend that the Republic is a partnership for justice and an agreement for the common good (*utilitas communis*). But because *ius* and *utilitas* are often overlooked by the multitude, *consilium* must lie with those few who can master their principles.[150] Expert knowledge of *ius*, in turn, is by definition distinct from common opinion, coming "by virtue of the decision, not of the Roman People, but of the wise, not by any obligation of the civil law, but by the common law of Nature."[151] As we have seen earlier in this chapter, Cicero is building on an *optimate* tradition regarding the higher-order authority of *ius* and the expertise required to apprehend it. What may be special in Cicero's claim is the argument that Roman tradition is *already* grounded in the natural law explicated by the Stoics.[152] The special knowledge of statesmen – illustrated by the college of Pontiffs – is thus not only distinct from but often contrary to what the *populus* desires: "Where does your literature as well praise that ruler of his native land who consults the interests of his people more than their will [*qui populi utilitati magis consulat quam voluntati*]?" (5.8).[153] The state's trustees are not parrots of public opinion.[154] And yet, he concludes, their expertise is the only guarantee that the *populus* remains a *populus* at all.[155]

We see, finally, why *voluntas populi* is the glue of Scipio's mixed constitution. He states that "there ought to be a supreme and royal

---

[149] Philus adds, in dialectic opposition to Scipio's earlier argument, that "not nature or will, but weakness, is the mother of justice [*iustitiae non natura nec voluntas, sed inbecillitas mater est*]"; *Rep.* 3.23.

[150] In the prologue, Cicero declares that he himself has endured the "severest storms" for the sake of *utilitas patriae*; ibid. 1.8.

[151] Ibid. 1.27: . . . *non Quiritium sed sapientium iure . . . nec civili nexo . . . sed communi lege naturae.* Cf. ibid. 5.5, where Scipio describes the educational regime required of a statesman (e.g. in history and civil law).

[152] Straumann 2016, 132, 180. Arena 2011, 317, argues that Stoicism may have provided a "philosophical substrate" to *optimate* arguments by Catulus and Philippus against Lepidus and Pompey in 78/77 and 67/66 BCE.

[153] Cf. *De or.* 3.138, Pericles spoke *contra voluntatem* of the Athenians but was popular because of this; *Sest.* 103, the desires of the masses often differed from *utilitas rei publicae*; *Sull.* 25, Cicero's opponents wrongly think him tyrannical for "consult[ing] the people's interests more than their will [*populi utilitati magis consulere quam voluntati*]."

[154] See Remer 2017, 138–40, 151, on the trustee/delegate distinction. Remer concludes that Cicero's orator-statesman is "double-sided" (i.e. both trustee and delegate). I disagree, for reasons discussed infra.

[155] Lévy 2012a, 264–65, concludes that Cicero incorporates the people's will into the elite pursuit of glory: "The *optimates* who commit to the struggle for *otium cum dignitate* and who harness the *voluntas populi* to achieve it, do this in the name of the social *oikeiōsis* Cicero revisits, but also with the hope of reward, since they are compensated by honors and glory, themes Cicero will theorize in the *De officiis* and *De gloria*."

element in the state, some power also ought to be granted to the leading citizens, and certain matters should be left to the judgment and will of the many [*esse quasdam res servatas iudicio voluntatique multitudinis*]" (1.69). This last phrase – *iudicio voluntatique multitudinis* – occupies the same term of the equation as *libertas populi* at 2.57. In other words, *voluntas populi* links together two central claims of Cicero's treatise: It is both the signifier of the people's freedom and their means to choose trustees to rule in their name. The quality of the people's will is seen not in its judgments about *ius* or *utilitas* – Cicero thinks it can apprehend neither – but rather in its selection of statesmen skilled in both. The *populus* can choose because it is free, and its choice elevates those who best preserve this freedom. The will of the people actualizes the Republic.

Indeed, at every stage of Scipio's history he ties the legitimacy of government to the people's consent. When power is in the hands of a dictator, it is because "our people have willed that all power should be granted to one man [*noster populus ... omne imperium nostri penes singulos esse voluerunt*]" (1.63). Even Rome's early kings differed from other monarchs in that the *novus populus* required them to be "freely chosen" (*deligendum*) according to merit (2.24).[156] In Cicero's retelling, therefore, the people's *potestas* has *always* lain not in the control of public affairs but in the elevation of others to rule.[157] Moreover, their will gives legitimacy not just to individual leaders but to the system as a whole. The predominance of the *principes* in the early Republic was justified because it was "conceded by the people" (*cedente populo*, 2.56); the senate held *summa auctoritas* "with the compliance and consent of the people [*populo patiente atque parente*]" (2.61).[158] Senatorial rule is thus triply justified: (1) on the grounds of reason – only those with access to *ius* and *utilitas* can preserve

---

[156] Cf. ibid. 2.31–32: "Tullius did not venture to assume even the insignia of royalty without the permission of the people"; 2.35: L. Tarquinius is chosen "by a unanimous vote" (*cunctis populi suffragiis*). Cicero finesses the question about whether or not the *populus* under Rome's kings was *liber*; ibid. 2.43–46. Cf. Schofield 2021, 46–47.

[157] Crucially, Cicero insists that the people's *voluntas* is manifest equally in passive consent as in active choice. When Servius Tullius takes power in a palace coup, Scipio affirms that his rule was "not by an order but rather by the will and acceptance of the citizens [*non iussu sed voluntate atque concessu civium*]"; ibid. 2.38, cf. 1.50. Scipio laments that the people's *voluntas* for Rome's kings would have lasted were it not for the nefarious Tarquin; ibid. 1.64. Schofield 1995, 80, notes that in Cicero's history of early Rome, "the *populus liber* is treated simply as one of the key elements in the republican system, which makes an indispensable input, albeit mostly passive, in all major developments."

[158] Cf. *Vat.* 36, regarding the senate's administration of provinces and the treasury: "[T]hese prerogatives the Roman People has never desired for itself, nor has it ever attempted to transfer to itself the control of high policy of state [*qui numquam ad se summi consilii gubernationem transferre conatus est*]."

the state; (2) by historical experience – only the right mixture of the three forms can forestall disaster; and (3) by consent of the people themselves, the "owners" of the Republic. An elected elite, serving *voluntate populi*, allows the people to remain sovereign, *liber*, and secure.

When this balance slips, *voluntas* once again guides a statesman's task. When Laelius asks Scipio which of the three forms of government is best, Scipio responds that "every State is such as its ruler's character and will make it [*et talis est quaeque res publica, qualis eius aut natura aut voluntas qui illam regit*]" (1.47). The measurability of *voluntas* – its variability in kind (*qualis*), in strength, and over time – makes it the ideal barometer of constitutional health. Intriguingly, Cicero anticipates the contemporary study of collective intelligence in his assertion that Rome's greatness resulted not from a semidivine founder but the accumulation of many acts of genius (*non unius esset ingenio, sed multorum*) (2.2).[159] As such, a *res publica* mitigates the risk shared by all autocracies: "The fortune of any people is therefore a fragile thing, as I have explained already, when it depends on the will or the character of one man [*voluntate vel moribus unius*]" (2.50). Nevertheless, the force of rational desire does not inevitably overcome the force of brutality. Cicero prophesies ruin when the nature of Roman rule changes "from one of justice to one of force" (*ad vim a iure traduxerit*) such that those subjects and allies "who up to the present have obeyed us by *voluntas* are held faithful by fear alone [*adhuc voluntate nobis oboediunt, terrore teneantur*]" (3.41). In the changeability of will lies both the promise and the peril of Cicero's republic. Only a statesman's reason and an orator's skill can guide the people to the right choice: the choice to let better men rule.

5.3.2 De legibus: *The Walls around Will*

In Book 2 of *De republica*, Scipio describes the balance of power in the early years of the Republic in which, "though the people were free, few political acts were performed by them, practically everything being done

---

[159] For an overview of the emerging field of collective intelligence (CI), see, e.g., Surowiecki 2004 (on conditions that produce a "wisdom of crowds"); Woolley et al. 2005 (on CI in small groups); Ober 2008 (on CI principles in Athenian democracy); Landemore 2013 (on CI and democratic theory); Malone and Bernstein 2015 (on computer-assisted CI); Noveck 2015 (on CI in public governance); Servan-Schreiber 2018 (on CI and prediction science); Mulgan 2018 (general overview). The author is a co-founder of the School of Collective Intelligence at the Université Mohammed VI Polytechnique in Morocco.

5.3 De republica *and* De legibus

by the authority of the senate."[160] Though never published and extant only in fragments, *De legibus* gives a blueprint for this balance.[161]

Prior to *De legibus*, Cicero does not openly oppose the people's legislative power *per se*. In fact, he appears to acknowledge that the *populus* regularly enacts its will in legislation, as when a certain land bill is amended *contionis voluntate*.[162] In *De legibus*, however, Cicero makes popular legislation an anathema. The supreme authority of Nature's law and its noncoincidence with public opinion are key points of continuity between the two treatises and represent a major departure from the attitude he had once taken toward the Stoics.[163] "True law is right reason in agreement with Nature," Scipio states in *De republica*, "and we cannot be freed from its obligations by senate or people."[164] Similarly, Cicero's point of departure in *De legibus* is the character Marcus'[165] lament that while all men are equally capable of apprehending justice, the majority simply do not. "Nay, if bad habits and false beliefs did not twist the weaker minds [*inbecillitatem animorum*] and turn them in whatever direction they are inclined, no one would be so like his own self as all men would be like all others."[166]

Because of the overwhelming prevalence of false belief, Cicero must distinguish "so-called" law, in which the *populus* "give[s] the name of law to that which in written form decrees whatever it wills [*quae scripta sancit, quod vult*]," from true law, which is "the highest reason, implanted in Nature, which commands what ought to be done and forbids the opposite" (1.18). The bravery of Cocles on the bridge and the wickedness of Tarquin's rape illustrate how the moral content of an action is prior to and independent of the rules of men (2.10). A *lex* that violates Nature's law is thus no law at all, even if "the people had accepted it" (*populus acceperit*, 2.13); stronger still, if true law is absent from a state, it must "for that

---

[160] *Rep.* 2.56.
[161] On the complementary relation of *Leg.* to *Rep.*, see generally Ferrary 1995, 17–39; Dyck 2004; Arena 2016. For a detailed discussion of the dating of *Leg.*, see Schmidt 1969, 41–69.
[162] *Att.* 1.19.4 (60 BCE). See *Inv.* 2.133–34 (91–88 BCE), discussed in Chapter 2; *Flac.* 15–16 (59 BCE), asserting that the ancestral tradition of assemblies is "now slipping out of our hands"; *Att.* 2.143.1 (49 BCE), Cicero's optimism based on the "will" of a certain public meeting (*voluntas contionis*). Cf. Schofield 2015, 116.
[163] Compare the youthful Cicero's dismissal of natural law at *Inv.* 2.67 as not relevant to the civil law and "removed from the perceptions of the crowd." Cf. Harries 2009, 55–56.
[164] *Rep.* 2.33.
[165] In contrast to *Rep.*, Cicero takes the lead role in this dialogue, joined by Quintus and Atticus.
[166] *Leg.* 1.29. Compare Scipio's rhetorical question at *Rep.* 1.29: "[W]ho believes that, though others may be called men, only those are men who are perfected in the arts appropriate to humanity [*cui persuasum sit appellari ceteros homines, esse solos eos, qui essent politi propriis humanitatis artibus*]?"

reason be considered no State at all" (2.12). Under this standard, Marcus asserts, certain *popularis* laws distributing land and grain to the *populus* were "not really laws [*leges nullas*]" – adding for safety, "especially as the Senate repealed them in one sentence and in a single moment" (2.14).[167] Though all manmade law is potentially discrepant from *ius naturae*, popular legislation is clearly the greater threat – a threat only an enlightened senate can check.[168]

The constitution Cicero proposes in Book 3 of *De republica* reflects this dim view of the people enacting its own will. While the character Marcus insists on preserving all institutions of the *maiores*, they must be reshaped to align with *recta ratio*.[169] Thus, while his code does not abolish the *contiones* or tribunes, their activities are placed under severe constraints. The tribunes – men theoretically of his own class – shall assist the state by tempering the people, since those who preside at assemblies "regulate not only the mind and will [*mentem ac voluntates*], but almost the facial expressions, of those in attendance" (3.40).[170] In the event that a tribune fails in this duty, augurs will have firmer authority to cancel an assembly (2.21), and an augur who casts his veto "shall be deemed a citizen of distinguished service."[171]

To meet the high standards of Nature's law, Cicero strengthens the primacy of the senate. Its *consulta*, formerly advisory opinions for magistrates of a single year, shall now be binding (*eius decreta rata sunto*, 3.10)

---

[167] Cf. ibid. 1.43–44: "But if the principles of Justice were founded on the decrees of peoples [*quodsi populorum iussis*] ... then Justice would sanction robbery and adultery and forgery of wills, in case these acts were approved by the votes or decrees of the populace [*multitudinis probarentur*]." We might also see here a response to the Clodian *popularis* legislation of the 50s BCE, including the *privilegium* targeting Cicero's home; see Rawson 1975, 116.

[168] Harries 2009, 58, argues that Cicero's stress on the universalism of *ius naturae* is part of what I call his conservative *popularis* stance: "[B]ecause the *ius naturae* was universal, it had the legitimacy of being based on the 'consensus' of everyone. In other words, it was really *popularis*, even though the real *populus* could not be expected to appreciate it." As such, "Cicero could claim ... that he, and his system of legislation, were the real representatives of the popular will."

[169] Cf. Powell 2001, 23–24, 32–35. On Cicero's constitutional innovations, see Keyes 1921, 309–23; Paulson 2014, 307–40.

[170] Cf. *De or.* 2.167. Under the code in *Leg.*, presiding officers are held personally responsible for any violence at a *contio*; *Leg.* 3.23–24. By the late 50s BCE, *contiones* had grown increasingly violent; see Crook 1967, 265. As in his arguments for popular liberty in *Rep.*, Cicero's defense of tribunes here takes a resignedly prudential tone; cf. 3.25: They are retained to help ensure "the senatorial order is not subject to envy, and the common people make no desperate struggles for their rights."

[171] Ibid. 3.11; 3.42–43. Cf. ibid. 3.27: The gods are called to put down such "unlawful assertions by the people" (*populi impetum iniustum*) through auspices; *Sest.* 33–34, against Clodius' attempt to abridge the Aelian and Fufian laws. On the augurs' power as a *de facto* aristocratic veto, see Polyb. 6.56.11; Lintott 1999, 187–90.

5.3 De republica *and* De legibus

and carry the force of *lex*.[172] Conversely, in what Marcus calls "certainly a populist measure" (*populare sane*), Cicero prescribes "that no one shall enter that exalted order except by popular election, the censors being deprived of the right of free choice" (3.27). And to help its *consulta* adhere to the standard of true law, each senator "shall be conversant with public affairs," "shall be free from dishonor, and ... be a model for the rest of the citizens" (3.10–11).[173] Again, rather than argue that power be shifted from the (still sovereign) people,[174] Cicero insists that his arrangement benefits all sides:

> For the fact is that if the Senate is recognized as the leader of public policy, and all the other orders defend its decrees, and are willing to allow the highest order to conduct the government by its wisdom, then this legal compromise [*ex temperatione iuris*], by which power is granted to the people and authority to the Senate [*cum potestas in populo, auctoritas in senatu sit*], will make possible the maintenance of that balanced and harmonious constitution I have described. (3.28)

We note that the *potestas* granted to the people is expressly not to make its own *leges*, but rather to elect honest men to a revitalized senate. Further, the supremacy of natural law leads Cicero to make certain guarantees unalterable – even, presumably, by the senate itself.[175] Among these are a citizen's right to appeal (*provocatio*, 3.6), the right to be heard in assemblies (*privatis magistratibusve audiendis*, 3.43), and the ban on *privilegia* – laws that single out one man for punishment (3.44). These protections of individuals from the will of a majority – even when enacted through proper legislative procedures – makes *De legibus* an essential, if barely recognized, precursor to contemporary human rights charters and bills of rights.[176]

---

[172] See Dyck 2004, 15. It is unclear whether under Cicero's constitution the popular assemblies would retain the right to veto a senatorial decree, even if a *contio* was no longer required to ratify it; see Lintott 1999, 63–64, 86–88.

[173] Cicero is more clear-eyed about the problem of senatorial virtue than this "rule" would suggest. When Atticus jests at *Leg.* 3.29 that the task of punishing all of the current senate's misdeeds "would wear out all the judges as well as the censors," Marcus reassures him, "for we are not talking about the present Senate or of the men of today [*qui nunc sunt*], but about those to come [*de futuris*]; that is, in case any of them ever are willing to obey these laws of mine."

[174] But cf. *Rep.* 2.56: At the moment of ideal balance in the early Republic, Scipio observes, "another principle that was most important to the retention of the power by the aristocracy was also strictly maintained, namely, that no act of a popular assembly should be valid unless ratified by the Fathers [i.e. the senate]."

[175] Despite his faith in the institution as a whole, Cicero remains lucid about his fellow senators' lapses of reason; cf. *Leg.* 3.29–32; *Fam.* 1.18.4.

[176] This thesis is powerfully elaborated by Straumann 2016, 18, 25, 43–47, 178–84. While concurring with Straumann on his main points, I lean toward the position of Atkins and Asmis

Where, then, is the people's *potestas*? Like *De republica*, *De legibus* recognizes only one expression of popular will: a controlled franchise. In Cicero's code, the electoral process gains new clarity. All senators must have served in magistracies elected by the people (3.27), sanctions against bribery are reinforced (3.46), and the position of aedile is officially made the first step toward higher office (3.7).[177] The *populus* is thus expected to bestow office on candidates of sufficient intellect and virtue, who thereafter join the senate for life. Here, the ex-consul arrives at a quandary. He has made popular election a requirement to join the sole body capable of upholding natural law. But if the electors are brimming with false beliefs, how will they choose the best men to rule?

Part of Cicero's solution is a novel, "semi-secret" ballot law.[178] "When elective, judicial, and legislative acts of the people are performed by vote," he decrees, "the voting shall not be concealed from citizens of high rank, and shall be free to the common people [*plebi libera sunto*]" (3.10). On the surface, the provision is so obscure that the character Atticus claims to have "no clear idea of its meaning" (3.33). The character Marcus then launches into the longest, most intricate defense given to any of his provisions.[179] At issue is the secret ballot, introduced by previous generations to curtail rampant bribery. While perhaps well-intentioned, this reform has instead, complains Quintus, "deprived the aristocracy of all its influence [*omnem auctoritatem optimatium*] ... [and was] never desired by the people when they were free [*populus liber numquam desideravit*]" (3.34). Marcus defends his new proposal by citing the balance struck between *libertas* and *auctoritas* in *De republica*:

> [L]et me explain – though Scipio has given a sufficient defense of these ideas in my former work – that I am granting this freedom to the people in such a way as to ensure that the aristocracy shall have great influence and the opportunity to use it. (3.38)

He insists that the provision will leave the people's freedom intact. Not only will they keep their ballots "as a safeguard of their liberty," by showing them voluntarily at a senator's request, they will gain the

---

that the code Cicero proposes in *De legibus* was intended to approximate or partake in natural law rather than be identical to it. The distinction is not critical to my argument here. See Asmis 2008, 2, 31; Atkins 2013, 199–223; Straumann 2016, 178–80.

[177] This provision would clarify some muddiness in the *cursus honorum*; see Lintott 1999, 228–29.
[178] The phrase is mine, not Cicero's.
[179] *Leg.* 3.33–40. The only passage of similar length is the debate between Quintus and Marcus at 3.19–27 on the latter's decision to preserve the tribunate.

5.3 De republica and De legibus

additional liberty of "honorably winning the favor of the aristocracy"[180] (3.39). With these rights secured, he concludes, "their will is managed by our authority and favor [*hoc retento reliqua voluntas auctoritati aut gratiae traditur*]" (ibid.). The *voluntas populi* is controlled, and the *populus* itself remains free.

Can a *libertas* so constrained still be *liber*? Neal Wood argues no: Cicero's constitution in *De legibus* is "above all else an ingenious mechanism to maintain the dominance of the large noble landholders in an age of mounting popular demand for more liberty and a greater role in government."[181] To Wood's point, though the character Marcus had earlier insisted that "real liberty, not a pretense of it, be given to the common people" (3.25), he concludes regarding the ballot, "our law grants the *appearance* of liberty (*libertatis species*), preserves the influence of the aristocracy, and removes the causes of dispute between the classes" (3.39, emphasis added).[182] Cicero once again uses the people's *voluntas* to evince their *libertas*, but we are right to wonder if this freedom is an eloquent sham.[183]

Bizarre as this proposal may be, it may be unfair to convict him of mere cynicism. As Scipio's pro-democracy argument shows, Cicero was not insensitive to the (prescient) critique that the people could retain the forms of liberty but lose its substance.[184] Nevertheless, his commitment to reason – as essential as liberty in his republic – leads him to imagine a different kind of relation between elector and elite. An illuminating point of comparison lies in Book 6 of Plato's *Laws*, a work Cicero had studied.[185] Concerning the magistrates for the ideal state of Magnesia, "the Athenian" advises that

---

[180] Cf. *Sest.* 103, regarding L. Cassius's law for the secret ballot: "The people thought that their liberty was at stake. The leaders of the state held a different opinion; in a matter that concerned the interests of the *optimates*, they dreaded the impetuosity of the masses and the license afforded by the ballot."

[181] Wood 1988, 171. Cf. Schofield 2021, 46.

[182] While "appearance" is the most probable sense of *species* here, it is interesting to note that Cicero later uses the same word to translates Plato's ἰδέα, the constant and eternal nature of an object that only disembodied souls can apprehend; see *Tusc.* 1.57–58. Thus, the "idea of liberty" may be an alternative and intriguingly different interpretation of his phrase.

[183] Behind Cicero's plea for interdependence one also senses an instinct to draw the sharpest possible line between himself and the *multitudo*. Though he has achieved unprecedented success as a *novus homo*, at no point in *Rep.* or *Leg.* does he mention this fact or even the phrase itself, when a compelling case could be made that more virtuous *novi* like himself could be just the thing to "refresh the colors" of the state; *Rep.* 5.2.

[184] *Rep.* 1.47. This prediction was borne out by the policies of Octavian in the years following Cicero's death. Rome's republican forms did indeed outlive their substance.

[185] Cicero was evidently aware of Plato's *Laws*; see *Leg.* 1.15. On the uncertain relationship between the two treatises, see Ferrary 1995, 58–60; Powell 2001, 18–20; Ryan 2012, vol. 1, 143; Atkins 2013, ch. 6; Annas 2017, ch. 7.

those who are to elect should have been trained in habits of law, and be well educated, that they may have a right [*orthos*] judgment, and may be able to select or reject men whom they approve or disapprove, as they are worthy of either. (751d)

Initially, this "education" is to be provided by the parent colony of the Cnossians, who "should take a common interest in all these matters" (754c). The votes are to be registered on tablets, with the name and choice of the voter clearly marked, and then be exhibited in the agora for not less than thirty days (753c). The resemblance to Cicero's proposal is striking: All votes should be displayed, and voters brought to reason with guidance from wise and sympathetic allies.

Whatever Cicero's debt to Plato, the differences between the two proposals speak as loudly as their similarities. Unlike Plato, for whom such guidance is a temporary measure to educate the citizens of a new city, Cicero does not allow that ordinary Roman citizens could *ever* choose rationally without guidance. One could even say that for Cicero the only relevant indicator of *ratio* in a rank-and-file citizen is that they vote as instructed. Doing so, in turn, enhances their own *dignitas* – a critical operation of public liberty for Cicero.[186] Though it may strain the credulity of readers, Cicero's position is clear: The people can be perpetually surveilled at no cost to their freedom.[187]

A deeper logic may be at work in Cicero's notion of interdependence. In the argument for monarchy, Scipio follows Plato in comparing the divided state to a divided soul; passion, when it contradicts "calm judgment," leads to "a sort of rebellion within the mind" (1.60). He argues that "the mind should be a kingdom, all of whose parts are to be ruled by reason" (ibid.). As such, the struggle between reason and passion in the mind is not mapped onto a struggle between senate and *populus* but rather an electoral contest between statesman and demagogue over what the *populus* will become. Here, again, the bivalence of *voluntas* is critical to Cicero's argument: With guidance, the people's will can be allied with *ratio* and *iudicium*,[188] but so, too, can it become *licentia* and *temeritas*.[189] Saying

---

[186] See *Verr.* 2.5.143; *Leg. agr.* 1.17, 2.25, 2.71; *QFr.* 2.3; *Dom.* 25; *Phil.* 2.27. See also Atkins 2018a, 769–70.
[187] Cf. Ferrary 1995, 58: "[B]y proceeding slowly and deliberately, the people can be persuaded that they really are free, and one can thus reinforce the unity of the city and the stability of the régime without running the risk of undermining its foundations." Perhaps this is the significance of the word "appearance" in the phrase *species libertatis* – not that the appearance belied reality, but rather that the balloting process would have symbolic value as a ritual of Roman liberty, and this value could be understood by even the most uneducated of Rome's citizens; cf. Schofield 2021, 92.
[188] See *Prov. cons.* 25; *Rep.* 1.69, 3.3.   [189] See discussion of *temeritas* in Chapter 3.

5.3 De republica *and* De legibus

that reason should rule passion is thus *not* to say that the senate should rule the people. Rather, it is that the people's power is legitimate only when infused with reason from above.[190] Reason rules when a virtuous senate wins over – and in fact, cocreates – the will of the people, checking the *temeritas* of demagogues.[191] Conversely, if their *voluntas* strays, the people become an "uneducated mob" (*multitudo imperita*), their *libertas* turning to *licentia*.[192] In this light, Cicero's ballot law makes greater sense: It symbolically enacts the interdependence of senate and people. Like Plato, and unlike Polybius,[193] Cicero thinks a stable rule of reason is achieved not by counterweight and competition but by consensus.

The consensus of senate and people is enacted in one way above all. In *De oratore*, the character Antonius counsels the orator-statesman to speak to the "social intercourse, precedent, tradition, *and the ways and wills* of his fellow-countrymen [*in moribus ac voluntatibus civium suorum*]" (2.131, emphasis added). He is not called to evangelize Stoic doctrine: He must rely upon "the language of everyday life, and the usages approved by common sense [*a vulgari genere orationis ... atque a consuetudine communis sensus*]" (1.12). An orator's language is *varia* because it must be "adapted to the feelings of common people [*ad vulgarem popularemque sensum accommodata*]" (1.108).[194]

In a "spoken" republic where most citizens neither read nor write, the great majority of political acts have an aural dimension – they are vocalized, heard, booed, or applauded.[195] And though the average citizen will never understand Nature's law, he does partake in the *sensus communis* – the body of phrases, stories, and traditions that *do* derive, as Cicero sees it,

---

[190] See *Inv.* 1.3: Cities are established when men of *ratio* use eloquence to persuade others to observe the norms of justice *voluntate*.

[191] Lévy 2012b, 64, comments on this passage: "This education of the will is presented to us as the means of moving on to a state of law through the renunciation of violence of those who possessed physical force. Eloquence is, in such a context, that which enables us to rationalize the will."

[192] *Flac.* 2; *Rep.* 1.44. Cicero's commitment to the skeptical suspension of judgment may be another reason why his ballot proposal, unlike Plato's, is designed to be permanent: Our judgments require perpetual surveillance because they may always turn out false. Cf. *Sest.* 105; *Planc.* 9–11.

[193] I believe Straumann errs in proposing that Cicero's constitution is one of "checks and balances" in the Polybian model; Straumann 2016, 160, 274 n.97. The senate is Cicero's indispensable actor, and nowhere in *Leg.* does he "balance" it with another. *Pace* Straumann and Connolly, even at his most generous Cicero accepts the tribunate in *Rep.* and *Leg.* as a lesser evil, not a positive good; *Rep* 4.8; *Leg.* 3.23, 3.26; cf. Connolly 2015, 33–48. On this point, Atkins' comparison to Aristotelian "blending" and Dyck's "strengthened control from the top" seem more just. Atkins 2018b, 28 (citing Lintott 1999, 220–25); Dyck 2004, 15. Perhaps tellingly, Straumann revises his phrase to "checks and constraints" at 167.

[194] Cf. *Part. or.* 15; *Para. stoic.* 4. See discussion in Chapter 2.

[195] Connolly 2015, 48–50, 156–68; Steel 2017a, 21–22; cf. Hölkeskamp 2010, 71–75.

from *ius naturae*. The *sensus communis* is thus what connects everyday citizens to the higher standards of *ius*: This "core political morality," in Remer's words, "originates in the wisdom of the ancients and is confirmed through long-standing communal acceptance."[196] While Cicero has very little faith in the common man's ability to reason, he has unwavering faith in his judgment of an orator's quality – including, and above all, his attunement to the *sensus communis*.[197] This judgment, though primarily aesthetic, incorporates *just enough* political substance – on the coherence of an orator's expression or the consistency of his words and character – to elect the right men to lead. When the voter errs, the "semi-secret" ballot corrects him. Asymmetrical as it may be, this relationship is profoundly moral; guiding the people's will is a duty of *decorum*, the accommodation of action to circumstance, one of the four cardinal virtues.[198] Perhaps as Cicero intended, *De oratore* thus completes the argument of its sister treatises.[199]

5.4 Ruin and Rebirth

De legibus would mark antiquity's final attempt at constitutional theory. Not long after Cicero drafts his code of laws, Caesar crosses the Rubicon and promulgates his own. Rome's new order will not be the mixed constitution of Scipio. As Cicero writes to Rufus in April of 45 BCE: "I should like us to ponder together how we should best pass through this present time, all of which must be accommodated to the will of a single man [*ad unius voluntatem accommodandum*]."[200] Caesar's will, as we saw in Chapter 3, is a vector of brutality, not reason, and serves no ends but its own.

What place now for the people's will? Cicero's *voluntas populi* combined the rational force of all good citizens to select magistrates and hold them accountable. Once granted his emergency powers, Caesar no longer needs

---

[196] Remer 2017, 19, 149; cf. Annas 2017, 177.
[197] *De or.* 2.178: It is imperative for the orator to move the audience by "strong emotional impulse rather than by reasoned judgment." Conversely, the crowd can judge an orator as well as any expert; ibid. 3.195–97. See also *Brut.* 185; *Orat.* 24, 70–74; *Amic.* 95–96. Atkins 2018b, 120–21, aptly associates the civic and aesthetic qualities of this judgment.
[198] Remer 2017, 151–52. *Off.* 1.93–94, 96. Cf. Atkins 2018b, 28: "Republican institutions that channel conflict are not enough if a republic lacks justice, consensus, and concord – and virtuous statesmen who can bring them about through education and persuasion."
[199] On the three treatises' relation to one another, see Rawson 1975, ch. 9; Zetzel 2003, 137; Atkins 2013, 59; Remer 2017, 4, 80–81; Steel 2017b, 8–13.
[200] *Fam.* 2.249.3.

5.4 Ruin and Rebirth 141

this will as the people's "specific choice." Alternatively, Cicero's *voluntas populi* and *voluntas mutua* also signified the people's *goodwill*, a bond that underwrote his personal authority in matters of state. This discourse of will as "special relationship" Caesar gladly adopts. Writing to Cicero, Balbus encloses a letter from Caesar in which he restates his policy of clemency to captured adversaries, so that "by this means we can win back the goodwill of all [*omnium voluntates recuperare*] and enjoy a lasting victory."[201] Caesar adds that in this he "do[es] not propose to imitate" the example of Sulla, a man whom in Cicero words had imposed his will *voluntate populi*.[202] For his part, Cicero seems to play along with this reading of the people's will not as their lawful choice but rather their personal goodwill toward Caesar. In his defense of Ligarius, he implores the dictator that his client be restored to a place in the loyal *populus*, "whose goodwill you have ever held most dear [*cuius voluntatem carissimam semper habuisti*]."[203] Intended or not, Caesar has benefited from Cicero's implication that the people's will can be "conceded" and that an elite figure may legitimately embody it.[204] But whereas the force of Cicero's *voluntas populi* was renewable only by election, Rome's new dictator does not just represent but replaces the people's will. Caesar is not the people's trustee, subject to their sovereignty, but the supreme leader in whom they repose their faith.[205]

As Caesar subsumes the *voluntas populi* into his will, he severs the connection Cicero made between *voluntas* and *libertas*. In Cicero's republic, "nothing ought to be so free from corruption in a State as the vote and the expression of opinion."[206] Serving the *voluntas* of Rome's new sovereign, however, is to annul one's own *libertas dicendi*.[207] No longer subject to the rule of law and the senate's guidance, the *voluntas populi* falls from its place of respect. Cicero and his friends must keep the favor of those close to Caesar, "whose word is law [*qui plurimum potest*]," and to this "we

---

[201] *Att.* 3.174C.1.
[202] Ibid.; *Verr.* 2.3.82. Cicero comments that Caesar's is "a sane letter so far as there can be any sanity in such madness [*sana mente scriptas litteras quo modo in tanta insania*]"; *Att.* 3.174.3.
[203] *Lig.* 37.   [204] *Rep.* 2.56.
[205] Caesar's apparent mildness and clemency create an apparently inverse relation to the strength of his will, a dynamic Cicero anticipates in his description of an orator's power at *De or.* 1.255. See Lévy 2012a, 258: "Crassus' power of speech was initially a force that let itself be seen as such, but as his glory grew, it had become *lenis* [mild], not because it was excluded from the play of combined or antagonistic forces, but because the weight of his own representation, of his *persona*, permitted the orator to attenuate the tension, the *contentio*, of his former voice."
[206] *Rep.* 5.11. Cf. *Clu.* 118; *Sest.* 60.
[207] *Fam.* 2.190.3: Freedom of speech is gone, and he must "say nothing offensive to [Caesar's] sentiments or those of people he likes [*nihil loqui quod offendat aut illius aut eorum qui ob illo diliguntur voluntatem*]." See Schofield 2015, 115.

can add the will of the crowd, or rather the consensus of all [*vulgi voluntas, vel potius consensus omnium*]."²⁰⁸

Needless to say, agreement with Caesar is not the *consensus bonorum* Cicero had extolled in *Pro Sestio*. Gone is the uncoerced will of a rationally constituted people: Cicero's meager hope is that "mild and merciful" Caesar will "[defer] to the wills of the many [*multorum ... voluntatibus*], when they are just and principled, not frivolous or self-interested."²⁰⁹ Interestingly, Cicero's loss of faith in the *voluntas populi* means he is no longer obliged to pretend its unanimity. Recounting many setbacks in the war effort against Antony, he sighs, "I might add, 'in the face of a unanimous Senate and People' [*in tanto senatus populique consensu*], were it not that the mischief within the gates remains so strong."²¹⁰ In *Pro Sestio*, he had noted with irony that the *optimates* of old had considered the people's approval to be a sign they had done something amiss.²¹¹ In his late treatises, written principally under Caesar's rule, Cicero takes his skepticism of popular judgment to its logical conclusion: Honor belongs not to those who heed the *voluntas populi* but to those who reject it.²¹²

But *voluntas*, an interior force, cannot be stripped as easily from Rome's citizens as their freedoms to speak and vote. Urging Decimus Brutus to pursue Antony without formal authorization, Cicero declares that "the will of the Senate [*voluntas senatus*] should be accepted in lieu of authority [*auctoritas*] when its authority is trammelled by fear."²¹³ The interior durability of will allows the senate to retain a latent power even when brute force has silenced it. When Cicero returns from exile, he is reassured that, with respect to his allies, their *voluntas* endured even when their *libertas* was stolen.²¹⁴

Something of the *voluntas populi* lasted until the end. In the waning months of his life, the restored leader of the senate blows on embers Caesar had stamped out. Cicero declares to Antony that in the many chants and ovations heard in public shows, "is not all this enough to signify the extraordinary consensus and will of the whole Roman people [*incredibiliter consentientem populi Romani universi voluntatem*]?"²¹⁵ Though the senate sends an envoy to Antony with terms, Cicero assures the people that war will follow, "for he is a man who has always flouted the judgment and authority of the senate, as he has your will and power [*semper voluntatem*

---

²⁰⁸ *Fam.* 2.225.5.   ²⁰⁹ Ibid. 2.234.8.   ²¹⁰ *Ad Brut.* 24.2.   ²¹¹ *Sest.* 105.
²¹² Cf. *Tusc.* 5.54, 5.106; *Off.* 1.65.   ²¹³ *Fam.* 3.354.2.   ²¹⁴ See *Sest.* 69.   ²¹⁵ *Phil.* 1.36.

vestram potestatemque contempserit]."²¹⁶ For all the skepticism Cicero had voiced in his treatises, in this brief moment the people's will outlasted a tyrant.

Cicero's ideal of rational interdependence failed in its own time. The Republic collapsed and his code of laws fell into obscurity. And yet as I explore in the Epilogue, Cicero's notion of *voluntas populi* made an essential, if highly problematic, mark on the modern world. In the tradition he inherits from Polybius, the mixed constitution apportions powers among distinct groups and sets them in constructive competition. Cicero transfigures this idea, replacing the metaphor of partition with one of trusteeship. The will of the people, expressed in elections, enacts their sovereignty over the whole republic, not their power over a part; their will, both as specific command and special relationship, elevates a properly educated elite into power; and elite guidance, in turn, ensures that reason rules. Whether professed or not, these are the principles that lie at the heart of what we today call "democracies" but what always were, and remain, republics: the people's sovereignty expressed through elections only, with special rules – from the electoral college to judicial life tenure²¹⁷ – that "safeguard" public freedom by constraining the people's power to govern. Though he could not save his republic, Cicero has enormously shaped our own.

---

²¹⁶ Ibid. 6.5. In what could be read as a reference to Caesar's assimilation of popular will into his own *voluntas*, Cicero adds: "Doubtless [Antony] will find it an easy matter to obey this order to submit to your control [*potestate*] and that of the senators – a man who was never in control of himself! What did he ever do by his own choice [*umquam arbitrio suo fecit*]?"
²¹⁷ Two noteworthy examples from the US Constitution.

PART II

The Philosophy of Voluntas

The rise of Caesar eclipses Cicero from his former place in the firmament of Roman power. Though doing what he can to win clemency for his allies, the engine of Cicero's genius shifts into a new gear. In his twelve late treatises, the ex-consul tracks an enormous terrain of ideas, from the history of Roman oratory to the principles of religion, friendship, and moral improvement. If these treatises served merely to preserve Hellenistic debates otherwise lost, this alone would commend them. And yet, as increasingly affirmed by modern scholars, Cicero's was no mere translation project to fill idle hours.[1] With the political and ethical system of the *maiores* in ruins, Cicero recreates it within the individual. The old qualities of the *populus Romanus* – its free judgment, resilience, and drive to excel – he rebuilds in the single human subject. Each citizen must win the autonomy over himself that the Roman people had lost over its Republic. Putting pen to paper is itself an act of resistance, an insistence that *libertas* of thought might flourish as the freedoms of senate and people expire.

These final chapters center upon two of Cicero's abiding obsessions: responsibility for the past and prescriptions for the future. In the year of his consulship, Cicero had proclaimed: "There is no evil from outside, of other's causing, that can make its way into our country; if you desire that country to be immortal ... it is against *our own passions* that we must be on our guard, against men of violence and revolutionaries, against evils from within, against plots devised at home."[2] If philosophy lets the ex-consul expand the frontiers of Roman knowledge, it also sheds light on his griefs and grievances – and, in particular, how those who murdered the Republic can be held to account. This problem takes Cicero into the recesses of the human mind, to the origin of reckless impulses and evil acts; equally, it

---

[1] See Barnes and Griffin 1989; Lévy 1992; Powell 1995; Nicgorski 2012; Baraz 2012; Steel 2013; Woolf 2015.
[2] *Rab. Perd.* 33–34 (emphasis added).

takes him skyward, to consider how the laws of the universe might excuse or affirm the deeds of mortals. Academic and Stoic texts give Cicero an arsenal of ideas with which to treat this problem. The Republic's new tyrants are not victims of insanity but are driven by "willing disturbances" (*perturbationes voluntariae*); the root cause of the crisis was not fate but "a matter of will."[3] So, too, does the notion of will become a way for the victims of the crisis to save their honor, their "conscience of a righteous will" (*conscientia rectae voluntatis*) a solace in political failure.[4]

With the old course of honors in ruins, what milestones will mark a worthy life? Cicero's ascent was sped by the favor of juries and the acclamation of crowds, but this path to glory depended on fragile laws and fickle men. From his library in Tusculum, the ex-consul seeks a new foundation for the public-spirited self. Here, *voluntas* is the driver of independent personhood and the engine of moral progress. In the *Tusculan Disputations*, he harnesses Roman courage to Greek ideals; it is by harnessing the force of volition and resisting evil "with all our might and main" that the good life is won (3.25). In the *De officiis*, adapting the Stoic Panaetius, *voluntas* drives the fourth of man's four *personae*, the one role depending solely on ourselves. Cicero's final text shows how a negotiated tension between nature, fortune, and will forms the crucible of a conscious self.

These chapters propose no Ciceronian "theory of the will." While his *voluntas* is abundant and illuminating, it is not systematic. It is the Roman way to open fields of inquiry and transmit them to future generations, not circumscribe and close them.[5] Nevertheless, it is my contention that Cicero's place in the history of the will – of political will and of free will – merits recognition. His Greek predecessors counseled their students to think better; Cicero exhorts his own to try harder. His explanation of virtue as the product of present effort continually renewed – the rational force of willpower – transposes Platonic and Stoic reason into a Roman key. My aim is that the present study, rather than resolve these questions, opens a path for Cicero's contribution to be explored anew.

---

[3] *Fam.* 2.181.2. [4] Ibid. 2.244.2.
[5] Cf. Sen. *Ep.* 45.4: "For these men, too, have left to us, not positive discoveries, but problems whose solution is still to be sought [*Nam illi quoque non inventa, sed quaerenda nobis reliquerunt*]."

CHAPTER 6

Willpower

In Book 5 of *De finibus*, a young Cicero strolls the grove of the Academy with a handful of fellow students. Fresh from a lecture by the great Antiochus of Ascalon, his friend Piso reports that virtue, in Antiochus' view, sits at the top of the hierarchy within each of us. Translating into Latin, he gives the following scheme: (1) Man's body (*corpus*) is ruled by his soul (*animus*); (2) within the soul, the mind (*mens*) is superior to the senses (*sensus*) and rules man's entire nature (*tota hominis natura*).[1] Which part of us, then, can properly be called virtuous? Here, Antiochus clarifies that (3) our *mens* is itself divided, containing both natural gifts (*virtutes*), which are *non voluntariae*, and, finally, the four cardinal virtues, which are "placed in the will" (*in voluntate positae*).[2]

This passage is the first where Cicero names the will as part of the human soul. Moreover, will occupies the top rung of this inner ladder: It is where the four cardinal virtues are placed (*positae*), which are both *ex ratione* and *divinae* (5.38).[3] Is this *voluntas* a "faculty" of the mind, in the sense of Plato's *thumos* or *epithumia*?[4] The juxtaposition of *voluntas* with *voluntaria* adds uncertainty to the question. In the passage from Antiochus, *voluntaria* simply names a quality absent from certain virtues.[5] Cicero could have continued that the four cardinal virtues, being "voluntary," are of special importance – but he does not do this. Instead, he

---

[1] *Fin.* 5.34.
[2] Ibid. 5.36. He ascribes this view to Antiochus of Ascalon, a syncretic thinker who weaves together Stoicism, Platonism, and Aristotelianism in his work. See generally Glucker 1978; Lévy 2010; Sedley 2012.
[3] Piso adds that these virtues, being *voluntaria*, are to be preferred to inborn talents; *Fin.* 5.38.
[4] Long 2015, 24, observes that these "thing-like" descriptions of the soul (*psukhē*) and its division into parts, while unknown to Homer, dominated the post-Socratic schools (with Aristotle "a partial exception").
[5] Frede 2011, 6–9, 19–20, 26–29, 42–48, emphasizes the important conceptual distinctions between "willingly," an "act of willing," and "the will" with regard to Aristotle and the Hellenistic schools.

concludes that Antiochus has put the most important virtues in a specific place: They are *in voluntate positae*, "placed in the will."[6]

This passage in *De finibus* marks a step in the gradual emancipation of *voluntas* from other terms in Cicero's psychology. In the *Tusculan Disputations*, Cicero pairs will with judgment (*iudicium*), suggesting its rootedness in reason – and recalling his admission in *De republica* that something be left to the "will and judgment" of the masses.[7] Written just after the *Tusculans*, *De natura deorum* (45 BCE) depicts "mind and will" (*mens ac voluntas*) as a joint force.[8] Cicero uses a similar phrase in *De fato*, written a year later, after Caesar's death, but now implying that "mind" and "will" are separable: "[T]hose who bring in an everlasting series of causes rob the human mind of free will and fetter it in the chains of a fated necessity [*ei mentem hominis voluntate libera spoliatam necessitate fati devinciunt*]."[9] Only in his final treatise, *De officiis*, does the will clearly stand on its own; Of man's four *personae*, the one we choose for ourselves "sets forth from our will [*a nostra voluntate proficiscitur*]."[10] These passages do not amount to a cohesive mental system with a fixed place for the will; they are suggestive, not definitive. But what they suggest is a growing importance of the will in Cicero's account of the mind. In his orations and earlier treatises, *voluntas* had offered Cicero a means to make a "subject" in the state – the "will of the people" was his base of support and the catalyst of Scipio's constitution.[11] In the wake of Rome's civil wars, the will that had once constituted the Republic now must bring order to the individual soul.

It is in the *Tusculan Disputations* that Cicero gives his most detailed blueprint for our inner lives. In Book 4, he makes a curious double announcement: He will "follow the time-honored distinction made first by Pythagoreans and after him by Plato, who divide the soul into two parts." However, he will also "employ the definitions and subdivisions of

---

[6] I find the phrase more significant than Gill 2006, 222, who characterizes the Antiochan scheme as subdividing "psychological qualities ... into non-volitional and volitional ones." For the centrality of the four cardinal virtues to Cicero's thought, see Powell 2012, 17. I examine infra the plausibility of whether *voluntate* is a mere stylistic variant of *voluntaria*.

[7] See *Tusc.* 3.66–67, 4.65, 4.82; *Rep.* 1.69.

[8] At *Nat. D.* 3.70, the skeptic Cotta aims to refute Stoicism on its own terms: "If therefore the divine mind and will [*mens voluntasque divina*] displayed care for men's welfare because it bestowed upon them reason [*ratio*], it cared for the welfare of those only to whom it gave virtuous reason, whom we see to be very few." See ibid. at 3.92, in which Cotta again says, "as man's limbs are effortlessly moved merely by his mind and will, so, as you say, the gods' power can mold and move and alter all things [*ut enim hominum membra nulla contentione mente ipsa ac voluntate moveantur, sic numine deorum omnia fingi moveri mutarique posse*]."

[9] *Fat.* 20, discussed in Chapter 7.   [10] *Off.* 1.115.   [11] See discussion in Chapter 5.

the Stoics" on the passions – doctrines arising from a monist view of the soul (4.11). Here, he gives the will an explicit role: *Voluntas* is one of the four *eupatheia* or "good passions," equivalent to the Stoic *boulēsis*, and defined as "that which desires something with reason" (*quae quid cum ratione desiderat*, 4.12).[12] He further affirms, as Plato and Aristotle had not, that our agitations of mind are all "willing disturbances" (*perturbationes voluntariae*) (ibid.). The will emerges in the *Tusculans* as the driving force of a virtuous life, the necessary complement of rational understanding. In this original philosophical braid, Cicero weaves *voluntas* and *voluntarius* into Greek notions of *boulēsis*, *prohairesis*, and *hekōn*, inflecting old debates and opening new fields of meaning.

We note that Cicero's notion of the will is developed by blending monistic and dualistic accounts of the soul, two seemingly incompatible viewpoints.[13] Why does he do this? Illuminating hints lie in the *Academica* and *De finibus*. Written just prior to the *Tusculans*, these dialogues contain extended arguments for and against the positions of the major schools. These exchanges provide insight into the ideas of Platonism and Stoicism that may have captured Cicero's interest as he readied his own account. Cicero names Plato as the "font" (*fons*) of his view on the soul (4.11) and his unquestioned authority on political matters; indeed, Plato's analogy of the city and individual soul may have been the core insight underlying his philosophical project in the 40s BCE. In Plato's division of the soul, we find a familiar Ciceronian embrace of hierarchy and competition. Yet it is the Stoics and their uncompromising stance on virtue that come closest to "the idea we all have of bravery" (4.53): Our soul is fully responsible for its vices, which we have a duty to recognize and overcome. Nevertheless, the character "Cicero" airs serious grievances with the Stoic account in *De finibus* Book 4: their rejection of common-sense beliefs, their poverty of style, and their "all or nothing" view of moral progress, among other complaints.[14] With the *Tusculans*, finally, Cicero declares "the birthday

---

[12] In their theory of human emotion, the Stoics lauded the *eupatheia* or "proper feelings" of the wise man, including joy (*terpsis*), good intent (*eunoia*), and reverence (*hagneia*). On *eupatheia*, see generally Graver 2007, 51–60.

[13] Cicero informs us at *Tusc.* 4.10–11 that Plato is the *fons* or source of his account but adds, "let us *nevertheless* in depicting these disorders employ the definitions and subdivisions of the Stoics who, *so it seems to me*, show remarkable acuity in addressing this problem [*utamur tamen in his perturbationibus describendis Stoicorum definitionibus et partitionibus, qui mihi videntur in hac quaestione versari acutissime*]" (emphasis added). The *tamen* and *qui mihi videntur* are hints that Cicero sees and embraces the apparent incongruity.

[14] I take no position in the rich debate as to the relation in these dialogues between the positions of the character Cicero and those of their author; see, e.g., Lévy 1984 and 1992; Schofield 2009; Baraz 2012, 128–49; Brittain 2015, 12–40; Woolf 2015, 125–29; Wynne 2019, 44–45. What is relevant

of philosophy in Latin" (2.5), offering a path to virtue more vivid and convincing than any predecessor. Front and center is the force of willpower, by which his Roman readers must mobilize their reason and win the battle for a better self.

6.1 Cicero on Platonic and Stoic Souls

The Academy's founder supplied Cicero with both his dialectical method, learned from Philo,[15] and a source of doctrines about man's inner life. Of particular interest was a thorny problem Plato had inherited from his own master. Socrates insisted that to know the good was to perform the good, with no exceptions.[16] This theory of action, though coherent, seemed to leave no room for *akrasia* or incontinence – the common experience of knowing something to be in our interest but failing to do it. Plato's solution, developed in Book 4 of the *Republic*, is that *akrasia* is evidence of a basic conflict between our rational and nonrational desires, which must therefore arise from different parts of the soul (*psukhē*).[17] Reason cohabitates with spirit (*thumos*) and appetite (*epithumeia*), whose impulses can conflict with our duties and best interests.[18] Just as enlightened guardians rule over Plato's imagined *politeia*,[19] reason must rule by right in each man, and spirit and appetite obey.[20]

Cicero may have seen much to admire in these hierarchies. It would be difficult, in fact, to find principles more attractive to a conservative exconsul who preached *concordia ordinum* and claimed that citizens should

---

here is that *Acad.* and *Fin.* illustrate what Cicero may have found to be the stronger and weaker arguments of the various schools as he prepared *Tusc.*, a text generally considered to represent the views Cicero held or found most probable; see Graver 2002, xiv, xxv; Schofield 2013, 81–83.

[15] See *Tusc.* 2.9.   [16] See, e.g., Pl. *Prt.* 345a–55b.
[17] See Long 2015, 39: "The principal basis for [Plato's] division of the soul is the fact that we sometimes find ourselves at the same time, or seemingly at the same time, subject to desires pro and contra the same thing." Cf. Frede 2011, 22.
[18] Pl. *Resp.* 4.434c–45e, 4.411a, 8.550b. Cf. Cic. *Acad.* 2.124: "[D]o we know if it has three parts, as Plato held, reason, passion and appetite, or is it a simple unity [*si est, trisne partes habeat, ut Platoni placuit, rationis irae cupiditatis, an simplex unusque sit*]?"
[19] Pl. *Resp.* 4.428e–29a: The city as a whole is wise "because of the smallest class and part in it, namely, the governing or ruling one."
[20] Ibid. 4.430e–33d: "It makes the weakest, the strongest, and those in between ... all sing the same song together. And this unanimity, this agreement between the naturally worse and the naturally better as to which of the two is to rule both in the city and in each one, is rightly called moderation [*sophrosunē*]." Cf. ibid. at 4.442c: Justice exists when "each does his own work and doesn't meddle with what is other people's"; 4.441e: "[T]herefore isn't it appropriate for the rational part to rule ... and for the spirited part to obey it ...?" See Long 2015, 10–11, 127–60.

be weighed, not counted.²¹ Plato's rule of reason earns consistent praise from the character Cicero, who adds in *De finibus* that the Stoics, by contrast, "were either unable or unwilling" to treat these political questions.²² After giving Antiochus' system at 5.34–36 (placing cardinal virtues "in the will"), Piso declares that his teacher regarded politics second only to philosophy as an activity worthy of man's gifts.²³ The Academy's authority is exemplified in a memorable passage of the *Tusculans* in which Cicero's characters agree that they would sooner be wrong with Plato than right with anyone else.²⁴

A further subject of interest to Cicero is Plato's argument, first enunciated in the *Phaedrus*, that the human soul moves itself.²⁵ All material things that owe their existence to external causes must perish, but our self-moving souls will live on. Plato's arguments for an immortal, automotive soul seem to figure heavily in the *Consolatio* composed after Tullia's death in 45 BCE,²⁶ and they become the centerpiece of the *Tusculans* Book 1.²⁷

The self-moving soul gives Plato and his successors a potentially appealing view of moral progress.²⁸ In Piso's retelling, Antiochus explains our growth into virtue as a fact of human biology. While every creature seeks completion according to its *summum bonum* or highest good,²⁹ animals differ from plants in *sensus, appetitus*, and the ability *per se ipsa moveatur.*

---

²¹ *Rep.* 6.1.1. See also Cicero's self-deprecating comment at *Acad.* 2.125: "[Y]ou know I have always been a devotee of rank [*studiosus nobilitatis fui*]." On the harmony posited by Plato between parts of the soul, see *Resp.* 4.442d; cf. Long 2015, 146–48. On the importance of *concordia* to Cicero's theory of the Republic, see *Rep.* 1.32, 1.49, 2.69. On distinctions of rank, see *Rep.* 1.43, 1.51–53.
²² *Fin.* 4.7, 4.61.   ²³ *Fin.* 5.58, 5.65–66.   ²⁴ *Tusc.* 1.39–40.
²⁵ Pl. *Phdr.* 245e–54e: "For the body which is moved from without is soulless; but that which is moved from within has a soul, for such is the nature of the soul. But if this be true, must not the soul be self-moving, and therefore of necessity unbegotten and immortal?"; cf. *Phd.* 69e–84b. For possible origins of the idea in Heraclitus, see Long 2015, 82–85.
²⁶ See *Tusc.* 1.65–66; cf. 1.76, 3.76, 4.63.
²⁷ See, e.g., *Tusc.* 1.24–81, 1.97–100. Cf. ibid. 1.52, "every act of your soul is an act of yours [*ab animo tuo quidquid agitur, id agitur a te*]"; 1.53–54, only that which is self-moving is eternal; 1.55, the soul is conscious that "it is self-moved by its own power and not an outside power." Cf. *Div.* 2.139; *Rep.* 6.28.
²⁸ With respect to their views on the soul, Cicero tends to treat Academics and Peripatetics as heirs to a single tradition. See, e.g., *Acad.* 1.17–24, 2.15; *Fin.* 5.7–14, 5.21. Of course, Cicero was aware that Plato's and Aristotle's metaphysics were hardly identical (see, e.g., *Acad.* 1.33–34) and at times separates out the skeptical Academy as mediator of doctrinal disputes between Peripatetics and Stoics (see, e.g., *Tusc.* 4.6, 4.47). This chapter, however, focuses on several key doctrines that Cicero presents as common to Aristotle and Plato, most notably: (1) the division of the human soul into rational and nonrational parts or potentialities; (2) the self-moving nature of the soul; and (3) the importance of education and conditioning to the exercise of reason. Cicero's debatable fidelity to these sources is not my main concern. I concur with Frede 2011, 19, that the Stoic notion of the mind may have been understood as "in opposition to Plato and Aristotle's notion"; it is this opposition that is at play in *Acad.* and *Fin.* See generally Runia 1989, 23–38.
²⁹ *Fin.* 5.25–27; cf. *Acad.* 1.20–21. Cicero discusses various possible translations of *telos* at *Fin.* 3.26.

Humans are additionally distinguished by the ability to perfect themselves "by the mind's reason" (*ex mentis ratione*).³⁰ Though perfectible by reason, we are born unaware of our true nature. Only by gradually "coming to know ourselves" (*nosmet ipsos cognoscimus*) do we approach the *telos* that nature intends for us: namely, a life of reason and virtue.³¹ We note that the teleology attributed to Antiochus has a somewhat determinist tone: Humans progress not by deliberate decision or sustained effort but because this is simply the type of creature we are.³² Nevertheless, the soul's ability to move itself is what puts virtue within its reach.

Does a good life depend on virtue alone? The *Academica* and *De finibus* feature sharp debates on this question. For some followers of Plato, satisfying our "animal" needs is natural and ethically acceptable. External goods such as health, education, and even good looks may thus be necessary for us to flourish.³³ For the Stoics, in contrast, these externalities have nothing to do with living well – the wise man is just as happy on the torture rack as in a palace.³⁴ For some Academics, Cicero continues, this dispute was more semantic than substantial; Even Peripatetics assigned far greater value to the morally honorable (*honestum*) than to health or beauty.³⁵ Even still, their commitment to a divided soul leads one to ask: Can "natural appetites" override our reason, and if so, are we responsible for the results? From the evidence that survives, the Peripatetics seem to have accepted that nonrational desires can indeed drive us to act, independently of our rational beliefs and even "against our choice [*prohairesis*]."³⁶ The Stoics, on the other hand, rejected any notion that

---

[30] *Fin.* 5.40; cf. *Acad.* 2.48. For the Peripatetic roots of this hierarchy of faculties or potentialities of soul, attributed here to Antiochus, see, e.g., Arist. *De an.* 413a23.

[31] *Fin.* 5.41–42. See also *Fin.* 5.24; cf. Arist. *Eth. Nic.* 1141a27–28. Frede 2011, 50–51 (emphasis in original), observes that Aristotle inherits Plato's "highly restrictive notion of reason and knowledge, a notion which involves understanding *why* what one believes one knows is, and cannot but be, the way it is." On different views of ethical teleology in the Hellenistic period, see generally Giusta 1967, vol. 1, 64–74, 84–89; ibid. vol. 2, 43–54.

[32] *Fin.* 5.59–60: Antiochus held that though nature gave us senses already near-complete, it "gives us only a germ" of virtue (*inchoavit*); it thereby rests with us (*nostrum est*) to develop it. See generally Irwin 2012.

[33] Cf. *Acad.* 1.33–34, 2.134 (Theophrastus), 2.131 (Hieronymus and Diodorus), 2.133 (Antiochus); *Fin.* 2.19 (Aristotle).

[34] See, e.g., *Fin.* 3.26, 3.36–39; *Tusc.* 4.35, 5.22–23. See generally Sedley and Long 1987, vol. 1, 377–86.

[35] Cf. *Acad.* 1.22, 1.35–36, Zeno's "alteration of terminology rather than of substance"; *Fin.* 2.68, "a battle rages between the Stoics and the Peripatetics" on this question; 3.10–11, 3.41, Cato rejects Carneades' proposed reconciliation of the two positions; 4.49, Peripatetic distinction between the good (*bonum*) and praiseworthy (*honestum*); 4.57–58.

[36] Frede 2011, 23–29. For actions "against *prohairesis*," see Arist. *Eth. Nic.* 1148a9; cf. 1111b5–13a33, 1139a31–b13, 1145b21–46b5. See also Graver 2007, 74; Long 2015, 158.

6.1 Cicero on Platonic and Stoic Souls 153

our reason could be bypassed or countermanded by another force in the soul.[37] As we will see later in this chapter, when he returns to this question in *Tusculans* Book 5, Cicero sides with the Stoics and their stricter view of moral responsibility.[38]

The *Academica* and *De finibus* trace how Cicero's two great philosophical influences – Platonism and Stoicism – align and diverge on moral questions.[39] Contra Plato and Aristotle, for the followers of Zeno and Chrysippus no evil act can occur solely from passion. Human reason can be neither bypassed nor preempted, only misused.[40] This argument about ethics is, for a Stoic, really about physics. The universe, fully material and thoroughly rational, unfolds in time as a perfect chain of cause and effect.[41] The human *psukhē*, animated by *pneuma* or breath, is thus neither immaterial nor immortal.[42] In such a strictly governed, Swiss-watch universe, what room is left for human freedom? Platonists could locate moral responsibility in the self-moving nature of the soul; this solution was unavailable to a Stoic. Instead, Chrysippus locates human freedom in our ability to ratify or reject the impressions we receive from the world. Each of our actions, excluding those from coercion or ignorance,[43] is the result of *synkatathesis* or assent. The moral soundness of these actions depends, in turn, on the quality of our beliefs.[44] Emotions like rage and jealousy do not arise from a separate, unreasoning part of the human soul – no such "part" exists. However ridiculous or self-destructive someone may be, their soul is rational through and through. The Stoic sage, he of perfected reason, will never – *can* never – act otherwise than virtuously;[45]

---

[37] See Graver 2007, 5–6.
[38] *Tusc.* 5.32–34. Embarrassed by the "sealed evidence" of *Fin.*, Cicero concludes, "for my part, let the Peripatetics and the Old Academy make an end to their stuttering and have the courage to say openly that happy life will step down into the bull of Phalaris"; *Tusc.* 5.75–76. On whether this inconsistency hints at a more radical skepticism in Cicero's dialogues, see Brittain 2015, 16–34.
[39] Again, I refer here to the positive doctrines of Platonism and Aristotelianism regarding the soul, not to the skeptical outlook of the New Academy that was itself a source of deep interest for Cicero.
[40] *Acad.* 1.37–38. Cf. Pl. *Resp.* 413a: "[P]eople are voluntarily deprived of bad things, but involuntarily deprived of good ones ... I do think that people are involuntary deprived of true opinions"; Frede 2011, 33: "According to the Stoics, the division of the soul threatens the unity of the person and obscures the responsibility we have for our supposedly nonrational desires"; Graver 2007, 5–6.
[41] *Acad.* 2.119; *Div.* 1.125–26. Cf. Sext. Emp. *Math.* 9.211 (SVF 2.341); Aët. 1.28.4 (SVF 2.917); Gell. 7.2.3 (SVF 2.1000). See generally Sedley and Long 1987, 340–43; Frede 2011, 78–88.
[42] *Fin.* 4.36. See Annas 1992, 37–56; Graver 2007, 15–28.
[43] For example, killing someone by unwittingly serving them a poisoned cake.
[44] Cf. Graver 2007, 24–34; Frede 2011, 32.
[45] See, e.g., Plut. *Comm. not.* 1046E–F (SVF 3.299); Stob. 2.66.14–67.4 (SVF 3.560); Diog. Laert. 7.127. Cf. Frede 2011, 78–83.

and though the rest of us let passions (*pathē*) spoil our reason, we are no less responsible for our failings.

The Stoic sense of responsibility is a recurrent topic in Cicero's dialogues. As part of a brief history of ethics, he recounts that

> whereas the older generation said these emotions [*perturbationes*] were natural and non-rational, and placed desire and reason in different regions of the mind, ... [Zeno] thought that even the emotions were voluntary [*nam et perturbationes voluntarias esse putabat*] and were experienced owing to a judgment of opinion [*opinionisque iudicio suscipi*].[46]

That every emotional response is "in our power and voluntary" (*in nobis positae et voluntariae*) is an idea Cicero outlines in *De finibus* and endorses in the *Tusculans*.[47] It commits him to an ethical system that, given his long experience with political compromise, is bracingly absolute.[48] No amount of distress, grievance, or temper can excuse a man from responsibility – not ever, not one bit. Cicero's letters from the period hint at the personal stakes involved here. The Stoic view allowed him to assert, for example, that crimes against the Republic could not be excused by passion or folly: These acts were all *voluntarii* and thus worthy of the highest censure.[49] Conversely, the wrenching grief Cicero felt for his daughter, Tullia, was also in this sense "up to him" and in his power, finally, to subdue.[50]

But can we simply think our way to a moral life? In the anti-Stoic refutations of *De finibus* Book 4, the character Cicero dismisses the Stoic notion of moral action as "consisting solely of pure intellect."[51] Human beings are part of nature, and as such, our desires should not be neglected but harnessed:

> Your friends [the Stoics] ... came to behold virtue in all her beauty, and forthwith flung aside all they had ever seen besides virtue herself, forgetting that the whole instinct of appetite [*naturam omnem appetendarum rerum*] is

---

[46] *Acad.* 1.39. [47] *Acad.* 1.40. Cf. *Fin.* 3.35; *Tusc.* 4.14, 4.35, 4.76, 4.79, 4.82–83.

[48] But see Brittain 2015, who argues that Cicero may have embraced a more radical Carneadan skepticism, situating *Tusc.* in a larger and more intractable *aporia* across his late philosophical works.

[49] Cf. *Cat.* 2.18; *Sull.* 28; *Red. pop.* 10.24; *Dom.* 115; *Phil.* 1.15, 10.19. On correspondences between the psychology of Cicero's treatises and his political invective, see generally Lévy 1998, 139–57.

[50] See *Tusc.* 3.64–66: "When actual cessation of sorrow has ensued and it is thus realized that nothing is gained by mourning, isn't it proof that all this is voluntary [*totum illud voluntariam*]? ... Therefore it is in one's power to throw grief aside when one will [*in potestate est abiicere dolorem, cum velis*]." Cf. ibid. 3.71–76, 4.63.

[51] *Fin.* 4.28-29. The sources of Book 4, and Cicero's attitude toward them, is a question that has long occupied scholars. See, e.g., Hirzel 1877–83, vol. 2, 620–69; Lorcher 1911, 120–35. Again, we cannot conclude that "Cicero's" positions in Book 4 are Cicero's; given what follows in *Tusc.*, the critique of Stoic cognitivism is illuminating nevertheless.

so wide in its range that it spreads from the primary objects of desire right up to the ultimate Ends, and not realizing that they are undermining the very foundations of the graces which they so admire. (4.42)

Importantly, "Cicero" does not take the position that virtue lacks supreme value or is an unworthy *summum bonum* (compared to, say, Epicurean *hēdonē*).[52] Nor is he unaware of the Stoic *eupatheiai*; "Cato" notes that "even the passion of love when pure is not thought incompatible with the character of the Stoic sage" (3.68). The criticism levied in Book 4 is rather that the Stoics rely on cognition alone to act rightly rather than the full range of forces with which nature has endowed mankind.[53] For the Stoa, achieving wisdom and virtue is a matter of correcting false belief.[54] But for "Cicero," a wise man sent by a tyrant to the rack, rather than merely deciding that pain is irrelevant, "would feel that he had a severe and searching ordeal before him, and seeing that he was about to encounter the supreme antagonist, pain, would summon up all his principles of courage and endurance ..." (4.31). It is by his strength of will and not by reason alone that the wise man wins his virtue.[55]

A philosophy of life, Cicero continues, must be both coherent and compelling. By this measure the school of Zeno and Chrysippus falls short:

> [F]or my own part, as regards all these Stoic syllogisms, I should have thought that to be worthy of philosophy and of ourselves, particularly when the subject of our inquiry is the Supreme Good, the argument ought to amend our lives, purposes, and wills, not just correct our terminology [*vitam nostram, consilia, voluntates, non verba corrigi*].[56]

For Cicero, inferior style cannot be a trivial point. As Raphael Woolf observes, "[t]hese things matter because to change people's outlooks one

---

[52] In fact, he characterizes Zeno as having taken his *summum bonum* of living according to nature from the accounts of "Xenocrates and Aristotle" (i.e. the Academics and Peripatetics); *Fin.* 4.14–20.

[53] The debate centers upon the Stoic doctrine of *oikeiōsis* or self-appropriation, which provides that at a certain stage of life humans actualize their capacity for reason and thus break definitively from a "pre-rational" childhood during which self-preservation is paramount. See generally Gill 2006, 221–43; Bénatouïl 2016, 216–17.

[54] Cf. *Acad.* 1.38: Unlike the Academics, for whom "certain virtues are perfected by nature or by habit," Zeno "placed all the virtues in reason."

[55] Compare Cicero's question at *Fin.* 4.33: How could it be that "mankind alone should relinquish man's nature, forget the body, and find its chief good not in the whole man but in a part of man [*quae summum bonum non in toto homine sed in parte hominis ponerat*]?" On Cicero's recurring opposition to *apatheia*, see Gildenhard 2011, 37.

[56] *Fin.* 4.52. See also ibid. 3.3: The Stoics' "rather crabbed style of argument" presents an opportunity as Cicero "invent[s] new terms to convey new ideas"; 4.5–7: "[T]heir meager little syllogisms are mere pin-pricks; they may convince the intellect, but they cannot convert the heart, and the hearer goes away no better than he came." Cf. *Tusc.* 2.42: Their syllogisms "fail to make any impression on the mind."

must, in the colloquial sense, speak to them, whereas the Stoic style of argument, even when it gains superficial assent, fails, as Cicero puts it, to change listeners in their hearts ... [I]n ethics, style is to an important extent inseparable from substance."[57] Cicero's stances on moral virtue thus reflect the lifelong convictions of a Roman orator. To be worthy of its name, philosophy must not only locate the truth but give it force; it must stir its listeners to action; it must ignite the will.[58]

In this light, the Stoic account of progress can seem empty, even discouraging. In Book 3 of *De finibus*, Cato posits that just as it makes no difference whether a drowning man is a mile or an inch below the surface, "similarly a man that has made some progress towards the state of virtue is none the less in misery than he that has made no progress at all" (3.48).[59] In Book 4, "Cicero" is sharply critical of the idea

> that all men's folly, injustice and other vices are alike and all sins [*peccata*] are equal; and that those who by nature and training have made considerable progress towards virtue, unless they have actually attained to it, are utterly miserable ... so that the great and famous Plato, supposing he was not a wise man [*sapiens*], lived a no better and no happier life than any unprincipled scoundrel. (4.21)

Arguing that the Republic's *maiores* were deluded[60] and its current citizens no better than slaves[61] will not help Stoic prospects in Rome.[62] Such views make a nonsense of politics, "as though it were admitted that all foolish people possess an equal degree of vice, and that L. Tubulus was exactly as weak and unstable as P. Scaevola who brought in the bill for his condemnation ..." (4.77). Though laudable on the question of moral responsibility, the Stoic "corrections" of Aristotle and Plato, so proposed,

---

[57] Woolf 2015, 159.
[58] *Fin.* 3.19: Cicero to Cato: "[T]o my mind, any clear statement of an important topic possesses excellence of style"; ibid. 4.22–23: The Stoics' "peculiar terms" are a smokescreen for their lack of novelty. Cf. *Tusc.* 4.66: "[W]e are at present suiting our language to ordinary thought [*sed loquimur nunc more communi*]."
[59] Cf. Sen. *Ep.* 75.8 (everyone not yet a *sapiens* counts as a *stultus*); Diog. Laert. 7.101 (SVF 3.92); Stob. 2.66.14–67.4 (SVF 3.560); Alex. *Fat.* 199.14–22 (SVF 3.658). Cf. Frede 2011, 75: "It is clear from the Stoic claim that only the wise are free, that freedom, like wisdom and virtue, does not admit of degrees."
[60] *Fin.* 4.62–64.
[61] Ibid. 4.74; cf. *Para. Stoic.* 33–41; Alex. *Fat.* 28.17–22 (trans. Sharples 1983). Frede 2011, 66, argues "[o]bviously [the Stoics] do not mean that we are all slaves in the legal or political sense or that only the wise person is politically free." *Pace* Frede, Cicero's insistence on the political unsuitability of the Stoic view suggests that the Romans of his day did not naturally distinguish metaphysical from political freedom.
[62] *Fin.* 4.62–64; *Tusc.* 5.13: "[T]here is more delight in a sip than a draught of this Stoic vintage." Cf. Brittain 2015, 38.

would win few converts in the forum or senate. At Murena's trial, Cicero remembers, he scored against Cato on this point (4.74).[63] A ringing, Roman exhortation to virtue is the task set for Cicero's magnum opus.

6.2 *Tusculan Disputations*: Cicero's Struggle for Reason

How, then, to tame our passions and overcome our pain? For Cicero, we cannot vanquish these foes without first seeing them for what they are. Since the freedom of a skeptic lets him combine doctrines that appear most probable,[64] he declares that he will

> follow the time-honored distinction made first by Pythagoreans and after him by Plato, who divide the soul into two parts: to the one they assign a share of reason, to the other none ... Let this then be the starting-point [*fons*]; let us nevertheless in depicting these disorders employ the definitions and subdivisions of the Stoics, who, it appears to me, show great penetration in addressing this problem. (4.10–11)

Having enlisted both Stoa and Academy in his project, Cicero defines his key terms. He renders the Stoic *pathos* as *perturbatio*, "an agitated movement of the soul [*animi commotio*] alien from right reason and contrary to nature [*aversa a recta ratione contra naturam*]" (4.11).[65] Desire leads all men naturally to what they believe is good, and though unguided appetite leads to lust (*libido*) and greed (*cupiditas*), so too may desire be deployed "in an equable and wise way." In this latter case, he announces that where the Stoics call this rational kind of appetite (*eius modi appetitionem*) *boulēsis*, he will now use *voluntas*, "that which desires something with reason [*quae quid cum ratione desiderat*]" (4.12).[66]

After hundreds of appearances in Cicero's corpus, *voluntas* has its first proper definition.[67] Its correspondence to *boulēsis* is, at first glance, quite

---

[63] Cf. *Acad.* 1.43, 2.15. Cicero exempts the great Panaetius, "a worthy member of the famous circle of Scipio and Laelius," from his criticism of Stoic absolutism. Instead of arguing that pain was not an evil, Cicero recounts, he rather "prescribes the method by which it is to be endured"; *Fin.* 4.23. See also *De or.* 3.65.
[64] *Tusc.* 4.7.   [65] Cf. Graver 2002, xxxviii–xxxix.
[66] The full passage reads: "[F]or by a law of nature all men pursue apparent good and shun its opposite ... Where this takes place in an equable and wise way – the Stoics employ the term *boulēsis* for this sort of longing – we should employ the term *will*. This, they believe, is found in the wise man alone and they define it thus: will is that which desires with reason [*natura enim omnes ea, quae bona videntur, sequuntur fugiuntque contraria; ... Id cum constanter prudenterque fit, eius modi appetitionem Stoici boulēsin appellant, nos appellemus voluntatem. Eam illi putant in solo esse sapiente, quam sic definiunt: voluntas est, quae quid cum ratione desiderat*]" (emphasis added).
[67] The subjunctive *appellemus* ("we should employ" or "let us call") suggests that this is an original definition proposed by Cicero himself. Cf. Begley 1988, 128.

logical. *Boulēsis* is one of the Stoic *eupatheiai*, emotions that accord with right reason. Accordingly, in this passage Cicero includes *voluntas/boulēsis* as one of three *constantiae* or "still states" of the soul.[68] The definition thus asserts in theory what he has argued in practice for decades: Will, properly considered, is the force by which reason orders the world. Yet the fit is imprecise. For one thing, *voluntas* in Cicero is not "still" but kinetic, a force in motion toward an identified goal. A *boulēsis*, on the other hand, can be a stable and rational longing for something beyond view.[69] I can have a *boulēsis* for world peace, but – at least in Cicero's usage – I could not have a *voluntas* for it. As some scholars have noted, a less "kinetic" Latin equivalent for *boulēsis* would be *consilium*, in the sense of a settled opinion regarding a desirable end.[70] Yet, perhaps recalling the opposition of *voluntas* and *vis* in his politics, Cicero situates will as a positive, rational force in competition with disruptive, irrational ones.[71] The originality of Cicero's usage (whether intended or not) is that *voluntas* combines the rational judgment of *boulēsis* with the impulsion of *hormē*, two concepts that the Stoics strictly separated.[72] The result is a rational force-in-motion – willpower – that can be considered original to Latin thought.

A second problem is that *voluntas* in its common use is often not rational at all. For the Stoics, *boulēsis* is *eulogos orexis*, the rational desire of the wise, to be contrasted with the appetite (*epithumia*) of the fool, which moves "contrary to right reason [*aversa a recta ratione*]" (4.11). A *boulēsis* can never be evil. By contrast, Cicero on many occasions has

---

[68] The others are *gaudium* (rational joy) in contrast to *laetitia* (excessive delight), and *cautio* (rational aversion) in contrast to *metus* (irrational fear). There is no "wise" counterpart to "present distress" (*aegritudo*), yielding three *constantiae* and four *perturbationes*. *Tusc.* 4.12–14; Diogenes Laertius reports that Chrysippus gave *boulēsis* as one of the three *eupatheiai*, 7.115–16. See Graver 2007, 51–60; Koch 2006, 103–04.

[69] Cf. Graver 2007, 58–59, 203–04; Frede 2011, 20.

[70] See Hatinguais 1958, 54, 56–58. Hatinguais concludes, "no doubt because its structure designated more clearly a master faculty of the human soul, Cicero preferred the substantive *voluntas* to represent both an inclination lucidly tested by reason and a firm declaration, by a creative step in the order of language."

[71] See also *Tusc.* 2.31, as long as honor exists, "pain will lead to virtue and grow fainter by the onrushing of soul [*animi inductione*]"; 2.58, "it is from this rush, this impulse of our souls towards true renown and reputation [*cursu atque impetu animorum ad veram laudem atque honestatem*] that the dangers of battle are encountered"; 4.34, disorders are "troubled and agitated movements of the soul alien from reason [*turbidi animorum concitatique motus*]." See Lévy 2007, 26–30.

[72] The precise status of *hormē* in Stoic psychology and its precise relation to assent remain subjects of intense debate; see Ioppolo 1988, 397–24; Graver 2007, 26–27. Ioppolo 2016, 191, argues that, for certain Stoic thinkers, the "animal" connotation of *hormē* may have made it problematic as an element of mature human psychology.

denounced his enemies for their wicked wills[73] and has claimed that *voluntas* can be righteous or vicious depending on its user.[74] As he observes later in Book 4, "virtue is an equable and harmonious disposition of the soul ..., there spring from it honorable willings [*voluntates honestae*], opinions, actions, and all that makes right reason [*omnisque recta ratio*]" (4.34). If *voluntates* can be *honestae*, they may of course be *inhonestae* as well. It is not surprising, then, that Cicero pairs *voluntas* with *iudicium*, implying (as he did with *voluntas populi*) that will, *properly considered*, is a force put to rational ends.[75] This is not to assume that Cicero wants his definition of *voluntas-as-boulēsis* to cover all possible contexts; as we have seen in previous chapters, the word's polysemy was not only well-established but extremely useful for Cicero. Here, whether intended or not, the bivalence of Roman *voluntas* – its potential to serve either good or evil – sets it interestingly apart from the "desire of reason" of the Stoic sage.[76]

A final ambiguity of Cicero's definition is whether *voluntas* and *boulēsis* imply a single instance of rational desire ("a willing") or something more. Margaret Graver renders *voluntas* as "a volition," in accordance with the scheme of *eupatheiai* ("a joy," "a caution," etc.).[77] This is the most plausible reading, as it comports with the plural use of *voluntates* at 4.34. Yet Cicero's syntax – *quae quid cum ratione desiderat* – introduces uncertainty. A simpler formulation for *eulogos orexis* would be something like *appetitio cum ratione* or *desiderium cum ratione*; instead, he makes *voluntas* the subject of a relative clause, "*that [thing] which* desires something with reason" (4.12, emphasis added). The phrase situates will as a durable subject oriented to various objects over time, suggesting not merely a dynamic force but an ongoing presence akin to *voluntas mutua* or *populi*.[78] Is this the moment when "the will" as mental faculty enters Western thought?

---

[73] See, e.g., *Verr.* 1.95, 1.104, 2.3.57, 2.3.220, 2.3.198; *Cat.* 2.16, 2.18, 4.13; *Sull.* 28; *Red. pop.* 24; *Dom.* 116; *Planc.* 33; *De or.* 2.54.302; *Fam.* 1.73.6; *Lig.* 4.
[74] See, e.g., *Scaur.* 15–16; *Part. or.* 49.
[75] See *Tusc.* 3.66–67, 4.65, 4.82; *Rep.* 1.69. Throughout his corpus, Cicero adjoins *iudicium* to *voluntas* at points where it is helpful to stress the rationality of individual or collective will. See, e.g., *Verr.* 1.10; *Att.* 1.17.7; *Sest.* 106; *Rab. Post.* 45; *Brut.* 42.156–57; *Fam.* 3.362.1.
[76] Frede 2011, 21, notes that *boulesthai*, while etymologically linked to the Latin *velle* and English "will," refers to "a highly specific form of willing or wanting which we no longer recognize or for which we tend to have no place in our conceptual scheme," shared by Academics and Stoics alike. "Thus it is assumed that there is such a thing as a desire of reason and hence also that reason by itself suffices to motivate us to do something. This is an assumption which is made by Socrates, Plato, Aristotle, the Stoics, and their later followers."
[77] Graver 2007, 51–60, 203–04. [78] See Hatinguais 1958, 58; cf. Chapters 4 and 5.

These ambiguities are compounded in the next argument, the keystone of his treatise: All disturbances of the soul are *voluntariae*. Against the idea that anger and grief are beyond our control, Cicero asserts that a disturbed soul "contain[s] nothing either natural or necessary" (4.60). All *perturbationes*, both pleasant and painful, are "in our power, are all subject to our judgment, are all voluntary [*in nostra potestate, omnes iudicio susceptas, omnes voluntarias*]" (4.65).[79] Several distinct Greek concepts are potentially at play here, from *hekon* and *hekousiōn* to *prohairetikos* and *eph'emin*. Broadly speaking, *voluntarius* fits Cicero's argument in that he has used it before to emphasize willingness that would not typically be expected, such as *mors voluntaria* for suicide.[80] And yet *voluntarius* and *voluntas*, though etymologically linked and serving the same argument, enter it at right angles. *Voluntas* advances Cicero's positive account of virtue: It is the force that makes reason effective, product of a self-moving soul, antithetical to the "lust or unbridled desire found in all fools" (4.12). In contrast, *voluntarius* features in his negative account of responsibility, making a more disconcerting if necessary point. What is "voluntary" here is not virtue but vice – our most painful and immoral impulses, the flaws we would soonest disavow. Here, the moral insight works "from the outside in," pointing out these lusts and desires and tying them back to a voluntary if unwitting choice. Conquering our pain and correcting our flaws require the same uncomfortable insight: "[T]hey are all deliberate and willing" (*omnes opinabiles esse et voluntarios*, 4.83).

For this insight to be of real use, Cicero wants to go beyond the Greeks. While Stoic thinkers correctly named these disorders, "their treatment of the subject where they claim to *cure* the soul and hinder it from being disquieted is quite small" (4.9, emphasis added).[81] It is up to the Roman, therefore, to "spread the sails of eloquence" (*panderem vela orationis*) and finish the work that the Stoics began.[82] These pernicious disorders within the self must not simply be recognized, they must be attacked (*medendi*) and stifled (*tollendi*) (4.62). The quest for a moral life is not a thought experiment; it is a fight.

---

[79] See also *Tusc.* 3.7–8: "[W]hat the Greeks call *pathē*, I call *perturbationes* ["disorders"] and not *morbi* ["diseases"]; they are movements of the soul which are not obedient to reason [*motus animi rationi non obtemperantes*]"; ibid. 4.76: No instance of love is "not subject to judgment, and not voluntary [*nisi iudicio susceptum, nisi voluntariam*]."

[80] See Introduction, note 31, and Chapter 2, note 73.

[81] But compare his own praise of Panaetius at *Fin.* 4.23 for having done exactly this. Having presented their views thoroughly and faithfully in his dialogues, Cicero may now be (gently) denigrating his predecessors to create more room to shine.

[82] Ibid. See Lévy 2007, 19.

Virtue, he continues, is not simply a matter of decision. Since distresses and passions are fully in our power, we must harness our volition to defeat them, resisting them with "all our might and main" (3.25).[83] We assume total responsibility for our souls, in the Stoic sense, then exert ourselves again and again in its care. "Strength of soul resembl[es] the strength and sinews and potency of the body [*viribus corporis et nervis et efficacitati similes similibus quoque verbis animi vires nominantur*]" (4.31). Just as athletes condition their bodies, so must we train our souls to withstand passion and pain. Like a weightlifter, "the soul must strain every nerve [*animi est adhibenda contentio*]," and "by its intense effort throw off all the pressure of burdens [*intentione sua depellit pressum omnem ponderum*]" (2.54–55).[84] In this, he draws upon the Stoic view that moral distress is physical weakness, and only by increasing the "soul's tension" (*intensio animi*) do we achieve true wisdom.[85] But Cicero rejects the Stoic goal of *indolentiam*,[86] an emancipation from feeling, saying that this would deprive our souls of their humanity (*immanitatis in animo*, 3.12). Even as we tear out our misery at its roots (*miseriarum ... omnes radicum fibras evellere*), we must watch over our impulses and appetites (3.12–13).[87] Such training is not reserved for athletes and soldiers. Wistfully, the ex-consul asks: "[W]hy should I speak of our candidature at elections, our desire for offices of State? Would fire and water stop the men who once used to gather in such prizes vote by vote?" (2.62).[88] Republican vigor thus completes Greek learning. "Therefore let us put ourselves in the hands of philosophy for treatment, since we have made a beginning: we shall be cured if we will it [*sanabimur, si volemus*]" (ibid.).

His Republic in ruins, Cicero makes the soul a new locus of *Romanitas*. The echo of *virtus* as virility is as inescapable in Latin as it is absent from the Greek *aretē*.[89] Of all Greeks, the Stoics come closest to Roman manliness: They are "true philosophers" (*soli philosophi*) because

---

[83] ... *si volumus hoc, quod datum est vitae, tranquille placideque traducere* ... [*perturbationibus*] *omnibus viribus atque opibus repugnandum est.* Cf. *Tusc.* 2.39–41.
[84] Cf. *Fin.* 1.33: "[E]qual blame belongs to those who fail in their duty through softness of soul [*mollitia animi*], which is the same as saying through shrinking from toil and pain."
[85] See, e.g., *Tusc.* 2.47, 2.54, 2.65, 4.15, 4.60. See Graver 2007, 19–20, 26.
[86] The Greek term is *analgēsia*; see *Tusc.* (Loeb ed.), 239 n.4.   [87] Pace Woolf 2015, 227.
[88] Cicero includes oratorical force in other kinds of physical effort; see *Tusc.* 2.56–57. Cf. Lévy 2012a, 250–65.
[89] Though some lexicons propose that *aretē* is "excellence" in a notably male sense, it is etymologically distinct from *anēr* ("man") and applied to women as early as Homer; see *Od.* 2.206, 18.251. Cf. "ἀρετή," Liddell and Scott, which mentions "manly qualities" of *aretē* and cites early cases of the word's use to describe women, and "ἀρετή," Autenrieth 1958, each of whose citations refer to women.

they support "the idea we all have of bravery" (4.53). Courage is "a disposition of soul in suffering and enduring, obedient to the supreme law of our being without fear [*adfectio animi in patiendo ac perferendo summae legi parens sine timore*]." The ex-consul boasts that the Republic's centurions – even its lowly gladiators – can outperform weak-willed Greeks, "such is the force of training, practice, and habit [*tantum exercitatio, meditatio, consuetudo valet*]" (2.39–41). As Romans open themselves to philosophy, they take equal inspiration from those ancestors who suffered *sua voluntate*.[90] These great men, Cicero insists, succeeded not through airtight syllogisms but through training and endurance.[91] As we build and sustain this rational force, new distresses will affect us less severely (3.67) and the traumas of the past will heal (3.74). Just as the sea is calm when no wind disturbs it, the struggle for reason is won "when no disturbance is strong enough to ruffle the soul [*cum perturbatio nulla est qua* [sc. *animum*] *moveri queat*]" (5.17). While not theorizing the will, Cicero defines it and shows it in action. With the *Tusculans*, it is fair to say that the ex-consul and *imperator* of Cilicia earns a different accolade: the father of willpower.

We can only speculate, finally, why Cicero chooses to merge Stoic and Platonic accounts of the soul. The hybrid argument of the *Tusculans* is exactly the one to make, however, if your goal is to maximize both autonomy and accountability by all available means.[92] His case for responsibility is essentially Stoic: Distress and disturbance lie not in nature but entirely in our own beliefs (3.31). In this, the Stoics have made the right diagnosis, says Cicero, but the wrong prescription. Pain is indeed our responsibility, but it is to be confronted and conquered, not reasoned away (2.28–29). The selection of beliefs must be matched by an intensity of commitment to put them into practice. With no hope of progress toward wisdom – a wisdom reserved, in any case, for a remote few – a listener is discouraged before he begins. Thus, the Stoics' absolutism, their cognitivism, and their poverty of style are three expressions of the same flaw: Their ethical system is coherent but uncompelling.

Cicero, the orator, means to compel. Competition is what galvanizes the Roman mind, and here the Academy is indispensable. By writing *in utramque partem*, Cicero endorses a vision of philosophy not as the

---

[90] See *Tusc.* 2.52–53, 4.63. Cf. *Fin.* 2.65; *Off.* 3.105; *Sest.* 127. Cf. Bénatouïl 2016, 220.
[91] See *Tusc.* 2.28, 2.33, 2.37–38, 5.76–79. Cf. Brittain 2015, 35; Woolf 2015, 218–19. On echoes of Roman martial values in Cicero's philosophy, see generally Lévy 2005.
[92] Cf. Graver 2002, xiv, xxv.

reception of wisdom but as a contest of ideas. This agon of rational forces glorifies author, audience, and Rome as a whole.[93] Though drawing principally on Stoic ethics, Cicero turns to Plato's divided soul to frame this contest with metaphors of hierarchy and rule. The division of the soul into "two selves, one to rule, the other to obey," creates the possibility for "reason to conquer recklessness [*ratio coerceat temeritatem*]" (2.47).[94] It is up to us whether our *perturbationes* will be beaten back by the rational force of will. "It is from this rush," he declares, "this impulse of our souls towards true renown and reputation, that the dangers of battle are encountered" (2.58).[95] Though Plato's division of soul enables this contest, it is waged in Roman terms.

If the Republic's freedoms have been lost, a new philosophically grounded freedom must be born. Even under a tyrant's rule, the Academy's dialectics empower us to choose among a host of possibilities.[96] The Stoic sage is free because he has recognized, confronted, and suppressed all disturbance: "[N]o bondage can enchain his soul."[97] But Cicero's is a distinctly Roman freedom, made manifest in endurance, in glory won by combat, in *imperium* for those with the right to rule ("it remains for you to rule over yourself [*ut tute tibi imperes*]," 2.47). But in the age of Caesar, this struggle for virtue can owe nothing to brutal tyrants or foolish mobs. Should you win public fame, Cicero advises, you should nevertheless not be "dependent on the judgment of the crowd," nor "accept their view of what is fairest," but "use your own judgment" (2.63–64).[98] Virtue thus earned will be not only a victory over the self, but "over the world of men and things" as well.

---

[93] See *Tusc.* 2.5: "I encourage all who have the capacity to wrest from the now failing grasp of Greece the renown won from this field of study and transfer it to this city"; 4.5: Rome had ability to outcompete Greece in all human arts "as soon as they conceived the will to do so" [*simul ut velle coepissent*]; *Fin.* 1.3: "If Wisdom be attainable, let us not only win but enjoy it." Cf. Zetzel 2003, 137; Koch 2006, 111–12; Remer 2017, 81.

[94] Pigeaud 1981, 275, observes: "Dualism does not signify the parallelism of body and soul; it designates a hierarchy with a conflictual state always possible … Cicero's stroke of genius is to have practiced a dualist reading of a monist philosophy."

[95] Bénatouïl 2016, 218–19 (emphasis in original), presents an intriguing alternative: "Zeno's move from natural things to virtue [in the theory of *oikeiōsis*] is analogous to the Platonist break from the senses and pursuit of a higher form of knowledge (and reality) … Stoics and Platonists can be compared because they value virtue as if they were *seeing* it, which leads them to forget everything else. This analogy seems to be an anticipation of the original blend of Stoicism and Platonism, with the leading role granted to the latter, offered in the *Tusculans*."

[96] *Tusc.* 2.8–9, 4.7, 5.32–33, 5.83. See Brittain 2015, 16–17.   [97] *Fin.* 3.75–76.

[98] Brittain 2015, 34, posits that Cicero may have intended his readers to apply this skeptical freedom even to his own conclusions in *Tusc.*

6.3 Conclusion: Willing, Willpower, and the Will

Relishing his skeptical freedom, Cicero may have taken liberties with his Greek sources that we are unable to measure. His readers may adopt a similar skepticism – sympathetic or less so – on the accuracy of several points upon which he is, inconveniently, the sole surviving witness. These caveats aside, I propose that in the *Tusculans* Cicero makes three key contributions to the notion of will that his posterity would inherit: He gives *voluntas* its primary shape as a term of philosophy; he preserves the flexibility and bivalence that distinguishes it from its Greek counterparts; and he gives willpower, not cognition, the lead role in moral progress.

First, drawing upon both Platonists and Stoics, Cicero brings *voluntas* into the philosophical vocabulary of Latin. Will becomes a proper object of study, associated with cognition and desire but distinct from each. In this, Hellenistic debates that had run in parallel are linked together for the first time. To demonstrate the myriad concepts united by this single term, consider Aristotle's theory of action.[99] A virtuous act begins as a *boulēsis*, the desire of reason for some virtuous end. If the intended course of action is "up to us" (*eph'emin*), we can make a choice (*prohairesis*) that validates this *boulēsis*, produces the action, and achieves the desired goal. Our ability to choose is determined not by present effort or deliberation, but rather by an "attachment to reason" resulting from good education and conditioning. As a separate matter, we can only be held ethically responsible for acts that are *hekōn*, "of our own accord."[100] These exclude actions performed under duress or by ignorance but *include* those prompted by (nonrational) appetites – for example, taking a second helping of dessert. Crucially, not only is there no "choice" (*prohairesis*) involved in such an action, but eating the dessert may actually be *against* our *prohairesis*.[101] For this reason, even children and animals can be punished or rewarded for acting "of their own accord" (*hekōn*), though their actions do not come from a (rational) *prohairesis*. Arguing that "the will" is not present in Aristotle, Charles Kahn observes that "there is no one concept that ties together the

---

[99] In this short summary of Aristotle's theory of action, I follow the reading of Kahn and Frede. See Kahn 1988, 239–41; Frede 2011, 19–30.
[100] See Arist. *Eth. Nic.* 1110b18–1121.
[101] Ibid. 1148a9. Frede 2011, 26, concludes for this reason that "there is no notion of the will, or a willing, in Aristotle." There are admittedly key points of overlap in Aristotle's accounts of virtue and of responsibility. Aristotle's criterion of a just action is that it must be *prohairoumenos* (1105a30–34), like friendship, which must be *kata tēn prohairesin* (1164b1–3). But concepts remain distinct; acts of *prohairesis* in friendship must be *hekōn* (1163a2, 1167a5–22).

6.3 Conclusion

voluntary [*hekousiōn*], *boulēsis* or desire for the end, and *prohairesis*, deliberate desire for the means. But it is precisely the role of *voluntas* to perform this work of conceptual unification."[102] Kahn credits Augustine with unifying these concepts, but by the evidence of these treatises, he built on Cicero's foundation.

Several scholars have argued that in translating *hekousiōs* as *voluntarius*, Cicero is simply making a mistake.[103] Whether an act is *hekousiōs* hinges on facts and knowledge ("Was there force or ignorance?"), not deliberate intent; *voluntarius*, on the other hand, denotes precisely this. Is the mismatch merely due to "a lack of psychological refinement in the Latin vocabulary"?[104] Hardly. Cicero had the phrase *sua sponte* available to denote actions "of one's own accord" generated without a rational choice.[105] If *sua sponte* does not figure in his account of moral responsibility, this is surely not due to negligence.

Rather, for Cicero, intention *should* matter in judging others. As we saw in Chapter 1, as a student he had sought out and compared frameworks of moral responsibility. *De inventione* shows his keen concern for the role of emotion in the law and how passion might prove or disprove a criminal motive. His analysis of *concessio* turned on the idea that the *voluntas* or righteous intent of a defendant might exculpate him when the principal evidence suggested guilt.[106] Conversely, Cicero's late treatises on jurisprudence align with the strict responsibility proposed in the *Tusculans*: Even seemingly "unwilling" acts are not excusable.[107] Most likely, the evolution from *hekousiōn* to *voluntarius* signifies Cicero's endorsement of a new standard for Roman law, one of deliberate intent (i.e. the "desire-in-motion" present in Latin but absent in Greek). With the help of Stoic ethics, the through lines of responsibility are clarified: Passion and recklessness are no excuse. Conversely, as we will see in the next chapter, a *recta voluntas* offers the hope of clemency to those who fail despite their "righteous will."

Second, the moral bivalence of *voluntas*, present in decades in practice, is reinforced in his treatise on the soul. In the *Tusculans*, Cicero must

---

[102] Kahn 1988, 240. Frede 2011, 25–26, effectively refutes the claim that *hekōn* denotes a "voluntary" act but notes that many modern translators have repeated the mistake.
[103] Frede 2011, 25, calls Cicero's translation of *voluntarius* for *hekōn* "misleading." Gauthier 1970, 260f., calls it a *maladresse*. Cf. Dihle 1982, 133; Kahn 1988, 248.
[104] See Dihle 1982, 133.
[105] See, e.g., *Verr.* 2.5.18; *Clu.* 79, 138; *Att.* 1.1, 6.2; *Cat.* 1.13; *Dom.* 12; *Fin.* 1.25.
[106] See *Inv.* 2.101: "[I]n all things one should look to *voluntas* . . ."; ibid. 2.24: A criminal can be said to lack legal intent (*voluntas*) if his mind is shown to be "free of such crimes and unsullied [*si animus a talibus factis vacuus et integer esse*]." See discussion in Chapter 2.
[107] Ibid.

finesse a point of bitter disagreement between the Peripatetics and Stoics: namely, whether immoral appetites were nonrational (as Aristotle argued) or the result of a weak or perverse use of reason (as the Stoics insisted).[108] On the one hand, Cicero appears to side firmly with the Stoa: All such *perturbationes* are voluntary and thus under reason's control.[109] Yet the four types he lists include disturbances "destitute of reason" (*rationis expers*), "contemptuous of reason" (*rationem aspernans*) and "disobedient to reason" (*rationi non oboediens*) (3.24). Though disassociated from reason, these can still be overruled by using our reason correctly.[110] However, when Cicero says that anger can kindle the soul *invita ratione* (4.78), we have clearly passed beyond Stoic doctrine into a framework of competing forces where each person has "two selves" and *ratio* can conquer *temeritas* (2.47). It is Plato's account that allows the sense of doing battle with our negative impulses, where the Stoics would have simply recommended thinking better or correcting our false beliefs. This sense of the self as moral battleground is a core quality of Cicero's *voluntas* – the possibility that the will, though fully in our power, can be put to *inhonestae* ends (cf. 4.34). This notion of "sheer volition," potentially guided by reason but not always, becomes a key idea in Christian thought.[111] Part of this ambiguity reflects the orator's concern for ordinary language,[112] describing certain acts in a way most natural to his listeners (e.g. an angry man "has lost his mind," cf. 3.11).[113] Undeniably, though, these ambiguities of *voluntas* arise from the merging of Stoic and Academic doctrines based on opposing premises about the soul.

---

[108] This ambiguity is captured nicely in the English "irrational," which can be used to signify either the absence of reason or its misuse; cf. Graver 2007, 24. Frede 2011, 21–22, draws a distinction between "nonrational" and "unreasonable" acts in Aristotle.

[109] This orthodox framework is most cleanly given in Cicero's phrase that disturbances are *aversa a recta ratione*, implying that a poor or perverse use of reason is to blame; *Tusc.* 4.11. Cf. ibid. 3.4: A good *voluntas* is distinct from good reasoning and can still produce an *error cursus* in those seeking the best (*petentes optima*).

[110] See Pigeaud 1981, 278–91.

[111] See Dihle 1982, 20: "The word 'will' ... as applied to the description and evaluation of human action denotes sheer volition, regardless of its origin in either cognition or emotion." Cf. Frede 2011, 182 n.5: "Dihle is primarily interested in arguing that early Christian theologians developed a new psychology and anthropology in order to register a person's individual commitment to God."

[112] Cf. *Tusc.* 4.66: "[W]e are at present suiting our language to ordinary thought [*sed loquimur nunc more communi*]."

[113] Cf. *Tusc.* 3.11: Those under the power of lust or wrath are called "unbridled" because they "are not under the control of mind [*non sunt in potestate mentis*]"; the furious mind is influenced "by the stronger power of wrath or fear or pain." Here, Cicero distinguishes the qualities of *insanus* (which can never beset the wise man) and *furiosus* (which can beset anyone).

6.3 Conclusion

Cicero's most important departure from his predecessors, finally, is his argument that moral progress is a matter of will. In the *Republic*, Plato stresses the importance of *askēsis* – the practice required to achieve health in the soul.[114] To choose those worthy of rule, "we must also look for someone who has got a good memory, is persistent and is in every way a lover of hard work. How else do you think he'd be willing to carry out both the requisite bodily labors and also complete so much study and practice?" (7.535c).[115] For Aristotle, the possession of wisdom and virtue is principally a function of inborn ability or past conditioning, not present effort.[116] If a man acts unreasonably, "it is this past failure, rather than a specific mental event, a choice or decision, which in Aristotle accounts for *akratic* action."[117] And the Stoics, by denying gradations of wisdom, "insist that all fools are mad in the same way that all mud stinks."[118]

The freshness of Cicero's account is unmistakable. Whereas Plato implies *askēsis* to be the inborn gift of a select few and the Stoics limit virtue to the sage alone, Cicero exhorts *all* his readers to use and develop willpower.[119] In the *Tusculans*, he adds the "onrushing" power of *hormē* to *boulēsis*, a rational desire, and replaces the Stoic "drowning man" with a patient who progressively recovers his eyesight.[120] Like Plato's *thumos*, *voluntas* gives force to reason's commands; nevertheless, for Cicero, will is not merely reason's natural servant but a force to be trained and brought into alignment with it. Whereas Aristotle and Antiochus made moral progress a function of biology and conditioning, Cicero makes it a matter of present effort, continually renewed. As with the Stoics, there is no part of the self that cannot be governed; as with the Platonists, the soul is explicitly self-moving and can be said, in Hannah Arendt's phrase, to "bring about something new."[121]

---

[114] Pl. *Resp.* 4.444d.
[115] Plato's analogy to athletics is another point of correspondence with Cicero; cf. Pl. *Resp.* 7.535b: "They must be keen on the subjects and learn them easily, for people's souls give up much more easily in hard study than in physical training, since the pain – being peculiar to them and not shared with their body – is more their own." Cf. *Phd.* 64a: Philosophy is training for dying; *Grg.* 491e, 505a: Self-restraint and self-improvement are essential (no training process is described). On *askēsis* in Plato, see generally Long 2015, 109–16.
[116] See Frede 2011, 22–24: "Aristotle's view is never that, if we are confronted with [*akrasia*, it is] … because there is a mental event, namely, a choice or decision to act in this way … It is, rather, a long story about how in the past one has failed to submit oneself" to the training required "that one acts for reasons, rather than on impulse."
[117] Frede 2011, 24.   [118] *Tusc.* 4.54.   [119] See Lévy 2007, 29–30.   [120] *Fin.* 4.65.
[121] Arendt 1971, vol. 2, 6. The idea is nicely expressed by Bergson 1921, 6: "Thus our personality sprouts, grows, and ripens without ceasing. Each of its moments is the new which augments what came before. Let us go further: it is not only the new, but the unpredictable."

Frede posits that only in Epictetus does the will, as *prohairesis*, become a deliberate object of cultivation and training within the self. Though he did not directly influence Epictetus, Cicero offers a similarly innovative model of moral progress – one whose resonance, as we shall see in the Epilogue, is felt in Augustine five centuries later. In this call to willpower, Cicero's unique life experience cannot be ignored. The resilience he extols in the *Tusculans* was, in a sense, his greatest asset in winning the consulship and enduring the reversals that followed. The great orator's message is that moral integrity is decided not by birth or conditioning but present choice – or more precisely, an unfolding series of choices that form what can be called our character. To reinforce our will, we draw upon a trove of resources: the values bred into us; the insights of philosophy; the examples of heroes, both historical and literary; and, finally, the wealth of our own experience. As Cicero goes on to elaborate in *De fato* and *De officiis*, it is this *voluntas* that best encapsulates our freedom and by which we create a unique, and uniquely conscious, self.

CHAPTER 7

Free Will and the Forum

The debate over free will is a thicket one may justly hesitate to enter. A rare if little-noticed point of agreement in this debate is that its most-cited classical sources say little of freedom. The key terms in Aristotle's account of human agency are *hekōn* – whether an act is performed "of our own accord" – and then whether a *prohairesis* or choice led to it.[1] The Hellenistic schools seem to have sparred over human autonomy, but evidence from later texts suggest that their key term was *eph'emin* – what is "up to us."[2] Why not freedom? Frede and Schofield, among others, have observed that the Greek *eleutheria*, like the Latin *libertas*, is unshakably political at its root. It connotes a civic status of nondomination: A free city makes laws for itself, and a free man is not enslaved to another.[3] With the death of the classical *polis* and rise of the Hellenistic empires, their new subjects may well have sought accounts of the good life that did not depend on "freedom" as such. In Frede's estimation,

> [t]he lack of clarity about the relation between the political notion and this personal notion of freedom in part is due to a lack of clarity about the relation between the good life one is able to have when one is politically free and the good life one can live if one has personal freedom. The tendency among ancient philosophers, needless to say, is to claim that one can live a good life even under a tyrant or as a slave.[4]

---

[1] For *hekōn*, see Arist. *Eth. Nic.* 1110b18–1112a1; for *prohairesis*, see ibid. 1148a9. I concur with Frede 2011, 19–30, that Aristotle's *prohairesis* and *hekōn* do not amount to a notion of "willing" and thus Aristotle has no notion of a will, properly understood. On *prohairesis*, see generally Merker 2016.
[2] See Arist. *Eth. Nic.* 1112a30–34; *De interpret.* 9; Epicurus, *Ep. Men.* 133–35; Diogenianus in Euseb. *Praep. evang.* 6.8.25–29 (SVF 2.998). Cf. Graver 2007, 81; Lévy 2007, 26. The term *eph'emin* has itself been mistranslated as "free will"; see, e.g., Huby 1967, 353–62. Cf. Bobzien 1998b, 135, and Kahn 1988, 242, noting this problem.
[3] As Schofield 2014 observes, the Greek and Latin terms for freedom do not map neatly onto one another; *eleutheria* had specific historical connotations – including of *parrhēsia* and *isagoreia*, freedoms to speak in public – that *libertas* did not necessarily have for Cicero.
[4] Frede 2011, 9–10.

In the Greek texts Cicero most likely read, therefore, debates over causality and responsibility were as fierce as they are today, yet "freedom" was nowhere to be found.

Cicero seems to have written *De fato* in 44 BCE, just after the Ides of March and a little more than a year before his own death. Ostensibly a dialogue between Cicero and Hirtius, consul-designate for 43 BCE, its extant passages take the form of a continuous exposition by the author. In the skeptical manner, Cicero compares the views of Epicurus, Chrysippus, and Carneades to see which school can reconcile the laws of physics with human autonomy. His language shows deference to his Hellenistic forebears, with the Latin *in nostra potestate* or *in nobis* featuring nineteen times. But Cicero also uses *voluntas* or *voluntarius* eleven times and *libertas* or its cognates seven times, beginning with the observation that the discussion took place on a day "freer than usual" (*liberiore quam solebat*, 2). The phrase is suggestive not only of the seriousness of the burden on Cicero's shoulders after Caesar's death, but also of the implied kinship between his freedom to inquire and his duty to find political solutions.[5] In what remains of the dialogue, Cicero rejects the Epicureans, both vaunts and chides the Stoics, and aims to improve the Stoic view with help from Platonist doctrine and Roman common sense. Throughout all this, the lodestar of *De fato* is *libertas*. Freedom is never dearer to Cicero than at the brink of political ruin. As he wrote in *De republica*, *voluntas* and *libertas* once defined the *populus Romanus*;[6] amid tyranny and chaos, free will must make the good man. In this technical treatise on fate, the political stakes of 44 BCE ring loudly.

The last battles of the Republic coincide with the opening salvo of the free will debate in the West. On opposite sides are two Roman proponents of Greek wisdom: Cicero and Titus Lucretius Carus. I begin by briefly examining Lucretius' *De rerum natura*, the first work of theory in which "free" and "will" are brought into orbit. Written in the 50s BCE, the poem is one that Cicero read and may even have edited. In any event, the Epicurean argument that human autonomy derives from a "swerve of atoms" (*clinamen*) is one that Cicero confronts and emphatically rejects. I propose that the notion of free will Cicero develops in 44 BCE is intended both to refute the Epicureans and to affirm civic duty at this turbulent

---

[5] It is significant as well that whereas Pansa, the other consul-designate for 43 BCE, had declared for the "liberators," Hirtius' allegiances remained, for Cicero, worryingly uncertain; see *Att.* 4.383.1. On the philosophical significance of Cicero's *proemia* to the main arguments of his treatises, see generally Lévy 1992, 140–80 and *passim*; Baraz 2012, ch. 5.
[6] See *Rep.* 1.51, 1.69, 2.39–40, 2.55–57, discussed in Chapter 5.

moment. As we will see later in this chapter, Cicero's letters underscore the metapolitical stakes of his treatise on fate.[7] At its core, this notion of free will helps him make three crucial arguments: that the Republic was not fated to fall; that his enemies bear full responsibility; and that a "righteous will" (*recta voluntas*) excuses his own failures.[8]

7.1 Lucretius' *Libera Voluntas*

De rerum natura was among the few works of Epicureanism to survive antiquity, and it is certainly its best known. For such a widely admired text, we know very little about its author. Cicero evidently knew and appreciated the poem; he writes to Quintus in 54 BCE: "Lucretius's poetry is as you say – sparkling with natural genius, but plenty of technical skill as well [*multis luminibus ingeni, multae tamen artis*]."[9] There was a belief in antiquity that Cicero even helped edit the younger man's work.[10] No direct evidence supports the claim, but it would not clash with a host of examples that show Cicero, foe of Epicureanism, as generous and affectionate toward the Epicureans he knew.[11]

In Book 2 of his poem, Lucretius introduces the Epicurean theory of *atoma*, the indivisible bodies that compose his universe. "While the first bodies [*corpora*] are being carried downwards," he writes, "by their own weight in a straight line through the void, at times quite uncertain and uncertain places, they swerve a little from their course [*depellere paulum*] ..." (2.217–20). How does this *inclinatio*[12] help make sense of the universe? In the first instance, the swerve is what allows otherwise straight-falling atoms to collide and combine, creating all matter as we know it (2.221–24). To deny that such an *inclinatio* is possible, Lucretius continues, is also to accept a universe in which all human acts are determined by an infinite chain of causes:

> *Denique si semper motus conectitur omnis*
> *et vetere exoritur motu novus ordine certo*
> *nec declinando faciunt primordia motus*
> *principium quoddam quod fati foedera rumpat,*

---

[7] See Lévy 2007, 20–21.   [8] *Fam.* 2.244.2.   [9] *QFr.* 14.3.
[10] See Saint Jerome's entry for 94 BCE in Eusebius, *Chronicon eusebii v. 2*, A. Schöne, ed. (Berlin, 1875), at 133; see extended discussion in Smith 1975, x–xiv.
[11] See generally Lévy (2020a).
[12] Lucretius' rendering of *clinamen*. See 2.243–44: "[T]he bodies must incline a little" (*paulum inclinare necessest corpora*). The term is also rendered as *declinatio* by Lucretius and Cicero; cf. Lucr. 2.221, 2.250, 2.253, 2.259; Cic. *Fat.* 22–23, 46–48.

> *ex infinito ne causam causa sequatur,*
> <u>*libera per terras unde haec animantibus exstat,*</u>
> <u>*unde est haec, inquam, fatis avolsa voluntas,*</u>
> *per quam progredimur quo ducit quemque voluptas,*
> *declinamus item motus nec tempore certo*
> *nec regione loci certa, sed ubi ipsa tulit mens?*

> [Again, if all motion is always one long chain, and new motion arises out of the old in order invariable, and if the first-beginnings do not make by swerving a beginning of motion such as to break the decrees of fate, that cause may not follow cause from infinity, *whence comes this free will in living creatures all over the earth, whence I say is this will wrested from the fates* by which we proceed whither pleasure leads each, swerving also our motions not at fixed times and fixed places, but just where our mind has taken us?] (2.251–60)[13]

Though he gives no definition for *voluntas* nor explains in what sense it is *libera*, we can make a few observations. We notice, as Cicero evidently did,[14] that Lucretius does not explain how the swerve of atoms could cause free will; instead, he merely poses the rhetorical question of how something could be "up to us" *without* the contingency that the swerve provides.[15] From a more poetic point of view, we also note the line symmetry of *voluntas* and *voluptas* (pleasure), the central ethical principle of the Epicurean universe.[16] Will is a means to pleasure, and in Lucretius' description, not just humans but "all living creatures" (*haec animantibus*) make use of it (2.256). Nevertheless, the nonrecurrence of the phrase "free will" in this lengthy work may suggest it was not a concept Lucretius felt worthy of special attention.[17] Rather, the phrase serves his broader ethical argument about bodies in motion; just as the

---

[13] Trans. Rouse, emphasis added.   [14] *Fat.* 47–48.
[15] See Frede 2011, 13: "Epicurus's doctrine of the swerve, it seems to me, has been widely misunderstood as a doctrine which is meant to explain human freedom, as if a postulated swerve of atoms in the mind could explain such a thing. Epicurus's point is, rather, that, since the world is not deterministic in this way, it does not constitute a threat to the idea that some of the things we do are genuinely our own actions, rather than something which happens to us or something we are made to do." Cf. Gauthier 1970, 256; Sedley 1983, 12–14.
[16] There remains some disagreement over whether *voluntas* is an interpolation for *voluptas* at Lucr. 2.257. See Büchner 1956, 227–29; Gauthier 1970, 256; Bollack 1976, 163–89; Avotins 1983, 286–91 (comparing Lucr. 2.251–58 to *Fat.* 20); Combeaud 2015, 531–33. I take no position on this debate but will analyze the passage as if *voluntas* is the correct reading.
[17] In the poem's 7,415 lines, *liber* and its cognates appear ten times and *voluntas* eleven. The sole pairing of *liber* and *voluntas* is at 2.256–57; *liber* and *velit* are brought into contact at 2.1046–47. *Voluntas*: 2.251–76 (four occurrences); 3.46, 3.174, 4.781, 4.883, 4.984, 4.1045, 6.389. *Liber*: 1.456, 1.1048, 2.256, 2.1047, 2.1091, 3.569, 4.398, 4.720, 5.79, 6.727.

swerve of atoms creates the world of nature, so does *inclinatio* allow living things to seek their pleasure.[18]

In the lines that follow, Lucretius traces the path by which the will of living things produces motion:

> For undoubtedly it is his own will in each that begins these things, and from the will movements go rippling through the limbs ...

> For all the mass of matter must be stirred up together through the whole body, in order that thus stirred up together it may all with one combined effort follow the inspiration of the mind; thus you may see that the beginning of motion is made in the heart, and the action moves on by [the force of] soul and will, to be passed onwards through the whole body and limbs ... (2.261–62, 265–71)[19]

The account is vivid, if a bit obscure. Parsing his poetic syntax, Lucretius' sequence is as follows: (1) An inspiration (*studium*) forms in the mind (*mens*), which sits in the heart (*cor*); (2) this beginning of motion (*initum motus*) proceeds from the heart via the "soul and will" (*ex animi voluntate*);[20] by this force of will, (3) man's whole body (*totum corpus*) is activated. In this way, a fully cognitive (but physical) *studium* is transformed by *voluntas* into motion: Will bridges thought and action.[21] The precise status of *voluntas* – is it a faculty of soul or merely an activity of it? – is unclear. What is clear is its quality of motion, and motion with an ethical purpose: Will is the force that allows us to go forth "where pleasure leads each" (*quo ducit quemque voluptas*, 2.258).[22]

These passages open interesting correspondences to Cicero's notion of will. *Voluntas*, in Lucretius, is the force by which creatures like us "project"

---

[18] Cf. 4.984–86: "Of so great import are devotion and will, and what those things are which not men only, but indeed all creatures, are in the habit of practicing [*Usque adeo magni refert studium atque voluntas/et quibus in rebus consuerint esse operati/non homines solum, sed vero animalia cuncta*]."

[19] *nam dubio procul his rebus sua cuique voluntas*
principium dat et hinc motus per membra rigantur ...
omnis enim totum per corpus materiai
copia conciri debet, concita per artus
omnis ut studium mentis conixa sequatur;
ut videas initum motus a corde creari
ex animique voluntate id procedere primum,
inde dari porro per totum corpus et artus. (2.261–62, 265–71)
I amend Rouse and Smith's translation slightly.

[20] The ablative following *ex* could imply that this motion is "by way of" (i.e. the means), "out of" (i.e. from the place), or "in accordance with."

[21] See also Lucr. 3.161–76, 4.881–84.

[22] In this Lucretius includes sexual desire, with *voluntas* as the "will to emit [our seed] towards that whither the dire craving tends [*voluntas eicere id quo se contendit dira lubido*]"; 4.1045–46.

themselves (*exstare*) and "march forward" (*progredior*); our "swerving" breaks the chain in which "new motion arises out of the old in order invariable"; our will is thus what "wrests" living creatures from fate (*fatis avolsa voluntas*).[23] As we have seen in previous chapters, this sense of motion and force had long been part of the polysemy of *voluntas*. But as we have also seen, this dynamic quality of *voluntas* – and its measurability in strength and duration – is not present in the closest Greek equivalents to will: *boulēsis* and *prohairesis*. With Lucretius as well as Cicero, therefore, the transfer of ideas from Greek into Latin allows new ways of conceiving man's place in the universe.

Yet Lucretius' *libertas* is not Cicero's. His freedom is, first, the shedding of superstitions to see the real "nature of all things." It is a freedom by which the mind of man projects itself "beyond the walls of the world," a mind that "continually wills to look forth."[24] This freedom to inquire leads us to the truth that nature and all living things are free from the indifferent will of the gods.[25] This truth liberates us, in turn, from our fear of death and divine punishment. To stay free, men must reject the temptation to "revert back again to the old superstitions, and take to themselves cruel taskmasters, whom the poor wretches believe to be almighty [*dominos acris adsciscunt, omnia posse/quos miseri credunt*]" (5.86–88). Crucially, this Epicurean freedom of the mind is not a freedom to act as a citizen or preserve a republic.[26] Rather, Lucretius recommends his readers find "lofty sanctuaries serene, well fortified by the teachings of the wise, whence you may look down upon others and behold them all astray ... [T]he strife of wits, the fight for precedence, all laboring night and day with surpassing toil to mount upon the pinnacle of riches and to lay hold on power" (2.7–13). As we will see later in this chapter, this attempt to sever man's *libertas* from civic duty and reorient it toward pleasure was not something an ex-consul of Rome could abide.

---

[23] Cf. 2.274–76: When we are pushed from outside, "then it is clear that all the matter of the whole body moves and is hurried against our will, until the will has curbed it back through the limbs [*nam tum materiem totius corporis omnem/perspicuumst nobis invitis ire rapique,/donec eam refrenavit per membra voluntas*]."

[24] Ibid. 2.1044–47.

[25] See ibid. 6.387–95: "[I]f lightning comes from the gods, who can strike whomever they will [*quo cuiquest cumque voluntas*], why do they not smite the unjust?" Cf. ibid. 2.1090–93, 5.77–81.

[26] Epicurus did apparently allow that individuals with a natural inclination for politics should follow it; nevertheless, he added, friendship exists on a higher ethical plane than politics, and politicians rarely have friends. Cf. Epicurus, *RS* 6.7.14; Phld. *Rhet.* 2, 158–59, fr. 19.6–22; Roskam 2009, 181–82.

7.2 Cicero's *Libera Voluntas*

Cicero is the first author we know definitively to have juxtaposed "freedom" and "will." Its first extant occurrence comes in Cicero's second speech against Verres in 70 BCE. Arguing that he has not brought this case rashly, he gives the example of Lucius Crassus, great orator of the previous generation, who after a similar star-making turn "*had willings less free in all things*, knowing that his life was being watched by more eyes than he would wish [*minus enim liberas omnium rerum voluntates habebat, et vitam suam pluribus quam vellet observari oculis arbitrabatur*]" (2.3.3, emphasis added). In Cicero's phrase, free will is not yet a constituent of the human subject. The price of Crassus' new fame are "willings less free" – specific desires, not a mental faculty. Importantly, this self-imposed constraint is part of a patriotic *voluntas virtutis atque officii* (2.3.2), his commitment to a life of duty and virtue. This negotiation of freedom and necessity happens in public, for a public cause, submitted to public judgment. Though admitting the force of *necessitas* in his life (2.3.2), Cicero enacts his autonomy by circumscribing it, limiting his future freedom for the Republic's sake.

Written two and a half eventful decades later, the extant passages of *De fato* return to this debate, bringing new intellectual resources to bear. At first glance, the treatise is something of a mystery. It is one of three late works, along with *De natura deorum* and *De divinatione*, in which Cicero explores religious or cosmological themes. Though submitting each view to dialectical challenges (in the skeptical Academic tradition), Cicero's aim is to show that philosophy not only resonates with Roman tradition but can reinforce it as well.[27] In Schofield's view, *De natura deorum* was "necessary to bring philosophy to Rome,"[28] and *De divinatione* concerned a highly visible topic on which Cicero had a unique perspective as augur. The role of *De fato* in this triad is not immediately evident. What good was a technical treatise on logic and causality to Roman readers in 44 BCE?

Cicero's method is to weigh in turn the accounts of moral responsibility offered by the various schools.[29] To the Epicureans, he offers less a critique than a direct frontal attack:

---

[27] See generally Wynne 2019, ch. 1.
[28] Personal notes from conversation with M. Schofield, Cambridge, UK, October 2016. On the place of *Fat.* in Cicero's late works and its relation to the debates of *Div.* and *Nat. D.*, see also Sharples 1991, 1–5, 23–25.
[29] Cicero, applying the methods of the Academic skeptic, passes back and forth among the arguments proposed by the Epicureans, the Stoics, and the "view of Carneades." In what follows, I group these

The reason why Epicurus introduces the "swerve" of atoms was his fear lest, if the atom were always carried along by the natural and necessary force of gravity, we should have no freedom whatever [*nihil liberum*], since the movement of the mind was controlled by the movement of the atom. (23)[30]

Importantly, Cicero does not question the premise he ascribes to Epicurus – that total causal necessity would deprive humans of *libertas*. In fact, this part of his account is a nearly word-for-word paraphrase of the key passage from Lucretius. Nevertheless, Cicero finds the *clinamen* ridiculous on its face. Epicurus and his Roman followers entertain simultaneously "two utterly inexplicable propositions, one that something takes place without a cause ... the other that when two atoms are travelling through empty space, one moves in a straight line and the other swerves" (18–19).[31] The Epicureans are oriented toward the correct goal – the protection of *libertas* – but their idea fails the basic tenets of physics. When he returns to Epicurus at the end of the text, it is to reaffirm that "one should not seek assistance from atoms that roam and swerve out of their path" (46).

Cicero's notion of free will emerges in the counterpoint of two Hellenistic innovators. Most of our extant text concerns the Stoics, and more precisely the pioneering theories of Chrysippus on causality and assent. At several points where Chrysippus' ideas seem to fall short, they are contrasted with – or perhaps completed by – those of Carneades, leader of the skeptical New Academy. In particular, it is Carneades' notion of the self-moving human soul that Cicero seizes upon in making his case for free will.[32] The common adversaries of Chrysippus and Carneades are those thinkers who argue that the universe operates in "an everlasting series of causes" (20; i.e. the strict determinists).[33] One alleged proponent of this view is the logician Diodorus Cronus, who held that since any proposition

---

arguments together and examine them in the order that best illuminates Cicero's position on free will.

[30] *Hanc Epicurus rationem induxit ob eam rem, quod veritus est, ne, si semper atomus gravitate ferretur naturali ac necessaria, nihil liberum nobis esset, cum ita moveretur animus, ut atomorum motu cogeretur.* Sedley 1983, 40–41, calls Cicero's reading of the doctrine, and its estimation of the mechanistic view Epicurus was trying to refute, "a thoroughly plausible explanation of the swerve."

[31] See also *Fin.* 1.19–20.

[32] Attributed to the leader of the skeptical New Academy, the "view of Carneades" is understood not to represent a positive doctrine but rather an argument developed in dialectical opposition to another position – here, as often, the Stoic view. Though Carneades would have been ready to accept the view ascribed to him as the most probable one, he would be equally free to trade it for another. Cf. Frede 2011, 91–92; Brittain 2015, 18–20.

[33] Among these "old philosophers" he includes Democritus, Heraclitus, Empedocles, and – oddly – Aristotle, ascribing to them the position "that everything takes place by fate ... [and] that assent is given perforce as the result of necessity"; *Fat.* 39–40.

7.2 *Cicero's* Libera Voluntas

is either true or false, a true statement that an event will happen is the same as saying it *must* happen. The consequence of this logical position, Cicero thinks, is a chain that man is powerless to break (12–13). Cicero then explains why such a view would be unacceptable:

> [T]hose who say that a true future event cannot be changed into a false one, are not asserting the necessity of fate but explaining the meaning of terms; whereas those who bring in an everlasting series of causes *rob the human mind of free will* and fetter it in the chains of a fated necessity [*ei mentem hominis voluntate libera spoliatam necessitate fati devinciunt*]. (*Fat.* 20, emphasis added)

Freedom arrives center stage. In contrast to Cicero's earlier use of the phrase in the *Verrines*, *libera voluntas* no longer signifies a "free willing," one desire among many, but a faculty of "the mind of man" (*mens hominis*). Suggestively, his antithesis to human freedom, "an everlasting series of causes," again corresponds to Lucretius' choice of words.[34] But where the Epicurean speaks equably of abridging fate's "decrees" (*fati foedera rumpat*, 2.254) and "plucking" will from it (*fatis avolsa voluntas*, 2.257), Cicero reprises his role as legal advocate, charging theft and wrongful enslavement. As if to sharpen the importance of freedom, in this lengthy section on logic *libertas* is literally Cicero's final word: "[R]eason itself will insist both that certain things are true from all eternity and that they are not involved in a nexus of eternal causes but are *free* from the necessity of fate [*et a fati necessitate esse libera*]" (38, emphasis added).

Why does Cicero insist upon the will's freedom? He agrees with Lucretius that a fully determined world deprives man of *libertas* – an argument no Greek appears to have made. But Cicero's *libertas* is decidedly un-Epicurean. His own notion emerges in the demolition of *ignava ratio*, the so-called Lazy Argument. This apparently well-known critique of determinism held that in a world of perfect cause and effect there would be no need, for instance, to call a doctor when sick, because our living or dying would be a matter of fate alone (28–29). Chrysippus, according to Cicero, attempts a solution via the idea of "condestination" or "co-fatedness" (*confatalia*).[35] Cicero agrees with Chrysippus that the Lazy Argument

---

[34] Cf. Lucr. 2.255, ... *infinito ne causam causa sequatur*; *Fat.* 20, ... *qui introducunt causarum seriem sempiternam*.

[35] The idea, which Cicero struggles to elucidate, is that certain events are "complex" (*copulata*), such that an act can be both fated *and* chosen by the actor; *Fat.* 11. Thus, the statement "you will recover whether you call in a doctor or do not" is captious, "for calling in a doctor is just as much fated as recovering. These connected events, as I said, are termed by Chrysippus 'condestinate' [*confatalia*]"; ibid. 30.

is no mere thought experiment, but a question upon which turns "the entire abolition of action from life" (29). The Stoa's founders, "those old philosophers," had held that "assent is given perforce as the result of necessity."[36] Under this framework, Cicero observes, neither assent nor action can truly be considered in our power. Why does this matter? The *ignava ratio* would "abolish action" because if man is not the true cause of his actions, "there is no justice in either praise or blame, either honors or punishments [*nec laudationes iustae sint nec vituperationes nec honores nec supplicia*]" (40).[37] Praise and blame, honors and punishments: The same civic order from which the Epicureans want to secede,[38] Cicero wants desperately to preserve.

To defeat the Lazy Argument, Chrysippus reframed the Stoic position: There are not one but two kinds of causality. He suggested the image of a cylinder rolling across a room: The "auxiliary and proximate" cause of the cylinder's motion is the push given to it from outside, but the "perfect and principal" cause is its own round shape (43). Accordingly, while the Stoic *phantasiai* are the auxiliary and proximate causes of action, human nature – our "shape," wise or foolish – is the perfect and primary cause (41–42). For Chrysippus, our actions are thus *in nostra potestate* because, like the roller, we move by our own *vis et natura* (43). In distinguishing these two types of causation, Chrysippus ingeniously managed "to escape necessity and to retain fate" (41).[39] But why does Cicero, defender of *libertas*, care about "retaining fate"? By preserving the logic of causality, Chrysippus assists Cicero in dispatching the Epicureans while leaving room for prophecies and divination – institutions precious to Rome and to Cicero's career.[40]

Yet Cicero is not quite content with the Stoic account. There is both a surface objection, I believe, and a deeper one. As he did in *De finibus* and the *Tusculans*,[41] Cicero reproaches the Stoics for their second-rate style. Using "formulae peculiar to himself," Chrysippus has undermined the will

---

[36] *Fat.* 39. Cf. Chrysippus' departure from his teacher Cleanthes on an issue of formal logic; ibid. 14.
[37] Cf. *Acad.* 2.38–39: "Where is virtue, if nothing is up to us [*ubi igitur virtus, si nihil situm est in ipsis nobis*]?"; cf. *Off.* 1.28: An action is just only if it is voluntary (*voluntarius*).
[38] See, e.g., Lucr. 2.37–61, 3.59–93, 5.1105–60. This is not to say that the Epicureans thought no acts were worthy of praise or blame, but rather that from their point of view most societies, Rome included, praise and blame the wrong things. Tellingly, Lucretius does not mention Rome by name in these passages, giving Cicero his opening. I am grateful to David Sedley for this observation.
[39] Cf. Sedley and Long 1987, 61–62.
[40] See *Div.* 1.7–9. *De divinatione*, structured as a dialogue, spares Cicero – himself a member of the college of augurs – the unpleasant task of having to side with skepticism over tradition or vice versa. His aim is clearly to retain the institution in some form; see *De legibus* Book 2, discussed in Chapter 5. Cf. Lévy 2020b, 12–14.
[41] See *Fin.* 3.3, 3.19, 4.5–7, 4.22–23, 4.52; *Tusc.* 2.29, 2.42.

"against his will" (*invitus*), handing ammunition to his intellectual opponents (39–40).[42] Graver still, according to the Stoic doctrine of assent, all human action must be preceded by an external force (*vi extrinsecus*, 42). We are, they insist, coauthors of our actions – though these are triggered from outside us and, following Chrysippus, determined by our "shape." In contrast, Plato's doctrine of the self-moving soul allows that the operations of our will are not only "up to us" (*in nostra potestate*), but ascribable *only* to us.[43] We remember that, for Plato, "every act of your soul is an act of yours."[44] This apparently stronger view of autonomy offers an attractive corrective to the Stoics' dependence on past conditioning and external stimulus. Carneades lets Cicero develop a notion of will based instead on independent choice and present effort: Free will manifests a self-moving soul.

A trained Stoic would undoubtedly object that Cicero has done violence to their position and that their account of fate is similarly robust and more coherent.[45] But Cicero's objection to the Stoics has never been a lack of coherence. Rather, they have failed to align their theories with the lived experience of their listeners. In an early passage, he takes aim at Chrysippus' view that the differences between men are explained by varieties of climate or the positions of heavenly bodies (7).[46] "All the same," Cicero ripostes, "the rarefied air of Athens will not enable a student to choose among the lectures of Zeno, Arcesilas and

---

[42] He also teases Chrysippus for trying to correct the syntax of Chaldean diviners; *Fat*. 15–16. After his analysis of the Stoic's doctrine of "condestination," he adds that Carneades achieved the same result "but did not employ any trickery [*nec ullam adhibebat calumniam*]"; ibid. 31.

[43] Cicero argues that by allowing "the possibility of some voluntary movement of the mind [*quendam animi motum voluntarium*]," the Academics "could easily have withstood Chrysippus, for in admitting that no motion is uncaused they would not have been admitting that all events are due to antecedent causes, as they would have said that there are *no external and antecedent causes of our will* [*voluntatis enim nostrae non esse causas externas et antecedentes*]" (23–24, emphasis added). Cicero makes an analogy from physics: The laws of nature allow atoms to move through the void by their own gravity and weight, with no additional external force required (24–25). "Voluntary motion possesses the intrinsic property of being in our power [*in nostra potestate*] and of obeying us, and its obedience is not uncaused, for its nature is itself the cause of this [*enim rei causa ipsa natura est*]" (25–26). Cf. Frede 2011, 16, arguing that in earlier antiquity explanations from "natural causes" still left room for the world to "remain in our sense causally undetermined, leaving enough space for us to live our life as we see fit."

[44] *Tusc*. 1.52: *ab animo tuo quidquid agitur, id agitur a te*. Cicero translates the famous passage from *Phaedrus* twice in his corpus; *Rep*. 6.25, *Tusc*. 1.53–54. On the persistence of this doctrine in the Hellenistic period, see Lévy 2007, 31.

[45] See Frede 2011, 91. Frede dismisses Cicero's use of the phrase *motus voluntarii* as irrelevant to later notions of free will but does not mention his phrase *libera voluntas*; ibid. 93.

[46] Cicero is equally critical of divine omens as he is of "climatic" determinism: Posidonius' arguments for the destiny of omens over simple natural explanations, or even mere chance, are *absurda*; *Fat*. 7–8.

Theophrastus" (ibid.). Differences of climate, however keenly observed, do not determine where we choose to walk on a certain day, or in which friend's company (9). For Cicero, the simplest daily choices – strolling here, sitting there – are common-sense, irreducible evidence of human freedom. As Woolf observes, "the upholding of common sense is, I think, one reason why he emphasizes his role as orator [in *De fato*], and the connection of oratory with the scepticism of the New Academy. The orator needs to take seriously ordinary ways of thinking; and the Academic sceptic is primed to look critically at philosophical doctrine."[47] Cicero encourages his readers to adopt a common-sense understanding, instead of a strict construction, of "willing something without cause": We mean not that our volition is uncaused but that we ourselves are causing it.[48] Intuitively, as compared to the Stoics, the Academic "will" seems a good deal more free.[49]

Now we can surmise why Chrysippus' "two causes" may be insufficient for Cicero. The "perfect and primary" cause of the cylinder's motion is its *natura*, not its *voluntas*. A cylinder does not strive to roll through a room. Chrysippus' position, his answer to the Lazy Argument, is that simply moving by *vis et natura* puts these movements in our power (43). For Cicero, by contrast, our will is manifest – is in a sense "at its most free" – where it does not merely reflect our *natura* but overcomes it. Though born with a predilection for liquor and women, Stilpo the Megarian strives fiercely to "master and suppress his vicious nature by study [*vitiosam ... naturam ab eo sic edomitam et compressam esse doctrina*]" (10). Though nature gave him certain traits, he is not doomed by these defects. Freedom is not the sole province of the sage but lies in the "will, effort, and training [*voluntate studio disciplina*]" practicable by all (11). This is Cicero's way of knowing: not in pristine logic but in present action, friction, the contest of

---

[47] Woolf 2015, 87. See *Fat.* 3: "[T]here is a close alliance between the orator and the philosophical system of which I am a follower," where the latter's subtlety adds to and is made more persuasive by the former's style.

[48] The Carnadean position appears to have some resonance in contemporary physics. See Rovelli 2015, 73: "When we say that we are free, and it's true that we can be, this means that how we behave is determined by what happens within us, within the brain, and not by external factors. To be free doesn't mean that our behavior is not determined by the laws of nature. It means that it is determined by the laws of nature acting in our brains ..."

[49] See *Fat.* 31: Cicero finds Carneades' position "rigidly conclusive" that "if everything takes place with antecedent causes ... all things are caused by necessity; if this is true, nothing is in our power. But *something is in our power* [*Est autem aliquid in nostra potestate*]" (emphasis added). In other words, our lived experience, the self-evident sensation shared by philosopher and layman alike, is evidence too rich to be disregarded. Strolling the agora, attending lectures, resisting temptations – these are *voluntatis*, matters of will. If we feel free, then, in some very important sense, we are.

forces.⁵⁰ Only by overcoming our inborn flaws, as Stilpo did, do we repay the gift of a *libera voluntas*; only in struggle does freedom become real.

7.3 The Politics of Free Will

As pioneers of Latin philosophy, Lucretius and Cicero each deserve mention as godfathers of free will. It must be added that sharing this accolade with the Epicurean would be, for Cicero, a nasty shock. Whatever warmth he may have felt for Lucretius personally, *De fato* reveals a vehement distaste for his school. The Epicureans "stand in terror of fate and seek protection against it from the atoms ..." (18). Their theories are motivated by fear (*veretur*, 21, 23) and "wishful thinking" (*optare*, 47); their incapacity for logic is "shameful" (*impudens*, 37). In the treatise's closing lines he concludes, "no one did more to abolish the voluntary movements of soul [*motus animi voluntarios*], than has the philosopher who confesses that he has been unable to withstand fate in any other way than by taking refuge in these fictitious swerves" (48). In other words, the Epicurean position is not merely wrong, it is shameful. Strictly speaking, isn't this beside the point?

Not at all. The manliness of the Epicurean position matters because in 44 BCE the Republic's *virtus* is at stake. Whereas the Garden preaches quiet extrication from politics, the Lazy Argument must be opposed because it leads "to the entire abolition of action from life" (29). If we are not the true authors of our actions, Cicero declares, then "there is no justice in either praise or blame, either honors or punishments [*nec laudationes iustae sint nec vituperationes nec honores nec supplicia*]" (40). For the Epicureans, *voluntas* is the force by which all creatures, human or beast, seek *voluptas*, including the fulfillment of sexual desire.⁵¹ For Cicero, will is exemplified in the specifically human self-mastery of Stilpo and the heroism of Regulus, who suffers for the Republic *sua voluntate*.⁵² The apparently esoteric debate of *De fato* thus has urgent and present consequences. A cosmology with no room for honor is a grave threat: Strip these from Roman life and nothing remains.⁵³

---

⁵⁰ Cf. Lévy 2007, 26: "[In *De fato*], *voluntas* appears as a force independent of *natura* and capable of transforming it. Stilpo and Socrates are evoked as examples of persons having surmounted by will the naturally determined qualities they do not deny."
⁵¹ Lucr. 2.258, 4.1045–46. ⁵² See *Fat.* 10; *Sest.* 127; *Fin.* 2.65; *Off.* 3.105.
⁵³ Cf. *Fin.* 1.23–25, 2.73, the example of Roman heroes refutes Epicurean ethics; 2.67–68, there is no mention of Greek heroes in the school of Epicurus; 2.74, a Roman orator could not endorse Epicurus in public; 2.76, Roman values that Torquatus should respect. Cicero continually grounds his account of virtue in civic duty; cf. *Nat. D.* 1.110; *Off.* 1.19; see also Powell 2012, 18.

In this sense, one can see why Cicero may have wanted to place freedom at the heart of this debate. At this knife-edge moment in history, the Epicureans cannot be allowed to redefine Roman values. Lucretius' *libertas* is a freedom expressed in detachment, a "freedom *from*" social convention and public duties.[54] The *libertas* of *De fato* and *In Verrem*, on the other hand, is a freedom of patriotic commitment, a "freedom *to*" correct one's faults, win the praise of fellow citizens, and sacrifice oneself for the common good.[55] Against the tyrants, Cicero wields the skeptical Academy to redeem a silenced republic. "Let everyone defend his views," he declares, "for judgment is free [*sunt enim iudicia libera*]."[56] This venerable debate on the cosmos can no longer be simply about "antecedent causes" or what is "up to us"; the citizen can regain in his soul what he has lost in the Republic. Though civil war rages and despots rule, in this inner battlefield reason can prevail.

His notion of free will helps Cicero advance three claims critical to the action of 44 BCE. First, against the necessity of fate he stresses the contingency of politics. The setting of *De fato* is a conversation with the consul-designate Hirtius just after the Ides, when "it had seemed as if a search was being made for every possible means of causing fresh upheavals, and we thought resistance must be offered to these tendencies [*eisque esse occurrendum putaremus*]" (2). Political urgency thus launches their examination of fate – and as Cicero frets to Atticus, Hirtius' will is hesitating between the Caesarians and liberators.[57] The course of history, as he writes to Varro in 46 BCE, depends not on fate but on the character of those in power:

> It is one thing to put up with what has to be put up with, another to approve what ought to be disapproved – though for my part I don't any longer know what to disapprove of, except *the beginnings of it all, which were a matter of will* [*quid non probem quidem iam scio, praeter initia rerum; nam haec in voluntate fuerunt*]. I saw (you were away) that our friends were

---

[54] This is understood in context rather than by his syntax, which otherwise resembles Cicero's; see discussion supra.

[55] This is not to say that Lucretius lacks a notion of moral self-improvement. See, e.g., 3.320–22: "[S]o trivial are the traces of different natures that remain, beyond reason's power to expel, that nothing hinders our living a life worthy of gods [*usque adeo naturarum vestigia linqui/parvola quae nequeat ratio depellere,/ut nil impediat dignam dis degere vitam*]." Whether or not Cicero reads Lucretius fairly, the antipolitical views of the Garden are in evidence throughout his poem; cf. Lucr. 2.37–61, 3.59–93, 5.1105–60.

[56] *Tusc.* 4.7. See ibid. 5.33: "I live from day to day, I say anything that strikes me as probable, and so I alone am free [*itaque soli sumus liberi*]." Cf. *Acad.* 2.8–9, 2.105; *Tusc.* 5.83.

[57] *Att.* 4.374.4. See Lévy 2007, 20–21.

7.3 The Politics of Free Will

desirous of war, whereas the person we are expecting [sc. Caesar] was not so much desirous as unafraid of it. That then came within the scope of design, all else followed inevitably [*ergo haec consili fuerunt, reliqua necessaria*]. And victory had to fall to one side or the other.[58]

The laws of causality were clearly operative in the clash of Caesar and Pompey, but behind the apparent necessity of events lay an incipient *voluntas* for war. Though allied to reason, Cicero's *voluntas* remains morally bivalent, potentially *honesta* or *inhonesta*.[59] The future of the Republic, he insists, will not be determined by climate or prophecy[60] but by the integrity of Rome's leaders.[61] If they guide their wills by reason, the Republic can last forever.[62] Conversely, if the Republic fails, no external force is to blame:

> No king is left, no nation, no tribe to cause you fear; there is no evil from outside, of other's causing, that can make its way into our country; if you desire that country to be immortal ... it is against our own passions that we must be on our guard, against men of violence and revolutionaries, against evils from within, against plots devised at home.[63]

No "everlasting chain" precipitated Rome's disaster; the Romans did.

Secondly, free will sharpens the responsibility of Cicero's enemies. Throughout his career, he uses *voluntas* to describe how wicked men put themselves above the law: The corrupt Verres had foregone the lawful exercise of power by his *voluntas* and *avaritia*;[64] the agrarian decemvirs betray the state by selling land *ex sua voluntate*;[65] and though nature made Catiline prone to madness, his *voluntas exercuit*.[66] And yet, by the force of his invective, the orator risks dehumanizing his opponents. Are such monsters truly free to act otherwise?[67] Employing the Stoic doctrine of "willing disturbance," Cicero affirms in the *Tusculans* that no matter how unhinged a man like Antony may seem, he is still responsible for his acts.[68]

---

[58] *Fam.* 2.181.2 (emphasis added).   [59] See *Tusc.* 4.34.
[60] Cf. *Fam.* 2.242.5 (46 BCE), to Torquatus regarding the civil war: "When I foretold what has come about, I had no prophetic vision: perceiving what *could* happen, and would be disastrous if it did, I feared it ..." (emphasis added).
[61] See Ferrary 1995, 56: "[F]or Cicero the death of a city is never due to natural causes"; Powell 2012, 25: "[E]ven though Rome has had and still has a constitution of the best possible kind, it is at risk precisely because of great faults in the rulers." Cf. *Rep.* 1.47: "[E]very State is such as its ruler's character and will make it [*et talis est quaeque res publica, qualis eius aut natura aut voluntas qui illam regit*]."
[62] *Rep.* 3.34. Cf. Cicero's assurance to Marcellus: "I believe there is nothing except lack of will to hinder you from the enjoyment of all that is yours [*nihil tibi arbitrer ad tuas fortunas omnis obtinendas praeter voluntatem*]"; *Fam.* 2.230.3 (46 BCE).
[63] *Rab. Perd.* 33–34 (63 BCE).   [64] *Verr.* 2.3.220.   [65] *Leg. agr.* 2.64.   [66] *Cat.* 1.25.
[67] See generally Lévy 1998.   [68] See *Tusc.* 4.60, 4.65, 4.83.

All crimes against the state are willing and thus fully deserving of blame. In arguing that their wills are free – that they abuse a faculty given to all men – Cicero intensifies their guilt.

Finally, a free will lets Cicero retain his own honor. In *De finibus*, he presents the Stoic view that actions should be judged not by results alone but also by the *voluntas* behind them.[69] Despite his exclusion from the conspiracy against Caesar, he partakes of its glory: "[A]ll decent men killed Caesar so far as it was in them to do so: some lacked design, some courage, some opportunity; none lacked the will [*aliis consilium, aliis animus, aliis occasio defuit; voluntas nemini*]."[70] And despite his failure to prevent the Republic's destruction, in the one matter truly "up to him" the statesman can hold his head high. In the same year as *De fato*, Cicero writes to Torquatus, a fellow republican lamenting Caesar's rise to power:

> I must admit that I find no consolation for our common calamities, save one; but that one, if we can make it ours, is sovereign [*maxima*], and I myself have recourse to it more and more every day. I mean that *the consciousness of a righteous will* is the greatest consolation in adversity [*conscientiam rectae voluntatis maximam consolationem esse rerum incommodarum*] . . . [O]ur hearts have always been in the right place, and the outcome of our course of action is deplored rather than the course itself [*eventusque magis nostri consili quam consilium reprehendatur*].[71]

If philosophy cannot save the *res publica*, it can help reconcile Cicero to his failures.[72] *De fato* helps him demonstrate that Romans are not prisoners of necessity, nor will their careers be measured solely by their defeats. "I shall never regret my will," he writes to Atticus, "merely the course I adopted [*voluntatis me meae numquam paenitebit, consili paenitet*]."[73] In the ashes of the Republic, a *recta voluntas* is all Cicero is left with, and philosophy shows him it is enough.

In the light of his speeches and letters, we see how Cicero's treatise on fate signals more than a retreat into contemplation. Through the clash of doctrines, Cicero gives new meaning to his political convictions: that the

---

[69] *Fin.* 3.22, 3.32.
[70] *Phil.* 2.29. Cf. *Vat.* 26: The whole world had repudiated Cicero's opponents "not just willingly but in open reproaches [*non voluntate sed convicio*]."
[71] *Fam.* 2.244.2 (emphasis added). See also ibid. 2.182.2 (46 BCE): Cicero takes refuge in "the conscience of my counsels" (*conscientia consiliorum meorum*). Shackleton Bailey translates the phrase as "political conscience." The phrase *recta voluntas*, the counterpart to the Stoic *orthos logos*, implies that the will, however free, must still be held to the strictest ethical standards.
[72] Cf. Lévy 2007, 75, who observes that "it was easier for him to emphasize the autonomy of will [in *De fato*] than to give a clear account of the use he made of it."
[73] *Att.* 3.217.2 (48 BCE).

Republic was not fated to fall; that those who destroyed it deserve real blame; and that his own failed efforts deserve honor. At the Republic's end, there was no stronger case he could wrest from his library, yet his own lived experience was just as important as the texts of Carneades and Chrysippus. In *libera voluntas*, Cicero joins man's struggle for reason to his freedom from necessity. Though this vision had failed to prevent disaster, it gives Cicero the means to explore a final sense of *voluntas*: the force that generates a conscious self.

CHAPTER 8

The Fourfold Self

Rarely can we witness a figure from antiquity suffer something like a nervous breakdown in real time. This is, nevertheless, the experience offered by Cicero's letters of spring and summer 58 BCE. Though one hesitates to use the modern term, the letters to Atticus following his exile from Rome leave little doubt as to the depth of his suffering. For it was not merely the ex-consul's estate on the Palatine that Clodius set out to demolish, but his very sense of self.

Cicero had lived a resplendently public life. He had staked his fortune to the people's will, and in return they had shielded him from his enemies. Against the mounting threats of 58 BCE, Cicero insists to Atticus that he is "protected by a most steadfast bastion of goodwill [*firmissima benevolentia hominum muniti sumus*]."[1] With the bill for exile and no public outcry in his favor, this illusion is shattered. He appears to have considered suicide; but for the intervention of his best friend, Cicero's story might well have ended here.[2] Though "stricken and dejected" and pleading for Atticus' company,[3] he makes his way from Rome to the Adriatic and from there to Thessalonica. The man who spent years in the forum now "hate[s] crowds and shun[s] my fellow creatures" (1.52.1); he thinks himself "a ruined and broken man" (1.55.2). Exile forces a question upon him even more painful than political betrayal and separation from family: With the "public Cicero" gone, who remains?

During a moment of resilience, he implores Atticus "since you have always loved me for my own sake, not to change. I am the same man.

---

[1] *Att.* 1.45.2.
[2] See *Att.* 1.47: "I hope I may see the day when I shall thank you for making me go on living. So far I am heartily sorry you did [*Utinam illum diem videam cum tibi agam gratias quod me vivere coegisti! adhuc quidem valde me paenitet* . . .]." Cf. ibid. 1.52.2.
[3] Ibid. 1.47–49.

My enemies have robbed me of what I have, but not of what I am."[4] This flash of courage gives way to despair:

> And if you, who still enjoy your status in the community, feel my absence, how do you think I feel the loss of that very status? ... [N]o man has ever lost so much or fallen into such a pit of misery ... I mourn the loss not only of the things and persons that were mine, but of my very self [*sed me ipsum*]. What am I really [*quid enim sum*]? (1.60.2, emphasis added)

This simple, devastating question is the crux of his crisis. His concluding plea: "[W]ish me to be somebody, since I can no longer be what I was or what I might have been [*velis esse aliquem, quoniam qui fui et qui esse potui, iam esse non possum*]" (1.60.8).

Cicero's return to Italy in the following summer offers some relief to these existential doubts. He exults to Atticus at having "attained what I thought would be most difficult to recover, namely my public prestige, my standing in the Senate, and my influence among the honorable men, in larger measure than I had dreamed possible" (1.73.3). In a formal speech of thanks, he announces that the "old" Cicero, though eclipsed in exile, has reemerged: "Behold me then, fellow-citizens, restored to myself, to my own, and to the republic [*mihi, meis, rei publicae restitutus*]."[5] Rather than start anew, he carries the old identity of private and public to its logical extreme: Not only has the ex-consul been "restored to himself," but the entire Republic, extinguished in his exile, now reignites.[6] This bravado may have thrilled his audience, but given the torment of his letters, Cicero may have had a harder time convincing himself.

The Republic's collapse causes him to reckon again with his identity. Just as he resituates civic freedom within a skeptical independence of mind, Cicero reanchors public duty in a new relation with oneself. The great Scipio, though ceaselessly occupied with public business, was "never less lonely than when he was alone";[7] the equally talented Demosthenes relied overmuch on fortune and failed "to commune with himself."[8] For

---

[4] Ibid. 1.50: *tantum te oro ut, quoniam me ipsum semper amasti, ut eodem amore sis; ego enim idem sum. inimici mei mea mihi, non me ipsum ademerunt.*
[5] *Red. pop.* 18.
[6] Ibid. 14; *Dom.* 87: "I, who went forth unstained, taking the republic with me, and who returned at the height of my prestige [*in me, qui profectus sum integer, afui simul cum re publica, redii cum maxima dignitate*] ..."; cf. *Sest.* 49; *Para. Stoic.* 27–29. On Cicero's rhetorical responses to his exile, see Gildenhard 2011, 46–49.
[7] *Off.* 3.1.
[8] *Tusc.* 5.103. See also *Fin.* 5.44, "Accordingly the Pythian Apollo bids us 'learn to know ourselves'; but the sole road to self-knowledge is to know our powers of body and mind, and to follow the path of life that gives us their full employment"; *Tusc.* 5.70, the goal of study is "that the mind should

Cicero, this care for the self does not substitute for the *vita activa*; rather, it offers a prophylaxis against the shocks of public life. What distinguishes a good man is not only his passion for truth but "for independence ... From this attitude comes greatness of soul and a sense of superiority to worldly conditions."[9] Could philosophy serve as the armor for a new model of the self?

This question is the centerpiece of the treatise that would be Cicero's last. The central problem of the *De officiis* is how to act, and in particular how to square the demands of principle with the messy circumstances of life. Composed in the form of a letter to his son, Marcus, then a twenty-one-year-old student in Athens, the treatise seems intended for a broader audience of young Romans contemplating a public career.[10] Its focus is thus not the metaphysics or first principles of ethics, already treated in *De finibus*, but their application in a particular place and time.[11] Cicero's main reference is the Stoic Panaetius and his work *Peri tou kathēkontos* ("On Duty"), published nearly a century before.[12] With illustrations from ancestral tradition and recent events, Cicero weighs the claims of honorable and beneficial action and how a man of integrity should respond when these appear to conflict. His principal recommendation is to act with *decorum*, a word often translated as morally fitting, proper, or appropriate.[13] Cicero holds *decorum* to be inseparable from what is *honestum* or morally fine,[14] though with this particularity: *Decorum* involves both an ongoing adjustment to circumstance and an unwavering consistency with oneself.[15] With the ethical ideal of *decorum*, observes Remer, "Cicero transmutes the orators' need to adapt their speech to circumstance from a pragmatic precept into a moral virtue."[16]

---

know its own self [*ipsa se mens agnoscat*] and feel its union with the divine mind [*coniunctamque cum divina mente se sentiat*]."

[9] *Off.* 1.13. Cf. ibid. at 1.72: "Statesmen, too, no less than philosophers – perhaps even more so – should carry with them that greatness of spirit and indifference to outward circumstances ... if they are to be free from worries and lead a dignified and self-consistent life."

[10] *Att.* 4.417.2; *Off.* 1.157–60, 2.12–15; cf. Remer 2017, 67. Laird 1999, 18–25, argues that such treatises, ostensibly addressed to a single person, were actually intended for a wider audience or "superaddressee."

[11] *Off.* 1.7, 3.20; Griffin and Atkins 1991, xxii. [12] *Off.* 3.7; Griffin and Atkins 1991, xix.

[13] Schofield 2012, 43 (emphasis in original), notes the difficulty in translating the word, concluding that "*decorum* is what both *is* and *looks* just right."

[14] *Off.* 1.93–94.

[15] See *Off.* 1.113: "[T]he thing most appropriate for each of us is what is most his own"; cf. ibid. 1.110, 1.125. Remer 2017, 29, 66, highlights the sensitivity to context inherent in *decorum*, as well as its rootedness in the shared values of a community. On the importance of self-consistency to *decorum*, see Schofield 2012, 49–50.

[16] Remer 2017, 54; see generally Kapust 2011.

To act with *decorum*, we must realize that each of us is made up of four *personae* – "roles" that, when properly understood, guide us to the right actions. The first *persona* is the reason shared by all mankind, from which "all morality and propriety are derived" and upon which the "rational method of ascertaining our duty" depends (1.107). The second consists in the distinctive qualities of body and soul that Nature gives us at birth (108). Third is the *persona* that "chance or circumstance imposes," including wealth, status, and the loss thereof (115). The fourth and final role is "that which we ourselves choose, which sets forth from our will [*ipsi gerere quam personam velimus, a nostra voluntate proficiscitur*]." A key instance of this *persona* is our choice of profession, but so, too, does it encompass "the virtues themselves," for which "one man prefers to excel in one, another in another" (115). As we have seen in Chapters 6 and 7, the will emerges in the *Tusculans* and *De fato* as the locus of inner liberty and the key to moral progress. Volition, here as well, is the father of virtue: To act with *decorum*, we must decide "who we want to be, and what kind of person, and in what way of life; and this is the most difficult problem in the world" (117).

But is there a deeper self, a *nos*, behind the roles we play?[17] How do the four roles cooperate in practice? And how indeed will playing them help us tackle "the most difficult problem in the world"?

8.1 The Four *Personae*: Background and Problems

Of the four *personae* Cicero presents, the one most fully under our control – that which tackles "the most difficult problem" – is ascribed to *voluntas*, our will. This notion of an inner force by which we navigate our moral lives may sound quite familiar to us, for reasons I explore in the Epilogue. Nevertheless, the ex-consul's account has much to puzzle contemporary readers. For one thing, he does not begin his four-*persona* scheme by saying, as one might expect, that there are four *personae*. He begins by evoking the (single) *persona* endowed by nature to all humans (1.97), then states that "we are invested by nature with *two personae*" (1.107, emphasis added), examines these two over more than a hundred lines and appears to conclude (1.114), before "adding" (*adiungitur*) the previously unmentioned third and fourth "roles."[18] Cicero gives few clues

---

[17] Cf. Lévy 2003, 129: "When, as in Cicero's text, the *personae* are those of the human subject, we are right to wonder what is the nature of this *nos* that Cicero presents as the bearer of these successive masks."

[18] See Gill 1988, 174–76; Dyck 1996, 285; Lévy 2003, 128–29; Schofield 2012, 47–54. The argument that Cicero himself added the third and fourth *personae* was offered by Schmekel 1892,

as to how each role interacts with the others, or indeed how four *personae* can compose a single self.[19] Finally, there is reason to doubt how closely Cicero embraces his own theory, given that he applies it to the example of Cato the Younger, but not to the equally noteworthy example of Regulus (3.99–108) or, really, anywhere else in his treatise.[20]

To understand Cicero's final and most intriguing reference to the will, we must situate his notion of *personae* in the broader stream of antique thought. The earliest attested sense of *persona*, like the Greek *prosōpon*, is an actor's mask. The idea that proper behavior in society depends on one's "role" is an analogy taken up by several of the schools familiar to Cicero. Yet not every account of *personae* suggested – as he would in *De officiis* – that these roles constitute our identity, or even that they help us live a good life.

As De Lacy observes in his seminal article,[21] the *persona/prosōpon* analogy gave rise to two types of ethical argument. The first focused on the distinctiveness of a given mask, qualities that applied to one dramatic role but not another: "[I]t is not possible for Agamemnon to behave like Thersites, or Thersites like Agamemnon."[22] The Stoics in particular found this reading useful in delineating which actions were *kathēkonta*; that is, appropriate for the mass of men who cannot perform the *katorthōmata* of the sage.[23] Seneca refers to a debate of the early Stoic masters Cleanthes and Ariston over whether philosophy should prescribe universal standards only or instead "give precepts proper to each role [*dat propria cuique personae praecepta*], such as how a husband should conduct himself towards his wife, how a father should bring up his children, or how a

---

39–41. As I explore later in this chapter, these critiques have largely failed to note that the exposition begins with a *single persona* at 1.97 (*nobis autem personam imposuit ipsa natura*), then introduces the first and second together at 1.107, and finally the third and fourth at 1.115. The incremental scheme is first < second < fourth *personae*, an "unfolding" that nicely mirrors its overall theme of progress and reevaluation.

[19] *Pace* Guérin 2011, 399, Cicero neither states nor implies that the four *personae* are meant to be treated "according to a strict hierarchy."

[20] See Gill 1988, 198–99. Cicero employs *persona* only twice in Book 3 and not at all in Book 2; *Off*. 3.43, 3.106.

[21] De Lacy 1977, 163–72.

[22] Ibid. 164, paraphrasing Diog. Laert. 7.160: "The wise man he compared to a good actor, who, if called upon to take the part of a Thersites or of an Agamemnon, will impersonate them both becomingly" (trans. R. D. Hicks); cf. Lévy 2003, 132. The Agamemnon/Thersites trope dates back at least to Demades, a 4th-century BCE Athenian orator and rival of Demosthenes. See Diod. Sic. 16.87.2; De Lacy 1977, 165.

[23] See *Off*. 1.8; cf. Diog. Laert. 7.107–09; Stob. 2.85.13–86.4 (SVF 3.494); see generally Sedley and Long 1987, 364–68.

8.1 The Four Personae

master should rule his slaves."[24] This distinctiveness is not absolute; though the mask may affix to exceptional individuals like Agamemnon, so too can it signal a "type" (e.g. the sighing lover or cunning slave) that situates the character in a well-known class. A distinct role is not necessarily or even typically a unique one.

An alternative view of *persona* stressed not its distinctiveness but its artifice. An actor may "give an excellent performance of a worthless character, and he laughs or weeps not according to his own inclination but as the play requires."[25] This is the reading given, for example, by the Epicurean Lucretius in arguing that adversity shows our worth, "for then alone/Are the true voices conjured from his breast/The mask off-stripped, reality remaining [*nam verae voces tum demum pectore ab imo/Eliciuntur et eripitur persona, manet res*]."[26] Rather than constituting our character, here *persona* marks the *gap* between what we profess and who we are: Though the role be well played, the mask is not the man.

Cicero is capable of playing on both senses of *persona*, the "distinct" and "detached." In the *Tusculans*, written about a decade after *De rerum natura*, Cicero turns Lucretius against his master, asserting that Epicurus "merely puts on the mask of a philosopher and has bestowed the title on himself ... [*An Epicuro, qui tantum modo induit personam philosophi et sibi ipse hoc nomen inscripsit* ...]."[27] In *De oratore*, similarly, the character Antonius insists on the distinction between an orator and actor. Whereas an actor may simulate emotions on the stage, an orator must express emotions he truly feels, such that "I am not the actor of another's *persona*, but the author of my own [*neque actor essem alienae personae, sed auctor*

---

[24] Sen. *Ep.* 94.1–4. On this question, the Stoics may well have been influenced by the Cynics. In his treatise *On Self-sufficiency*, Teles proposes that fortune is like a poetess who gives out at one time the *prosōpa* of king and wanderer; just as the good actor must play well whatever role the poet gives him, so the good man must play whatever role fortune has given him; De Lacy 1977, 165 (citing *Teletis Reliquiae* at 3 = Stob. vol. 3, 37–38). See generally Fuentes Gonzalez 1998. For a later Stoic use, see Epic. *Disc.* 2.10.1–9; cf. Lévy 2003, 135. On Epictetus' use of *prosōpa*, see De Lacy 1977, 166–67.

[25] De Lacy 1977, 164, cites Plut. *Lys.* 446D and *Dem.* 856A. See also Plut. *Quaest. conv.* 711C, suggesting that each *prosōpon* implies a certain *ethos*.

[26] Lucr. 3.57–58. Cf. Moreau 2002, 17; Lévy 2003, 132. Plutarch would later apply a similar critique in the context of Roman politics, in which it would be "shameful for aging statesmen to exchange one political *prosōpon* for another"; Plut. *An seni* 785C. Here as well inhabiting a public *persona* can signal moral emptiness rather than propriety, as with Arrhidaeus, who "only has the name and *prosōpon* of a king"; ibid. 791E. Though he likely read *Off.*, Seneca also employs the artificial or "detached" reading of the *persona* analogy rather than Cicero's framework; see Sen. *Ep.* 24.13.

[27] *Tusc.* 5.73. To underscore the difference between his view and that of Lucretius, Cicero adds that Epicurus' view of pleasure and pain "differs but little from the instinct of the beasts [*huic ... non multum differenti a iudicio ferarum*]." The Epicureans are thus ignorant of the *logos* that, in the Stoic view Cicero adopts, distinguishes man from his fellow creatures and comprises the first of his four *personae*.

meae]."[28] In the mouth of his exemplar, Cicero both acknowledges the potential falseness of a public *persona* and the corresponding duty of self-consistency, a key tenet of *decorum*. *De officiis* Book 3 shows Cicero's awareness of the "distinctive" reading as well. Justifying the general Regulus' voluntary submission to torture, Cicero denies that oaths to a wicked enemy can be forgotten, a view voiced in drama by Atreus: "None have I giv'n ; none give I ever to the faithless."[29] He continues that "it was proper for the poet to say that, because, when he was working out his Atreus, he had to make the words fit the role [*personae serviendum fuit*]," yet he warns readers against "adopting it as a principle … that it not be a mere loophole for perjury that they seek" (3.106). Here lies the Stoic dilemma: How do we distinguish sensitivity to moral context from *ad hoc* indulgence? Though Atreus may be a monster, Cicero's even-handed approach is to give measured praise to his precept while signaling danger if its context is removed.

Why *four* roles? Nothing like Cicero's framework survives elsewhere in ancient thought.[30] As noted earlier in this chapter, its primary inspiration appears to have been Panaetius' "On Duty," available to us only in a few fragments.[31] Early Stoics taught that because man is gifted with reason, he must participate in the *logos* of the universe by living virtuously. As we saw in Chapter 6, the problem for orthodox Stoicism lay in providing moral guidance to the great majority of humans, at all levels of society, who will never achieve the perfected reason (*recta ratio*) of the Stoic sage. The framework of four *personae* seems to have been Panaetius' invention, his attempt to reconcile human variety with the standard of universal *logos*.[32] From the testimonials that survive, Panaetius had a more agreeable style

---

[28] *De or.* 2.193–94.
[29] *Off.* 3.103. The play is by the Roman poet Accius; Ribbeck 1875, fr. 227–28.
[30] See De Lacy 1977, 163: The framework in the first book of *De officiis* is "so far as I know, unparalleled in ancient philosophical writings." Cf. Lévy 2003, 135: "[B]y its systematic character and the variety of approaches to the notion of *persona*, the passage in *De officiis* constitutes a *unicum*."
[31] *Off.* 3.7; *Att.* 4.420.4. See De Lacy 1977, 163; Gill 1988, 169. The most comparable extant passages in Stoicism all postdate Cicero, such as Epic. *Disc.* 1.2, 2.10; Hierocles (Von Arnim at 59 = Stob. vol. 4, 660–61). Cf. De Lacy 1977, 166–71.
[32] See Gill 1988, 175; De Lacy 1977, 168: "The fourfold scheme thus provides a theoretical basis for analyzing conduct at all levels, and to this extent it deemphasizes the sage. And inasmuch as it recognizes the variables in human life, it prepares the way for practical advice on how to deal with these variables." Speculation as to precisely how Panaetius' scheme differed from those of his predecessors is limited by the fact that the most relevant testimony on earlier Stoic debates comes from later sources such as Seneca, Diogenes Laertius, or Epictetus; see Sen. *Epp. mor.* 94.1–4; Diog. Laert. 7.160; Epic. *Disc.* 1.2, 2.10.

8.1 *The Four* Personae

than most Stoics,[33] and was interested in giving practical advice to the good man who was not a sage.[34] In the traditional theory of four virtues, Schofield explains, "we start with general consideration of what fine behavior to others or of what the pursuit of truth (for example) requires. *Personae* theory, by contrast, makes the *persona* or *personae* of particular individuals or types of individual the starting point for determining one's *officium* ..."[35] The metaphors of role and mask were Panaetius' key to unlocking the problem of everyday morality.

Scholarship has tended to downplay Cicero's contributions to these ideas,[36] yet the role he claims in *De officiis* is not merely that of a faithful scribe. Indeed, his point of departure is a gap in Panaetius' work; to Cicero's surprise, he has failed to define *officium* (1.7)! Moreover, while he has treated *honestum* and *utilitas* individually, the Stoic has "never fulfilled his promise" in advising how to resolve conflicts between them (3.7).[37] Given the state of the evidence, we cannot be sure where *De officiis* may have enriched or departed from Panaetius' ideas. Nevertheless, if we take him at his word, Cicero clearly wants to make his own contribution to this critical debate on how to live well. In Gill's reading, Cicero employs the *persona* analogy primarily to situate his readers within "the norms and conventions of a specific social milieu" – that of a Roman gentleman. The fourth *persona* simply "consists of the career or *métier* we adopt," though he grants that "Cicero seems to conceive of this choice in broad terms."[38] The roles work in sequence: "[B]earing in mind" his rationality, distinctive talents, and social status, a young man will "choose his *métier* and way of life," which will then entail its own duties. Gill locates a "problematic" tension between what he sees as Cicero's universalist pretensions and his conventional Roman outlook, concluding that his "rather minimal

---

[33] *Fin.* 4.79.
[34] *Fin.* 4.23; Sen. *Ep.* 116.5. Cf. Erskine 1990, chs. 7 and 8; Griffin and Atkins 1991, xx; Burchell 1998, 105.
[35] Schofield 2012, 47.
[36] An early hypothesis by Schmekel 1892, 39–41, that Cicero added the third and fourth *personae* has gone largely unaccepted. De Lacy 1977, 171, presumes that Cicero gives Panaetius' framework without significant modification ("the distinctive features of the scheme, however, and specifically the formulation in terms of *personae*, remain Panaetius's own"). Gill 1988, 171, posits simply that Cicero "follows Panaetius" in Books 1 and 2, adding that the original material in Book 3 is "notoriously unsatisfactory" from a critical perspective.
[37] See also *Off.* 1.6: "I ... follow chiefly the Stoics, not as a translator, but, as is my custom, I shall at my own option and discretion draw from those sources in such measure and in such manner as shall suit my purpose [*Sequemur ... potissimum Stoicos non ut interpretes, sed, ut solemus, e fontibus eorum iudicio arbitrioque nostro, quantum quoque modo videbitur, hauriemus*]."
[38] Gill 1988, 174.

conception of personality" falls short of the self-creation envisioned by Nietzsche centuries later (171–82).

As Lévy points out, Gill's argument treats the four-*persona* theory in an exclusively ethical framework, whereas for the Stoics (unlike, say, the Peripatetics) ethics, logic, and physics formed an indissociable braid (136–37). In Lévy's view, the four *personae* can better be understood in relation to the four Stoic categories of any object: (1) its substrate (*hypokeimenon*), (2) its quality or disposition (*poion*, both shared and distinctive), (3) its disposition at a moment in time (*pōs ekhon*), and (4) its disposition in relation to another object (*pōs ekhon pros ti*) (137). Because these categories are not "descriptive and static," so too should the four *personae* be interpreted in a "dynamic manner," not as rigid constraints but as starting points for moral progress (ibid.). Though the *persona* of will does not seem to fit neatly into any category, Lévy draws on the "circular" orientation of Stoic thought to propose that the fourth *persona* actualizes the first: "The only rational being is he who decides to *realize* his rational nature by the choice of virtue."[39] In this reading, Cicero's "masks" are both distinctive *and* detached: distinctive, in that they allow *decorum* to be expressed differently by different people; and detached, in that we all must confront the unresolved duality between a world of appearances and a *logos* we cannot see, but with great effort – or, more neatly, an act of will – can apprehend.[40]

It may be fruitful to carry this idea of activation and interrelation a step further. Just as the linkage of ethical roles to physical categories suggests the circling back of will (role #4) to reason (role #1), Cicero may have embedded a circular or recursive quality in each of *De officiis*'s four *personae*. Indeed, Cicero has already made such a move in his discussion of *decorum*, ostensibly part of the fourth cardinal virtue, which he then holds to "[belong] to each division of moral rectitude [*pertinet quidem ad omnem honestatem*]" (1.95).[41]

In what follows, I aim to show that will is essential to each of life's four roles, just as *decorum* belongs to each of the four virtues. The recursive quality of will is seen more clearly, in my view, by reading *De officiis* in light of passages in other Ciceronian texts. Care should admittedly be taken in such an approach, especially with regard to a Carneadean skeptic

---

[39] Lévy 2003, 138 (emphasis added).
[40] At *De or.* 2.193, Antonius is struck by how an actor's eyes "seem to blaze forth from his mask," suggesting a quasi-physical fusion of actor and role; see Garsten 2006, 161. Cf. Lévy 2003, 137: "The unity of *nos* is physical, the entire problem thus being to make its ethical unity coincide with this physical unity."
[41] See Schofield 2012, 51–53.

ready to abandon one "probable" doctrine for another.[42] Nevertheless, *De officiis* is full of allusions to Cicero's recent works on ethics (1.6), glory (2.31), old age (1.151), and friendship (2.31). Griffin and Atkins are struck by "how closely it mirrors Cicero's views elsewhere," and they argue that the work joins its sister treatises in a larger purpose to instruct Rome's rising generation in virtue.[43]

As we will see in this chapter, for Cicero this virtuous self is best understood relationally. If Panaetius' four roles are his key to reconciling the demands of reason with the pluralities of human experience, then will is the catalyst that brings these roles into alignment. It is the power that drives self-awareness, enables rational choice, and, in the reciprocal tension between actor and mask, creates an evolving but coherent "character" for each of us. The unique self of Cicero's four *personae* emerges not from Nietzschean self-separation but in a recursive web – temporally to past choices, socially to friends and fellow-citizens, and ontologically to the *logos* that no man can alter.[44] This multiform play is his blueprint for a public-minded yet invulnerable self.

8.2 Will and the Four *Personae*

8.2.1 *The Role of Reason*

What does it mean to play the "role of reason"?[45] Cicero writes that man's first *persona* "is universal, arising from the fact of our being all alike endowed with reason and with that superiority which lifts us above the brute." "From this," he continues, "all morality and propriety are derived [*trahitur*], and upon it depends the rational method of inquiring into our duty [*ratio inveniendi officii*]" (1.107). A first clue lies in comparing this passage to a similar one from *De finibus*. Cato notes in Book 3 that just as our limbs and appetites were fashioned

> not for any kind of life one may choose, but for a particular mode of living, ... the same is true of reason and perfected reason [*perfecta ratio*]. For just as an actor or dancer has assigned to him not any but a certain particular part or dance, so life has to be conducted in a certain fixed way, and not in any way we like. (3.23–24)

---

[42] Baraz 2012, 133–34; Brittain 2015, 18–20. [43] Griffin and Atkins 1991, xvii; cf. *Div.* 2.3–5.
[44] Cf. De Lacy 1977, 171: "[T]he Stoics do not explain individuation in terms of some unique essence or substance but rather in terms of a unique set of relations. The four *personae* express these relations so far as they pertain to moral action, and collectively they identify the moral agent."
[45] Cf. Schofield 2012, 48 (emphasis in original): "Making a *role* out of our shared humanity obviously stretches the notion of a *persona* to the limit."

Each passage uses a theater analogy in its argument for reason, but their emphasis is quite different. Cato's argument seems to reflect the orthodox Stoic view; he stresses the perfection of reason (*perfecta ratio*) through fixed (*certus*) and constrained behavior (the twice-repeated "not in any way we like"). The passage in *De officiis*, by contrast, emphasizes the *opportunity* offered by reason rather than its constraints; from the starting point of reason, we can derive (*trahere*) and inquire into (*invenire*) our moral duty. Taking a step back, we see that this embrace of inquiry and progress is built into the structure of Cicero's argument in Book 1: (1) his observation that Nature endows man with a (still single) *persona* setting him apart from other animals (1.96–97); (2) the pairing of the roles of reason and nature at 1.107; and finally (3) the adjoining [*adiungitur*] of the third and fourth *personae* at 1.115. This incremental unfolding, which has appeared odd to some readers, may in fact be Cicero/Panaetius modeling the "role play" of reason that they prescribe.[46]

Cicero's mask analogy works by marking human beings out from what they are not: irrational beasts governed by their urges. To give in to appetite, therefore, is to lose the most distinctive quality of mankind, the "superiority and dignity of our nature" (1.106). This distinctiveness is again not presented as a command or constraint but a truth to be "borne in mind," such that we "realize how wrong it is to abandon ourselves to excess … and how right it is to live in thrift, continence, simplicity, and sobriety" (1.106). He brings this *persona* of "surpassing excellence" further into relief by comparison to playwrights who write what is suitable for "a great variety of characters … even for the bad" (1.98). To human beings, however, Nature gives the "parts" of consistency, moderation, self-control, and consideration of others (*constantiae, moderationis, temperantiae, verecundiae partes datae sint*). In this we must not be careless (*non neglegere*) of our fellow men and must show reverence (*reverentia*) to all (1.98–99). These "parts," we infer, operate within the single "role" evoked above, just as different qualities of a character are foregrounded in a given scene. Though orthodox Stoicism seems to have emphasized the "vertical" aspect of human reason and its kinship with the divine,[47] the Panaetian enacts his *persona* of reason "horizontally" by caring for and listening to others.

---

[46] See Lévy 2003, 133–37: *Off.* concerns the *progressant*, not the sage; reason is the substrate of moral action, not its final achievement; and Cicero presents reason "as an open determination," whereas for Cato it is "the order that must imperatively govern human life." Cf. Schofield 2012, 48–50.

[47] See, e.g., *Nat. D.* 2.23–30; Cleanthes *apud* Hermias, *In gent. phil.* 14 (SVF 1.495); Plut. *Comm. not.* 1052C-D (SVF 2.604); Epic. *Disc.* 2.6.9; Sextus Emp. *Math.* 9.75–76 (SVF 2.311). See generally Sedley and Long 1987, 319–20; Annas 1992, 43–56; Frede 2011, 83–86.

The inquiry that our reason sets in motion is thus worked out relationally, in the moral behaviors we enact or fail to enact toward our neighbors and loved ones.

A thorny problem remains. As "natural" as is the *persona* of reason, the Stoics are equally clear that most of us fail to achieve it. The truth of human nature is available to all, but actualizing our reason – "playing the role" – requires a choice. With reference to the four Stoic categories, Lévy proposes that this actualizing force is *voluntas*: Man's rational nature is the substrate, "*le don de logos-providence*," a gift realized only in an individual's choice of virtue (138). If this is so, doesn't the progressive structure of Book 1 suggest that the choice of virtue must follow an earlier choice to *inquire into* our duties (1.107)? If inquiry is necessary for rational choice, then virtue would depend on a *voluntas* for philosophy itself. Cicero suggests elsewhere that this is the case: From his earliest days of manhood, he writes in the *Tusculans*, "my will and enthusiasm compelled me" (*voluntas studiumque nos compulisset*) to the bosom of philosophy, and "in my present heavy misfortunes, tossed by the fury of the tempest, I have sought refuge in the same haven from which I had first set sail."[48] Conversely, those young Romans who seek virtue and glory without philosophy's aid are "misled in their quest of the best, not so much in *voluntas* as by a mistake in direction [*non tam voluntate quam cursus errore*]" (*Tusc.* 3.4).

Voluntas does not merely lead one "to the gates" of the Academy or Stoa; it is a force that philosophy must organize and direct. Here, the ex-consul may have intended to surpass the Stoics, who have excelled in insight but failed in presentation: "[A]s regards all these syllogisms, I should have thought that to be worthy of philosophy and of ourselves, particularly when the subject of our inquiry is the Supreme Good, the argument ought to *amend our lives, purposes, and wills*, not just correct our terminology [*vitam nostram, consilia, voluntates, non verba corrigi*]."[49] In other words, each of us owes nature a will to learn – to activate our *persona* of reason – but we are owed in return an account of truth that inspires us.

---

[48] *Tusc.* 5.5. Cf. *Fin.* 2.96, where Cicero quotes a farewell letter of Epicurus to his pupil Hermarchus: "I charge you, by the *voluntas* which from your youth you have shown toward myself and philosophy, to protect the children of Metrodorus [*sed tu, ut dignum est tua erga me et philosophiam voluntate ab adulescentulo suscepta, fac ut Metrodori tueare liberos*]." Here, *voluntas* carries the double sense, impossible to render in English, of will as adherence to a cause and goodwill toward an individual.

[49] *Fin.* 4.52 (emphasis added). See also ibid. 3.3; 4.5–7. As noted in previous chapters, while I take care not to assume the views of the character "Cicero" are Cicero's, his repetition of the criticism at *Tusc.* 2.29 and 2.42 (their syllogisms "fail to make any impression on the mind") may be suggestive.

What the Stoics have begun, a great orator may complete: *Voluntas* is the force by which reason, well taught, is inscribed upon the world. The "choice of life" Cicero arrives upon is not binary but reciprocal: philosophy as a complement and catalyst of public action.⁵⁰

Though the force of reason should be supreme, it is not alone in Cicero's scheme. "Twofold are the force and nature of souls [*duplex est enim vis animorum atque natura*]; one of these is appetite (that is, *hormē* in Greek), which pulls a man this way and that [*quae hominem huc et illuc rapit*], and the other is reason, which teaches and explains what should be done or left undone. This being so, reason should preside and appetite comply."⁵¹ This play of competing forces echoes Cicero's unusual choice in the *Tusculans* to combine the Platonic division of the soul with Stoic ethical responsibility.⁵² Cicero goes as far as to say that the division of our soul into two parts leads us to express our inner conflicts "just as if we had two selves, one to be master and one to obey: still the phrase shows insight [*quasi duo simus, ut alter imperet, alter pareat; non inscite tamen dicitur*]."⁵³ We achieve self-mastery, in Cicero's view, when "reason conquers recklessness [*ratio coerceat temeritatem*]."⁵⁴

Why the emphasis on division and conflict? Perhaps it is because in the great crisis of his lifetime the Republic's forces of reason struggled against those of brutality and lost.⁵⁵ In *De officiis*, too, the contest of our brutal and rational tendencies is reflected in politics: "[T]here are two ways of settling a dispute, first by discussion [*per disceptationem*]; second, by physical force [*per vim*], and since the former is characteristic of man, the latter of the brute [*beluarum*], we must resort to force only in case we may not avail ourselves of discussion" (1.34). Looking back on his decades

---

⁵⁰ *Off.* 1.19: "[A]ll these professions are occupied with the search after truth; but to be drawn by study away from active life is contrary to moral duty. For the whole glory of virtue is in activity; activity, however, may often be interrupted, and many opportunities for returning to study are opened." Cf. Lévy 2012b, 58–78.
⁵¹ *Off.* 1.101.   ⁵² See *Tusc.* 4.10–11 and discussion in Chapter 6.
⁵³ *Tusc.* 2.47. The passage in full: "For the soul is divided into two parts, one of which is gifted with reason, while the other is destitute of it. When then we are directed to be masters of ourselves, the meaning of the direction is that reason should conquer recklessness [*est enim animus in partes tributus duas, quarum altera rationis est particeps, altera expers. Cum igitur praecipitur, ut nobismet ipsis imperemus, hoc praecipitur, ut ratio coerceat temeritatem*]."
⁵⁴ Ibid.
⁵⁵ See *Off.* 1.35, 1.38. Cf. ibid. 1.26, referring to Caesar: "[T]he trouble about this matter is that it is in the greatest souls and in the most brilliant geniuses that we usually find ambitions for honors, power, and glory springing up; and therefore this type of error is to be most avoided." The Republic's fall may well have been perceived by Cicero as a case of Platonic *stasis*, the "revolt" of city and soul; such a reading may have inspired or reinforced his desire to refound the values of the Republic at the level of the soul; cf. Pl. *Resp.* 351d–52a.

in public life, Cicero may be suggesting that the drama his readers have witnessed on the political stage is also occurring within each of them. It is a drama in which *voluntas* has played a central, if persistently ambiguous, role. When infused with reason, it is the force that animates and stabilizes society; and yet the models of Caesar and Catiline show how far it can carry evil men.[56] The wills of Cicero's readers, of Rome's rising generation, are the battleground upon which the Republic's fate will be decided.

8.2.2 The Role of Nature

"We must so act as not to oppose the universal laws of human nature," Cicero continues, "but, while safeguarding those, to follow the bent of our own particular nature [*ea tamen conservata propriam nostram sequamur*]" (1.110). The notion of "following the bent of one's own nature" is not the flexible license it might appear. Nature gives each man a set of qualities at birth, he explains, but equally gives him the capacity – indeed, the duty – to augment certain qualities and correct others. While Cicero does not expand on the correction of "natural" faults in *De officiis* Book 1, related passages from *De fato*, *Orator*, and the *Brutus* suggest the importance of will to this task.

In his explanation of the second *persona*, Cicero illustrates a range of natural differences, progressing from differences of body to those of "personality" (notably, gravity or wit) and what we might call "moral temperament" (shrewd versus plain-spoken and direct). No matter how nature has fashioned us, *decorum* "can be nothing more than uniform consistency [*aequabilitas*] in the course of our life as a whole and all its individual actions" (1.111).[57] But consistency is not achieved in passive acceptance. Rather, "it is each man's duty to weigh well what are his own peculiar traits of character, to regulate these properly, and not to wish to try how another man's would suit him" (1.113). In these three phrases lie the complex negotiation that the role of nature entails: (1) a careful self-evaluation; (2) a correction of "natural" vices (*vitiosa*); and, thereafter, (3) acting consistently with the "character" that is authentically ours. This self-critique is echoed in his discussion of the fourth *persona*: A choice of career should be made not by parental influence or popular opinion but from

---

[56] Cf. *Off.* 1.63: "Even the courage that is prompt to face danger, if it is inspired not by public spirit, but by its own selfish purposes, should have the name of effrontery rather than of courage [*si sua cupiditate, non utilitate communi impellitur, audaciae potius nomen habeat quam fortitudinis*]." See discussion of *temeritas* in Chapter 3.
[57] Cf. *Fin.* 5.44; Hawley 2020, 94–98.

"each individual's natural bent ... just what is proper for him [*in qua deliberatione ad suam cuiusque naturam consilium omne revocandum*]" (1.118–19). Playing any role – and thus playing all four together – is an essentially recursive task. To "show himself a critical judge of his own merits and defects" (1.114), a moral agent plays both judge and performer, examining the mask as he wears it.[58]

But how to escape our faults (*vitia fugiamus*)? Though Cicero does not expand on the point, two other texts of 45–44 BCE provide clues. In *De fato*, Cicero writes that the Megarian philosopher Stilpo had a famous proclivity for liquor and women, but that his associates "do not record this as a reproach but rather to add to his reputation," for he had "mastered and suppressed his vicious nature by instruction [*doctrina*]" (10). Socrates, too, was diagnosed by Zopyrus, a physiognomist, as being naturally "stupid and thick-witted" because a certain area of his neck was "blocked and stopped up."[59] Thus the path to virtue lies not in acceptance of "defects due to natural causes," but in applying "will, effort, and training" (*voluntate studio disciplina*) to eradicate them (11). Vice is corrected by reason's force: *Voluntas* marks its presence; *studium*, its intensity; and *disciplina*, its training and persistence. Interestingly, the foil for Cicero's argument in *De fato* is Chrysippus, the chief architect of Panaetius' school, whom he accuses of attributing "our wills and desires ... to natural and antecedent causes," leaving "nothing in our power" (9). Assuming Cicero's criticisms of Chrysippus in *De fato* are not wildly eccentric, might they in fact be Panaetius'? If so, could it be that the Cicero/Panaetius scheme departs from orthodox Stoicism by foregrounding the will – presumably *prohairesis* – in the correction of natural vice?[60] While the paucity of evidence limits us to speculation, the link Cicero draws between free will and personal integrity is one that later

---

[58] Each man must "show himself a critical judge of his own merits and defects" and "correct the faults [he has]"; *Off.* 1.114. Cf. Dyck 1996, 283, on the "self-reflexive" quality of this passage. An interesting question concerns the point in life at which this "critique" is performed and one's "character" set in place. On the one hand, Cicero acknowledges that life-altering decisions are too often taken at a moment of immaturity (1.117–18); on the other, nowhere does he acknowledge that this "character" of early manhood could later be altered – the trials of Cato and Ulysses being to sustain, not amend, the qualities of character that defined them (1.112–13). One wonders whether Cicero would counsel acting "consistently" with an early estimation of one's own character if that estimate proved unwise or incomplete.

[59] "He added that [Socrates] was addicted to women – at which Alcibiades is said to have given a loud guffaw!"; *Fat.* 10–11.

[60] The other obvious candidate would be Carneades, an elder contemporary of Panaetius and regular foil for orthodox Stoicism. See Sedley and Long 1987, 455–60.

8.2 Will and the Four Personae

thinkers would place at the heart of their moral teaching.[61] Cicero wants to say that only by overcoming natural flaws, as Socrates did, do we play the role that Nature intends.

Cicero illustrates our "natural" differences by recalling the styles of speaking associated with famous men.[62] His list of exemplars includes Scipio and Laelius, eminent men and great friends, whose differing characters led to similar heights of glory (1.108). In his rhetorical treatises, the development of a distinct style in harmony with one's natural gifts (literally a "will of speaking," *voluntas dicendi*) is critical to an orator's education. In *Orator* (46 BCE), when asked for his opinion on the ideal way of speaking, Cicero replies that the problem is "the hardest of all ... for not only is language soft, pliant, and so flexible that it follows wherever you turn it, but also the varieties in nature and will [*et naturae variae et voluntates*] have produced styles widely different."[63] In the tradition he inherits, *voluntas dicendi* is something akin to a school of rhetorical thought.[64] Antonius, the leading orator of Cicero's youth, posits in *De oratore* that nearly every age has produced its own distinctive style of oratory (*singula genera dicendi*). Since "our own orators" left very few writings, this is most clearly observed in the case of the Greeks,

> from whose works the method and tendency of the oratory of every generation may be understood [*ex quorum scriptis, cuiusque aetatis quae dicendi ratio voluntasque fuerit, intellegi potest*]. (2.92–93)

Here, *voluntas dicendi* indicates adherence to a style with distinct traits – vigorous or pointed, terse or "rich in ideas." In the case of the Greeks, these styles are linked to the generation into which a speaker was born.[65] The many students of the "master" Isocrates, "while differing in natural gifts, yet in will resemble one another and their master too [*naturis differunt,*

---

[61] See, e.g., August. *Conf.* 7.3.4, 7.16.22, 7.21.27, 9.2.4.
[62] *Off.* 1.108: "Lucius Crassus and Lucius Philippus had a large fund of wit; Gaius Caesar, Lucius's son, had a still richer fund and employed it with more studied purpose ..." Besides styles of speaking, Cicero illustrates various character traits such as shrewdness, straightforwardness, and social grace; ibid. 1.108–09.
[63] *Orat.* 52–53. An orator's training involved certain "theatrical" elements with which Cicero was no doubt familiar. The exercise of *prosōpopoia*, for example, required the repetition of a speech as if given by different characters. See, e.g., Quint. *Inst.* 3.8.49–50, 6.1.25–27, 11.1.39–42.
[64] See Guérin 2011, vol. 2, 399–400.
[65] Thus, the generation of Pericles and Alcibiades differed from the subsequent one of Critias and Isocrates; ibid. 2.94. See also *De or.* 3.55–56: The true orator's commitment to join eloquence to integrity and reason was not "the result of instruction but owing to a similarity of intention and of will [*sed impetus mentis simili et voluntate*]," shared by Greeks and Romans alike. Cf. Guérin 2011, vol. 2, 359–62.

voluntate autem similes sunt et inter sese et magistri]" (ibid.). In Cicero's history of Roman oratory, however, the individual takes center stage. He elaborates in the *Brutus* on the qualities of Laelius that set him apart from the equally remarkable Scipio: "And indeed, as in habits of speech and style there are varying likes and dislikes [*cum in dicendo variae voluntates*], it would seem that Laelius had a greater fondness for the antique and took pleasure in using words of older stamp."[66] Laelius' particular interests and temper of mind, not adherence to a school, are the foundation upon which his *voluntas dicendi* operates.[67]

Laelius' individuality is not praised for its own sake. Rather, Cicero wants to show how self-awareness can be harnessed to practical effect. Knowing his cerebral style to be unsuitable for a certain murder trial, Laelius recommends that the more bombastic Galba argue it, to great success. Laelius is thus a model for Cicero's readers not because his is the ideal *voluntas dicendi*, but because he is aware which tasks best suit his gifts.[68] "There was in those days a habit of mind," Cicero concludes, "better in all respects, and in this one thing worthier of our human nature, of granting readily to each his own [*ut faciles essent in suum cuique tribuendo*]."[69] Individual excellence depends on attunement to others:

> The eloquence of orators has always been controlled by the good sense of the audience, since all who desire to win approval have regard to the goodwill of their auditors [*omnes enim qui probari volunt, voluntatem eorum qui audiunt intuentur*], and shape and adapt themselves completely according to this and to their opinion and approval. (*Orat.* 24–25)[70]

---

[66] *Brut.* 83.
[67] In the construction of rhetorical style, one's natural gifts and conscious choices may blend together, as in the case of Demetrius of Phalerum, whose florid style was "his natural bent or perhaps his deliberate choice [*natura quaedam aut voluntas*]"; *Brut.* 285. Nevertheless, Cicero affirms that will is needed to bring natural gifts to fruition, as in the case of T. Manlius Torquatus, a young man with natural gifts worthy of a consulship who fell short because "his ability to speak was greater than his will [*plus facultatis habuit ad dicendum quam voluntatis*]"; ibid. 245.
[68] See *Off.* 1.110: "[E]ven if other careers should be better and nobler, we may still regulate our own pursuits by the standard of our own nature"; 1.111–12: Acting consistently means not "introducing anything foreign into our actions or our life in general"; 1.114: Actors "select, not the best plays, but the ones best suited to their talents."
[69] *Brut.* 85. Compare Dyck 1996, 281, on Cicero's adaptation of the Greek *prepon* ("standing out"). Guérin 2011, 359–83, 394–406, argues that Cicero gives greater flexibility to "individual excellence" in *De oratore* relative to the later *Brutus*, by which point oratory had lost nearly all of its political utility. In the latter work, Cicero's more rigid *persona oratoris* serves a broader argument against the "Atticist" school.
[70] Cf. *Orat.* 162, where Cicero makes an almost identical juxtaposition: "We had thus either to neglect the favor of those whom we were striving to please [*voluntas eorum quibus probari volebamus*], or find some art of winning it"; *Part. or.* 15: "[T]he prudent and cautious speaker is controlled by the reception given by his audience – what it rejects has to be modified."

Attunement and adaptation to the *sensus communis*, skills fundamental to oratory,[71] lie at the heart of the ethical system Cicero recommends.

8.2.3 The Role of Fortune

Though "chance and circumstance" could apply to the full measure of human experience, in the third *persona* Cicero is tellingly specific: "regal powers and military commands, nobility of birth and political office, wealth and influence, and their opposites ..."[72] Of the four *personae*, Cicero's role of fortune is most overtly political. To this point in Book 1, readers have tasted the ex-consul's famous blend of patriotism and despair. Though "nothing remains" of the Republic (1.38), he nevertheless insists that

> those whom Nature has endowed with the capacity for administering public affairs should put aside all hesitation, enter the race for public office, and take a hand in directing the government; for in no other way can a government be administered or greatness of spirit made manifest. (1.72)

The persona of *casus* thus aims at a consistency of self in the changing winds of political fortune. "It is only a madman," Cicero writes, "who, in a calm, would pray for a storm; a wise man's way is, when the storm does come, to withstand it with all the means at his command" (1.83). The goal of equanimity is common to all professions, but as Cicero wants to show, politics poses a unique challenge to the harmonious self.[73]

Our first hint: If a change in fortune thrusts us "into some uncongenial part," we must "devote to it all possible thought, practice, and pains, that we may be able to perform it, if not with propriety, at least with as little impropriety as possible ..." (1.114). Public service adds a complexity to ethical practice with which few philosophers would have had Cicero's

---

[71] Remer 2017, 54, 59–60, 77.
[72] *Off*. 1.115. A key reference for the third *persona* may be the Cynic Bion of Borysthenes, who compared fortune to a poetess assigning one man the role of king and another the role of beggar; see Kindstrand 1994, frg. 16a. Lévy 2003, 133–34, notes that whereas for Bion fortune (*tukhê*) constitutes "the testing of a character who, no matter what happens, must stay the same," for Cicero it merely provides one of the elements that must be borne in mind in selecting the decorous act; cf. *Off*. 1.117. A still closer kinship may exist with the heterodox Stoic Ariston, who had argued that "the wise man plays every role to perfection." Importantly, Cicero targets the moral striver (*progressant*), whereas Ariston addresses the wise man only, a difference Lévy says "cannot be considered as indifferent."
[73] Cf. *Off*. 1.71: "Statesmen, too, no less than philosophers – perhaps even more so – should carry with them that greatness of spirit and indifference to outward circumstances to which I so often refer, together with calm of soul and freedom from care, if they are to be free from worries and lead a dignified and self-consistent life."

familiarity.[74] To his exposition of the four *personae* the ex-consul adds a passage on the special duties of old and young, citizen and stranger. Whereas all citizens must treat their neighbors justly, elected officials must meet an even higher standard:

> It is, then, peculiarly the place of a magistrate to bear in mind that he plays the role of state [*se gerere personam civitatis*] and that it is his duty to uphold its honor and its dignity, to enforce the law, to dispense to all their constitutional rights, and to remember that all this has been committed to him as a sacred trust. (1.124)

Is the "role of state" Cicero's fifth *persona*? Not quite. The four *personae*, as Cicero makes clear, are shared by all human beings, and only a vanishing few will be magistrates.[75] Nevertheless, treating elected office as a *persona* – a "choice of life" specially subject to the whims of chance – lets Cicero make a delicate point about politics and the self.

At the portal of his argument stands the younger Cato, a hero in both the traditional Roman and specifically Panaetian sense: His is a life for others, led with perfect consistency. In the face of the bitterest fortune, his suicide is triumphant: Rather than "look upon the face of tyrants," he dies at his own hand, his *personae* in perfect alignment (1.112). Why, then, is Cato not a model for Cicero and us all? Here we must tie together several strands. Cicero's first principle of public service is that individual interest must bow to the greater good. If the times and our country demand, we may need to sacrifice not only our material well-being, but the "inner wealth" of reputation and honor as well.[76] We remember his admonition that the greatest harm is not physical pain or poverty but disharmony with oneself.[77] Second, unlike with the other *personae*, Cicero stresses that

---

[74] Panaetius, too, had a rare vantage point, if he was in fact, as tradition held, an intimate friend of Scipio Aemilianus. See generally Grimal 1953.

[75] The term *commissi/commissa* at *Off.* 1.124 echoes what Cicero has said regarding the duties of a magistrate at 1.85: "For the administration of the government, like the office of a trustee, must be conducted for the benefit of those entrusted to one's care, not of those to whom it is entrusted [*Ut enim tutela, sic procuratio rei publicae ad eorum utilitatem, qui commissi sunt, non ad eorum, quibus commissa est, gerenda est*]." In this context, *persona civitatis* serves to explain the nature of a magistrate's duties when he takes up the "role of state." I am grateful to Malcolm Schofield for guiding me to this point.

[76] *Off.* 1.83: "The dangers attending great affairs of state fall sometimes upon those who undertake them, sometimes upon the state. In carrying out such enterprises, some run the risk of losing their lives, others their reputation and the goodwill of their fellow-citizens [*benevolentia civium*]. It is our duty, then, to be more ready to endanger our own than the public welfare and to risk honor and glory more readily than other advantages."

[77] Ibid. at 1.125: "There is nothing so essentially proper as to maintain consistency [*servare constantiam*] in the performance of every act and in the conception of every plan"; 1.111–12: "... thus we must not introduce any inconsistency [*nullam discrepantiam*] into our actions or our

8.2 Will and the Four Personae

fortune may render *decorum* – that is, acts consistent with oneself – impossible.[78] That this is true does not in any measure excuse us from our duties to the Republic.[79] He adds, tellingly, that this duty may require us to behave with greater strictness than is in our personal interest.[80] It is scarcely possible that Cicero's own consulship – a subject upon which he still may "boast" to his son (1.77–78) – is not the example foremost in mind. An oration from that period reveals his larger point.

Publius Sulla's was a rather incongruous brief to take. The dictator's nephew had been associated with Catiline, and his prosecutor in 62 BCE for political violence was a protégé of Cicero's, L. Torquatus.[81] Tasked with inconsistency between his record as consul and his present calls for lenience, Cicero protests:

> If you characterize the whole of my life, Torquatus, on the basis of my consulship, you are very much mistaken ... My will and nature [*voluntas et natura*] have now caused me to shed that harsh and stern role [*personam vehementem et acrem*] which circumstances and republic imposed at the time [*tum tempus et res publica imposuit*]. (8)

An unsympathetic reading would be that he uses the mask analogy to distance himself from his record as consul by implying that his brutal treatment of the conspirators belied his "true" nature. But this is not what he says. He does not claim that the *persona* imposed by chance and country was false (i.e. that the Republic forced an evil upon him, a glaringly unusual and probably ineffective argument), but rather that this role does not "characterize the whole of my life."[82] His *persona* of sternness was both "distinct" and "detached": distinct, in that all Romans can recognize the

---

lives." Cf. *Tusc.* 4.28–33: True evil is not physical pain but sickness of soul, and "health of the soul means a condition when its judgments and beliefs are in harmony."

[78] *Off.* 1.114.
[79] We recall Cicero's hard-won admission in *De republica* that "the essential nature of the commonwealth often defeats reason [*sed tamen vincit ipsa rerum publicarum natura saepe rationem*]"; *Rep.* 2.57. See generally Atkins 2013.
[80] *Off.* 1.88: Living as a free and lawful people requires mental poise and a "gentleness of spirit" (*mansuetudo*). Nevertheless, "strictness may be exercised for the good of the state; for without that, the government can not be well administered." Such strictness is applied only with "regard for the welfare of the state [*rei publicae utilitatem*], not the personal interest of the man administering the punishment or reproof."
[81] *Sull.* 2.
[82] See also Cicero's defense of L. Junius Brutus and Scipio Nasica, each of whom committed acts for the sake of the Republic that appeared to conflict with conventional morality; *Off.* 3.40; *Dom.* 91. Remer 2017, 67–88, situates these cases in Cicero's "distinct role morality for politicians," allowing that moral duties may change as danger to the Republic increases. Remer argues – convincingly in my view – that Cicero intends these departures from everyday morality to themselves be moral, since *decorum* originates in collective norms and the community may give *ex post* approval or disapproval of exceptional acts.

unique burdens that fall on a consul's shoulders; detached, in that he may still "shed" those qualities (*detraxit*) once these duties are complete – especially if, as in this case, his other *personae* incline him to lenience. The critical point is that the role of consul, like all of these others, is genuine – as much a part of himself as his rationality, his natural gifts, and his will. The intricacy of his argument suggests that Cicero was making full use of Panaetius at this high point in his career.[83]

That public service forced him out of harmony with himself is something Cicero does not hide but embraces. Why? This returns us to Cato, the man who Cicero once accused of speaking "as if he dwelled in Plato's republic rather than Romulus's cesspool."[84] Cicero reveres Cato's patriotism, but the equivocal praise of his suicide shows how different is Cato's vision of politics from his own – and, indeed, why Cicero is memorializing Cato instead of the other way around.[85] If politics requires us to stand firm, so too does it require us to adjust to meet the moment. This, Cicero implies, Cato was unwilling or unable to do.[86] In his suicide, Cato achieves self-consistency at the cost not only of his life but of any future service he could give his country. If Cato is the "Chrysippean" politician, showing the absolutism of the Stoic sage, Cicero is fully a Panaetian, a moral work in progress, aware that pure principle must be tailored to impure circumstance. If the public role assigned by fortune puts us out of harmony with our nature and will, this too is a sacrifice for the greater good.[87] Cato's

---

[83] This likelihood is made more so by a nearly identical use of *persona* at *Mur.* 6: "I have always been happy to play this role of leniency and mercy which I learned from Mother Nature. I have not sought the part of sternness and severity [*illam vero gravitatis severitatisque personam non appetivi*], but when I had it thrust upon me by the state I have sustained it as the majesty of this realm demanded in her citizens' supreme peril." Here, too, *voluntas* is the contrary force: To take on the harsher role, Cicero "did overcome my natural inclination, though it was not what I wanted [*vici naturam . . . non quam volebam*]."

[84] *Att.* 1.21.8: . . . *dicit enim tamquam in Platonis* politeia, *non tamquam in Romuli faeci, sententiam.*

[85] *Off.* 1.112: "Did Marcus Cato find himself in one predicament, and were the others who surrendered to Caesar in Africa in another? And yet, perhaps, they would have been condemned if they had taken their lives; for their mode of life had been less austere and their characters more good-natured [*propterea quod lenior eorum vita et mores fuerant faciliores*]." Cf. Hawley 2020, 99–100.

[86] It is a complex question as to whether Cato is merely "unwilling" or, given the "natural" stringency he reinforces, functionally unable to adjust. Does his character "harden" at a certain point, after which any "willings" that depart from this character are *ipso facto* rejected? He is presumably freest to change course at a younger age, before his role of nature is fully established – and yet, at a young age he is also least able to act with far-seeing wisdom, a paradox explored later in this chapter.

[87] As if in memory of the struggle he evokes in *Sull.* and *Mur.*, Cicero adds reassuringly that between the roles of nature and fortune, nature is so much more stable and steadfast (*firmior . . . et constantior*) that "for Fortune to come into conflict with Nature seems like a combat between a mortal and a goddess"; *Off.* 1.120. While the role of fortune is not ontologically inferior to the role of nature, its changeability and unpredictability limit its "force" upon us in cases of inner conflict.

patriotism, in other words, is not the only kind. Dissonance with oneself – the sacrifice Cicero made as consul[88] – will never earn the plaudits of a heroic martyrdom, but this is the point. The greatest sacrifices are those we make knowing full well they gain us no glory. Cicero's *persona* of state perfectly captures this truth. Politics enlivens us to the tension between private will and public duty, causing us at times to feel "alienated from ourselves." But Cicero teaches that the duties we owe to others, to the community, are a part of ourselves coequal with our individual needs. Politics is maddening and incoherent, but so, too, is it our birthright and highest duty. And in this negotiation of the space between actor and mask, a conscious self takes shape.

8.2.4 The Role of Will

Though our political duties may be decided by chance, "the role we ourselves may choose sets forth from our will [*a nostra voluntate proficiscitur*]." Each of these four words illuminates. First, just as *ratio* is not the alpha but the omega of rational inquiry, *voluntas* is depicted as a durable capacity, the stage upon which our fourth role is played. This reification of will, unattested before Cicero, further strengthens the notion elaborated in *De finibus* (virtues *in voluntate positae*, "placed in the will"), the *Tusculans* (*quae quid cum ratione desiderat*, "that which desires something by reason"), and *De fato* (*libera voluntas*, "free will").[89]

Proficiscor, "to depart, spring forth, or set out on a journey," lends dynamism to Cicero's phrase, the preposition *a* carrying the double sense of "from" and "by way of." Just as a vector in mathematics is a starting point plus a direction, *voluntas* is both harbor and vessel, a durable capacity and a force in motion.[90] It must integrate, in turn, the forces of the other three *personae*: of nature and fortune, with nature the stronger;[91] and, if we must alter our way of life, of reason as well.[92]

---

[88] In this, the promise made in the Verres case – that his offering to the Republic was a "less free" *voluntas* henceforth – comes to fruition. Cf. *Verr.* 2.3.3 and discussion in Chapter 7.
[89] *Tusc.* 4.12; *Fat.* 9, 20; cf. *Top.* 64: Throwing a weapon is "by will" (*voluntatis*), but hitting someone unintentionally is "by fortune" (*fortunae*).
[90] The progress implied by *proficiscor* reinforces Lévy's argument regarding the second *persona* that the gap between actor and mask is a spatial representation of a person's development through time. See Lévy 2003, 130.
[91] *Off.* 1.120: ... *ad hanc autem rationem quoniam maximam vim natura habet, fortuna proximam* ...
[92] Ibid. 1.121: "To change one's way of life requires all of one's reason [*omni ratione curandum est*], so that the change may be seen to have been made by sound thinking [*ut id bono consilio fecisse videamur*]."

The fourth word, *nostra*, marks the force as ours. It is our own in a very special way: Unlike reason, natural gifts, or circumstances, our will is fully ours to control – and thus is a fitting locus of human freedom (*De fato*) and virtue (*De finibus*). Our will not only belongs to us; as it catalyzes and negotiates these four roles, it constitutes us. *Nos* emerges in the space that *proficiscor* opens, when we turn our telescope back from the ship's deck and examine the harbor. It is this motion through space and the turning back – the gap between actor and mask – that allows us, finally, to determine "who we want to be, and what kind of person, and in what way of life; and this is the most difficult problem in the world [*quos nos et quales esse velimus et in quo genere vitae, quae piniontion est omnium difficillima*]" (1.117). As Plautus had hinted a century earlier, self-consciousness is a space opened between "me" and "my will."[93]

We find hints of this idea earlier in Cicero's career. Returning from exile and seeking absolution by the pontifical college, Cicero strays outside the legal question to recount his suffering "at greater length than the general feeling, or indeed my own will, would approve [*me plura extra causam dixisse quam aut pinion tulerit aut voluntas mea*]."[94] When called to serve as governor of Cilicia, he explains that "contrary to my own will [*contra voluntatem meam*] and quite unexpectedly, I find myself under the necessity of setting out to govern a province."[95] Inversely, when at the end of his tenure he must defend his accounting, he concludes, "I believe I replied in as human a fashion as I could, in accordance with my mind and will [*pro animi mei voluntate*], and with my financial expectations."[96] In each of these cases, Cicero is not merely expressing his *voluntas* but examining, evaluating, even ironically distancing himself from it. More properly, "himself," the ironic or earnest subject of each phrase, is a consciousness created in recursion, in an intention to examine his intentions. His linguistic gifts, as ever, are aimed at highly practical goals: In matters where his integrity has been challenged, these turns of phrase offer him a subtler, more convincing story to tell to friends and fellow citizens.[97]

Some modern readers have characterized the fourth *persona* as merely the choice of profession.[98] Admittedly, following his definition, Cicero highlights this specific instance of will: "And so some turn to philosophy,

---

[93] Plaut. *Merc.* 321–22; see discussion in Chapter 1.
[94] *Dom.* 32. Cicero's syntax leaves some ambiguity as to whether the *opinio* is "general" or personal; regardless, the will at issue (*mea voluntas*) is his own.
[95] *Fam.* 1.65.1.   [96] *Fam.* 2.128.8.   [97] Cf. Kaster 2005, ch. 2.
[98] See Gill 1988, 174; Dyck 1996, 286–87; Woolf 2015, 178–79; Remer 2017, 55.

8.2 Will and the Four Personae

others to the civil law, and still others to oratory" (1.115).[99] Because Cicero is advising his student-aged son and the "choice of *bios*" theme is a venerable one, it is easy to miss his joke: *Ius civile, philosophia, eloquentia* – in this supposedly exclusive "choice," Cicero picked all three! Behind the jest is an insight that, as with the other three roles, *voluntas* does not manifest in a single "choice of career," but rather in iterative exploration.[100] Here, Cicero confronts what we might call the "immaturity paradox." Some of the most consequential decisions in our lives are made at an age when we are least equipped to do so: "[F]or it is in the years of early youth, when our judgment is most immature, that each of us decides his calling in life shall be that to which he has taken a special liking" (1.117). Instead of deliberating carefully – using our reason, bearing in mind our circumstances, following our "natural bent" (1.119) – as young adults we too often take the obvious path, following currents of popular opinion or copying our parents.[101] Wisdom in one's choice of career inevitably arrives too late to be of use: We are cursed to live life forward and understand it backward.

It is a problem for which Cicero shows a precocious understanding. Prosecuting Verres at thirty-six years of age, his detractors accuse him of political opportunism. On the contrary, Cicero retorts, taking this brief will be more constraint than opportunity. Recall Lucius Crassus, the great orator of the previous generation, who, after prosecuting Gaius Carbo as a young man, was carefully watched for the vices he had condemned in others, making him "less free in his willings."[102] In contrast to the self-serving *cupiditas* of so many young Romans and unlike Crassus (who stumbled into his problem), Cicero freely and willingly gives Rome a less free will (2.3.2). As it did with Crassus, the force of necessity will constrain his *voluntas* going forward; our early life choices may foreclose as many options as they open.[103] This act of will was decidedly *not* a "choice of

---

[99] On the relationship of virtue to "honorable professions" in late republican Rome, see Atkins 2018b, 73–79.
[100] There is additional resonance in the *novus homo*'s observation that a man may "[decline] to follow in the footsteps of his fathers and [pursue] a vocation of his own," adding that "those very frequently achieve great success who, though sprung from humble parentage, have set their aims high"; *Off*. 1.116. Cicero has achieved his own success via personal will, not parental example – another reason to elaborate the notion of *voluntas* for his readers.
[101] Dyck 1996, 291–92, observes that not all young people are afforded Hercules' solitude to make their decision, which is thus naturally influenced by parents and peers.
[102] *Verr*. 3.1.3. See discussion in Chapter 7.
[103] Though ridding Rome of the vile Verres is service enough, still more praise is due to the prosecutor "for the assurance and guarantee he gives them that his own life will, and must be, upright and honorable, both from his *voluntas* for virtue and duty and even more so from the force of necessity

career" – he rarely prosecuted thereafter – but something closer to Hercules' choice of a "value system" or way of life (*via vivendi*).[104] Because of the importance of this case in his public *parcours*, Cicero would be obliged to cultivate the virtues – frugality and justice – that Verres lacked.

Even for a precocious orator, later adjustments could be necessary. Cicero offers a guide as to how to do this in more serious cases:

> [L]et him go on consistently – for that is the essence of *decorum* – unless he should discover that he has made a mistake in choosing his life path. If this should happen (and it can easily happen), he must change his manners and mode of life [*facienda morum institutorum mutatio est*]." (1.120)

"To change one's way of life," he continues, "requires all of one's reason [*omni ratione curandum est*], so that the change may be seen to have been done by sound thinking [*ut id bono consilio fecisse videamur*]" (1.121). The recursive quality of *voluntas* – that good or bad "willings" strengthen or weaken our capacity to will – serves as a warning to Cicero's readers. At the moment it becomes clear that our life must change, we may find our will weakened by past failures to act.[105] If our will is not so diminished, we must still align it with the role of *ratio*.[106] We must further account for the force of *casus*, in that how we bring about the change depends on "if circumstances will aid it [*eam mutationem si tempora adiuvabunt*]" (1.120). *Videamur* ("let us be seen") shows the importance of a final dimension: We must not only satisfy our own reason but recognize how our change of life is perceived by others – starting presumably with the friends and loved ones whose wills are most closely tied to our own.[107]

Though we should follow our own nature, discovering who we are is no solitary task. Cicero declares earlier in Book 1 that of all the bonds of *societas* there is none nobler (*praestantior*) nor more powerful (*firmior*) than friendship (1.55).[108] Though traditional Stoic accounts put friends in the

---

[*sed etiam vi quadam magis necessaria recte sit honesteque vivendum*]"; *Verr.* 2.1.2–3. Here, I keep the original *voluntas*, which I interpret to signify both "choice in this matter" and "lifelong adherence."

[104] *Off.* 1.118.

[105] This insight is reflected in Cicero's emphasis on training and toughening as part of his ethical regimen in the *Tusculans* and here; cf. *Off.* 1.17–19, 1.83. See discussion in Chapter 6.

[106] The alignment of will and reason is, as I argued in Chapter 6, a normative one for Cicero. As a matter of description, he knows that this is not the case for many of his fellow Romans, whose *voluntates* are less than *honestae*; cf. *Tusc.* 4.34.

[107] Cf. *Fam.* 1.65.1; *Brut.* 245. The sentiment aligns with the (probably Panaetian) accent Cicero puts on horizontality in the role of reason (i.e. that we reason best by considering and exchanging with those around us). See *Off.* 1.99; cf. Dyck 1996, 258.

[108] See also discussion of *De amicitia* and *De officiis* in Chapter 4.

8.2 Will and the Four Personae

middle of a series of concentric circles radiating from the self and immediate family,[109] Cicero gives friendship exceptional praise. Why? Because friends are made not by accident of blood or geography but by compatibility and choice: "[F]or when two people have the same ideals and the same wills [*in quibus enim eadem studia sunt, eaedem voluntates*], it is a natural consequence that each loves the other as himself; and the result is, as Pythagoras requires of ideal friendship, that several are united in one [*ut unus fiat ex pluribus*]" (1.56). For Cicero, friendship is not merely affection or admiration but fusion: Men are "joined together" (*coniuncti*, 1.55), they are "united in one" (1.56) and "cemented by congeniality of character" (*similitudo morum coniugavit*)" (1.58). (We remember an earlier characterization of friendship as "gluing our wills together."[110]) The bond of two wills is both virtuous in itself and critically useful. Though he credits the fundamental claims of family and country, he insists that "intimate relationship of life and living, counsel, conversation, encouragement, comfort, and sometimes even reproof flourish best in friendships" (1.58). Why be grateful for reproof? If we happen to be prominent statesmen, the frank advice of friends is a welcome antidote to sycophants (1.91). A more universal reason emerges in dialogue between Cicero and his own best friend.

Near the end of 61 BCE, Cicero and Atticus' friendship was in danger. The marriage between Cicero's brother and Atticus' sister had badly deteriorated, and a rift between Quintus and Atticus was nearly public. Atticus sends a letter to Cicero complaining of Quintus' *varietas voluntatis*,[111] and in his defense cites certain opportunities given up for the sake of his friend's career. In reply, Cicero assures Atticus that the rift with Quintus is not beyond repair, but he feels that the strain on their own friendship must also be addressed:

> Your generosity and greatness of soul are evident to me, and I have never felt any difference between us except in the modes of life we have chosen [*voluntatem institutae vitae*]. What may be called ambition has led me to seek political advancement, while another and entirely justifiable way of thinking has led you to an honorable independence. In the things that really

---

[109] The best testimony for the ethical doctrine of concentric circles is from Hierocles in Stob. 4.671.7–73.11; see Sedley and Long 1987, 353.
[110] The example also shows how the force of *casus* can intervene in the merging of wills. See *Fam.* 3.348.2: "[Y]our subsequent departure for a long period, together with my pursuit of a political career and the difference between our modes of life, debarred us from 'gluing our wills together' by constant contact [*voluntates nostras consuetudine conglutinari*]."
[111] *Att.* 1.17.1.

matter [*vera quidem laude*] – uprightness, integrity, conscientiousness, fidelity to obligation – I put you second neither to myself nor to any other man ...[112]

We see how much broader than "choice of career" is Cicero's fourth *persona*. The "natural bents" of the two men, their respective roles of nature, have led to an apparent division between them – that of their *voluntas institutae vitae*. But behind this discrepancy between public and private career, a deeper will unites them: a kinship of values, of "the things that really matter," reinforced by the *beneficia* each friend has shown the other.[113] Thus, Cicero's notion of *voluntas mutua*, the reciprocal goodwill linked to the Greek *eunoia*, undergirds the *voluntas* of deliberate choice, the *prohairesis kai boulēsis* that may have been Panaetius' fourth *prosōpon*.[114] In Cicero, these Greek tributaries – latent disposition and present choice – meet in a common sea.

Rereading *De officiis* in light of these letters, we understand why Atticus' worth to Cicero goes beyond shared values and mutual service. The more subtle gift of this merged *voluntas* is that one consciousness can midwife another. "Your congratulation has often given me pleasure in success," Cicero tells Atticus, "and your comfort consoled my apprehensions. Indeed at the present time I badly miss in your absence not only your excellent advice but also our habitual exchange of talk, which is such a delight to me."[115] Several times he gives this paired phrase: Cicero values not just Atticus' advice, but the "talk" [*sermo*] itself.[116] This is not merely for companionship – as Cicero writes in his next letter, he is never more lonely than surrounded by his many "friends"[117] – but for the personal insight that intimacy unlocks. "Delicacy [*verecundia*]," he writes, "has often kept both you and me from putting these things into words."[118] And yet in friction, in the

---

[112] Ibid. 1.17.5.
[113] For the resonance in Atticus' claims of past service to Cicero, see the discussion of *voluntas mutua* in Chapter 4 and the lengthy passage concerning reciprocity in friendship at *Off.* 1.42–60, just prior to introducing the four *personae*.
[114] De Lacy 1977, 170, sees a possible anticipation of the *persona* of *voluntas* in a passage from the *Magna Moralia*, which proposes that human beings can be the "cause" (*arkhē*) of their actions by "choice and wish and all that is in conformity with reason [*prohairesis kai boulēsis kai to kata logon pan*]." Arist. [*Mag. Mor.*] 1187b4–30, 1188a38–b24.
[115] Cic. *Att.* 1.17.6.
[116] Cf. ibid.: "In short, whether working or resting, in business or in leisure, in professional or domestic affairs, in public life or private, I cannot for any length of time do without your affectionate advice and the delight of your conversation."
[117] See *Att.* 1.18.1.   [118] Ibid. 1.17.7.

8.2 *Will and the Four* Personae

tension of competing forces (this time, the aberrant will of Quintus), comes the possibility to crystallize and "overhear" what lay invisible to Cicero before.[119] In exile he writes, "I am reproaching myself far more than you, and if I do reproach you it is as my 'other me' [*deinde te quasi me alterum*]; also I am looking for someone to share the blame."[120] Just as the Verres case spurred a difficult self-awareness, Atticus makes Cicero's will – his *voluntas institutae vitae* – the object of conscious reflection. Atticus did more than keep him alive in exile. With Atticus, and perhaps Atticus alone, Cicero can examine his own intentions, flaws, and possibilities, aiding his constitution as a moral subject.[121] It is the "other me" that makes "me" possible.

We remember that this metaphysical play would be described by the Stoics in physical terms.[122] Combining the many threads of Cicero's *voluntas*, self-consciousness thus emerges in a play of four dimensions. Our will "sets forth" (*proficiscor*) from a point of choice, a two-dimensional vector allowing a reflective loop or "turning back." A third dimension arises from other minds – the reference point for virtuous choice, and, in the case of our closest friends, the spur and helpmate of our reflection.[123] And finally, in the fourth dimension of time, each act of will can strengthen this reflective loop, just as a failure of will can weaken it. These metaphysics of will are opened by implication, not theory; as ever, Cicero probes and suggests more than he defines. But the recursive elements of *De officiis* are all the more striking given their echoes in the study of consciousness today.[124] Cicero did not travel to these horizons, but he pointed us in their direction and set us forth.

---

[119] See Bloom 1998, xix: "[S]elf-overhearing is the royal road to individuation." In antiquity, as Foucault 1981–82, 342, observes, this was literally the case: "It was a habit – and a recommended one – when one had read, to write, and when one had written to reread what one had written, and to reread necessarily out loud since, as we know, in Latin and Greek writing the words ran together." Randall 2018, 17–36, explores the ideals of conversation as exemplified in Cicero's letters and treatises.

[120] *Att.* 1.60.4. Cf. ibid. 8.14.2, 3.15.4 (to Caesar); *Amic.* 80, 92.

[121] Foucault 1981–82, 343, observes regarding the exchange of intimate letters between friends (the "*correspondance d'âme*"): "And in these supple exchanges of gifts and benefits, in these supple exchanges of soul where one tries to aid the other along his path toward the good and toward himself, you understand that the activity of writing is important." Incredibly, Foucault gives the letters between Cicero and Atticus as a *counterexample* to this type of correspondence, implying that Cicero's letters served only "to give news of the political world," but not of himself. On this point Foucault is simply incorrect.

[122] Diog. Laert. 7.139; Stob. *Ecl.* 2.64.18–23. See Schofield 2012, 51.

[123] An elegant expression of this idea in modern times is found in Smith 1759, sec. 1, chs. 1–4.

[124] See, e.g., Hofstadter 2007; Corballis 2011; Dennett 2017.

8.3 Conclusion: Scipio and Foucault

Does the self begin where politics end? In his 1981–82 lectures on the history of Western subjectivity ("*L'herméneutique du sujet*"), Michel Foucault proposes the "Hellenistic and imperial" age as a crucial pivot point. What he calls the Hellenistic "culture of self" (*culture de soi*) differs radically from what comes before it – the classical notion exemplified by Plato – and what comes after: Christianity's "conversion" (*metanoia*), a renunciation and rebirth into divine truth.[125] Foucault proposes that the Hellenistic *conversion du regard* differed from the Platonic "care for the self" in four important ways: (1) Its essential truths are immanent, not transcendent (201–02); (2) its "turn toward the self" is not a liberation to another world but from what does not depend on us to what does (202); (3) it is characterized not by knowledge as reminiscence but by *askēsis*, perpetual training and practice (202); and (4) its purpose is to equip, protect, and honor the self – not instrumentalize it, as Plato did, for the good of the city (170, 198).[126] This final abandonment of a politically constructed self anticipates what Gill calls the evolution from "personhood" to "personality" in Western thought.[127] The achievement of the Hellenistic *conversion*, Foucault concludes, is "*auto-finalisation de soi par soi*" (170), total self-completion and liberation. Though including properly Hellenistic thinkers like Epicurus in his argument, he focuses principally on post-republican thinkers such as Seneca, Epictetus, and Marcus Aurelius.[128] Cicero and his abundant pen are absent.[129]

---

[125] Foucault 1981–82, 203, characterizes the Christian conversion or *metanoia* as follows: (1) "*une mutation soudaine*," "*un événement unique . . . à la fois historique et métahistorique*"; (2) "*un passage d'un type de l'être à l'autre . . . de la mortalité à l'immortalité, etc.*"; and (3) "*une rupture . . . le soi qui se convertit est un soi qui a renoncé à lui-même.*"

[126] He observes for example that, whereas Plato's "*connais-toi toi-meme*" applied equally for political and "cathartic" ends in his own time, by the 3rd and 4th centuries CE, "*connais-toi toi-meme*" is an "*embranchement*," a choice between political action and cultivating one's true self; ibid. 167.

[127] Gill 1988, 169–73. See, e.g., 169–70: "Those who are concerned with 'personhood,' as I understand this notion, are interested in persons as a class, and are, especially, concerned to define the nature and boundaries of this class by reference to normative criteria of personhood . . . By a concern with 'personality,' I understand an interest in persons as individuals, and, especially, an interest in what makes each individual distinctive and unique."

[128] Philo of Alexandria, Plutarch, Musonius Rufus, and Lucan each make philosophical cameos as well. For a full index, see ibid. 537–40.

[129] Foucault occasionally cites Cicero on minor points: at 92–95 (translation), 343 (correspondence with Atticus), 367 (contribution to rhetoric), and 424 (Stoic reflection turns apparent evil into nonevil). Lévy 2003, 127, notes that Foucault and Hadot located the key turning point in the Imperial period and did not give much attention to the Republic. Cf. Foucault 1981–82, 502 n. 21, where Gros (ed.) cites Lévy's observation that skepticism is missing from Foucault's analysis.

8.3 Conclusion

Yet *De officiis* reveals the existence of another waystation in Foucault's genealogy. Cicero stands – alone, or nearly so – at the crossroads of Plato's "self for the city" and the Hellenistic/imperial "self for oneself alone."[130] The "Hellenistic/imperial" designation is especially illuminating in that the Greek and Roman thinkers Foucault cites have something in common with one another that they do not have with Cicero: Their theories come *after* the definitive failure of a political order – the end of the plural, self-governing *polis* and Republic, respectively. Cicero, unlike Seneca or Epictetus, dedicates his life to a society of normatively free and active citizens. However successful the tyrant or submissive the elite, Cicero is adamant that these new rules shall never replace the old, and that "the wise man should turn to the Republic's care [*sapiens ad rem publicam tuendam ... transeat*]."[131] Public service is service to one's highest self, "for in no other way can a government be administered or greatness of spirit be made manifest."[132]

Yet Cicero's inward turn just as certainly anticipates the recursion or conversion that Foucault finds in later Stoics: in the actor who must both play and judge his role and in the dynamic of *proficiscor*, what Foucault calls the "trajectory from self to self" (214). Indeed, the trajectory of *voluntas* sparks the conscious mind in Foucauldian terms: "[T]he presence of self to self, due precisely to the distance that remains between self and self; the presence of self to self *in* the distance of self to self" (ibid., emphasis added).[133] Critically, Cicero's self-sufficiency is not characterized as a withdrawal into oneself or from city to countryside.[134] It is "indifference to outer circumstances"; that is to say, a practiced courage nourished by experience but also by lucidity as to our essential nature (what "depends on us" or not).[135] It emerges not in isolated reflection but in the friction and contest of life's many forces: fortune and brutality and nature and will. Cicero's vision of moral independence is not the "*détournement des autres*"

---

[130] Cf. MacIntyre 1988, 147–48; Burchell 1998, 104–05; Hawley 2020, 88–89, 100–01.
[131] *Tusc.* 5.72.   [132] *Off.* 1.72.
[133] Another correspondence, worthy of its own analysis, is Cicero's anticipation of Foucault's idea that "it is toward the self that he must turn his gaze" in the admonition that the ideal statesman passes his time regarding himself as if in a mirror; cf. Foucault 1981–82, 204; *Rep.* 2.69. There is also an intriguing analogy with Roman legal practice; cf. Seneca's eighth letter to Lucilius (letter 8.7, vol. 1; cited by Foucault at 204): "[P]hilosophy makes the subject turn toward himself [*la philosophie fait tourner le sujet sur lui-même*]," echoing the traditional gesture in Roman law by which a master frees a slave.
[134] See Foucault 1981–82, 212.
[135] *Off.* 1.66: "[W]hen the soul is disciplined [by indifference to external circumstances], one should do deeds not only great and in the highest degree useful, but extremely arduous and laborious and fraught with danger both to life and to many things that make life worth living."

advised by Marcus Aurelius,[136] but, somewhat paradoxically, a self-sufficiency that others assist. Alone among Earth's creatures, man can refine his reason socially; he progresses by "overhearing" his intimations to another.[137]

All of this is enough to show that Gill's critique of *De officiis* – that it falls on the wrong side of "personhood and personality" – presents a false choice. It is a frame that makes sense to an individualist and "post-Christian" age,[138] but not to Cicero's. The natural tension between universal rules and particular contexts – among the roles of reason, fortune, and state – is not "problematic," as Gill says; it is the engine of self-creation. The instinct that Cicero apparently shared with Panaetius is that universal principles, if they are to be understood at all, can be understood only in particular lives.[139] Only in a specific time, in concrete actions, in our own society and culture do we realize the gift of reason common to all places and times. Our will is the force by which these negotiations of *decorum* unfold: in public duties, for which self-consistency may be our greatest sacrifice; in dialectic with friends who "join forces" with us; and in emulation of ancestors, philosophers, and heroes. Cicero's is a struggle within that is proved by public action, seeking harmony with oneself and honoring the values of the *maiores*. As De Lacy eloquently puts it,

> the element of detachment implicit in the notion of a role helps to remind us that we are not discrete entities. We are parts of a far greater unity to which we are related in a variety of ways, and moreover in ways that change with time. To identify ourselves with any one of our roles, to the exclusion of the others, would lead us into error.[140]

Tension and crisis do not weaken us. They improve us by heightening our awareness of the spaces between actor and mask, of the negotiation of roles from which our *nos* comes to be.

We are left with the image of Scipio, the great general and statesman, upholder of ancestral legacy, Laelius' friend and Panaetius' patron. Despite a life of public glory, Cicero writes, Scipio was "never less lonely than when

---

[136] See Foucault's translations of M. Aur. Med. 2.8: "*on n'est jamais malheureux parce qu'on ne prête pas attention à ce qui se passe dans l'âme d'autrui*"; 3.4, "*N'use pas de la part de vie qui t'est laissé à imaginer ce que fait autrui*"; 4.18. Foucault 1981–82, 211.

[137] Foucault 1981–82, 341, observes that by the 1st and 2nd centuries CE, "writing has already become, and would not cease from affirming itself thereafter, as an exercise of the self."

[138] Here, I do not mean to suggest that Christianity and other monotheisms are relics of the past, but rather that in the West, modern secularism – and especially the notion of a "unique personality" – owes much to Judeo-Christian, and particularly Protestant, notions of individual autonomy. See generally Henrich 2020.

[139] Cf. Hawley 2020, 94–98.   [140] De Lacy 1977, 172.

8.3 Conclusion

he was alone." "Even in leisure hours," he relates, "his thoughts were occupied with public business, and he communed with himself [*in solitudine secum loqui solitum*]."[141] This is Cicero's vision: civic duty and self-knowledge in mutual completion. He is, with the near-exception of Seneca, the last ancient thinker to uphold politics as an arena of self-mastery. That the construction of self became a private, individual endeavor owes as much to the failure of politics as to the evolution of wisdom. Cicero wants his readers to understand, finally, that the purposes of the self and those of the city may be achieved together. The failures of his own life take nothing away, in my view, from the power of his insistence that such a self is both desirable and possible. In the ashes of the Republic and "often alone," Cicero reaffirms his fidelity to Scipio's ideal, an example he follows not *imitatione* but *voluntate* (ibid.). It is for us to decide whether we, too, can dedicate our wills, and discover ourselves, in the same fragile cause.

---

[141] *Off.* 3.1; cf. *Rep.* 1.27. Compare Cicero's praise of Cato the Elder at *Planc.* 66: "I have always thought that a sublime and noble sentiment which Marcus Cato expresses in the opening passage of his *Origines*, where he says that great and eminent men should attach as much importance to their hours of relaxation as to their hours of toil [*clarorum virorum atque magnorum non minus otii quam negotii rationem exstare oportere*]." See Garbarino 1973, fr. 292, 141–42.

Conclusion

It was often said of Cicero that he was eclectic rather than systematic; that his treatises are devoid of originality; that even to call him a philosopher is overgenerous. In the eyes of these critics, his primary contribution to Western thought is as a translator, more prolific than precise. Thankfully, the shadow of anti-Ciceronian sentiment cast by 19th-century scholars – the caricature of grandiose orator, failed statesman, and unserious thinker – has lifted in recent years. In this moment of resumed appreciation of his philosophy, I hope this study has affirmed two major innovations for which he deserves credit.

Cicero's foundational role in Latin's philosophical lexicon has long been in evidence. These contributions are not limited, however, to coinages like *qualitas*, *adsensio*, and *humanitas*. The choices of a translator are legion, and his generation sets the high-water mark of Greek proficiency in the long river of Latin culture. It is in this context that we appreciate both Cicero's challenge – translating Greek for peers who likely knew it – and his ingenuity. *Voluntas* comes to him with a centuries-old pedigree from Roman law and the comic stage. Its dynamic quality – Varro links it to *volo*, both "I want" and "I fly"[1] – unsettles the Greek concepts it approaches. Identifying it with Stoic *boulēsis*, Cicero takes a calculated risk. "How can *voluntas* be the wise man's desire of reason," Brutus might have asked, "when it is also the evil scheme of Clodius or Catiline?" Equally bold is his choice to make a "free will" the key to moral autonomy in a centuries-old debate in which freedom (*eleutheria*) had never figured. The ex-consul sits at the crossroads of Greek and Latin thought, adept of the former and architect of the latter.

Yet the real story of *voluntas* is not one of translation but of transformation. Cicero's regard is double: As practitioner and strategist, he develops the will descriptively, inventing new shades of expression; as

---

[1] Varro, *Ling.* 6.6.47; see discussion in Chapter 1.

Conclusion

thinker and scholar, he develops it normatively – insisting, against all the evidence of his age, that will should be stabilized by reason. In treatises, orations, and letters, Cicero lays the foundation for an idea – the will and its freedom – with tremendous consequence for the West. Before him, *voluntas* was a "willing" but not yet a "will"; it was a desire-in-motion, a force in competition with others. Cicero inherits this venerable force – the *voluntas populi, patris,* and *deorum* – and situates it in a *rational* political order and, when that order fails, in the human subject. His "will" varies in strength, in type, and in time, as *boulēsis* or *prohairesis* had not. And, of course, his normative arguments – a will fully rational and oriented to virtue – collide with decades of invective, yielding a rich ambiguity: a power of mind caught between good and evil.

None of these contributions can be seen in a vacuum; as he affirms in *De natura deorum*, Cicero had thought through these questions at times when he seemed furthest from philosophy (1.6–7). Complex and contradictory, his ideas are the fruits of a long career in a most turbulent age. His skeptical method served a sacred mission: to preserve the Republic's virtues when its institutions were no more. Certainly, his *voluntas* had antecedents of great significance. Certainly, it would take others to explore and systematize the paths he had opened. But it would be difficult to imagine these systems without the contributions Cicero provided. Virtuoso of Latin prose and pioneer of Latin thought, Cicero has always repaid the interest given him. He will continue to do so as long as *voluntas philosophiae* exists in humankind.

Epilogue
The Afterlife of Cicero's Voluntas[1]

He was swordless and shieldless, but the young man from Thagaste had a battle to fight. The late 4th century CE was home to a cacophony of schools and sects, each offering their own account of the universe and mankind's place in it. The protagonist of the *Confessions*, written in a "concentrated burst" in 397 CE,[2] is a young man making his way through this intellectual *mêlée*, gifted with rare talent and deeply disturbed. This situation was not new, but Augustine of Hippo describes his unsettlement and ensuing quest as no one in the West had done before. His journey, from an obscure corner of North Africa to the imperial court of Milan and back, announces the autobiography as literary genre and soon joins the canon of Christendom. Augustine's is a battle for insight, a pilgrimage toward a truth beyond dispute. Less grandly, he is a young man struggling with self-control. For his mind, mystifyingly, does not follow its own commands:

> Whence is this strange situation? And why is it so? The mind orders the body, and the body obeys; the mind orders itself, and it resists. The mind orders a hand to be moved, and this is accomplished with such ease that its authority can scarcely be discerned from that of a master over his slave. The mind orders the mind to will; it is only one mind, but it does not do as ordered [*imperat animus, ut velit animus, nec alter est nec facit tamen*]. Whence is this strange situation? And why is it so? (8.9.21)

Augustine's dramatic conversion at Milan is sparked by a passage from Saint Paul, his decisive spiritual influence. In the Apostle he finds a kindred struggle for godliness against temptations of the flesh. But whereas

---

[1] A complete genealogy of *voluntas* from antiquity to the present would take in more thinkers and texts than is possible here. For the development of notions of will in the imperial period, see, e.g., Pohlenz 1948, 1964, 159; Voelke 1973, 161; Dihle 1982, 134–35; Inwood 2000, 44–60; Zöller 2003, *passim*.
[2] Fox 2001, xv.

Paul pits man's immortal soul against his corrupted body, Augustine's battleground is within the soul itself:

> [A]s I endeavoured to raise my mental sight from the depths, I was drawn down again; and often as I tried, I was drawn down again and again. What raised me up towards your light was the fact that I knew that I had a will just as much as I knew I was alive [*quod tam sciebam me habere voluntatem quam me vivere*]. Thus, when I willed or did not will something, I was wholly certain that it was I and no one else who was willing it or not willing it; and I was now on the point of perceiving that therein lay the reason for my own sin. (7.3.4)

What is the *voluntas* of which Augustine is so sure? To the river of ink on this subject,[3] I can only add a drop or two here. In my view, the "will" he reveals in *Confessions* has four key qualities that bear attention. The first is ontological: Augustine's *voluntas* is not merely an "instance of willing" but a durable capacity or power of mind.[4] Human will is, secondly, a reflection of God's will, the primary cause of our universe. Among all living creatures, only man has a *voluntas* and thus participates in some small way in the divine will that governs all.[5] Third, human will is a critically important part of ourselves for which we bear full moral responsibility. One person's capacity of will does not necessarily resemble another's, and it may be directed to better or worse ends. It is our duty, therefore, to use and improve this capacity as best as we are able, in accordance with God's plan.[6] Finally, having a will does not mean that it is free. In fact, most people do *not* have a free will, and they will make disastrous choices – choices for which they are nevertheless responsible – from ignorance of the truth, accumulation of bad habits, or both.[7]

In consideration of the above, many have credited Augustine with inventing the will.[8] This premise, with deep roots in Christian and secular scholarship, is now being reexamined. In his painstaking study, Frede argues that all four elements of Augustine's will are present in the works of Epictetus, three centuries before the conversion at Milan. Frede

---

[3] In English, the classic study of Augustine's life and works remains Brown 1967. An illustrative list of contributions include Deane 1963; O'Donnell 1992; Goulven 1996; Büttgen 2001; Stump 2001; Teske 2001; O'Donnell 2005; Sellier 2009.
[4] See August. *Conf.* 7.3.4, 7.16.22, 7.21.27, 8.5.10, 8.8.19–20, 8.9.21, 8.10.23–24.
[5] Ibid. 7.4.6, 7.9.14, 10.37.60, 11.6.8, 11.10.12, 12.15.18, 12.23.32, 12.28.38, 13.4.5, 13.9.10, 13.15.18, 13.16.19, 13.22.32.
[6] Ibid. 7.3.4, 7.16.22, 7.21.27, 9.2.4.   [7] Ibid. 1.6.8, 4.7.12, 7.3.4, 7.16.22, 8.5.10.
[8] See Arendt 1971, vol. 2, 84, calling Augustine "the first philosopher of the Will"; Dihle 1982, 144: "St. Augustine was, in fact, the inventor of our modern notion of will"; Kahn 1988, 255–59; King 2010, xxxi; Brann 2014, 23–37, calling Augustine "discoverer of the will."

marshals impressive evidence for his thesis, drawing from a wide range of Peripatetic, Stoic, and Neoplatonic texts. We are shown how Epictetus' *prohairesis* has the same durability as a power of mind, is shared by mortals and the divine, varies widely, and is generally abused.[9] These texts suggest a strong, perhaps decisive influence of Stoicism on Augustine's notion of the will. But did he get them from Epictetus?

Here, Frede's argument hits rough going. The Stoa was defunct by the 4th century CE, and few of its seminal texts had been translated into Latin.[10] As Augustine himself admits in the *Confessions*, he did not enjoy Greek and never mastered it.[11] Frede admits that it is not "fully clear through what channels the Stoicism reached Augustine," but he offers the following idea: "In large part, of course, it came through Cicero, who, though he was an Academic skeptic, had espoused the kind of Philonean skepticism which allowed for the qualified adoption of philosophical views; these, for the most part, turned out to be Stoic, or inspired by Stoicism."[12] Indeed, Augustine is hardly bashful about his debts to Cicero. He credits the *Hortensius*, now lost, not only with having inspired a deep love of philosophy, but in "chang[ing] my prayers and turn[ing] them to you, O Lord" (3.4.7). In Cicero's philosophy, Augustine continues, "there was one thing that I loved especially, namely that his words aroused me and set me on fire not to be a lover of this or that sect, but of wisdom itself, whatever it may be" (3.4.8). Though Augustine regrets that Cicero was not – indeed, could not have been – a follower of Christ,[13] he does not hesitate to cite him favorably in the course of his spiritual journey. Now bishop, he quotes lines from the *Tusculan Disputations*,[14]

---

[9] See especially Frede 2011, 31–48, 66–88.

[10] See Gill 2003, 33–58. Gill notes the "Latin" Stoicism of Seneca and a Stoic influence on Roman poetry, but Greek appears to have remained the school's predominant language in the period following Cicero; ibid. 49–50, 57–58.

[11] See *Conf.* 1.13.20: "As for the reason why I hated the Greek literature in which I was steeped as a boy – for that I have still found no satisfactory explanation. I had fallen in love with Latin literature …"; 1.14.23: "It was the sheer difficulty of gaining a thorough grasp of a foreign language that cast gall, so to speak, over the sweet allurements of Greek myth and epic."

[12] Frede 2011, 154. He continues, "in Augustine's time the study of Cicero was perhaps the most crucial part of any higher education for Westerners, especially for a professional rhetorician, as Augustine was in his early career. But we also have to remember in this context that by his time Platonism had absorbed large doses of Stoicism." Cf. *Conf.* 5.6.11: Augustine criticizes Faustus' patchy knowledge of Cicero. See generally MacCormack 2013, 251–306.

[13] Augustine continues: "And there was one thing that damped my ardour, namely that the name of Christ was not in that book"; *Conf.* 3.4.8. Cf. ibid. 8.7.17.

[14] Ibid. 1.16.25. Regarding Jove the adulterous "Thunderer," Augustine observes, "these things are all Homer's invention, says Cicero. 'He conferred upon the gods attributes that are properly human; I would rather he had ascribed divine qualities to us men.' But it would be truer to say that Homer did indeed make up the stories he tells, but ascribed divine attributes to depraved humans."

Academica,¹⁵ and, perhaps improbably, the *De natura deorum*.¹⁶ He even refers to a gentlemanly debate *de finibus bonorum et malorum* with his friends Alypius and Nebridius in Milan (6.16.26). Indeed, Augustine's very first treatises – dialogues set at a countryside villa in summer 386 CE – bear a striking resemblance to those Cicero imagined at Tusculum four centuries before.¹⁷ Regarding the great minds of Augustine's era in the Latin-speaking West, his recent biographer, James O'Donnell, observes:

> Greek was now Greek to them, so to speak, and Cicero their best philosopher. His philosophical writings had very little success or imitation between his death and the fourth century, but he came into his own as a philosopher – not just an orator – when the elites could no longer read Greek, and the philosophical treasures of the Greeks were opaque to them. Arnobius, Lactantius, Ambrose, Augustine – these writers of the fourth century are the most sophisticated, interested, and interesting disciples of Cicero from all antiquity.¹⁸

Next to Paul, Cicero was probably the greatest influence in Augustine's intellectual life. What role might he have played in Augustine's "invention" of the will?

The question merits its own full-length study. What a closer look may reveal is that Cicero's *voluntas* prefigures Augustine's in each of its most important respects – though as we will see in this Epilogue, the bishop widens certain fields of meaning while foreclosing others. We have explored at length how Cicero guides *voluntas* from "a willing" to an engine of human subjectivity. Cicero's will is "that which desires something with reason [*quae quid cum ratione desiderat*]";¹⁹ it is the faculty by which we change ourselves and mark the world.²⁰ Secondly, Cicero proposes a correspondence between human and divine will. In *De natura*

We note not only the favorable treatment of Cicero's text, but that the context is one of the nature of kinship between the human and the divine.

¹⁵ Ibid. 6.10.18: "... and all the time I said, 'Wisdom? I will discover it tomorrow. It will appear before my eyes, and I will lay hold on it.' – 'Faustus will come, and will explain everything.' – 'What heroes the Academics are! Is it true that "nothing pertaining to the blessed life be apprehended as a certainty?"'" (quoting Cicero, *Acad.* 2.18, 2.31).

¹⁶ Ibid. 6.5.7: "... for no amount of fighting talk, name-calling, or ruthless questioning on the part of the various conflicting philosophers I had read, had ever forced me not to believe that you were what you are (though I did not know what you were), or that 'the governance of human affairs' was not your concern" (quoting Cicero, *Nat. D.* 2.3).

¹⁷ See O'Donnell 2015, 218. Cf. *Conf.* 5.14.25: "[T]he views of the philosophers seemed to me much more plausible ... [therefore] I followed what is believed to be the Academic practice; reserving judgment on all questions and wavering between all points of view ..."

¹⁸ O'Donnell 2015, 235.   ¹⁹ Cic. *Tusc.* 4.12.

²⁰ Cf. *Fat.* 9. See especially the example of Regulus; *Sest.* 127; *Fin.* 2.65; *Off.* 3.99–115.

deorum, Cotta asserts that if the Stoics are correct, the gods could create a just world as effortlessly as humans move their limbs, "by their mind and will [*mente ipsa ac voluntate*]."[21] In turn, a man expands his *magnitudo animi* by turning his mind to the *numen, consilium,* and *voluntas* of the gods.[22] Thirdly, the will is, for Cicero as well as Augustine, the critical locus of human morality and progress. The *persona* that "sets forth from our will [*a nostra voluntate proficiscitur*]" is the one by which we choose our value system and life path.[23] Our *voluntas* is where nature has "placed" (*positae*) the cardinal virtues,[24] and is the focal point of legal responsibility and cosmological freedom.[25] And though Cicero argues that the will is normatively rational and *honestae*,[26] he finds abused and evil wills everywhere he looks. A Stoic *prohairesis* can stumble and err, but the Devil's *mala voluntas*, like Catiline's, is quite literally a force for evil.[27]

Does a sinful world disprove divine providence? Cicero's *De natura deorum* is evidence that Christian theologians, however innovative their answers, were not the first to pose the question. In debate with his Stoic friend Balbus, the skeptic Cotta grants that "many men make bad use of their inheritances, but this does not prove that they have received no benefit from their fathers."[28] Though Cotta's fellow skeptics argue that the "divine mind and will" (*mens voluntasque divina*) neglected humankind by endowing them with capacities the vast majority would abuse, Balbus will insist that the gift itself does not disclose "the will of him who gave"

---

[21] *Nat. D.* 3.92. Cotta, as a skeptic, is not endorsing the Stoic view. Nevertheless, the evocation of will on the "human" and "divine" plane is present in both sets of arguments; cf. ibid. 2.44: "[T]he motion of all living bodies is due to one of three causes, nature, force, or will [*omnia quae moventur aut natura moveri censuit aut vi aut voluntate*]." See also *Rosc Am.* 136: "I am aware that all these results are due to the will of the gods, the zeal of the Roman people, and the wisdom, power, and good fortune of Sulla [*deorum voluntate, studio populi Romani, consilio et imperio et felicitate L. Sullae*]"; *Leg.* 1.24: "[H]ence we are justified in saying that there is a blood relationship between ourselves and the celestial beings [*agnatio nobis cum caelestibus*]; or we may call it a common ancestry or origin;" *Tusc.* 5.38: "... the soul of man, derived as it is from the divine mind [*humanus autem animus decerptus ex mente divina*], can be compared with nothing else, if it is right to say so, save God alone."

[22] *Fin.* 4.11.   [23] *Off.* 1.115.   [24] *Fin.* 5.36.   [25] *Top.* 64; *Fat.* 20.   [26] *Tusc.* 4.34.

[27] August. *Conf.* 7.3.4: "But if the Devil himself changed by his perverse will [*ipsa perversa voluntate*] from being a good angel to being the Devil, what is the origin of the evil will [*voluntas mala*] by which he became the Devil ...?"; Augustine also uses the phrase *bona voluntas* (13.9.10), a phrase that never appears in Cicero's corpus. Augustine's ironic *malevola benevolentia* ("ill-willed goodwill," 3.2.3) also takes him beyond Ciceronian usage.

[28] Cic. *Nat. D.* 3.70–71. This debate seems already to have been well established in Stoicism, but Cicero and Lucretius may have been the first to examine the question in Latin. See Woolf 2015, 34–39, 51–62.

(*voluntas eius qui dederit*).²⁹ The corruption of man, for the Stoics, cannot refute the gods' benevolent will. Rather, if the gods give reason to man, "it is we who make it good or the reverse" (*bonam autem rationem aut non bonam a nobis*).³⁰

These correspondences, though ripe for exploration, are not even the most telling link between the two men. What is most striking is how emphatically Augustine describes his *voluntas*, like Cicero's, as a dynamic and measurable force. His will can *inclinare* to one side or another, an image Cicero develops in his oratory.³¹ It can shift dramatically from one type to another, as when Ponticianus' friends, fresh converts to a monastic life, "told them of their resolve and purpose, and how such a will as this had arisen and been confirmed in them [*quoque modo in eis talis voluntas orta esset atque firmata*]" (8.6.15). And, of course, the will can be perverse, literally "turned around" from good to evil, to which Augustine originally adds the imagery of "casting forth its innermost part" (*proicientis intima sua*) and "swelling outwards" (*tumescentis foras*).³²

Twelve years after Cicero's *Hortensius* kindled him to a search for wisdom, at age thirty-one he is certain of the truth of Christ. And yet being certain in the truth and wanting to follow it are still apparently not enough: "My soul resisted. She refused, and did not excuse herself; all her arguments were used up and shown to be false" (8.7.18). This, the ancient *akrasia* problem, Augustine frames anew. His ability from Cicero to explain *voluntas* in terms of competition and strength leads him to a new argument. Augustine's will to follow Christ is not his only will. His agony is the experience of a combat between *two* wills: an "iron will" (*ferrea voluntas*, 8.5.10), "weighed down by its habit" toward worldly appetites;

---

²⁹ *Nat. D.* 3.70. Cf. August. *Conf.* 13.26.41: "The fruit is the good and honest intention of the giver [*fructus autem bona et recta voluntas datoris est*]." On Cicero's phrase *mens et voluntas*, see his rendering of *kata noun* in the *Timaeus* as *ex sua mente et voluntate* (fr. 36d–e); *Nat. D.* 3.92: Both divine and human motion is achieved by *mens et voluntas*; *Cat.* 3.22: It was not Cicero alone who foiled the conspirators, but rather, "I received this mind and will from the immortal gods and have arrived at this ample evidence [*Dis ego immortalibus ducibus hanc mentem voluntatemque suscepi atque ad haec tanta indicia perveni*]."
³⁰ Cic. *Nat. D.* 3.71; cf. August. *Conf.* 7.21.27: "[J]ustly have you handed us over to the ancient sinner, the Lord of Death [*antiquo peccatori, praeposito mortis*], since he has persuaded our will to take on the likeness of his will; and he has willed not to stand fast in your truth [*quia persuasit voluntati nostrae similitudinem voluntatis suae, qua in veritate tua non stetit*]."
³¹ See *Conf.* 2.3.6: Like his father's joy at noticing Augustine's pubescence, so too is mankind "drunk on the invisible wine of its own will, perverse as it is and bent on lower things [*de vino invisibili perversae atque inclinatae in ima voluntatis suae*]." Cf. ibid. 2.5.10. For "inclination" of the will in Cicero, see *Cat.* 4.6; *Mur.* 53; *De or.* 2.129.
³² August. *Conf.* 7.16.22, 7.3.4. Cf. 10.22.32: "[T]heir will is not averse at least to some image of joy [*ab aliqua tamen imagine gaudii voluntas eorum non avertitur*]."

and a "will to progress," not yet "strong and whole throughout" (8.8.19). Thus divided, his will is "twisted and tossed around, wounded in part, caught in a struggle between rising and falling factions" (ibid.).

Anticipating that this idea could be exploited by the Manichaeans, he clarifies that these "two wills" do not represent "two Principles," one subject to God, the other outside his power.[33] Though Augustine is caught between an "upward" and "downward" will, it is possible for multiple evil and good wills to compete (8.10.23). In the latter case, such as when a Christian hesitates between reading the Apostle, singing a psalm, or proclaiming the Gospel,

> [a]ll these wills are good, and yet they strive against each other, until one course of action is chosen, and the whole will, which had been divided into several wills, is channeled into it [*et omnes bonae sunt et certant secum, donec eligatur unum, quo feriatur tota voluntas una, quae in plures dividebatur*]. So too, although eternity has a delight that draws us upwards, and pleasure in temporal good draws us back downwards, there is no one soul that wills with all its will either one or the other. It is torn in two by the weight of its troubles, as long as it prefers the former for truth's sake, but for familiarity's sake does not put aside the latter. (8.10.24)

Augustine, here as elsewhere, gives special attention to the role of time. In numberless daily choices, each human "will" accrues and hardens into habit, ultimately moving us with the force of necessity.[34] Though such an "iron will" does not excuse us from responsibility, it does not prevent us from feeling trapped and prevented from doing what we "really" want.[35] This thoroughly Stoic argument is the one Cicero had adopted in the *Tusculan Disputations*, fusing Stoic ethics to Plato's divided soul to bring "willpower" to life.[36] Augustine's innovation is the notion of a divided and reintegrated will and his quest to lead a Christian life with a "full will" (*plena voluntas*, 8.9.21, 9.2.4), "strong and whole throughout" (*fortiter et integre*, 8.8.19).[37] As in Cicero, a fertile ambiguity is preserved between

---

[33] Ibid. 8.10.22; cf. 3.6.10–11.20.   [34] Ibid. 8.7.17; cf. 4.7.12, 8.5.10–11, 8.7.17, 8.9.21.
[35] See ibid. 8.5.11: "From my own experience I realized that what I had read was true in myself: the flesh lusted against the spirit, and the spirit against the flesh. I was in both the flesh and the spirit, but I was more myself [*magis ego*] in that which I approved in myself, than in that which I disapproved in myself. By now it was rather not I who was in the flesh, since for the most part I was an unwilling sufferer rather than a willing doer [*quia ex magna parte id patiebar invitus quam faciebam volans*]. But it was my own doing that habit gripped me so fiercely, since I had arrived willingly at a place to which I had no wish to come."
[36] See discussion in Chapter 6; cf. Cic. *Tusc.* 2.28–29, 2.39–41, 2.47, 2.54–55, 2.62, 3.25, 4.31, 4.62.
[37] Cf. August. *Conf.* 10.21.31: "... everyone wishes to be blessed; and if we did not know it with such sure knowledge, we would not will it with such sure will [*quod nisi certa notitia nossemus, non tam certa voluntate vellemus*]."

"a willing" for a determined object and "the will" as a durable faculty.[38] For both men, the will contains multiple *voluntates*, which echo back and reshape the will producing them. If it was Paul whose words healed Augustine's will, the will he healed was Ciceronian.

This shared language of combat and relative strength brings the bishop of Hippo to a most un-Ciceronian conclusion. Though despairing of Rome's moral decline, Cicero clearly believed man capable of improvement without divine intervention. *Sanabimur si volemus*, Cicero had written in the *Tusculans*, "we will be healed if we will it."[39] Not so for Augustine. What marks his worldview most sharply from Cicero's is his rejection of worldly affairs and his pessimism for mankind. The *Confessions* poignantly trace the path to this conclusion: Augustine had acknowledged the truths of God; he had willed to follow them; and, with all his gifts, time and again he had failed.

His conclusion is that no human will can become "strong and whole" on its own. Though the model for our will, *voluntas dei* is different in two critical respects. First, it is incomparably greater in power. Borrowing from Plotinus, Augustine places God's will on a higher plane of causality: "[T]he Word, that is God, was born not of the blood nor of the will of man nor of the will of the flesh, but of God [*quia verbum, deus, non ex carne, non ex sanguine, neque ex voluntate viri, neque ex voluntate carnis, sed ex deo natus est*]" (7.9.14).[40] In comparison to man's *voluntas*, the will of God is untouched by time, "incorruptible and unchangeable, sufficient in itself for itself."[41] Why, then, does God not allow our wills to achieve their ends? Since He is unquestionably just, our weak and corrupted wills must be a deserved punishment for the abuse of His gifts. This leads Augustine, in turn, to his argument for original sin – that Adam's initial misuse of a free will effectively enslaved his descendants. As Frede points out, many Christians – including Augustine's archrival, Pelagius – dissented from his unforgiving view of man's helplessness. But against these fellow Christians and centuries of Stoic and Platonic tradition he is adamant: No man can perfect himself by reason.[42] Our will can be liberated and

---

[38] See ibid. 8.10.23: "... when a man ponders a course of action, then one soul wavers between various wills."

[39] *Tusc.* 2.62.

[40] He quotes Plotinus favorably here, though he adds, "but as for the fact that the Word was made flesh and dwelt among us, that I did not read."

[41] *Conf.* 13.4.5; cf. 11.10.12, 12.15.18, 12.28.38.

[42] Another striking departure from Stoicism in the sharp line Augustine draws between "nature's will" and God's. See ibid. 3.6.10: "The sun and moon are your works, and beautiful indeed; but they are your works and not you, nor the earliest of your works"; 5.10.19: "And when I wished to think of

made whole only by the greater force of God's will, and His grace to apply it in our favor.[43] And it is Augustine's idea of divine grace that ultimately becomes Catholic orthodoxy.

It is in his politics, finally, where Augustine's break from Cicero is most emphatic. The ex-consul's core commitment was the care of the Republic. Cicero adapts Plato to argue that Rome had been led to perfection by its extraordinary *maiores*, men who strove and sacrificed for their fellow citizens.[44] Though Augustine's view of natural law is reminiscent of Cicero's,[45] the bishop is firm that mankind will not and cannot achieve it. By Augustine's time, republican pluralism was a distant memory. In its place was the organizing principle of an emperor's absolute if all-too-human will. "Can we have any greater hope at Court," he asks, "than that of becoming Friends of the Emperor? And if we do, what will we then have that is not frail and beset with perils? How many perils must we endure to arrive at a greater peril?" (8.6.15). To the perpetual insecurity of imperial politics – already known to Seneca, and an immutable fact by the 4th century CE – there could be only one release: "If I will to become a friend of God, behold, I can become one now!" (ibid.).

Cicero had once said that a republic without *ius* and *libertas* was no republic at all. In the *City of God*, Augustine uses the strictness of Cicero's reasoning to argue against his hero:

> Thus, where there is no true justice there can be no human gathering brought together by a common sense of right and wrong, and therefore *there can be no people, as defined by Scipio or Cicero*; and if there is no people, then there is no common business of a people but only of some promiscuous multitude unworthy of the name of people. Consequently, if the republic is the people's common business ... then most certainly it follows that there is no republic where there is no justice. (19.21, emphasis added)[46]

---

my God, I did not know how to think of him except as some physical mass – for I thought there was nothing that was not physical – and, inevitably, this was the main and almost the sole cause of my error." For the association of divine will and the will of nature in Cicero, cf. *Fin.* 1.64, 5.55.

[43] Even for the "saved," divine grace is necessary to guard our wills against corruption. See *Conf.* 10.37.60: "I am tested by these temptations every day, O Lord; I am tempted incessantly ... You bid us be continent in respect of this sort of temptation also; give what you command and command what you will [*da quod iubes et iube quod vis*]."

[44] See Cic. *Rep.* 3.41: The Republic "might live on forever if the principles and customs of our ancestors were maintained"; cf. 2.55–56, 3.7, 3.33–34.

[45] See *Conf.* 3.7.13: "It is according to this Law that the customs of different times and places are shaped to fit their time and place; but the Law itself is everywhere and always, not one thing in one place and another in another." Cf. Cic. *Rep.* 3.33; *Leg.* 1.18–24.

[46] Here, Augustine rejoins the question he poses at *De civ. D.* 2.21–24; on his critique of Cicero's politics, cf. O'Donnell 2015, 231.

In other words, the disastrous inability of humans to achieve a just political order is proof that the only community worthy of our adherence is God's. In the twilight of antiquity, divine will is ascendant; the will of the people, defunct.[47]

It would take thirteen centuries and another author of *Confessions* to bring *voluntas populi* back to life. Jean-Jacques Rousseau was a native of the free city of Geneva, exceptional in a Europe of waxing monarchy. *Du contrat social*, published in 1762, rejoins a debate over sovereignty and legitimacy that had percolated through medieval and early modern Europe. The man Rousseau most directly addresses, Hugo Grotius, had argued against "divine right" that the political authority of monarchs derives from the people they govern.[48] An English philosopher of the previous century, Thomas Hobbes, posited that only the transfer of power from a mass of individuals to a unified "Leviathan" could rescue man from brutal nature.[49] Both Grotius and Hobbes argued that following this transfer of authority to a ruler, except under extraordinary conditions the people's duty was to obey.[50] Answering this argument is Rousseau's main task in *Du contrat social*.

For the young essayist, composer, and sometime seminarian, Rome's republic was a blueprint for a better state. In Rousseau's reading of history, its "elective aristocracy" was both more effective and more just than kingship on the one hand and unwieldy democracy on the other (3.5).[51] Rousseau is steeped in the technical details of Roman elections, examining its *comitia* and the fine points of tribal voting at great length (4.3–4). Yet the magistrates Rousseau endorses are not enlightened monarchs, or even legislators in the traditional sense; they are *commissaires* (3.1, 3.15). Their

---

[47] There is a faint echo of the *voluntas populi* at *De civ. D.* 14.1.8: "And thus it has come to pass, that though there are very many and great nations all over the earth, ... yet there are no more than two kinds of human society, which we may justly call two cities [*civitates duas*] ... The one consists of those who wish to live after the flesh, the other of those who wish to live after the spirit; and when they severally achieve what they wish, they live in peace, each after their kind [*Una quippe est hominum secundum carnem, altera secundum spiritum vivere in sui cuiusque generis pace volentium et, cum id quod expetunt adsequuntur, in sui cuiusque generis pace viventium*]." Though sympathetically framed, Augustine's main argument is that a community wishing or willing (*volentium*) to live for earthly purposes alone is in grave error. Cf. Brown 1967, 321–22. For an alternative view stressing the continuities of Cicero and Augustine's politics, see Atkins 2002.
[48] Grotius 1625, I.3.8.1, I.4.2.1; see Brett 2002, 31–51. For a general overview of Grotius, see van Holk and Roelofsen 1983. On his classical influences, see Blom and Winkel 2004.
[49] Hobbes 1651; see LeBuffe 2003, 15–39. On Hobbes' theory of sovereignty, see generally Shelton 1992; Kramer 1997; Skinner 2008.
[50] Grotius 1625, I.3.9–16; Hobbes 1651, pt. 2, ch. 18 ("Of the Rights of Sovereigns by Institution").
[51] Rousseau 1762.

commission, revocable at any time, depends upon their fidelity to a supreme and continuous force: *la volonté générale*.

Will is the keystone concept of *Du contrat social*. For Rousseau, politics is properly understood not as a mirror of divine ordonnance but as a competition – and, better, the reasoned integration – of *volonté*. Though man enjoys complete liberty of action in his primitive state, at a certain point the perils of nature prove too great for any one man to face. Rousseau continues:

> As men cannot engender new forces, but only unite and direct existing ones, they have no other means of preserving themselves than the formation, by aggregation, of a sum of forces great enough to overcome the resistance [of nature]. These they must bring into play by means of a single motive power, and cause to act in concert. (1.6)[52]

The aggregation of forces that makes a political community possible Rousseau calls the *volonté générale*. Importantly, this general will is not simply the sum of what its individual members desire at a given time. It is the will of a people to *be* a people and thus to choose a government, control a territory, and make laws for the general good. All other forces are subject to it because "the general will alone can direct the forces within the State toward the end for which it was instituted, which is the common good: for if the clashing of particular interests made the establishment of societies necessary, the agreement of these very interests made it possible"[53] (2.1). The *volonté générale*, once formed, is indivisible and inalienable (2.1). Whichever rulers or magistrates control the resources of state, the general will remains sole Sovereign (1.6–8). The people alone has the power to make laws (2.2, 2.6), and these apply equally to all (2.4, 2.6). All other uses of state power are merely "decrees" or applications of the people's law (2.2, 2.6), what Rousseau calls *émanations* of the general will (2.2). The *volonté générale* determines the form of government proper to serve it (3.1), and though such decisions should be made carefully (3.8), they can nevertheless be revoked or amended by the general will at any time (3.11, 3.13).

---

[52] "*Or, comme les hommes ne peuvent engendrer de nouvelles forces, mais seulement unir et diriger celles qui existent, ils n'ont plus d'autre moyen, pour se conserver, que de former par agrégation une somme de forces qui puisse l'emporter sur la résistance, de les mettre en jeu par un seul mobile et de les faire agir de concert.*"

[53] "*... la volonté générale peut seule diriger les forces de l'Etat selon la fin de son institution, qui est le bien commun; car si l'opposition des intérêts particuliers a rendu nécessaire l'établissement des sociétés, c'est l'accord de ces mêmes intérêts qui l'a rendu possible.*"

Epilogue 231

From where does Rousseau derive his notion of will? As with Augustine, it is a complex question.⁵⁴ Judging from the text, however, Rousseau does not share Augustine's warm feelings for Cicero. Rousseau names him in *Du contrat social* exactly twice: Once to refute his criticisms of the secret ballot (4.4), then regarding his consulship he asserts that the suppressor of Catiline, "loving his own glory better than his country, sought, not so much the most lawful and secure means of saving the State, as that which would give sole honor to himself." Thus, he concludes, Cicero was "justly honored as the liberator of Rome and justly punished as a law-breaker" (4.6).⁵⁵ What, then, does the *volonté générale* owe to *voluntas populi*? As we have seen in Chapter 5, Cicero's fullest analysis of political will was in *De republica*, a text only republished in 1822.⁵⁶ On the other hand, Cicero's orations were required reading in a liberal education, and the *voluntas populi* features heavily in *In Verrem*, *Pro Murena*, and *Pro Sestio*.⁵⁷ More proximate influences included the 17th-century works of Pascal and Malebranche – each heavily influenced by Augustine – and ultimately the article "La Volonté Générale" in Diderot's *Encyclopédie*, to which Rousseau had enthusiastically contributed.⁵⁸ These lines of influence have been well explored and will no doubt be further clarified.

---

⁵⁴ See Groethuysen 1949; Salomon-Bayet 1968; Manin 1985; Riley 2011, 124–53; Bertram 2012, 403–20. On Rousseau's classical influences, see Brooke 2011, 94–123.
⁵⁵ "... aimant mieux sa gloire que sa patrie, ne cherchait pas tant le moyen le plus légitime et le plus sûr de sauver l'Etat, que celui d'avoir tout l'honneur de cette affaire ... Aussi fut-il honoré justement comme libérateur de Rome, et justement puni comme infracteur des lois." Tellingly, the passage appears in the section of Book 4 dedicated to "*la Dictature*" (i.e. those magistrats of Rome who acted contrary to the normal rule of law). The case of Caesar is discussed just before that of Cicero in a similarly critical tone (4.6).
⁵⁶ Only Book 6 of *De republica* (the "dream of Scipio"), in which *voluntas* does not occur, was available to Western Europeans in the medieval and early modern period. John Adams laments, "[t]he loss of [Cicero's] book upon republics is much to be regretted ... As all the ages of the world have not produced a greater statesman and philosopher united in the same character, his authority should have great weight"; Adams 1787, vol. 1, xix–xx, xxi. Angelo Mai's discovery of additional fragments in 1818 – fittingly, in a palimpsest of a work by Augustine – restored *De republica* to the still-partial version we have today; see Grimal 1984, 88–89.
⁵⁷ See discussion in Chapter 5. On Cicero's reception in the 18th century, see generally Fox 2013.
⁵⁸ Diderot 1750–65, see especially the articles "*Autorité Politique*," "*Cité*," and "*Droit Naturel*." Diderot's notion of *volonté générale* is, in brief: (1) All legitimate power is based on consent of the citizen body; (2) men enter a social pact to leave the state of nature, characterized by the violent rule of the strongest; (3) this social pact delegates political authority to a *souverain physique* (the ruler or rulers) and *l'être moral public* or *volonté générale*; (4) the *volonté générale* is infallible and demands universal obedience of its laws; (5) legislative power can be permanently alienated to a representative body; and (6) an equal rule of law, not a transformation of human nature, is its primary purpose. It is on these final two points especially where Rousseau's *volonté générale* diverges from Diderot's. The two men took very different positions on the state of nature and natural law as well. See generally Riley 1986; Fabre 1961; Deguergue 2015, 107–26.

Returning to the texts, it is difficult to ignore the kinship between Cicero's and Rousseau's notions of political will. Rousseau shares Cicero's conviction that not all communities deserve the name of republic, but only those governed by free citizens treated equally under law.[59] Both men narrate the founding moment of a republic as an act of collective volition; by reciprocal consent, free individuals leave the state of nature behind.[60] Both identify political freedom with popular sovereignty, expressed equally in the people's active decision and by their passive consent.[61] Both insist that in a republic the wills of individual politicians (what Rousseau calls *volontés particulières*) must be directed to the public good and subordinate to the will of all.[62] Both locate the main threats to the people's will in the ambitions of would-be despots (2.1) and the self-interested will of factions (3.18).[63]

More interestingly, perhaps, Rousseau's *volonté générale* has the "personhood" of Cicero's *voluntas*. At its moment of birth, "this act of association yields a collective and moral body [*corps moral et collectif*], composed of as many limbs [*membres*] as the assembly has voices, which by this act receives its unity, its common 'me,' its life and its will" (1.6).[64] The 'I' of the state, its sovereign will, must then craft a government to enact its laws and fulfill its ends. This government also must have "a particular 'me,' a sensibility common to its members, and a force and will of its own making for its preservation" (3.1).[65] The personality of government is expressed through the arrangement of councils, titles, and institutions that together create its "identity." But the government's will is subsidiary to the will of the whole, such that

> it in no way alters the general constitution by affirmation of its own, and always distinguishes the particular force it possesses, which is destined to aid in its preservation, from the public force, which is destined to the

---

[59] *Contrat social* 1.5, 2.6; cf. Cic. *Rep.* 3.43. See also Schofield 1995, 76.
[60] *Contrat social* 1.2–4, 1.6; cf. Cic. *Inv.* 1.3.
[61] On the connection established between *libertas/liberté* and *voluntas/volonté*, see *Contrat social* 1.4, 4.2; cf. Cic. *Rep.* 1.39, 1.69, 2.57, 3.43. On the active expression of *voluntas/volonté*, see *Contrat social* 2.6 (in lawmaking); cf. Cic. *Planc.* 54, *Mur.* 1 (in elections). On its passive expression, see *Contrat social* 2.1, 4.2; cf. Cic. *Verr.* 1.10; *Cat.* 4.14; *Sest.* 124; *Rep.* 1.50, 1.64, 2.38.
[62] See *Contrat social* 1.6–7; Cic. *Verr.* 2.3.82 (with regard to Sulla); *Fam.* 2.234.8, 2.249.3 (with regard to Caesar).
[63] On the will of despots, see Cic. *Fam.* 2.190.3, 2.249.3. On the will of factions, see *Cat.* 2.18; *Sest.* 96, 114, 122.
[64] "... cet acte d'association produit un corps moral et collectif, composé d'autant de membres que l'assemblée a de voix, lequel reçoit de ce même acte son unité, son moi commun, sa vie et sa volonté."
[65] "... un moi particulier, une sensibilité commune à ses membres, une force, une volonté propre qui tende à sa conservation."

preservation of the State; and, in a word, is always ready to sacrifice the government to the people, and never to sacrifice the people to the government. (3.1)[66]

In this, Rousseau relates will to personality, linking together psychology and political thought as Cicero had. And the will constitutes the personal and political in precisely the same manner as it did for Cicero: It is the force, proper to me, by which I inscribe my reasoned judgment on the world.

Indeed, Rousseau's arguments in *Du contrat social* both reflect and extend Cicero's physics of will. As for Augustine, the measurability of *voluntas/volonté* – and specifically its strengthening or weakening over time – helps advance his main thesis. For Rousseau, politics begins at the moment when the "natural forces" that pit man against man yield to the unified power of the *volonté générale*. Here, he specifies – as Cicero did not – that interdependence of will solidifies over time: When "each citizen is nothing and can do nothing without the rest, and the force acquired by the whole is equal or superior to the sum of each individual's natural force, it may be said that legislation is at its highest perfection" (2.7).[67] Rousseau takes the three classical forms of government in turn, examining how the forces of *volontés particulières*, the *volonté* of government, and the *volonté générale* interact in each.[68] Originally, he posits that a magistrate's will can be more or less "concentrated" as a function of his institutional power and the physical growth of the state (3.1).[69] And, intriguingly, as Augustine had, Rousseau develops the idea that multiple wills vie for control within a single person. For the Genevan, a magistrate partakes of his own individual will, the shared will of all magistrates, and the *volonté générale* (3.2). The true master of political arts, Rousseau's *législateur*, is he who knows "how to fix the point at which the power and the will of the Government, which

---

[66] "... il n'altère point la constitution générale en affermissant la sienne; qu'il distingue toujours sa force particulière, destinée à sa propre conservation, de la force publique, destinée à la conservation de l'État, et qu'en un mot il soit toujours prêt à sacrifier le gouvernement au peuple, et non le peuple au gouvernement."

[67] "... en sorte que si chaque citoyen n'est rien, ne peut rien que par tous les autres, et que la force acquise par le tout soit égale ou supérieure à la somme des forces naturelles de tous les individus, on peut dire que la législation est au plus haut point de perfection qu'elle puisse atteindre."

[68] See sections 3.4 ("*De la démocratie*"), 3.5 ("*De l'aristocratie*"), 3.6 ("*De la Monarchie*"), and 3.7 ("*Des Gouvernements mixtes*").

[69] Ibid. at 3.1; With regard to the "Prince's dominant will," his power is only "the public force concentrated in himself"; 3.2: "Thus, as particular wills converge into the general will ... the force to punish must increase. And so the government, to be good, must become relatively stronger as its people grow more numerous."

are always in inverse proportion, coalesce in the relation most advantageous to the State" (3.2).[70]

Still, his political disagreements with Cicero are nearly as deep as Augustine's. The veteran of many tough elections, Cicero praised the people's sovereignty while knowing how capricious their will could be.[71] For Rousseau, the proud political amateur, la *volonté générale* is by definition infallible (2.3).[72] Its individual members may err (4.2), it may weaken in relation to other forces (4.1), but the general will is never corrupted.[73] On the question of its durability, Rousseau is perhaps the more pragmatic of the two; whereas Cicero insists that a well-designed and virtuous republic can last forever,[74] Rousseau allows that even the best constituted State will have an end (3.11).[75] In Ciceronian fashion, he describes this decline as a loss of equilibrium between competing wills; the natural tension among them "is the unavoidable and inherent defect which, from the very birth of the body politic, tends ceaselessly to destroy it, as age and death end by destroying the human body" (3.10).[76] But the gravest difference between the two men is on the matter of representation. Cicero argues that a rational and virtuous elite, the trustees of the people, are the best guarantors of their liberty.[77] Rousseau takes precisely the

---

[70] "... *savoir fixer le point où la force et la volonté du Gouvernement, toujours en proportion réciproque, se combinent dans le rapport le plus avantageux à l'Etat.*"

[71] See Cic. *Planc.* 10: "For it is the privilege of free peoples, and above all this people, whose conquests have given it paramount sway over the whole world, that by its votes it can bestow or take away its offices as it likes. We too have our part to play; tossed as we are upon the stormy billows of popular favor, we must bear contentedly with the people's wills [*ferre modice populi voluntates*], win them back when estranged, hold them when won, and pacify them when in turmoil." *Voluntates populi* in the plural is a very rare usage for Cicero; here, the plural serves his point that the people's will may shift without warning.

[72] See section 2.3 ("*Si la volonté générale peut errer*"). In his preface Rousseau writes, "I am asked if I am a prince or legislator worthy to write on Politics? I answer no, and this is why I write. If I were a prince or legislator, I would not waste my time saying what should be done; I would do it, or I would hold my tongue."

[73] Cf. Cic. *Rep.* 3.45: "There can be nothing more horrible than that monster which falsely assumes the name and appearance of a people [*nihil ista, quae populi speciem et nomen imitatur, immanius belua est*]."

[74] Ibid. 3.7, 3.33–34, 3.41.

[75] See *Contrat social* 3.11: "It is not in men's power to prolong their own lives; but it is for them to prolong as much as possible the life of the State, by giving it the best possible constitution."

[76] The passage in full: "*Comme la volonté particulière agit sans cesse contre la volonté générale, ainsi le gouvernement fait un effort continuel contre la souveraineté. Plus cet effort augmente, plus la constitution s'altère; et comme il n'y a point ici d'autre volonté de corps qui, résistant à celle du prince, fasse équilibre avec elle, il doit arriver tôt ou tard que le prince opprime enfin le souverain et rompe le traité social. C'est là le vice inhérent, et inévitable qui, dès la naissance du corps politique, tend sans relâche à le détruire, de même que la vieillesse et la mort détruisent enfin le corps de l'homme.*"

[77] See Cic. *Rep.* 1.51: "But if a free people [*liber populus*] chooses the men to whom it is to entrust its fortunes, and, since it desires its own safety, chooses the best men, then certainly the safety of the

Epilogue 235

opposite view. In his republic, the freedom of citizens is expressed in their intense commitment to collective legislation; they "fly to the assemblies" (3.15). Elected officials, correctly viewed, do not legislate; they are only *commissaires*, merely adapting or executing the laws the *volonté générale* has set in place (3.15).[78] "Sovereignty," Rousseau declares,

> being nothing less than the exercise of the general will, can never be alienated, and that the Sovereign, who is no less than a collective being, cannot be represented except by himself: the power indeed may be transmitted, but not the will. (2.1)[79]

Only when the people get lazy and selfish do they need "representatives." Thus, notes the adopted Frenchman, except for rare days when they elect their parliament, the English who so prize their freedom are political slaves.[80] What is more, Rousseau's reading of Roman history would have made Cicero blue in the face: The fate of Europe was "decided in the people's assemblies" (4.4); any idea of representation was unknown to Romans (3.15); and Cicero's beloved senate "was nothing at all" (3.14)!

This leads us to a subtle but essential point: Why *la volonté générale* and not *la volonté du peuple*? Amid the text's many references to the general will, Rousseau invokes "the will of the people" exactly twice.[81] Near the beginning of Book 3, he describes the "three wills" that coexist within each magistrate: Alongside the individual and the collective will of all magistrates is "*la volonté du peuple ou la volonté souveraine, laquelle est générale*" (3.2). Why does the "will of the people" make its first appearance here? It is possible, given that he composed the work over ten years, that the lapse of time between Books 2 and 3 had brought new phrases to mind.[82] More likely, something in the nature of this topic prompts him to introduce the

---

State depends on the wisdom of its best men"; cf. ibid. 1.39, 1.43, 1.69, 2.57. See discussion in Chapter 5.

[78] Cf. Cic. *Rep.* 2.56: In the Republic's golden age, "the government was so administered by the senate that, though the people were free, few political acts were performed by them, practically everything being done by the authority of the senate." See discussion in Chapter 5.

[79] "*Je dis donc que la souveraineté n'étant que l'exercice de la volonté générale ne peut jamais s'aliéner, et que le souverain, qui n'est qu'un être collectif, ne peut être représenté que par lui-même ; le pouvoir peut bien se transmettre, mais non pas la volonté.*" See ibid. 3.15: "At the moment that a People gives itself Representatives, it is no longer free; it is a People no longer."

[80] Ibid.

[81] Ibid. 3.2, 3.6. He contrasts "the will of an entire people" (*la volonté de tout un peuple*) to "the clamors of a faction" at 3.18. Other variants include "the sovereign will" (*la volonté souveraine*, 3.2), "the public will" (*la volonté publique*, 3.5), and "the will of all" (*la volonté de tous*, 4.1).

[82] There is also the matter of syntax; he says just above that the "common will of magistrates" is *générale* with respect to the Government and *particulière* with respect to the State. It may have seemed awkward to use *générale* twice in the following phrase (i.e. that *la volonté générale* is *générale* with respect to both Government and State), but it was certainly possible to have done so.

phrase. In Chapter 4, we saw how a double sense of *populus* helps Cicero reconcile popular sovereignty with elite power. The *populus* is *omnes*, "the whole," when Scipio gives the qualities shared by all citizens; they are *liberi*, and their association is based on a *ius* and *utilitas* that binds all and serves all.[83] But the *populus* is *multitudo*, "the masses," when seen in the traditional frame of monarchy, aristocracy, and democracy.[84] This fertile ambiguity makes Cicero's ideal possible: a republic in which the masses partake in universal liberty but whose powers are limited to endorsing an elite.

It is telling, then, that Rousseau brings in *la volonté du peuple* at the point when he describes the position of the magistrate and not before. Rousseau admits the necessity of magistrates as an "intermediate body" in the state, an executive power distinct from the legislative power of the *volonté générale* (3.1); indeed, he favors an "elected aristocracy" to execute the people's will.[85] Magistrates must exert the "repressive force" (*force reprimante*) necessary to enforce the laws and maintain a well-ordered state. But Rousseau confronts a problem whose existence Cicero would never admit. No magistrate, however wise, can be purely public-spirited; he has not one but three wills, including interests of his own and of his fellow magistrates. By the laws of "concentration," the relative force of his will as part of the whole people – the *populus* as *omnes* – will naturally be less than his will as part of the body of magistrates. The corporate will of elected officials, in turn, may conflict with the *volonté du peuple* – here, the *multitudo* – who lack their executive powers.[86] But the *générale* must prevail over the *particulière*: As his phrase makes clear, the *volonté du peuple* exactly *is* the *volonté générale*. With mathematical precision worthy of Plato, Rousseau declares that the number of magistrates must be calibrated inversely to the growth of the population (to conserve their *force reprimante*), while keeping them numerous enough to align their corporate will with the general one. Cicero used his notion of will to constrain the multitude; Rousseau uses his to control the elite.[87]

---

[83] See Cic. *Rep.* 1.39, 1.54–55. Cf. *Inv.* 2.67–68: Customary law (*consuetudo*) derives its legitimacy "from the will of all" (*voluntate omnium*).

[84] See *Rep.* 1.41–42, 1.65–66, 1.69, 5.8.

[85] See *Contrat social* 3.5: An elective aristocracy, unlike natural or hereditary ones, is "the best: this is Aristocracy properly called." He continues: "In a word, it's the best and most natural order when the wisest govern the multitude, when one is sure that they govern for its benefit and not for their own."

[86] Ibid. 3.2.

[87] Rousseau implies that inequalities among citizens, including those of wealth, are an inherent threat to political order; see ibid. 2.3, 3.15. There is no evidence that Cicero agreed and much to suggest that he did not.

Nevertheless, Rousseau's ambivalence on the capacities of the common citizen brings him closer to Cicero than he may have wanted to appear. Though the general will is supreme, the individual sees through a mirror darkly. "Our will is always for our own good," he writes in Book 2, "but we do not always see what that is; the people is never corrupted, but it is often deceived, and on such occasions only does it seem to will what is bad" (2.3).[88] In primitive societies, where peasants gather under oak trees to deliberate, their *simplicité* leads them to felicitous consensus (4.1); in more sophisticated states, though, "there are a thousand kinds of ideas that cannot be translated into the people's language" (2.7).[89] Here, Rousseau's prescription is not mass education but expert assistance. To become a people, a wise *législateur* – modeled on the "royal or civil man" from Plato's *Politicus* (2.7) – must intervene to rescue the mass of citizens from their bad old habits. This assistance is no gentle nudge:

> He who dares to undertake the making of a people's institutions ought to feel himself capable, so to speak, of *changing human nature*, . . . of altering man's constitution for the purpose of strengthening it; and of substituting a partial and moral existence for the physical and independent existence nature has conferred on us all. He must, in a word, take away from man his own resources and give him instead new ones alien to him, and incapable of being made use of without the help of other men. (2.7, emphasis added)[90]

As to this "mechanic" who undertakes this radical project and "invents the machine,"[91] Rousseau does not specify where he comes from or how he acquires his art. Nor is it clear if his expertise is limited only to exceptional moments or continues beyond them;[92] this same ambiguity has been noted with regard to Cicero's *rector rei publicae*.[93]

What is clearer is Rousseau's conviction that individual citizens often miss the bigger picture. When my opinion of the common interest is defeated by a majority, "this proves neither more nor less than that I was

---

[88] "*On veut toujours son bien, mais on ne le voit pas toujours: Jamais on ne corrompt le peuple, mais souvent on le trompe, et c'est alors seulement qu'il paraît vouloir ce qui est mal.*"
[89] "*. . . il y a mille sortes d'idées qu'il est impossible de traduire dans la langue du peuple.*"
[90] "*Celui qui ose entreprendre d'instituer un people doit se sentir en état de changer, pour ainsi dire, la nature humaine . . . d'altérer la constitution de l'homme pour la renforcer; de substituer une existence partielle et morale à l'existence physique et indépendante que nous avons reçue de la nature. Il faut, en un mot, qu'il ôte à l'homme ses forces propres pour lui en donner qui lui soient étrangères, et dont il ne puisse faire usage sans le secours d'autrui.*"
[91] "*. . . le mécanicien qui invente la machine . . .*"
[92] The principal sections where the legislator appears – 2.7 and 3.2 – focus on the formation of the Sovereign and the choice of a form of government; but cf. 3.5.
[93] For a general discussion of the problem, see Powell 1994, 19–29; cf. Powell 2001, 31–32.

mistaken, and that what I thought to be the general will was not so." Had I achieved what I thought I wanted, "I should have achieved the opposite of what was my will; and it is in that case that I should not have been free" (4.2).[94] Regardless of any such confusion regarding my "true" will, my continued residence in the state is tantamount to consent to any coercion against me, as long as it emanates from the *volonté générale*.[95] It bears repeating that in the face of these apparent contradictions, Rousseau does not propose mass education to raise the mean; his solution is the imposition of reason on the people from a superior position – using divine pretexts if necessary – that the people can then ratify.[96] This is all quite Ciceronian. Yet Rousseau's cast of mind is as radical as Cicero's is conservative. Violent revolutions may be desirable, he observes, to restore *la vigueur de la jeunesse* (2.8) in the state. This tacit endorsement of a revolutionary elite, who can "transform" shortsighted dissenters in the name of the general will, would become fodder for countless authoritarian projects, some still underway. Rousseau's text echoes ominously for all those who have been "forced to be free" (1.7).

Among Rousseau's avid readers was the third President of the United States. In Thomas Jefferson's inaugural address of March 1801, the resonance of ancient Rome is unmissable. America's "republican government," based on "equal and exact justice to all men," has "kept us free and firm."[97] The republic's glory is not territory or wealth but the triumph of reason over violence and the "supremacy of the civil over the military authority."[98] He offers tribute to America's *maiores*, "the wisdom of our sages and blood of our heroes"; the principles they established "should be the creed of our political faith, and text of civic instruction." A free and unified republic refutes the notion "that man cannot be trusted with the government of himself"; it is, in fact, the "world's best hope." Here is the republicanism that Cicero was first to theorize.

What does the author of the Declaration of Independence owe to the *voluntas populi*? The evidence, though not conclusive, is suggestive.

---

[94] "*Quand donc l'avis contraire au mien l'emporte, cela ne prouve autre chose sinon que je m'étais trompé, et que ce que j'estimais être la volonté générale ne l'était pas. Si mon avis particulier l'eût emporté, J'aurais fait autre chose que ce que j'avais voulu; c'est alors que je n'aurais pas été libre.*"
[95] Cf. ibid. 2.1, 4.2.
[96] Ibid. 2.7; cf. Cic. *Sest.* 33–34; *Leg.* 2.21, 3.27. Only a nonpolitician like Rousseau could propose without irony that "he who drafts the laws does not or should not have any legislative power [*celui qui rédige les lois n'a donc ou ne doit avoir aucun droit législatif*] ..." (2.7).
[97] First Inaugural Address (March 4, 1801), in Peterson 1984, 993–94.
[98] "Absolute acquiescence in the decisions of the majority" is "the vital principle of republics, from which is no appeal but to force, the vital and immediate parent of despotism"; ibid. 997.

Jefferson read Cicero's philosophical treatises as a young man,⁹⁹ though a letter from John Adams (himself an avowed Ciceronian) cautions that his political works were then only available in fragments.¹⁰⁰ Looking back at the American Revolution, Jefferson would later trace the "authority" of the Declaration of Independence to "the harmonizing sentiments of the day, whether expressed in conversation, in letters, printed essays, or in the elementary books of public right, [such] as Aristotle, Cicero, Locke, Sidney, etc."¹⁰¹ For Jefferson, moreover, the will of the people is the "mother principle" of politics. To Samuel Kercheval in 1816 he writes: "Governments are republican only in proportion as they embody the will of their people, and execute it."¹⁰² This principle, of course, came to him on a firm Enlightenment footing. Indeed, we see the clear imprint of Rousseau in Jefferson's idea of "the will of the nation" as the source of law, a general will that "creates or annihilates the organ which is to declare & announce it."¹⁰³ The questions of legitimate revolution and the protection of religious minorities were also concerns that Jefferson shared with Rousseau and other 18th-century thinkers but not with Cicero.¹⁰⁴

It is certainly possible that Cicero's influence on Jefferson was mainly through these intermediaries. Nevertheless, the republicanism Jefferson evokes is the tradition for which Cicero, in the late 18th and early 19th centuries, was antiquity's chief exponent.¹⁰⁵ We will recognize by now how the "proportion" Jefferson evokes – and that Rousseau elaborated – is made possible by the measurability Cicero had given to *voluntas*. It has been argued moreover that Jefferson's views on providence and the state of nature put him closer to the doctrines of Stoicism than to Rousseau.¹⁰⁶ In his First Inaugural we see how this preference, if true, may have colored his "will of the people." Whereas for Rousseau the *volonté générale* can never err, Jefferson strikes both a Stoic and Ciceronian note when he asserts "that though the will of the majority is in all cases to prevail, that will to be

---

⁹⁹ Wilson 1989, 56–61.   ¹⁰⁰ See Rahe 1994, 65.
¹⁰¹ Jefferson to Henry Lee (May 8, 1825), in Peterson 1984, 3225. See Rahe 1994, 75–76.
¹⁰² Jefferson to Samuel Kercheval (July 12, 1816), in Peterson 1984, 2986.
¹⁰³ Jefferson to Edmund Randolph, Monticello (August 18, 1799), in Peterson 1984, 2233.
¹⁰⁴ Jefferson asks for greater political tolerance from his audience, "having banished from our land that religious intolerance under which mankind has so long bled and suffered." First Inaugural Address (March 4, 1801), in Peterson 1984, 993.
¹⁰⁵ On Cicero's influence upon America's founding generation, see generally Middlekauf 1961; Arendt 1963, 197, 258; Wood 1969, 48–70; Richard 1994, 2008, chs. 6–7.
¹⁰⁶ See Holowchak 2016, 9: "Jefferson's natural-law theory is Stoical, not Hobbesian or Rousseauian. For Jefferson, the basal laws of nature that obtain when man is in the state of nature are roughly the self-same laws that obtain in civil society."

rightful must be reasonable."[107] Unlike Rousseau, Jefferson does not require the unanimity of the people's will at any moment.[108] He shares with Cicero the balanced view of a philosopher well seasoned by political life: A statesman may insist that the people's will be unified and rational, but he must act in a world where it is not.

Jefferson's answer to the will's fallibility is not, as Rousseau proposes, an all-seeing legislator to transform human nature. Rather, like Cicero, he maintains that the people's will, to be effective, must be represented. The representative principle first found in Cicero's orations is as axiomatic to Jefferson as it is anathema to Rousseau.[109] His core argument is practical: For the man who doubles the size of his country as President, America is simply too big to be ruled directly by its people. Though he admits that a government is "more" republican to the extent that it allows "the direct action of the citizens," the will of the people can justly be expressed through the men they elect.[110] But which men? To John Adams he declares:

> There is a natural aristocracy among men. The grounds of this are virtue and talents ... There is also an artificial aristocracy founded on wealth and birth, without either virtue or talents; for with these it would belong to the first class.[111]

What Jefferson calls the "natural *aristoi*" comprise "the most precious gift of nature for the instruction, the trust, and government of society." That government is best that allows for "a pure selection of these natural *aristoi* into [its] offices." With general education, one only needs "to leave to the

---

[107] First Inaugural Address (March 4, 1801), in Peterson 1984, 992–93. See discussion of Cicero's adaptation of Stoicism in *Rep.* and *Leg.* in Chapter 5.

[108] As one of the founders both of the United States and of its two-party system, Jefferson's ideal of political order is one of mutual tolerance and peaceful rotation, not unanimity of views. His "will of the people" is expressed in a majority and is thus not "general" as such. Cf. Letter to John Taylor (May 28, 1816): Jefferson's "precise and definite idea" of republicanism is "a government by its citizens in mass, acting directly and personally, according to rules established by the majority"; letter to Kercheval (July 12, 1816): the republic "functions according to the rules (periodically revisable) established by the majority of the citizens ..." in Peterson 1984, 1394–403. On Rousseau's requirement of unanimity in the formation of the *volonté générale*, see *Contrat social* 1.5, 2.1, 2.2, 4.2.

[109] In his First Inaugural Address Jefferson speaks of "our attachment to union and representative government," in Peterson 1984, 494.

[110] Letter to Taylor (May 28, 1816), ibid.; cf. Letter to Kercheval (July 12, 1816), ibid.: "A government is republican in proportion as every member composing it has his equal voice in the direction of its concerns (not indeed in person, which would be impracticable beyond the limits of a city, or small township, but) by representatives chosen by himself, and responsible to him at short periods."

[111] Letter to John Adams (October 28, 1813), in Peterson 1984, 1305–06.

citizens the free election and separation of the *aristoi* from the pseudo-*aristoi*," for "in general they will elect the real good and wise" (ibid.). This is precisely the representative ideal Cicero frames in *Pro Sestio* and that propelled the *novus homo* to the consulship. His linking of a virtuous elective aristocracy to broad-based education and a free press constitutes important progress by Jefferson over Cicero, an advance of the sort eighteen centuries should bring.[112]

Jefferson clearly thought he was improving on the Roman model. In a late letter to Adams, he asks himself: "[W]hat was that government which the virtues of Cicero were so zealous to restore, and the ambition of Caesar to subvert?" His answer:

> I do not say to *restore* [good government], because they never had it, from the rape of the Sabines to the ravages of the Caesars. If their people indeed had been, like ourselves, enlightened, peaceable, and really free, the answer would be obvious. "Restore independence to all your foreign conquests, relieve Italy from the government of the rabble of Rome, consult it as a nation entitled to self-government, and do its will."[113]

For Jefferson, truly fulfilling the people's will – empowering those whom history had excluded from the task of public reason – was America's chance to succeed where Rome had failed. Nevertheless, we would be right to wonder if the natural aristocracy he intended to govern the American republic ever emerged. The homogeneity of its political elite,[114] the current resentments and rebellions against them, and the worsening sclerosis of representative institutions should give us pause regarding the continued wisdom of the Jeffersonian model.[115]

The Universal Declaration of Human Rights in 1948 marked something new in the world: a global standard for sovereign states. "The will of the people," it states, "shall be the basis of the authority of government; this will shall be expressed in periodic and genuine elections which shall be

---

[112] See, e.g., Jefferson's letter to James Madison (December 20, 1787): "Above all things I hope the education of the common people will be attended to; convinced that on their good sense we rely with the most security for the preservation of a due degree of liberty," in Peterson 1984, 918. On his tombstone, Jefferson asked that he be remembered for three achievements: the Declaration of Independence, the Virginia Statutes on Religious Freedom, and the foundation of the University of Virginia.

[113] Jefferson to Adams (December 10, 1819), in Rahe 2017, 202 (emphasis in original).

[114] Among congressional candidates and elected officials of both parties, white men, the very wealthy, and lawyers are significantly overrepresented; see Herrnson 2019, ch. 2.

[115] In fairness to Jefferson, who advised each generation to remake the constitution anew, his posterity's lack of political creativity and initiative would surely appall him; Jefferson to Madison, Paris (September 6, 1789), in Peterson 1984, 1993–95.

by universal and equal suffrage ..."[116] The sovereign nation-state is the first political idea to reach every corner of Earth. The will of the people, first described by Cicero, is its criterion. Even despots in their farcical mock-elections admit his ideal of popular sovereignty, the tribute vice pays to virtue.

But how virtuous is the idea today? Unmistakably, the problems of modern republics – what since Jefferson we inaccurately call "democracies" – are growing worse. Rising populations have stretched the representative principle to its limit. In no age have politicians been paragons of virtue, but partisan, winner-take-all elections further narrow the people's scope of choice. In much of the "democratic" world, trust in government and turnout in elections are in sharp decline. Twice in recent years, "the will of the people" has elected US Presidents who earned fewer votes than their opponents. According to Pew Research, an average of 64 percent of people across 34 countries do not believe that elected officials care what ordinary citizens think.[117] Around the world, frustration with unresponsive and self-dealing elites has led to rising support for extreme and undemocratic alternatives. Like Augustine, many of the world's citizens have despaired of politics and place their hopes in the hereafter. These frustrations are not new. The core paradoxes of modern "democracy" were latent in Cicero's *voluntas populi* – and specifically its dependence on an elite class to shape, interpret, and fulfill it.

It may not be too late to refresh the colors of our republics. Since the 1990s, a small but growing movement of activists, academics, and elected leaders have begun experimenting with new modes of self-government. These initiatives enable citizens to participate directly in the form of deliberative assemblies, continuous feedback on public services, putting new issues on the public agenda, or proposing new policy ideas through hackathons and petitions.[118] These experiments have increasingly taken more binding, institutionalized form, such as participatory budgeting – pioneered by the city of Porto Alegre, Brazil, and now practiced in over 5,000 cities – where public funds are allocated to citizen-generated ideas;[119] or citizens' assemblies, composed by lottery and empowered to tackle a specific issue like climate change or reproductive rights.[120] These

---

[116] Article 21(3), *Universal Declaration of Human Rights* (1948). UN General Assembly 217 [III] A., Paris.
[117] Wike and Schumacher 2020.   [118] See Ryan et al. 2020.
[119] See, e.g., Sintomer 2008, 164–78; Dias 2014; Hagelskamp 2016.
[120] See Farrell and Suiter 2019; OECD 2020. Created in the wake of the 2008 financial crisis, the Irish Constitutional Convention brought sixty-six randomly selected citizens together with

Epilogue 243

experiments in participatory and deliberative democracy have shown not only that including citizens in public decisions can build empathy and trust,[121] it can also produce more innovative solutions to complex public problems.[122]

Such findings align with centuries-old ideas. Rousseauian arguments on the importance of independent judgment (*Du contrat social* 2.4) and structured deliberation (4.2) have been given new force by the emerging field of collective intelligence.[123] So, too, has the ancient practice of sortition – assisted in its own time by a "digital technology," the *klerotērion*[124] – reemerged buttressed by evidence that large, diverse groups systematically outperform "experts" on a range of complex tasks.[125] Digital tools have helped scale up participation, link thousands of citizens in a common conversation, and create resilience during a global pandemic.[126] But while some platforms have shown great potential to advance Jeffersonian ideals of mass education and free inquiry, others have polarized opinions, fueled hatred, and deepened the civil strife with which Cicero was all too familiar. If such platforms were carefully designed and publicly owned, critical thought and political savvy – his tools of art – could be mobilized in new ways to serve the common good.

thirty-three politicians to recommend reforms to the nation's constitution, leading to a public referendum that legalized marriage equality in 2015. In 2017, a Citizen's Assembly of ninety-nine citizens recommended ending restrictions on reproductive rights and taking new actions against climate change. The former proposal was ratified by a national vote in 2018, and the latter prompted a new government action plan for climate. In 2019, French President Emmanuel Macron created the *Convention citoyenne pour le climat* ("Citizen's convention for the climate") of 150 randomly selected French citizens, whose nine-month mandate was to develop proposals to reduce carbon emissions by 40 percent by 2030 in comparison to 1990 levels, "in a spirit of social justice." A version of their proposals, altered significantly by the "nation's representatives" in the Assemblée Nationale, was adopted in July 2021 in the form of the *Loi climat et résilience* ("Climate and Resilience Law").

[121] A growing body of evidence suggests that participating in a civic process may have positive effects on knowledge of public affairs and feelings of personal efficacy (Dryzek 2007; Eriksson et al. 2019; Spada 2019), on critical thinking skills (Goodin and Stein 2009; Fishkin 2018), on empathy and social trust (Kanra 2012; Grönlund et al. 2017), on behaviors like voting, volunteering, and charitable donations (Grönlund et al. 2017; Kukučková and Bakoš 2019), and on perceptions of government (Cutler et al. 2008; Webb 2013). These positive effects may extend beyond those directly participating to the public at large (Boulianne 2018).

[122] OECD 2020; Ryan et al. 2020.

[123] See Mulgan 2018; Servan-Schreiber 2018; Landemore 2020. Centers of reseach in this emerging field include the New York University Governance Lab (The GovLab), the Université Mohammed VI Polytechnique School of Collective Intelligence, the Nesta Centre for Collective Intelligence Design, the World Bank Open Government Unit, the newDemocracy Foundation, Santa Fe Institute's Collective Computation Group, the Collective Intelligence Group at the IT University of Copenhagen, the Max Planck Institute for Human Development, and the Organisation for Economic Co-operation and Development Innovative Citizen Participation Project.

[124] See Courant 2020. [125] See Hong and Page 2004; Woolley et al. 2005; Krause et al. 2011.

[126] See OECD 2020.

A universally educated and engaged citizenry was unthinkable to Cicero. It is nearly so today. But the core of the problem is not one of technology but, as Cicero would agree, of power: who is given access and how they are taught to use it. The senators and magistrates of today will not legislate themselves out of existence, but so, too, have collapsing trust and rising authoritarianism revealed an untenable status quo. Indomitable until its crash, Cicero's republic stands as a cautionary tale of the balance that must continually be struck between tradition and transformation, between emotion and reason, between the many and the few.

Could a world of elitist republics be refashioned on principles of collective intelligence? Events may leave us little choice. Confronting the challenges of ecological stress, economic inequality, and mass migration will require, as Cicero put it, "the genius not of one, but of many."[127] Moments of political imbalance, such as his and ours, are times of danger but also of invention and opportunity. The framework of a more inclusive and effective model is in sight; what remains is a matter of will.

---

[127] Cic. *Rep.* 2.2.

APPENDIX

Occurrences of Voluntas in the Works of Cicero

Opera Ciceronis		Voluntas	Voluntarius
Rhetorica		84	5
	De inventione	42	3
	De oratore	18	–
	Brutus	11	2
	De optimo genere oratorum	–	–
	Orator	5	–
	De partitione oratoriae	8	–
Orationes		280	15
	Pro Quinctio	3	1
	Pro Roscio Amerino	9	–
	Pro Roscio Comoedo	–	1
	In Caecilium and Verrines I	55	1
	Verrines II	36	1
	Pro lege Manilia	7	–
	Pro Caecina	8	2
	Pro Cluentio	8	–
	Pro Rabirio Perduellionis Reo	2	–
	De lege agraria	4	–
	In Catilinam	11	–
	Pro Murena	11	–
	Pro Sulla	8	–
	Pro Flacco	6	–
	Pro Archia Poeta	1	–
	Post reditum in Senatu	4	–
	Post reditum in Quirites	6	–
	De domo sua	5	–
	De haruspicum responsis	2	–
	Pro Plancio	11	–
	Pro Sestio	11	–
	In Vatinium	4	–
	Pro Caelio	2	–
	De provinciis consularibus	5	1
	Pro Balbo	7	–
	Pro Milone	3	–
	In Pisonem	3	–

(cont.)

Opera Ciceronis		Voluntas	Voluntarius
	Pro Scauro	1	1
	Pro Fonteio	4	–
	Pro Rabirio Postumo	2	–
	Pro Marcello	2	1
	Pro Ligario	8	–
	Pro rege Deiotaro	1	–
	Philippics	30	6
Epistulae		206	6
	Ad Atticum I	37	–
	Ad Atticum II	6	–
	Ad Atticum III	21	1
	Ad Atticum IV	7	–
	Ad familiares I	54	2
	Ad familiares II	31	1
	Ad familiares III	33	1
	Ad Quintum fratrem	11	–
	Ad Brutum	6	1
Philosophica		74	33
	De republica	12	1
	De legibus	3	1
	Paradoxa stoicorum	2	–
	De finibus	9	5
	Tusculan Disputations	10	8
	Academica	–	2
	De natura deorum	6	2
	Topica	8	5
	Cato maior de senectute	–	1
	Laelius de amicitia	7	1
	De divinatione	1	–
	De fato	6	5
	De officiis	10	2
Total		644	59

Contested occurrences:
(1) The Loeb edition uses *voluntas* but indicates an alternative reading: *Orator*, 68 (*voluptate*). I include this occurrence in my list.
(2) The Leob edition gives another reading but indicates *voluntas* as an alternative: *In Pisonem*, 59 (*hominem volitantem*), *De finibus* IV, 58 (*voluptatem*); *De amicitia*, 68 (*voluptatem*). I include neither these nor the 17 occurrences in the *Commentariolum petitionis* in my list.

References

Adams, J. (1787). *A Defence of the Constitutions of Government of the United States of America*, vol. 1. n.p.
Alexander, M. (2009). "The 'Commentariolum petitionis' as an attack on election campaigns," *Athenaeum* 97: 31–57, 369–95.
Annas, J. (1992). *Hellenistic Philosophy of Mind*. Berkeley: University of California Press.
  (2013). "Plato's *Laws* and Cicero's *de Legibus*," in M. Schofield & D. Sedley, eds., *Plato, Aristotle and Pythagoras in the 1st Century* BCE. Cambridge: Cambridge University Press.
  (2017). *Virtue and Law in Plato and Beyond*. Oxford: Oxford University Press.
Arena, V. (2011). "The consulship of 78 BC. Catulus versus Lepidus: an *optimates* versus *populares* affair," in H. Beck, A. Duplá, M. Jehne, & F. Pina Polo, eds., *Consuls and Res Publica: Holding High Office in the Roman Republic*. Cambridge: Cambridge University Press.
  (2012). *Libertas and the Practice of Politics in the Late Roman Republic*. Cambridge: Cambridge University Press.
  (2016). "Popular sovereignty in the late Roman Republic: Cicero and the will of the people," in R. Bourke & Q. Skinner, eds., *Popular Sovereignty in Historical Perspective*. Cambridge: Cambridge University Press.
Arendt, H. (1963). *On Revolution*. New York: Penguin Books.
  (1971, 2nd edition 1978). *The Life of the Mind*, vol. 2 "Willing." New York: Harcourt Brace Jovanovich.
Asmis, E. (2008). "Cicero on natural law and the laws of the state," *Classical Antiquity* 27(1): 1–33.
Atkins, J. W. (2013). *Cicero on Politics and the Limits of Reason*. Cambridge: Cambridge University Press.
  (2018a). "Non-domination and the *libera res publica* in Cicero's republicanism," *History of European Ideas* 44(6): 756–73.
  (2018b). *Roman Political Thought*. Cambridge: Cambridge University Press.
Atkins, M. (2002). "Old philosophy and new power: Cicero in fifth-century North Africa," in G. Clark & T. Rajak, eds., *Philosophy and Power in the Graeco-Roman World: Essays in Honour of Miriam Griffin*. Oxford: Oxford University Press.

Avotins, I. (1983). "Two observations on Lucretius 2.251–2.257," *Rheinisches Museum für Philologie* 126: 282–291.
Balsdon, J. (1963). "The *Commentariolum Petitionis*," *Classical Quarterly* 13: 242–50.
Baraz, Y. (2012). *A Written Republic: Cicero's Philosophical Politics*. Princeton, NJ: Princeton University Press.
Barnes, J. & M. Griffin, eds. (1989). *Philosophia Togata*. Oxford: Oxford University Press.
Beaulieu, P.-A. (2005). "World hegemony, 900–300 BCE," in D. Snell, ed., *A Companion to the Ancient Near East*. Oxford: Blackwell Press.
Begley, C. (1988). "Voluntas in Cicero." Unpublished doctoral thesis, University of North Carolina at Chapel Hill.
Bénatouïl, T. (2016). "Structure, standards and Stoic moral progress in De Finibus 4," in J. Annas & G. Betegh, eds., *Cicero's De Finibus: Philosophical Approaches*. Cambridge: Cambridge University Press.
Bergson, H. (1921). *L'evolution créatrice*. Paris: F. Alcan.
Bertram, C. (2012). "Rousseau's legacy in two conceptions of the general will: democratic and transcendent," *Review of Politics* 74(3): 403–19.
Blackwell, C. W. (2003). "The council," in C. W. Blackwell, ed., *Dēmos: Classical Athenian Democracy* (A. Mahoney & R. Scaife, eds., The Stoa: a consortium for electronic publication in the humanities [www.stoa.org]), edition of January 23, 2003.
Blom, H. W. & L. Winkel, eds. (2004). *Grotius and the Stoa*. Assen: Royal Van Gorcum.
Bloom, H. (1998). *Shakespeare: The Invention of the Human*. New York: Riverhead Books.
Bobzien, S. (1998a). *Determinism and Freedom in Stoic Philosophy*. Oxford: Clarendon Press.
  (1998b). "The inadvertent conception and late birth of the free-will problem," *Phronesis* 43(2): 133–75.
Bollack, M. (1976). "*Momen mutatum*, la déviation et le plaisir," *Cahiers de Philologie* I: 163–89.
Boulianne, S. (2018). "Mini-publics and public opinion: two survey-based experiments," *Political Studies* 66(1): 119–36.
Boyancé, P. (1941). "Cum dignitate otium," *Revue des Études Antiques* 43: 172–91.
Brann, E. (2014). *Un-willing*. Philadelphia, PA: Paul Dry Books.
Brett, A. (2002). "Natural right and civil community: the civil philosophy of Hugo Grotius," *The Historical Journal* 45(1): 31–51.
Brittain, C. (2015). "Cicero's skeptical methods: the example of the *De finibus*," in J. Annas & G. Betegh, eds., *Cicero's De finibus: Philosophical Approaches*. Cambridge: Cambridge University Press.
Brooke, C. (2011). "Rousseau's political philosophy: Stoic and Augustinian origins," in P. Riley, ed., *The Cambridge Companion to Rousseau*. Cambridge: Cambridge University Press.

Brown, P. (1967). *Augustine of Hippo: A Biography.* London: Faber and Faber.
Brunt, P. (1971). *Social Conflicts in the Roman Republic.* New York: W.W. Norton & Co.
  (1988). *The Fall of the Roman Republic and Related Essays.* Oxford: Clarendon Press.
Büchner, K. (1956). "Präludien zu einer Lukrezausgabe," *Hermes* 84(2): 198–233.
Burchell, D. (1998). "Civic personae: MacIntyre, Cicero, and moral personality," *History of Political Thought* 19(1): 101–18.
Burckhardt, L. A. (1988). *Politische Strategien der Optimaten in der späten römischen Republik* (Historia Einzelschrift 57). Stuttgart: Franz Steiner Verlag.
Büttgen, P. (2001). "Liberté et intériorité," in J.-M. Valentin, ed., *Luther et la réforme.* Paris: Éditions Desjonquères.
Cammack, D. (2021). "Deliberation and discussion in classical Athens," *Journal of Political Philosophy* 29(2): 135–66.
Cartledge, P. (2016). *Democracy: A Life.* Oxford: Oxford University Press.
Chavalas, M. (2005). "The age of empires, 3100–900 BCE," in D. Snell, ed., *A Companion to the Ancient Near East.* Oxford: Blackwell.
Combeaud, B. (2015). *Lucrèce: la naissance des choses.* Paris: Mollat.
Connolly, J. (2010). "Cicero's concordia ordinum: a Machiavellian reappraisal," paper delivered at American Political Science Association.
  (2015). *The Life of Roman Republicanism.* Princeton, NJ: Princeton University Press.
Corballis, M. (2011). *The Recursive Mind: The Origins of Human Language, Thought, and Civilization.* Princeton, NJ: Princeton University Press.
Corbeill, A. (2013). "The intellectual milieu of the late Republic," in C. Steel, ed., *The Cambridge Companion to Cicero.* Cambridge: Cambridge University Press.
Courant, D. (2020). "From *kleroterion* to cryptology: the act of sortition in the 21st century, instruments and practices," in L. Lopez-Rabatel & Y. Sintomer, eds., *Sortition and Democracy: History, Tools, Theories.* Exeter: Imprint Academic UK.
Crook, J. A. (1967). *Law and Life of Rome, 90 B.C.–A.D. 212.* Ithaca: Cornell University Press.
Cutler, F., R. Johnston, R. K. Carty, A. Blais, & P. Fournier. (2008). "Deliberation, information, and trust: the British Columbia Citizens' Assembly as agenda setter," in Mark E. Warren and Hilary Pearse, eds., *Designing deliberative democracy: The British Columbia citizens' assembly.* Cambridge: Cambridge University Press.
De Lacy, P. (1977). "The four Stoic *personae*," *Illinois Classical Studies* 2: 163–72.
Deane, H. A. (1963). *The Political and Social Ideas of St. Augustine.* New York: Columbia University Press.
Deguergue, M. (2015). "La conception de la Volonté Générale Chez Diderot," *Revue d'Histoire des Facultés de Droit* 35: 107–26.
Dennett, D. (2017). *From Bacteria to Bach and Back.* New York: Random House.

DeSanctis, G. & R. B. Gallupe (1987). "A foundation for the study of group decision support systems," *Management Science* 33(5): 589–609.
Dias, N., ed. (2014). *Hope for Democracy: 25 Years of Participatory Budgeting Worldwide*. Sao Bras de Aportel: In Loco Press.
Diderot, D., ed. (1750–65). *Encyclopédie, ou Dictionnaire raisonné des sciences, des arts et des métiers*. n.p.
Dihle, V. (1982). *The Theory of Will in Classical Antiquity*. Berkeley: University of California Press.
Dryzek, J. S. (2007). "Theory, evidence, and the tasks of deliberation," in S. W. Rosenberg, ed., *Deliberation, Participation and Democracy*. London: Palgrave Macmillan.
Dugan, J. (2012). "*Scriptum* and *voluntas* in Cicero's *Brutus*," in M. Citroni, ed., *Letteratura e civitas: transizioni dalla Repubblica all'Impero. In ricordo di Emanuele Narducci*. Pisa: n.p.
Dyck, A. R. (1996). *A Commentary on Cicero, De officiis*. Ann Arbor: University of Michigan Press.
  (2004). *A Commentary on Cicero, De legibus*. Ann Arbor: University of Michigan Press.
Dyck, A. R., ed. (2008). *Cicero: Catilinarians*. Cambridge: Cambridge University Press.
Enos, R. L. (2005). "*Rhetorica ad Herennium*," in M. Ballif & M. G. Moran, eds., *Classical Rhetorics and Rhetoricians: Critical Studies and Sources*. Westport, CT: Greenwood Press.
Eriksson, M., C. J. Van Riper, B. Leitschuh, A. B. Brymer, A. Rawluk, C. M. Raymond, & J. O. Kenter. (2019). "Social learning as a link between the individual and the collective: evaluating deliberation on social values," *Sustainability Science* 14(5): 1323–32.
Erskine, A. (1990). *The Hellenistic Stoa*. London: Gerald Duckworth & Co.
Fabre, J. (1961). "Deux frères ennemis: Diderot et Jean-Jacques," *Diderot Studies* 3: 155–213.
Farrell, D. M. & J. Suiter. (2019). *Reimagining Democracy: Lessons in Deliberative Democracy from the Irish Front Line*. Ithaca, NY: Cornell University Press.
Ferrary, J.-L. (1995). "The statesman and the law in the political philosophy of Cicero," in A. Laks & M. Schofield, eds., *Justice and Generosity: Studies in Hellenistic Social and Political Philosophy*. Cambridge: Cambridge University Press.
Finley, M. (1983). *Politics in the Ancient World*. Cambridge: Cambridge University Press.
Fishkin, J. S. (2018). *Democracy When the People Are Thinking: Revitalizing our Politics through Public Deliberation*. Oxford: Oxford University Press.
Fortenbaugh, W. W. & P. Steinmetz, eds. (1989). *Cicero's Knowledge of the Peripatos*. Abingdon-on-Thames: Routledge.
Foucault, M. (1981–82). *L'herméneutique du sujet*. Collège de France 1981–82, édition Gallimard, 2001. Paris: SEUIL.

Fox, M. (2013). "Cicero during the Enlightenment," in C. Steel, ed., *The Cambridge Companion to Cicero*. Cambridge: Cambridge University Press.
Frede, D. (1989). "Constitution & citizenship: Peripatetic influence on Cicero's political conceptions in the *De re publica*," in W. W. Fortenbaugh & P. Steinmetz (ed.), *Cicero's Knowledge of the Peripatos*. Abingdon-on-Thames: Routledge.
Frede, M. (2011). *A Free Will: Origins of the Notion in Ancient Thought*. Berkeley: University of California Press.
Fuentes Gonzalez, P. (1998). *Les diatribes de Télès*. Paris: Vrin.
Garbarino, G. (1973). *Roma e la filosofia greca dalle origini alla fine del II secolo a.c.* Turin: Paravia.
  (2014). *La letteratura latina*. Milan: Pearson Italia.
Garsten, B. (2006). *Saving Persuasion: A Defense of Rhetoric and Judgment*. Cambridge, MA: Harvard University Press.
Gauthier, R. A. (1970). *Aristote: l'éthique à Nicomaque*, 2nd ed. Paris, Louvain: Peeters.
Gavoille, E. (2000). *Ars: étude sémantique de Plaute à Cicéron*. Paris, Louvain: Peeters.
Gelzer, M. (1969). *The Roman Nobility*, trans. R. Seager. Oxford: Blackwell.
Gildenhard, I. (2011). *Creative Eloquence: The Construction of Reality in Cicero's Speeches*. Oxford: Oxford University Press.
Gill, C. (1988). "Personhood and personality: the four-*personae* theory in Cicero, *De officiis* I," in J. Annas, ed., *Oxford Studies in Ancient Philosophy*, vol. 6. Oxford: Oxford University Press.
  (2003). "The school in the Roman Imperial period," in B. Inwood, ed., *The Cambridge Companion to the Stoics*. Cambridge: Cambridge University Press.
  (2006). *The Structured Self in Hellenistic and Roman Thought*. Oxford: Oxford University Press.
Giltaij, J. (2016). "Greek philosophy and classical Roman law: a brief overview," in P. Du Plessis, C. Ando, & K. Tuori, eds., *The Oxford Handbook of Roman Law and Society*. Oxford: Oxford University Press.
Giusta, M. (1967). *I Dossografi di Etica* (2 vols.). Turin: Giappichelli.
Glucker, J. (1978). *Antiochus and the Late Academy*. Göttingen: Vandenhoeck & Ruprecht.
Goldberg, S. (1986). *Understanding Terence*. Princeton, NJ: Princeton University Press.
Goodin, H. J. & D. Stein. (2009). "The use of deliberative discussion to enhance the critical thinking abilities of nursing students," *Journal of Public Deliberation* 5(1): 5.
Goulven, M. (1996). *Saint Augustin et la philosophie: notes critiques*. Paris: Institut d'études augustiniennes.
Gourinat, J.-B. (1996). *Les stoïciens et l'âme*. Paris: Presses Universitaires de France.
Graver, M. (2002). *Cicero on the Emotions: Tusculan Disputations 3 and 4*. Chicago, IL: University of Chicago Press.

(2003). "Not even Zeus: a discussion of A. A. Long, Epictetus: A Stoic and Socratic Guide to Life," *Oxford Studies in Ancient Philosophy* 25: 341–61.
    (2007). *Stoicism and Emotion*. Chicago, IL: University of Chicago Press.
Griffin, M. (2007). "From Aristotle to Atticus: Cicero and Matius on friendship," in J. Barnes & M. Griffin, eds., *Philosopha Togata II: Plato and Aristotle at Rome*. Oxford: Oxford University Press.
Griffin, M. & E. Atkins, eds. (1991). *Cicero: On Duties*. Cambridge: Cambridge University Press.
Grimal, P. (1953). *Le siècle des Scipions. Rome et l'hellénisme au temps des guerres puniques*. Paris: Aubier.
    (1984). *Cicéron*. Paris: Presses Universitaires de France.
Groethuysen, B. (1949). *Jean-Jacques Rousseau*. Paris: Gallimard.
Grönlund, K., K. Herne, & M. Setälä (2017). "Empathy in a citizen deliberation experiment," *Scandinavian Political Studies* 40(4): 457–80.
Grotius, H. (1625). *De iure belli ac pacis libri tres*. Paris: Buon.
Guérin, C. (2011). *Persona. L'élaboration d'une notion rhétorique au Ier siècle av. J.-C. Volume II: Théorisation cicéronienne de la persona oratoire*. Paris: Les Belles Lettres.
    (2015). *La voix de la vérité: témoin et témoignage dans les tribunaux romains du 1er siècle av. J.-C.* Paris: Les Belles Lettres.
Hagan, T. & D. Smail. (1997). "Power-mapping: background and basic methodology," *Journal of Community & Applied Social Psychology* 7: 257–67.
Hagelskamp, C., C. Rinehart, R. Silliman, & D. Schleifer (2016). "Public Spending, by the People," *Public Agenda*, available at: www.publicagenda.org/wp-content/uploads/2019/11/PublicSpendingByThePeople_PublicAgenda_2016.pdf
Hahm, D. (2009). "The mixed constitution in Greek thought," in R. Balot, ed., *A Companion to Greek and Roman Political Thought*. Oxford: Oxford University Press.
Halbwachs, V. (2016). "Women as legal actors," in P. Du Plessis, C. Ando, & K. Tuori, eds., *The Oxford Handbook of Roman Law and Society*. Oxford: Oxford University Press.
Harries, J. (2009) "*Cicero and the Defining of the Ius Civile,*" in *Cicero and Modern Law*. Routledge.
    (2016). "Legal education and training of lawyers," in P. Du Plessis, C. Ando, & K. Tuori, eds., *The Oxford Handbook of Roman Law and Society*. Oxford: Oxford University Press.
Hatinguais, J. (1958). "Sens et valeur de la volonté dans l'humanisme de Cicéron," *Bulletin de l'Association Guillaume Budé: lettres d'humanité* 17: 50–69.
Hawley, M. (2020). "Individuality and hierarchy in Cicero's *De Officiis*," *European Journal of Political Theory* 19(1): 87–105.
Hellegouarc'h, J. (1963). *Le vocabulaire latin des relations et des partis politiques sous la république*. Paris: Les Belles Lettres.

Henrich, J. (2020). *The WEIRDest People in the World: How the West Became Psychologically Peculiar and Particularly Prosperous*. New York: Farrar, Strauss and Giroux.
Herrnson, P. (2019). *Congressional Elections: Campaigning at Home and in Washington*, 8th edition. Washington, DC: Congressional Quarterly Press.
Hilder, J. (2016). "Jurors, jurists and advocates: law in the Rhetorica ad Herennium *and* De Inventione," in P. Du Plessis, C. Ando, & K. Tuori, eds., *The Oxford Handbook of Roman Law and Society*. Oxford: Oxford University Press.
Hinard, F. (1985). *Sylla*. Paris: Fayard.
Hirzel, R. (1877–83). *Untersuchungen zu Cicero's philosophischen Schriften*. Leipzig: n.p.
Hobbes, T. (1651). *Leviathan: Or the Matter, Forme, and Power of a Common-Wealth Ecclesiasticall and Civill*. n.p.
Hofstadter, D. (2007). *I Am a Strange Loop*. New York: Basic Books.
Hölkeskamp, K.-J. (2010). *Reconstructing the Roman Republic*. Princeton, NJ: Princeton University Press.
Holowchak, M. A. (2016). "Thomas Jefferson," in *Stanford Encyclopedia of Philosophy*. Available at: https://plato.stanford.edu/entries/jefferson/
Hong, L. & S. Page. (2004). "Groups of diverse problem solvers can outperform groups of high-ability problem solvers," *Proceedings of the National Academy of Sciences of the United States of America* 101(46): 16385–89.
Huby, P. (1967). "The first discovery of the freewill problem," *Philosophy* 42: 353–62.
Ibbetson, D. (2015). "Sources of law from the Republic to the Dominate," in D. Johnston, ed., *The Cambridge Companion to Roman Law*. Cambridge: Cambridge University Press.
Inwood, B. (1985). "The psychology of action," in *Ethics and Human Action in Early Stoicism*. Oxford: Oxford University Press.
  (2000). "The will in Seneca the Younger," *Classical Philology* 95: 44–60.
Ioppolo, A.-M. (1988). "Le cause antecedenti in Cic. De Fato 40," in J. Barnes & M. Mignucci, eds., *Matter and Metaphysics: Fourth Symposium Hellenisticum*. Naples: Bibliopolis.
  (2016). "Sententia explosa: criticism of Stoic ethics in De Finibus 4," in J. Annas & G. Betegh, eds., *Cicero's De Finibus: Philosophical Approaches*. Cambridge: Cambridge University Press.
Irwin, T. (2012). "Antiochus on social virtue," in D. Sedley, ed., *The Philosophy of Antiochus*. Cambridge: Cambridge University Press.
Jakab, E. (2016). "Inheritance," in P. Du Plessis, C. Ando, & K. Tuori, eds., *The Oxford Handbook of Roman Law and Society*. Oxford: Oxford University Press.
Kahn, C. (1988). "Discovering the will from Aristotle to Augustine," in J. M. Dillon & A. A. Long, eds., *The Question of "Eclecticism": Studies in Later Greek Philosophy*. Berkeley: University of California Press.

Kanra, B. (2012). "Binary deliberation: the role of social learning in divided societies," *Journal of Public Deliberation* 8(1): 1.

Kapust, D. (2011). "Cicero on decorum and the morality of rhetoric," *European Journal of Political Theory* 10(1): 92–112.

Karakasis, E. (2008). *Terence and the Language of Roman Comedy*. Cambridge: Cambridge University Press.

Kaster, R. (2005). *Emotion, Restraint and Community in Ancient Rome*. Oxford: Oxford University Press.

  (2006). *Cicero: Speech on Behalf of Publius Sestius*. Oxford: Clarendon Press.

Kenny, A. (1979). *Aristotle's Theory of the Will*. New Haven, CT: Yale University Press.

Keyes, C. W. (1921). "Original elements in Cicero's ideal constitution," *American Journal of Philology* 42: 309–23.

Kindstrand, J. F. (1994). *Bion of Borysthenes: A Collection of the Fragments with Introduction and Commentary*. Uppsala: Acta Universitas Uppsalensis.

King, P., ed. (2010). *Augustine: On the Free Choice of the Will, On Grace and Free Choice, and Other Writings*. Cambridge: Cambridge University Press.

Koch, B. (2006). *Philosophie als Medizin für die Seele: Untersuchungen zu Ciceros Tusculanae Disputationes*. Stuttgart: Franz Steiner Verlag.

Konstan, D. (1997). *Friendship in the Classical World*. Cambridge: Cambridge University Press.

Kramer, M. (1997). *Hobbes and the Paradox of Political Origins*. New York: St. Martin's Press.

Krause, S., R. James, J. J. Faria, G. D. Ruxton, & J. Krause. (2011). "Swarm intelligence in humans: diversity can trump ability," *Animal Behaviour* 81 (5): 941–48.

Kukučková, S., & E. Bakoš. (2019). "Does participatory budgeting bolster voter turnout in elections? The case of the Czech Republic," *NISPAcee Journal of Public Administration and Policy* 12(2): 109–29.

Kunkel, K. (1966). *An Introduction to Roman Legal and Constitutional History*, 2nd edition. Oxford: Clarendon Press.

Laird, A. (1999). *Powers of Expression, Expressions of Power: Speech Presentation in Latin Literature*. Oxford: Oxford University Press.

Landemore, H. (2013). *Democratic Reason: Politics, Collective Intelligence, and the Rule of the Many*. Princeton, NJ: Princeton University Press.

  (2020). *Open Democracy: Reinventing Popular Rule for the Twenty-First Century*. Princeton, NJ: Princeton University Press.

LeBuffe, M. (2003). "Hobbes on the origin of obligation," *British Journal for the History of Philosophy* 11(1): 15–39.

Lepore, E. (1954). *Il princeps ciceroniano e gli ideali politici della tarda repubblica (Istituto italiano per gli studi storici in Napoli)*. Naples: Nella sede dell'Istituto.

Lévy, C. (1984). "La dialectique de Cicéron dans les livres II et IV du *De Finibus*," *REL*, 62, 111–27.

(1992). *Cicero Academicus. Recherches sur les Académiques et sur la philosophie cicéronienne*. Rome: Ecole Française de Rome.
(1998). "Rhétorique et philosophie: la monstruosité politique chez Cicéron," *Revue d'Etudes Latines* 76: 139–57.
(2003). "Y a-t-il quelqu'un derrière le masque? A propos de la théorie des *personae* chez Cicéron," *Itaca. Quaderns Catalans de Cultura Classica* 19: 127–40.
(2005). "Le philosophe et le légionnaire: l'armée comme thème et métaphore chez Lucrèce et Cicéron," in F. Bessone & E. Malaspina, *Politica e cultura in Roma antica, volume d'hommage à Italo Lana*. Bologna: Pàtron.
(2007). "De la critique de la sympathie à la volonté. Cicéron, *De Fato* 9–11," *Lexis* 25: 17–34.
(2008). "Cicéron, le moyen platonisme et la philosophie romaine: à propos de la naissance du concept latin de qualitas," *Revue de métaphysique et de morale* 57: 5–20.
(2010). "Cicero and the New Academy," in L. Gerson, ed., *The Cambridge History of Philosophy in Late Antiquity*. Cambridge: Cambridge University Press.
(2012a). "Acte de parole et ontologie du discours chez Cicéron," in *Genèses de l'acte de parole dans le monde grec, romain, et médiéval*. Paris: Brepols.
(2012b). "Philosophical life versus political life: an impossible choice for Cicero?" in W. Nicgorski, ed., *Cicero's Practical Philosophy*. Notre Dame, IN: University of Notre Dame Press.
(2016). "Lucilius et la fondation de la culture philosophique romaine," in P. Vesperini, ed., *Philosophari: usages romains des savoirs grecs sous la République et sous l'Empire*. Paris: Classiques Garnier.
(2018). "De la rhétorique à la philosophie: le rôle de la temeritas dans la pensée et l'œuvre de Cicéro," in G. M. Müller & F. M. Zini, eds., *Philosophie in Rom – Römische Philosophie? kultur-, literatur- und philosophiegeschichtliche Perspektiven. Beiträge zur Altertumskunde, 358*. Berlin: De Gruyter.
(2020a). 'Cicero', in P. Mitsis, ed., *Oxford Handbook of Epicurus and Epicureanism*, online edition, available at: https://doi.org/10.1093/oxfordhb/9780199744213.013.36
(2020b). "Some remarks about Cicero's perception of the future of Rome," in J. J. Price & K. Berthelot, eds., *The Future of Rome: Roman, Greek, Jewish and Christian Visions*. Cambridge: Cambridge University Press.
Lévy, P. (1997). *L'intelligence collective: pour une anthropologie du cyberspace*. Paris: La Découverte.
Lewis, A. (2015). "Slavery, family, and status," in D. Johnston, ed., *The Cambridge Companion to Roman Law*. Cambridge: Cambridge University Press.
Libet, B. (2002). "Do we have free will?" in R. Kane, ed., *The Oxford Handbook on Free Will*. Oxford: Clarendon Press.
Lintott, A. (1999). *The Constitution of the Roman Republic*. Oxford: Oxford University Press.

(2008). *Cicero as Evidence: A Historian's Companion*. Oxford: Oxford University Press.
(2015). "Crime and punishment," in D. Johnston, ed., *The Cambridge Companion to Roman Law*. Cambridge: Cambridge University Press.
Long, A. A. (2015). *Greek Models of Mind and Self*. Cambridge, MA: Harvard University Press.
Lörcher, A. (1911). *Das Fremde und das Eigene in Ciceros Büchern de Finibus Bonorum et Malorum und den Academica*. Halle: G. Olms.
MacCormack, S. (2013). "Cicero in late antiquity," in C. Steel, ed., *The Cambridge Companion to Cicero*. Cambridge: Cambridge University Press.
MacIntyre, A. (1988). *Whose Justice? Which Rationality?* Notre Dame, IN: University of Notre Dame Press.
Malone, T. W. & M. S. Bernstein, eds. (2015). *Handbook of Collective Intelligence*. Cambridge, MA: MIT Press.
Manin, B. (1985). "Volonté générale ou délibération ? Esquisse d'une théorie de la délibération politique," *Le Débat* 33: 72–94.
McConnell, S. (2014). *Philosophical Life in Cicero's Letters*. Cambridge: Cambridge University Press.
Mendelow, A. (1991). "Stakeholder mapping," in *Proceedings of the 2nd International Conference on Information Systems*. New York: Association for Computing Machinery.
Merker, A. (2016). *Le Principe de l'action humaine selon Démosthène et Aristote : Hairesis – Prohairesis*. Paris: Les Belles Lettres.
Middlekauf, R. (1961). "A persistent tradition: the classical curriculum in eighteenth-century New England," *The William and Mary Quarterly* 18: 54–67.
Millar, F. (2002). *The Roman Republic in Political Thought*. Hanover, NH: University Press of New England.
Moatti, C. (2015). *The Birth of Critical Thinking in Republican Rome*. Cambridge: Cambridge University Press.
Mommsen, T. (1871). *Römisches Staatsrecht* (vols. 1–3). S. Hirzel.
Moreau, P.-F. (2002). *Lucrèce. L'âme*. Paris: Presses Universitaires de France.
Morstein-Marx, R. (1998). "Publicity, popularity and patronage in the '*Commentariolum Petitionis*'," *Classical Antiquity* 17(2): 259–88.
(2004). *Mass Oratory and Political Power in the Late Roman Republic*. Cambridge: Cambridge University Press.
Mouritsen, H. (2001). *Plebs and Politics in the Late Roman Republic*. Cambridge: Cambridge University Press.
(2017). *Politics in the Roman Republic*. Cambridge: Cambridge University Press.
Mousourakis, G. (2003). *The Historical and Institutional Context of Roman Law*. Burlington, VT: Ashgate.
Move to Amend (n.d.). "A Guide to Power Mapping" by the advocacy network, available at: www.movetoamend.org/guide-power-mapping

Mulgan, G. (2018). *Big Mind: How Collective Intelligence Can Change Our World*. Princeton, NJ: Princeton University Press.

Murray, R. J. (1966). "Cicero and the Gracchi," *Transactions and Proceedings of the American Philological Association* 97: 291–98.

Nardo, D. (1970). *Il Commentariolum Petitionis : la propaganda elettorale nella "ars" di Quinto Cicerone*. Padua: Liviana Editrice.

Nicgorski, W., ed. (2012). *Cicero's Practical Philosophy*. Notre Dame, IN: University of Notre Dame Press.

Nippel, W. (1995). *Public Order in Ancient Rome*. Cambridge: Cambridge University Press.

Noveck, B. S. (2015). *Smart Citizens, Smarter State: The Technologies of Expertise and the Future of Governing*. Cambridge, MA: Harvard University Press.

Noy, D. (2008). "Power mapping: enhancing sociological knowledge by developing generalizable analytical public tools," *The American Sociologist* 39(1): 3–18.

O'Donnell, J. J., ed. (1992). *Augustine: Confessions*, 3 vols. Oxford: Oxford University Press.

(2005). *Augustine: A New Biography*. New York: HarperCollins.

(2015). *Pagans*. New York: HarperCollins.

Ober, J. (1989). *Mass and Elite in Democratic Athens*. Princeton, NJ: Princeton University Press.

(2008). *Democracy and Knowledge: Innovation and Learning in Classical Athens*. Princeton, NJ: Princeton University Press.

OECD (2020). *Innovative Citizen Participation and New Democratic Institutions: Catching the Deliberative Wave*. Paris: OECD Publishing.

Pagnotta, F. (2007). *Cicerone e l'ideale dell'aequabilitas: l'eredità di un antico concetto filosofico*. Cesena: Stilgraf Editrice.

Paulson, L. (2014). "A painted republic: the constitutional innovations of Cicero's *De legibus*," *Etica & Politica/Ethics & Politics* 16(2): 307–40.

Pereboom, P. (2011). "Free-will skepticism and meaning in life," in R. Kane, ed., *The Oxford Handbook on Free Will*, 2nd edition. Oxford: Oxford University Press.

Peterson, M., ed. (1984). *Thomas Jefferson: Writings*. New York: Library of America.

Pigeaud, J. (1981). *La Maladie de l'Ame: étude sur la relation de l'âme et du corps dans la tradition médico-philosophique antique*. Paris: Les Belles Lettres.

Pitkin, H. (1967). *The Concept of Representation*. Berkeley: University of California Press.

Pohlenz, M. (1948, 1964). *Die Stoa*, 2 vols., 3rd edition. Göttingen: n.p.

Polak, J. (1946). "The Roman conception of the inviolability of the house," in M. David, B. A. Van Groningen, & E. M. Meijers, eds., *Symbolae ad Jus et Historiam Antiquitatis Pertinentes J. C. Van Oven Dedicatae*. Leiden: E. J. Brill.

Powell, J. G. F. (1994). "The *rector rei publicae* of Cicero's *De Re Publica*," *Scripta Classica Israelica* 13: 19–29.

ed. (1995). *Cicero the Philosopher*. Oxford: Oxford University Press.
  (2001). "Were Cicero's *Laws* the laws of Cicero's *Republic*?" in J. G. F. Powell & J. North, eds., *Cicero's Republic*. London: Institute of Classical Studies, University of London.
  (2012). "Cicero's De Re Publica and the virtues of the statesman," in W. Nicgorski, ed., *Cicero's Practical Philosophy*. Notre Dame, IN: University of Notre Dame Press.
Powell, J. G. F. & J. Paterson, eds. (2004). *Cicero the Advocate*. Oxford: Oxford University Press.
Rahe, P. A. (1994). "Cicero and Republicanism in America," *Ciceroniana* 8: 63–78.
  (2017). *Republics Ancient and Modern, Volume III: Inventions of Prudence: Constituting the American Regime*. Chapel Hill: University of North Carolina Press.
Randall, D. (2018). *The Concept of Conversation: From Cicero's Sermo to the Grand Siècle's Conversation*. Edinburgh: Edinburgh University Press.
Rawson, E. (1975). *Cicero: A Portrait*. London: Allen Lane.
Remer, G. (2005). "Cicero and the ethics of deliberative rhetoric," in B. Fontana, C. Nederman, & G. Remer, eds., *Talking Democracy: Historical Perspectives on Rhetoric and Democracy*. University Park, PA: Penn State University Press.
  (2017). *Ethics and the Orator: The Ciceronian Tradition of Political Morality*. Chicago, IL: University of Chicago Press.
Rhodes, P. J. (1972). *The Athenian Boulé*. Oxford: Clarendon Press.
  (1986). *The Greek City States: A Sourcebook*. Cambridge: Cambridge University Press.
Ribbeck, O. (1875). *Die römische Tragödie im Zeitalter der Republik*. Leipzig: Teubner: n.p.
Richard, C. (1994). *The Founders and the Classics: Greece, Rome, and the American Enlightenment*. Cambridge, MA: Harvard University Press.
  (2008). *Greeks and Romans Bearing Gifts: How the Ancients Inspired the Founding Fathers*. Lanham, MD: Rowman and Littlefield.
Riley, P. (1986). *The General Will before Rousseau: The Transformation of the Divine into the Civic*. Princeton, NJ: Princeton University Press.
  (2011). "Rousseau's general will," in P. Riley, ed., *The Cambridge Companion to Rousseau*. Cambridge: Cambridge University Press.
Roberts, J. T. (1994). *Athens on Trial: The Antidemocratic Tradition in Western Thought*. Princeton, NJ: Princeton University Press.
Rosillo-López, C. (2020). "Informal political communication and network theory in the late Roman Republic," *Journal of Historical Network Research* 4: 90–113.
Roskam, G. (2009). *Plutarch's Maxime cum Principibus esse disserendum: An Interpretation with Commentary*. Leuven: Leuven University Press.
Rousseau, J.-J. (1762). *Du contrat social*. B. Bernardi, ed. Paris: Flammarion (2001).

Rovelli, C. (2015). *Seven Brief Lessons on Physics*, trans. S. Carnell. New York: Riverhead.
Ruelle, A. (2012). "Le citoyen face aux pratiques collectives de la honte à Rome," in R. Alexandre, C. Guérin, & M. Jacotot, ed., *Rubor et Pudor. Vivre et penser la honte dans la Rome ancienne*. Paris: Editions Rue d'Ulm.
Runia, D. (1989). "Aristotle and Theophrastus: conjoined in the writings of Cicero," in W. W. Fortenbaugh & D. Steinmetz, eds., *Cicero's Knowledge of the Peripatos*. New Brunswick, NJ: Rutgers University Studies in Classical Humanities.
Ryan, A. (2012). *On Politics: A History of Political Thought*. New York: Liveright.
Ryan, M., D. Gambrell, & B. S. Noveck. (2020). "Using Collective Intelligence to Solve Public Problems," Report by the NYU GovLab and Nesta, available at: www.nesta.org.uk/report/using-collective-intelligence-solve-public-problems/
Ryle, G. (1949). *The Concept of Mind*. London: Hutchinson's University Library.
Salomon-Bayet, C. (1968). *Jean-Jacques Rousseau ou l'impossible unité*. Paris: Seghers.
Schmekel, A. (1892). *Die Philosophie der mittleren Stoa*. Berlin: n.p.
Schmidt, P. (1969). *Die Abfassungszeit von Ciceros Schrift über die Gesetze*. Rome: Centro di Studi Ciceroniani Editore.
Schofield, M. (1991). *The Stoic Idea of the City*. Cambridge: Cambridge University Press.
  (1995). "Cicero's definition of *res publica*," in J. G. F. Powell, ed., *Cicero the Philosopher*. Oxford: Oxford University Press.
  (1999). *Saving the City: Philosopher-Kings and Other Classical Paradigms, Issues in Ancient Philosophy*. London, New York: Routledge.
  (2005). "Approaching the *Republic*," in C. Rowe & M. Schofield, eds., *The Cambridge History of Greek and Roman Political Thought*. Cambridge: Cambridge University Press.
  (2009). "Ciceronian dialogue," in S. Goldhill, ed., *The End of Dialogue in Antiquity*. Cambridge: Cambridge University Press.
  (2012). "The neutralizing argument: Carneades, Antiochus, Cicero," in D. Sedley, ed., *The Philosophy of Antiochus*. Cambridge: Cambridge University Press.
  (2013). "Cosmopolitanism, imperialism and justice in Cicero's republic and laws," *Journal of Intellectual History and Political Thought* 2(1): 5.
  (2014). "Liberty, equality, and authority: a political discourse in the later Roman Republic," in D. Hammer, ed., *Roman Political Thought. From Cicero to Augustine*. Cambridge: Cambridge University Press.
  (2021). *Cicero: Political Philosophy*. Oxford: Oxford University Press.
Seager, R. (1972). "Cicero and the word *popularis*," *The Classical Quarterly* 22(2): 328–38.
Sedley, D. (1983). "Epicurus' refutation of determinism," in Συζήτησις: *Studi sull'epicureismo greco e romano offerti a M. Gigante*. Naples.
  ed. (2012). *The Philosophy of Antiochus*. Cambridge: Cambridge University Press.

Sedley, D. & A. A. Long (1987). *The Hellenistic Philosophers*, 2 vols. Cambridge: Cambridge University Press.
Segal, E. (2001). *The Death of Comedy*. Cambridge, MA: Harvard University Press.
Sellier, P. (2009). *Augustinisme et littérature classique*. Paris: Les cahiers d'histoire de la philosophie.
Servan-Schreiber, E. (2018). *Supercollectif: la nouvelle puissance de nos intelligences*. Paris: Fayard.
Sharples, R. W., ed., trans. (1991). *Cicero, On Fate ("De Fato") and Boethius, The Consolation of Philosophy IV.5–7, V ("Philosophiae Consolationis")*. Warminster: Aris & Phillips.
Shelton, G. (1992). *Morality and Sovereignty in the Philosophy of Thomas Hobbes*. New York: St. Martin's Press.
Sillett, A. (2016). "Quintus Cicero's *Commentariolum*: a philosophical approach to Roman elections," in E. P. Cueva & J. Martinez, eds., *Splendide Mendax: Rethinking Fakes and Forgeries in Classical, Late Antique, and Early Christian Literature*. Eelde: Barkhuis.
Sintomer, Y., C. Herzberg, & A. Röcke (2008). "Participatory budgeting in Europe: potentials and challenges," *International Journal of Urban and Regional Research* 32(1): 164–78.
Skinner, Q. (2008). *Hobbes and Republican Liberty*. Cambridge: Cambridge University Press.
Smith, A. (1759). *A Theory of Moral Sentiments*. London: Andrew Millar.
Smith, M. F. (1975). *Lucretius, De Rerum Natura*, trans. W. H. D. Rouse, revised M. F. Smith. Loeb Classical Library. London: Heinemann.
Spada, P. (2019). "The impact of democratic innovations on citizens' efficacy," in S. Elstub & O. Escobar, eds., *Handbook of Democratic Innovation and Governance*. Cheltenham: Edward Elgar Publishing.
Steel, C. (2017a). "Defining public speech in the Roman Republic: occasion, audience and purpose," in C. Rosillo-Lopez, ed., *Political Communication in the Roman World*. Boston, MA: Brill.
  (2017b). "*Re publica nihil desperatius*: salvaging the state in Cicero's pre-civil war philosophical works," in G. Müller & F. Zini, eds., *Philosophie in Rom – Römische Philosophie*. Berlin: De Gruyter.
Steel, C. E. W., ed. (2013). *The Cambridge Companion to Cicero*. Cambridge: Cambridge University Press.
Straumann, B. (2016). *Crisis and Constitutionalism: Roman Political Thought from the Fall of the Republic to the Age of Revolution*. Oxford: Oxford University Press.
Strawson, G. (1986). *Freedom and Belief*. Oxford: Oxford University Press.
Stump, E. (2001). "Augustine on free will," in E. Stump & N. Kretzmann, eds., *The Cambridge Companion to Augustine*. Cambridge: Cambridge University Press.
Surowiecki, J. (2004). *The Wisdom of Crowds*. New York: Random House.
Syme, R. (1939). *The Roman Revolution*. Oxford: Oxford University Press.

Taylor, L. R. (1949). *Party Politics in the Age of Caesar*. Berkeley: University of California Press.
Tempest, K. (2011). *Cicero: Politics and Persuasion in Ancient Rome*. London: Bloomsbury.
Teske, T. (2001). "Augustine's theory of soul," in E. Stump & N. Kretzmann, eds., *The Cambridge Companion to Augustine*. Cambridge: Cambridge University Press.
Universal Declaration of Human Rights (1948). UN General Assembly 217 [III] A., Paris: n.p.
van de Mieroop, M. (1997). *The Ancient Mesopotamian City*. Oxford: Clarendon Press.
van Holk, L. E. & C. G. Roelofsen, eds. (1983). *Grotius Reader: A Reader for Students of International Law and Legal History*. The Hague: T.M.C. Asser Instituut.
Villey, M. (1945). *Le droit romain*. Paris: Presses Universitaires de France.
Voelke, A.-J. (1973). *L'idée de volonté dans le stoïcisme*. Paris: Bibliothèque de philosophie contemporaine.
Vogel, C. (2020). "Quintus Cicero and Roman rule. Networks between centre and periphery," *Journal of Historical Network Research* 4: 57–89.
Vuolanto, V. (2016). "Child and parent in Roman law," in P. Du Plessis, C. Ando, & K. Tuori, eds., *The Oxford Handbook of Roman Law and Society*. Oxford: Oxford University Press.
Webb, P. (2013). "Who is willing to participate? Dissatisfied democrats, stealth democrats and populists in the United Kingdom," *European Journal of Political Research* 52(6): 747–72.
Wegner, D. (2002). *The Illusion of Conscious Will*. Cambridge, MA: MIT Press.
Wieacker, F. (1988). *Römische Rechtsgeschichte, Erster Abschnitt: Einleitung, Quellenkunde, Frühzeit und Republik*. Munich: C.H. Beck.
Wike, R. & S. Schumacher (2020). "Democratic rights popular globally but commitment to them not always strong," *Pew Research Center*, available at: www.pewresearch.org/global/2020/02/27/attitudes-toward-elected-officials-voting-and-the-state/
Will, E. (1998). "Poleis hellénistiques: deux notes," in *Historica Graeco-Hellenistica: Choix d'écrits 1953–1993*. Paris: Boccard.
Williams, B. (1993). *Shame and Necessity*. Berkeley: University of California Press.
Williamson, C. (2005). *The Laws of the Roman People: Public Law in the Extension and Decline of the Roman Republic*. Ann Arbor: University of Michigan Press.
Wilson, D. L., ed. (1989). *Jefferson's Literary Commonplace Book*. Princeton, NJ: Princeton University Press.
Wirszubski, C. (1950). *Libertas as a Political Idea at Rome during the Late Republic and Early Principate*. Cambridge: Cambridge University Press.
  (1954). "Cicero's *Cum Dignitate Otium*: a reconsideration." *Journal of Roman Studies* 44(1–2): 1–13.
Wood, G. (1969). *The Creation of the American Republic, 1776–1787*. Chapel Hill: University of North Carolina Press.

Wood, N. (1988). *Cicero's Social and Political Thought*. Berkeley: University of California Press.
Woolf, R. (2015). *Cicero: The Philosophy of a Roman Sceptic*. New York: Routledge.
Woolley, A. W., I. Aggarwal, & T. W. Malone (2005). "Collective intelligence and group performance," *Current Directions in Psychological Science* 24(6): 420–24.
Wynne, J. P. F. (2019). *Cicero on the Philosophy of Religion: On the nature of gods and On divination*. Cambridge: Cambridge University Press.
Yavetz, Z. (1969). *Plebs and Princeps*. Oxford: Clarendon Press.
Zarecki, J. (2014). *Cicero's Ideal Statesman in Theory and Practice*. London: Bloomsbury Academic.
Zetzel, J. E. G., ed. (1995). *Cicero, De Re Publica. Selections. Cambridge Greek and Latin Classics*. Cambridge: Cambridge University Press.
  (2003). "Plato with pillows: Cicero on the uses of Greek culture," in D. Braund & C. Gill, eds., *Myth, History and Culture in Republican Rome: Studies in Honour of T. P. Wiseman*. Liverpool: Liverpool University Press.
Zöller, R. (2003). *Die Vorstellung vom Willen in der Morallehre Senecas*. Munich, Leipzig: K.G. Saur.

ANTIQUE WORKS CITED
Greek

Aeschylus, *The Suppliants*.
Aetius, *Opinions of the Philosophers*.
Alexander of Aphrodisias, *On Fate*.
Aristotle, *De anima, Constitution of the Athenians, Nicomachean Ethics, De interpretatione, Politics*.
Demosthenes, *Philippics*.
Dio Cassius, *Roman History*.
Dio Chrysostomos, *Orationes*.
Diodoros of Sicily, *Library of History*.
Diogenes Laërtius, *Lives of Eminent Philosophers*.
Epictetus, *Discourses*.
Epicurus, *Letter to Menoeceus, Sententiae Vaticanae*.
Eusebius of Caesaria, *Praeparatio evangelica*.
Herodotus, *Histories*.
Homer, *Odyssey, Iliad*.
Hyperides, *Speeches*.
Marcus Aurelius, *Meditations*.
Menander, *Dyscolos*.
Philodemus of Gadara, *On Rhetoric*.
Plato, *Gorgias, Lysias, Phaedo, Phaedrus, Republic*.
Plutarch, *Parallel Lives, De communibus notitiis adversus Stoicos, An seni respublica gerenda sit, Quaestiones convivales*.

Polybius, *Histories*.
Sextus Empiricus, *Adversus Mathematicos*.
Stobaeus, *Eclogæ physicæ et ethicæ*.
Thucydides, *The Pelopennesian War*.
Xenophon, *Hellenica*.

Latin

Augustine of Hippo, *Confessions*, *City of God*.
Aulus Gellius, *Attic Nights*.
Caecilius Statius, "Fragments," in E. H. Warmington, trans. (1935). *Remains of Old Latin*, vol. 1. Cambridge, MA: Loeb Classical Library.
Livius Andronicus, "Tereus," in M. Schauer, trans. (2012). *Tragicorum Romanorum Fragmenta, Vol. 1: Livius Andronicus; Naevius; Tragici minores; Fragmenta adespota*. Göttingen: Vandenhoeck and Ruprecht.
Lucilius, "Fragments," in E. H. Warmington, trans. (1935). *Remains of Old Latin*, vol. 3. Cambridge, MA: Loeb Classical Library.
Lucius Calpurnius Piso Frugi, *Annalium fragmenta in aliis scriptis seruata*.
Lucretius, De rerum natura.
Plautus, *Curculio, Menaechmi, Mercator, Miles gloriosus, Phormion, Pseudolus, Trinummus*.
Pliny the Younger, *Letters*.
Quintilian, *Institutio oratoria*.
Rhetorica ad Herennium.
Sallust, *De coniuratione Catilinae, Bellum Jugurthinum*.
Seneca, *Letters to Lucilius*.
Sisenna, *Histories*.
Suetonius, *De Viris Illustribus*.
Tacitus, *Annals*.
Terence, *Adelphoe, Andria, Heauton Timoroumenos, Hecyra, Phormio*.
Varro, *De lingua Latina*.

REFERENCE WORKS

Autenrieth, G. (1958). *A Homeric Dictionary*. Norman: University of Oklahoma Press.
Ernout, A. & A. Meillet, eds. (1960). *Dictionnaire étymologique de la langue latine*, 4th edition. Paris: C. Klincksieck.
Jones, H. S., ed. (1968). *A Greek–English lexicon: Compiled by Henry George Liddell and Robert Scott*, 9th edition. Oxford: Oxford University Press.
Meiggs, R. & D. M. Lewis. (1989). *Greek Historical Inscriptions*. Oxford: Clarendon Press.
Mommsen, T., P. Krueger, & A. Watson, eds. (1985). *The Digest of Justinian* (Vol. 1). Cambridge: Cambridge University Press Archive.

Simpson, J. A. & E. S. C. Weiner, eds. (1989). *The Oxford English Dictionary*, 2nd edition, vol. 20. Oxford: Clarendon Press.
von Arnim, H. (1903–05). *Stoicorum Veterum Fragmenta*. Leipzig: n.p.
Warmington, E. H. (1935). *Remains of Old Latin*, vol. 1. Cambridge, MA: Loeb Classical Library.
  (1938). *Remains of Old Latin*, vol. 3. Cambridge, MA: Loeb Classical Library.
My reference editions for Cicero's corpus are those of the Loeb Classical Library, Harvard University. For a complete list of these works, see the Appendix.

Index

Academy, New, *see also* Carneades
  skeptical freedom as substitute for civic freedom, 145
  skeptical methods of, 33, 194, 222
Aelius Stilo, 32
akrasia, 17, 150, 225
amicitia, 79, 98, *see also* friendship
  interpretations of modern scholars, 81
  Stoic accounts of, 210
animus
  correspondence with *voluntas* in Cicero, 44–45, 49, 147
Antiochus of Ascalon
  account of the soul, 147, 151
  division of world into two principles, 5
  role in Academic tradition, 5
  teleological view of moral progress, 151, 167
Antony (Marcus Antonius), 64, 68
Appius Claudius Pulcher, 95–96
Arendt, Hannah, 10, 167
Aristotle, 55, 108
  definition of the *polis*, 124
  influence of rhetorical works on Cicero, 43
  theory of action, 18, 23, 152, 164, 167, 169
  theory of friendship, 80–81, 83, 85, 88
Athenian democracy, 20–23, 57, 107
  absence of a governing class, 21
  Cicero's views regarding, 125
  dogmata tou dēmou (decisions of the people), 22, 108
  eunoia (goodwill), 22
  role of *boulē*, 21
Atticus, Titus Pomponius
  as character in *De legibus*, 136
  as correspondent with Cicero, 182, 184, 186
  his choice of life (*voluntas institutae vitae*), 211
  relationship with Cicero, 211–12
Augustine of Hippo, 1, 220–29
  influence of Cicero, 2, 222
  influence of Paul, 221
  notion of will, 168, 221–29
  original sin, doctrine of, 227
  political views of, 10, 228
  preference of Latin over Greek, 222
  role in historical accounts of will, 1, 17, 165

boulēsis, 19, 108, 167, *see also* Aristotle; Stoicism
  in Aristotle, 19, 80, 164
  correspondence to *voluntas* in Cicero, 9, 149, 157, 159, 174, 219
  in Homer, 19
  potential equivalents in Latin, 158
  in Stoicism, 9, 149, 157–58, 218
Brunt, Peter, 81, 83
Brutus, Marcus Junius, 94

Caelius Rufus, 61, 140
Caesar, Gaius Julius, 62, 90
  Bellum Gallicum, 75
  voluntas Caesaris, 4, 66, 75–77, 140
Calpurnius Piso (Roman historian), 26
Carneades, *see also* Academy, New
  as leader of Academy, 33
  skeptical methods of, 194
  views on fate and moral responsibility, 170, 176
Catiline (Lucius Sergius Catilina), 62, 66
Cato, Marcus Porcius (Cato the Younger)
  as character in *De finibus*, 155–56, 195
  as exemplar in *De officiis*, 190, 204, 206
  in political affairs, 62
  in Roman political affairs, 157
Chrysippus
  Cicero's appraisal of, 178–79, 200
  political views of, 124
  theory of causality (cylinder metaphor), 178
  views on fate and moral responsibility, 153, 170, 176–77, 200
Cicero, Marcus Tullius
  as *novus homo*, 46, 186
  as orator, 6
  attitude toward the common citizen, 46, 88, 93, 117, 137–40

265

Cicero, Marcus Tullius (cont.)
  period of exile, 186
  relationship with Atticus, 186, 211–12
Cicero, Quintus Tullius, 66
  views on friendship in *Commentariolum petitionis*, 99
Cicero, works of
  Academica, 5, 152–57
  Brutus, 202
  Consolatio, 151
  De amicitia, 84, 101
  De divinatione, 175
  De domo sua, 120
  De fato, 3, 148, 170, 200
  De finibus, 3, 8, 147, 152, 195
  De inventione, 9, 34–35, 39–41, 46–54, 98, 165
  De lege Manilia, 109
  De legibus, 3, 59, 100, 109, 132
  De natura deorum, 3, 148, 175, 223
  De officiis, 8, 10, 84, 102, 146, 148, 188
  De oratore, 43, 139
  De partitione oratoria, 54, 101
  De provinciis consularibus, 66
  De republica, 3, 59–60, 74, 123–32, 170
  Epistolae ad familiares, 182, 184
  Hortensius, 222
  In Vatinium, 37
  In Verrem, 35, 105–7, 175, 209
  Orator, 201
  Philippics, 64, 68, 184
  Pro Balbo, 37, 111
  Pro Cluentio, 36, 38
  Pro Flacco, 53, 114, 116
  Pro Fonteio, 53, 110
  Pro Lege Manilia, 120
  Pro Ligario, 4
  Pro Murena, 65
  Pro Plancio, 75, 83, 88, 99, 118
  Pro Quinctio, 35
  Pro Rabirio Postumo, 38, 53
  Pro rege Deiotaro, 86
  Pro Roscio Amerino, 99
  Pro Scauro, 54
  Pro Sestio, 67, 110, 118, 120–22, 142
  Pro Sulla, 205
  Topica, 55
  Tusculan Disputations, 3, 8, 146, 148, 157
Clodius Pulcher, Publius, 64, 66, 111
collective intelligence, 132, 244
Commentariolum petitionis, 99, see also Cicero, Quintus Tullius
concordia ordinum, 6, 106, 116, 121, 150
consensus bonorum, 6, 121, 142
consilium
  correspondence with *voluntas* in Cicero, 44, 53

controversia ex scripto et sententia, 26, 34, 38–41, 86
Cornelius Sisenna (Roman historian), 26

De Lacy, Phillip, 190, 216
decorum, 84, 102, 140, 188, see also *De officiis* (Cicero, works of) democracy, see Athenian democracy
Diodorus Cronus, 176

eleutheria
  absence from free will debate in Greek, 24
  absence from Stoic political theory, 124
  political connotations, 169
embassy of the philosophers (155 BCE), 5, 33
eph'emin, 24, 164, 169, see also *libera voluntas*
Epictetus, 168, 221, see also Stoicism
Epicureanism, 5
  Cicero's objections to, 81, 84, 96, 101, 155, 176, 191
  notion of freedom, 174, 176
  theory of *atoma*, 171
  theory of *clinamen* or swerve of atoms, 171, 176
eunoia, 212
  in Aristotle, 80, 88
  as a binary concept, 8, 82
  in political context, 22
  in Polybius, 22
  in theatrical context, 30

Foucault, Michel, 214–16
Frede, Michael, 23, 168–69, 221
freedom, see *libertas*
free will, see *libera voluntas*
friendship, see also *amicitia*
  Aristotle's theory of, 80, 83
  Cicero's evolving views on, 98–104
  Epicurean theory of, 84
  Stoic theory of, 84, 100

Gill, Christopher, 194, 214, 216
Gracchus, Gaius, 69, 107, 115, 118
Gracchus, Tiberius, 6, 58, 107, 115
Graver, Margaret, 159
Griffin, Miriam, 85
Grotius, Hugo, 229

hekōn, 24, 160
  in Aristotle, 80, 160, 169
  as a binary concept, 8, 23
  correspondence to *voluntas* in Cicero, 160
  different from "willing," 23
Hellenistic philosophy, see Academy, New; Epicureanism; Stoicism
Hobbes, Thomas, 229

hormē, 19
  in Cicero, 9, 167, 198
  correspondence to *volo*, 19
  differences with *boulēsis*, 19
  in Stoicism, 158
Hortensius, Quintus, 32

iudicium
  correspondence with *voluntas* in Cicero, 35, 44, 148, 159
ius naturae, 6, 13, 59, 100, 130, 133, 135, *see also* Stoicism; *De legibus* (Cicero, works of)

Jefferson, Thomas, 238–41
  embrace of political innovation, 241
  idea of "natural *aristoi*," 240
  notion of "will of the people," 239
    measurability of, 239
    need for representatives, 240
  republicanism of, 238
  views on Roman republic, 241

Kahn, Charles, 164

Laelius, Gaius
  as character in *De republica*, 61, 74, 124, 129, 132
  as exemplar of *voluntas dicendi*, 202
  as protagonist of *De amicitia*, 101
Lazy Argument (*ignava ratio*), 177, 180–81
Lévy, Carlos, 6, 194, 197
  distinction between notion and concept, 3
libera voluntas
  in Cicero, 175–81
  in Lucretius, 171–74
libertas
  in Cicero
    In Verrem, 175
  curtailed by Caesar, 76, 141, 145, 170
  etymology of, 169
  in *De fato*, 13, 170, 177
  in *De legibus*, 136, 139
  in *De republica*, 109, 123, 125–28
  licentia as outer limit, 125, 139
  in Lucretius, 174, 176, 182
  skeptical freedom of New Academy. See Academy, New
Livius Andronicus (Roman dramatist), 27
Lucretius (Titus Lucretius Caro), 170, 191
  personal relationship with Cicero, 170–71

Marius, Gaius, 33, 106–7
mixed constitution theory, 126, 129, *see also De republica* (Cicero, works of)
Moatti, Claudia, 33

Modestinus (jurist), 77, *see also* Roman law
mos maiorum, 32, 57, 60, 70, 72, 115, 134, 145

natural law, *see ius naturae*

Octavian Caesar, Gaius (later Augustus), 58

Panaetius, *see also* Stoicism
  association with Scipio Aemilianus, 29, 157, 216
  influence on *De finibus*, 160
  influence on *De officiis*, 189–94, 204, 216
  influence on idea of *decorum*, 84
  relationship to orthodox Stoicism, 157, 192, 196, 200
  theory of four *personae*, 10, 146, 189–95, 212
Peripatetics
  kinship with Academic tradition in Cicero, 151
  views on external goods, 152
perturbationes voluntariae, 9, 149, 160, 183
Peripatetic school, *see* Aristotle
Philo of Larissa, 33, 150, 222, *see also* Academy, New
Pitkin, Hanna, 128
Plato, 125, 139
  definition of the *polis*, 124
  importance of unity in the state, 116, 138
  "rule of reason," 138, 151
  theory of *askēsis*, 167
  theory of divided soul, 17, 138, 147, 149–50, 157, 163, 198
  theory of self-moving soul, 151, 153, 167, 176, 179
Plato, works of
  Phaedrus, 151
  Politicus, 237
  Republic, 17, 124, 150, 167
  The Laws, 138
Plautus, Titus Maccius, 4, 27–29, 32, 35, 68, 110, 208
  mutuom argentum, 82
political theory, *see De legibus, De republica, Pro Sestio* (Cicero, works of); *libertas*; mixed constitution theory; *voluntas populi*
Polybius, 22, 108, 125, 128, 139
Pompey (Gnaeus Pompeius Magnus), 61, 73, 113
potestas, 109, 112, 126
powermapping, 60
prohairesis, 108
  in Aristotle, 18, 80, 86, 152, 164, 169
  as choice of a manner of life, 67
  correspondence to *voluntas* in Cicero, 18, 149, 174, 219

prohairesis (cont.)
   in Epictetus, 168, 222
   etymology of, 20
   in Polybius, 22
   prohairesis kai boulēsis in Panaetius, 212
   in Stoicism, 200, 224
Pythagoreanism, 148, 157

Remer, Gary, 128, 140, 188
Rhetorica ad Herennium, 26, 34, 38, 41–42
republicanism, see *De legibus, De republica, Pro Sestio* (Cicero, works of); *libertas*; mixed constitution theory; *voluntas populi*
Rhodes, P. J., 21
Roman constitution, See *De legibus, De republica, Pro Sestio* (Cicero, works of); *mos maiorum*
Roman law, 24, *see also* Modestinus, Ulpian (jurists)
   Cicero's use of, 12, 32, 46–55
   emergence of "constitutional" claims in republican period, 70
   in imperial period, 77
   letter versus spirit of a law. See *controversia ex scripto et sententia*
   notion of trusteeship, 129
   voluntas patris (will of the father), 24
Rousseau, Jean-Jacques, 229
   ambivalence toward citizen judgment, 238
   arguments for direct citizen participation in government, 235
   desirability of revolution, 238
   notion of will
      as force or "desire-in-motion," 233–34
      basis of political sovereignty, 230
      infallibility of *volonté générale*, 234
      influence of Diderot, 231
      measurability of, 233
      role in origins of human society, 232
      volonté générale versus *volonté du peuple*, 235
   references to Cicero, 231
   role of will in the origin of society, 230
   views on Roman republic, 229, 235

Scaevola, Quintus Mucius, 32
Schofield, Malcolm, 124, 169, 175
Scipio Aemilianus, 32, 187
   as exemplar in *De officiis*, 216
   as exemplar of *voluntas dicendi*, 201
   as patron of Terence, 29
   as protagonist of *De republica*, 7, 123
Sedley, David, 11, 176, 178
skepticism, See Academy, New
Socrates, 200
   notion of *akrasia*, 17, 150

soul, See *animus*; Plato; Stoicism; *Tusculan Disputations* (Cicero, works of)
Stoicism
   account of moral progress, 154, 156, 160, 167, 179, 193, 196
   association of human and divine will, 224–25
   in Cicero's education, 33, 84
   circular orientation of Stoic thought, 194, 211, 215
   definition of the *polis*, 124
   four categories of an object, 194, 197
   influence on Jefferson, 239
   influence on *Tusculan Disputations*, 149
   materialist explanations of mental states, 153, 161, 213
   natural law, 13, 59, 100, 133
   poverty of argumentative style, 149, 155, 162, 178, 197
   role in historical accounts of the will, 18, 222
   Stoic sage or wise man, 153, 159, 163, 167, 180, 192, 206
   theory of assent (*synkatathesis*), 5, 153, 179
   theory of *eupatheiai*, 155, 158
   theory of friendship, 84, 210
   universe as rational being, 5, 192
   views on moral responsibility, 55, 149, 153, 161–62, 165, 167, 184, 198, 226
Strato (Peripatetic philosopher), 6
Straumann, Benjamin, 58, 69–70, 114, 120
sua sponte, 64, 165
Sulla, Lucius Cornelius, 33, 71, 76, 141
Syme, Ronald, 81

Taylor, L. R., 81, 83
temeritas, 61, 73–75
Terence (Publius Terentius Afer), 4, 29–32, 35
tribunate, 134
trusteeship, 109, 128

Ulpian (jurist), 77, *see also* Roman law
Universal Declaration of Human Rights
   notion of "will of the people," 241
utilitas, 123, 130

Varro, Marcus Terentius
   as correspondent with Cicero, 90, 182
   etymology of *voluntas* in *De lingua Latina*, 24, 218
Verres, Gaius, 71, 74, 105, *see also* In Verrem (Cicero, works of)
vis, 47
   duality with *voluntas*, 38, 61, 73, 97, 115, 132, 158
Voelke, André-Jean, 18

voluntarius, 23, 147
  as willingness where it would not be expected, 48, 55, 160
  in criminal intent, 48
voluntas
  as collective preference or intent, 115
  as designation of political support, 63–67
    contra voluntatem, 73
    sua and *summa voluntate*, 63–67
  as force or 'desire-in-motion', 24, 29, 119, 141, 158, 165, 207, 215, 219, 225
  as goodwill of an audience, 42, 110
    in court, 45
    at the theater, 30, 119, 122
  as lawful intent of a private individual, 27, 29, 36
    injured party in a lawsuit, 37, 74
    legal clients, 36
    paterfamilias, 24, 33, 72
    in renouncing citizenship, 74
    witness in a lawsuit, 54
  as lawful intent of a public official, 24, 33, 39, 58, 62, 71
  as mutual goodwill (*voluntas mutua*), 59, 79–104, 212
  as part of criminal intent, 49–50, 52–54, 74, 159
  as patriotism (*voluntas in rem publicam*), 93
  as personal affiliation
    to a manner of life (*voluntas institutae vitae*), 197, 211, 213
    to a party or cause, 67–69
    to a rhetorical style (*voluntas dicendi*), 201
  as willingness or absence of compulsion, 29–30
  as willpower, 160–63
  bivalence of, 8, 34, 68, 74, 138, 159, 165, 183, 219
  duality with *utilitas*, 121, 130
  durability of, 8, 40, 43–44, 55, 61, 71, 87, 93, 111–12, 142, 159, 207, 223
  etymology of, 17, 19, 24
  measurability of, 8, 53, 63, 88, 132, 225
  recta voluntas, good conscience, 184
  recursive qualities of, 210
  role in origins of human society, 73, 123
  temeritas as outer limit, 73–75
  usages in Latin prior to Cicero, 24–31
  voluntas deorum, "the will of the gods," 115, 122
  voluntas populi, "the will of the people," 43, 106

will, *See voluntas*
will of the people, *see also voluntas populi*
  absence from classical Greek usage, 20–23, 108
  approximation in Polybius, 22
  in Cicero, 7, 12–13, 23
    after Caesar's rise to power, 140
    De legibus, 132–40
    De republica, 123–32
    orations, 105–22
  in Jefferson, 238–42
  rejection of Ciceronian notion by Augustine, 229
  role in modern politics, 143, 242
  in Rousseau, 235–36
Woolf, Raphael, 155, 180

Zeno of Citium, 154, *see also* Stoicism
  political views of, 124

Lightning Source UK Ltd.
Milton Keynes UK
UKHW022010061222
413517UK00006B/35